Scholastic
Student
Thesaurus

Scholastic

Student Thesaurus

JOHN K. BOLLARD

Editorial Assistant: Catrin Lloyd-Bollard
Curriculum Consultant: Bob Stremme
Book design: Nancy Sabato
Composition: Kevin Callahan / BNGO Books

Library of Congress Cataloging-in-Publication Data

Bollard, John K.
    Scholastic student thesaurus/John K. Bollard
        p. cm.
    Includes index.
    Summary: Provides synonyms and antonyms for thousands of English words.
    1. English language—Synonyms and antonyms—Juvenile literature.
    [1. English language—Synonyms and antonyms.] I. Title
    PE1591 .B586 2002
    423'.1—dc21
    2001045766

ISBN 0-439-24882-5

10 9 8 7 6 5 4 3 2 1   02 03 04 05 06

Printed in the U.S.A.
First printing, August 2002

Contents

Introduction

The Web of Words

Imagine a large, beautiful spiderweb. Its strands run from point to point creating intricate and fascinating patterns wherever you look. The English language is just such a web, but it is a web of words. Many words are connected by strands of meaning to other similar words, called *synonyms*. Those words, in turn, are connected to still other synonyms, moving you gradually from one idea to another. How can you find your way around this web of words? How can you find just the right word when you need it? A thesaurus helps you to do just that. The *Scholastic Student Thesaurus* is designed to move you around in the web of words. If you start with a word you know, your thesaurus will help you find synonyms to choose from.

Why Use a Thesaurus?

You already know thousands of words. These words are usually all you need. But sometimes, even though you know you have a good idea, you just can't think of quite the right word to express it the way you want. Here are some of the ways in which the *Scholastic Student Thesaurus* can be helpful:

To avoid repetition. Suppose you have used the same word three or four times in one paragraph or page. Rather than use that word again, you would like to find a different way to express the same idea. Your thesaurus provides you with a variety of synonyms.

To make your meaning clear and precise. When you speak or write, you usually think about what you *mean*, not about the words you are using. But sometimes the meaning doesn't come out as easily or as clearly as you had hoped. Your thesaurus can help you find words that express your idea more effectively than the words you began with. You may find that looking through the synonyms of a word brings to mind different ways to express your idea. It may even help you understand the idea better yourself. Sometimes a word you have used may be too vague. Sometimes its meaning or its tone is not exactly what you want. You want your readers to understand exactly how you felt, what you saw, or what you thought. Your thesaurus can give you synonyms that are more precise and effective.

To avoid overused terms. There are a few words that get used so often in so many different ways that they have run out of energy. They no longer have a sharply defined meaning, even though they give a general impression of what we want to say. It may be easier just to use these words, but they don't say anything specific. Often they lead us into clichés or vague thinking. If you find yourself using such general words as **nice** or **pretty** or **good,** try to pin down your thoughts with synonyms that more specifically describe what you are talking about. Your thesaurus can help you replace those words with synonyms like "delightful," "striking," or "favorable." This will make your writing more energetic and original.

To achieve the proper tone. Sometimes the word you thought of is too informal to be used in a school assignment or for a letter you want to write. You want a more serious word, but can't think of one. Or the opposite may be true. You may be writing a story or poem in a conversational or informal style. The synonyms in your thesaurus cover a broad range of vocabulary from informal to colloquial to formal. Some words are labeled as *informal* in your thesaurus. You should avoid using these in your serious writing. For example, "chicken" and "yellow" are informal synonyms of **cowardly**. You may not want to use them in an essay or assignment, but they might be just right for a character's speech in a story. When selecting any synonym, you should always take a moment to consider whether it is suitable for the style in which you are writing or speaking.

You already know many of the words in the *Scholastic Student Thesaurus*, but you will also find many new words here. Your thesaurus will guide you through this web of words in order to make your writing more clear, more mature, and even more elegant. Most importantly, the *Scholastic Student Thesaurus* will help you to write accurately and precisely. In this way, you can communicate your thoughts more easily to others. And that is what you are always trying to do when you speak or write.

At-a-Glance

A thesaurus is a reference book that lists words that mean the same thing or almost the same thing. Such words are called *synonyms*. In some cases, your thesaurus also helps you find words that mean the opposite or almost the opposite. These words are called *antonyms*. The different parts of your *Scholastic Student Thesaurus* are identified in the sample page below.

Guide words give the first and last words alphabetically on each page, including both the main entries and the on-the-page index.

The **on-the-page index** alphabetically lists every synonym that is not a main entry. If a word you are looking up is not a main entry, you should look for it here. The black arrow points to the main entry word or words where you will find it and other synonyms.

Main entries are listed in alphabetical order.

Main entry words are set in blue type. Main entry words jut out a bit from the entry. This makes it easier for you to find the word you are looking for.

---

slant 1. *vb* tilt, lean, list, incline, slope, bank, sag, pitch, cant ➡ **bend**
2. *n* slope, incline, climb, ascent, rise, descent, declivity, grade, hill

slavery *n* bondage, servitude, enslavement, serfdom, subjugation, vassalage ⇨ *freedom*

sleep 1. *vb* slumber, doze, snooze, nod, nap, hibernate ➡ **rest**
2. *n* slumber, doze, rest, repose, siesta, nap, catnap, shut-eye (*informal*)

slide 1. *vb* glide, skim, coast, skid, slip, skate ➡ **push**
2. *n* ➡ **channel**
3. *n* ➡ **photograph**
4. *n* ➡ **avalanche**

slippery *adj* smooth, slick, glassy, icy, waxy, soapy

slow 1. *adj* leisurely, gradual, sluggish, deliberate, moderate, torpid ⇨ *fast*
2. *adj* dilatory, lackadaisical ➡ **passive**, lazy, listless
3. *adj* ➡ **dull, stupid**

sly 1. *adj* devious, crafty, cunning, shrewd, subtle, tricky, sneaky, wily, slick, shifty, artful, scheming, underhanded ➡ **dishonest**
2. *adj* secretive, furtive, sneaky, surreptitious, stealthy, elusive ➡ **private**

small 1. *adj* little, tiny, miniature, minute, diminutive, Lilliputian, compact ➡ **trivial** ⇨ *big*
2. *adj* scanty, meager, slight, spare, skimpy, stingy, paltry ➡ **inadequate**

smart 1. *adj* intelligent, clever, bright, wise, learned, brilliant, keen, acute, quick, alert, apt, astute, perceptive, insightful, discerning, incisive, canny, shrewd ➡ **precocious, educated, profound** ⇨ *foolish, stupid*
2. *adj* ➡ **fashionable**
3. *vb* ➡ **hurt**
In general, **smart**, **clever**, *and* **bright**, *which all suggest quickness in learning, are more often applied to young people than are* **intelligent**, **wise**, *and* **learned**, *which suggest the wisdom that comes from experience, education, and age.*

If the word you want is not a main entry above, look below to find it.

slam ➡ close
slammer ➡ jail
slander ➡ insult
slang ➡ dialect
slap ➡ punch, blow[1]
slash ➡ cut, decrease
slat ➡ board
slate ➡ gray, ballot
slather ➡ rub
slaughter ➡ kill, murder
slave ➡ servant, prisoner, work
slavish ➡ servile
slay ➡ kill
slayer ➡ killer
slaying ➡ murder
sled ➡ vehicle

sledge ➡ hammer
sledgehammer ➡ hammer
sleek ➡ shiny
sleeping ➡ asleep
sleepless ➡ awake
sleepy ➡ tired
sleet ➡ ice
slender ➡ thin, narrow, light[2]
slew ➡ abundance
slice ➡ cut, block
slick ➡ slippery, sly
slight ➡ small, thin, short, light[2], insult
slightest ➡ least
slightly ➡ partly
slim ➡ thin, narrow
slime ➡ dirt

sling ➡ throw
slink ➡ sneak
slip ➡ mistake, trip, dock, ticket, slide, fall
slip by ➡ elapse
slit ➡ cut
slither ➡ crawl
slogan ➡ saying
slop ➡ dirt
slope ➡ slant
sloppy ➡ messy
slosh ➡ splash
sloth ➡ laziness
slothful ➡ lazy
slouch ➡ bend
slough ➡ shed
slovenly ➡ messy

sludge ➡ dirt
slug ➡ hit, missile
sluggard ➡ loafer
sluggish ➡ slow, listless
sluice ➡ channel
slumber ➡ sleep
slumbering ➡ asleep
slump ➡ depression, fall, drop, bend
slush ➡ snow
slushy ➡ wet
smack ➡ hit, kiss, blow[1]
smaller ➡ less
smallest ➡ least
small-minded ➡ mean
smash ➡ break, hit, collide
smear ➡ rub, insult

8

Thesaurus Entries Close-up

Sense numbers separate the different meanings of an entry. This makes it easier for you to find the word use you are looking for.

Black arrows point to synonym cross-references. These synonyms have their own main entry. You can find more synonyms by looking up these entries.

slant ①. *vb* tilt, lean, list, incline, slope, bank, sag, pitch, cant ➡ **bend**
②. *n* slope, incline, climb, ascent, rise, descent, declivity, grade, hill

slavery *n* bondage, servitude, enslavement, serfdom, subjugation, vassalage ⇨ *freedom*

Part-of-speech labels in *italic (slanted)* type give the part of speech for each entry or sense.
n = noun
vb = verb
adj = adjective
adv = adverb
prep = preposition
conj = conjunction
interj = interjection
pron = pronoun

smart 1. *adj* intelligent, clever, bright, wise, learned, brilliant, keen, acute, quick, alert, apt, astute, perceptive, insightful, discerning, incisive, canny, shrewd ➡ **precocious, educated, profound** ⇨ *foolish, stupid*
2. *adj* ➡ **fashionable**
3. *vb* ➡ **hurt**

In general, **smart**, **clever**, *and* **bright**, *which all suggest quickness in learning, are more often applied to young people than are* **intelligent**, **wise**, *and* **learned**, *which suggest the wisdom that comes from experience, education, and age.*

White arrows point to antonym cross-references. Look up these entries to find more antonyms.

Usage notes in *italic* type give information about how some synonyms are used.

Small raised numbers tell you which entry to look up if two headwords are spelled the same.

slender ➡ thin, narrow, light²
slew ➡ abundance
slice ➡ cut, block
slick ➡ slippery, sly
slight ➡ small, thin, short, light², insult
slightest ➡ least
slogan ➡ saying
slop ➡ dirt
slope ➡ slant
sloppy ➡ messy
slosh ➡ splash
sloth ➡ laziness
slothful ➡ lazy

How to Use This Book

T he *Scholastic Student Thesaurus* will help you find synonyms for a word that you have in mind. The three main features of the thesaurus are explained below: **main entries**, **cross-references**, and the **on-the-page index**.

Main Entry Words

Synonyms are grouped together after **main entry words**. These **main entries** are listed alphabetically and printed in **blue boldface** type. Suppose you need a synonym for **exaggerate**. Your thesaurus has a main entry for **exaggerate** with nine synonyms:

exaggerate *vb* overstate, overdo, inflate, embellish, embroider, elaborate, gild, magnify, dramatize

If a main entry word has more than one sense or use, the synonyms are grouped in numbered senses, as in the entry for **boast**, which can be either a verb or a noun:

boast 1. *vb* brag, gloat, crow, show off, vaunt, swagger, exult
  2. *n* brag, bragging, vaunt, claim, assertion, bluster, swagger, bravado

If two main entries have the same spelling, a small raised number is used to tell them apart, as at **live¹** and **live²**. The same raised numbers are used in the index.

live¹ 1. *vb* exist, be, thrive, subsist, breathe ➡ **experience**
  2. *vb* survive, outlive, outlast, persevere,
  persist ➡ **continue** ⇨ *die*
  3. *vb* reside, dwell, stay, abide, inhabit, lodge,
  room, sojourn ➡ **occupy**

live² *adj* ➡ **lively, alive, active**

Part-of-speech labels

Each entry or numbered sense has a **part-of-speech label** that identifies the part of speech of the main entry and the synonyms of each sense. The part-of-speech labels are:

n	noun	*prep*	preposition
vb	verb	*conj*	conjunction
adj	adjective	*interj*	interjection
adv	adverb	*pron*	pronoun

Usage labels and usage notes

Some synonyms are followed by a **usage label** printed in *italics* inside parentheses. A usage label helps you recognize how that synonym is used. For example, there are two usage labels at the entry for **wig**:

wig *n* hairpiece, fall, toupee, periwig *(historical)*, rug *(informal)* ➡ **hair**

The *(historical)* label indicates that "periwig" is used in historical contexts. You can learn from a dictionary that it is a term for a type of wig popular in the 17th and 18th centuries. The *(informal)* label is the most common usage label in this thesaurus. It warns you that a synonym should not be used in serious or formal writing or speech. Other usage labels may indicate the language of origin of a term, such as "*adios (Spanish), au revoir (French)*" at the entry **good-bye**, or a field of reference to which it is restricted, such as "petrol *(British)*" at **gasoline**.

Some entries are followed by a usage note, which gives information about how the synonyms are used or how they are different from each other. For an example, see the usage note at **maybe**:

All of these words express uncertainty about something.
Maybe *and* **perhaps** *are very close synonyms and it usually makes no difference which one you use.*
Possibly *stresses the uncertainty more than* **maybe.**
Conceivably *and* **feasibly** *suggest even greater uncertainty.* **Perchance** *is a more formal and less common synonym.*

Cross-references

Many entries include a boldface cross-reference, indicated by an arrow, that directs you to a related main entry. If you don't find a synonym that you want at one main entry, the cross-references direct you to other entries where you will find more choices. There are two types of cross-references: ➡ **synonym cross-references** and ⇨ *antonym cross-references.*

➡ Synonym cross-references

Synonym cross-references direct you to other main entries that are related to the main entry you looked up. Synonym cross-references are printed in **boldface** type following a black arrow ➡, as at the entry for **patriotic:**

patriotic *adj* loyal, zealous, nationalistic, chauvinistic ➡ **faithful**

If the main entry you looked up does not have a synonym you want, the synonym cross-reference points you to another main entry that might be helpful.

Sometimes more than one synonym cross-reference is given, as at **tolerant:**

tolerant *adj* permissive, lenient, indulgent, easygoing ➡ **liberal, kind, patient**

In these cases, look first at the entry that seems closest to the idea you have in mind. And remember that the cross-reference itself may be a synonym for you to use.

In some main entries, you will find a sense number with only a cross-reference and no other synonyms. This cross-reference indicates that the synonyms for that sense are given at the cross-reference entry, as at the entry for **house:**

house 1. *n* ➡ **home**
  2. *vb* accommodate, board, lodge, put up, shelter, quarter, billet

At the entry for **home,** you will find the noun "house" with 17 other synonyms and two more cross-references.

⇨ Antonym cross-references

Sometimes you can find a clearer way to express your idea by putting it in opposite terms. **Antonym cross-references** direct you to main entries that are approximate opposites, or *antonyms*, of the entry where they are found. If you are not quite satisfied with any of the synonyms you have found, it may be helpful to check the antonym cross-references. Antonym cross-references are printed in **boldface italic** type following a white arrow ⇨, as at **punctual**:

punctual *adj* timely, prompt, precise, expeditious, punctilious ⇨ *late*

On-the-page Index

All of the synonyms in the *Scholastic Student Thesaurus* are listed alphabetically in the **on-the-page index** in the bottom portion of the page. Each word in the index is followed by a black arrow ➡ with one or more **main entries** where the index word is listed as a synonym:

> class ➡ course, elegance
> classic ➡ masterpiece, model
> classified ➡ secret
> classify ➡ arrange

If a word you are looking for is not a main entry, you should look in the **on-the-page index** on the same page where you looked for it as a main entry. Having the **on-the-page index** on the same pages as the main entries means that you will not have to look in two parts of the book just to get started in your search for the right word. For example, if you look up the word **silly**, you will find that it is not a main entry on page 169. The main entries go from **signature** to **skeptic**. On the bottom of that same page, however, you will find "silly" in the **on-the-page index**:

> silly ➡ foolish

All you need to do now is turn to the main entry for **foolish**, where there are 10 synonyms, including "silly," and three more cross-references.

Guide Words

The **guide words** at the top left and right corners of the pages give the first and last words alphabetically on each page, including both the **main entries** and the **on-the-page index**.

An Important Reminder

Teachers have one common complaint about the way thesauruses are used. They complain that often students will pick an unfamiliar synonym without realizing that it does not fit properly into the sentence where they put it. Remember that **no two synonyms mean *exactly* the same thing**. Sometimes synonyms are used in different grammatical constructions. If you have a feeling that a synonym is not quite right, trust your instincts. You can either look in a dictionary to find out more about it or pick another synonym that you are more sure of. Anytime you are not certain whether a synonym is just the one you want, or if you are not sure what it means, look it up in a dictionary. Or ask someone whose judgment and knowledge of the language you can trust.

A

abandon 1. *vb* quit, cease, discontinue, concede, abdicate, renounce, resign, forfeit, scuttle ➡ **surrender, discard**
2. *vb* ➡ **leave, betray**

abandoned *adj* deserted, desolate, forsaken, uninhabited, neglected, rejected, derelict ➡ **empty**

abbreviation *n* acronym, initialism, contraction, abridgment, shortening

ability *n* capability, capacity, competence, aptitude, proficiency, ingenuity, faculty, power, efficacy ➡ **strength, talent**

able 1. *adj* capable, competent, qualified, eligible, authorized, suitable, fit
2. *adj* accomplished, proficient, skillful, adept, clever, handy, dexterous, deft ➡ **smart, expert, practical**

abolish *vb* end, eradicate, exterminate, eliminate, revoke, cancel, obliterate, repeal, rescind, annul, nullify, countermand, disallow, veto, overrule ➡ **finish, destroy, erase** ⇨ *save*

about 1. *adv* approximately, around, roughly, nearly, almost ➡ **practically**
2. *adv* around, round, all around, everywhere, nearby
3. *prep* concerning, regarding, touching, relating to
4. *prep* around, near, at

above 1. *prep* over, on, higher than, upon ⇨ *under*
2. *prep* over, more than, beyond, exceeding
3. *adv* over, overhead, up, upward, upwards, aloft ⇨ *under*

abroad *adj* overseas, away, traveling, touring

abrupt 1. *adj* blunt, hurried, impetuous, brusque, curt, short, gruff ➡ **rude, thoughtless**
2. *adj* ➡ **steep**
3. *adj* ➡ **sudden, sharp**

absence 1. *n* nonattendance, truancy, absenteeism ⇨ *presence*
2. *n* deficiency, dearth, lack ➡ **want**

absent *adj* away, missing, elsewhere, astray, AWOL ➡ **lost** ⇨ *present*

If the word you want is not a main entry above, look below to find it.

abase ➡ shame

abash ➡ embarrass, confuse

abashed ➡ ashamed

abate ➡ decrease

abbess ➡ religious

abbey ➡ monastery

abbot ➡ religious

abbreviate ➡ condense

abbreviated ➡ short

abdicate ➡ abandon

abdication ➡ surrender

abdomen ➡ stomach

abduct ➡ seize

aberration ➡ oddity, departure

abhor ➡ hate

abhorrence ➡ hatred

abide ➡ bear, live[1], wait

abiding ➡ permanent

abject ➡ poor, servile

ablaze ➡ burning

abnormal ➡ strange

abnormality ➡ oddity

abode ➡ home

abominable ➡ bad

abominate ➡ hate

aboriginal ➡ primitive, native

abortive ➡ useless

abounding ➡ abundant

above all ➡ best

abrade ➡ rub

abrasion ➡ friction

abreast ➡ parallel

abridge ➡ condense

abridged ➡ short

abridgment ➡ abbreviation, summary

abscess ➡ sore

absentee ➡ runaway

absenteeism ➡ absence

---

absentminded *adj* forgetful, preoccupied, distracted, inattentive, oblivious, scatterbrained, spacey (*informal*) ➡ **absorbed**

absorb 1. *vb* soak (up), digest, suck up, sop up
2. *vb* ➡ **learn, interest**

absorbed *adj* engrossed, engaged, intent, involved, preoccupied, immersed
➡ **thoughtful, absent-minded**

abstain *vb* refrain, forbear, forgo, renounce, shun, eschew ➡ **avoid**

abstinence *n* temperance, forbearance, denial, self-denial, self-restraint, austerity, moderation, celibacy

abundance *n* profusion, wealth, surplus, plethora, excess, plenty, lot, peck, slew, load, ton, glut

abundant *adj* plentiful, copious, ample, profuse, plenteous, generous, voluminous, abounding, bountiful, bounteous, prodigal, much ➡ **big, enough**

abuse 1. *vb* misuse, mistreat, torment, oppress, suppress, repress, ill-treat, maltreat, torture, persecute, victimize, molest, harass ➡ **hurt, insult, punish**
2. *n* misuse, mistreatment, ill-treatment, injury, harm, punishment, torture

accent 1. *n* stress, emphasis, prominence, beat, cadence, diacritic
2. *n* pronunciation, inflection, drawl, twang, burr ➡ **dialect**
3. *n* ➡ **decoration**
4. *vb* ➡ **emphasize**

accident 1. *n* mishap, setback ➡ **collision, disaster, emergency**
2. *n* ➡ **chance**

accidental *adj* incidental, coincidental, unintentional, fortuitous, inadvertent, unplanned, chance ➡ **lucky**

accidentally *adv* unintentionally, inadvertently, unwittingly, unconsciously, fortuitously, incidentally ⇨ *purposely*

accompany *vb* escort, attend, chaperon, chaperone, convoy ➡ **lead**

accuracy *n* exactness, precision, correctness, exactitude ➡ **truth**

If the word you want is not a main entry above, look below to find it.

absolute ➡ complete, certain, unconditional, dictatorial

absolutely ➡ very, certainly

absolution ➡ forgiveness

absolutism ➡ tyranny

absolve ➡ forgive

absorbing ➡ interesting

abstinent ➡ celibate

abstract ➡ theoretical, summary

abstruse ➡ obscure

absurd ➡ foolish, illogical

absurdity ➡ nonsense

abut ➡ border

abutting ➡ adjacent

abyss ➡ hole

academic ➡ theoretical, intellectual, teacher

academy ➡ school

accede ➡ agree, surrender

accelerate ➡ hurry

acceleration ➡ speed

accentuate ➡ emphasize

accept ➡ agree, approve, believe, receive, bear

acceptable ➡ fair

acceptance ➡ approval

access ➡ door

accessible ➡ available, open

accession ➡ acquisition

accessory ➡ partner

acclaim ➡ approve, praise

acclamation ➡ praise

acclimatize ➡ adjust

accommodate ➡ adjust, house, contain, condescend

accommodation ➡ loan

accomplice ➡ partner

accomplish ➡ do

accomplished ➡ able, successful

accomplishment ➡ act, work, success

accord ➡ agree, agreement

accordingly ➡ therefore

accost ➡ approach, call

account ➡ story, description, supply

accoutrement ➡ equipment

accumulate ➡ gather

accurate ➡ correct, careful

accurately ➡ correctly

---

acquisition 1. *n* attainment, procurement, takeover, appropriation
2. *n* purchase, inheritance, possession, accession ➡ **property**

acrobat *n* gymnast, tumbler, aerialist, trapeze artist ➡ **athlete**

act 1. *vb* perform, work, function, operate, execute, stage, carry out, ply, serve, go ➡ **do**
2. *vb* behave, seem, appear
3. *vb* perform, play, enact, stage, portray, dramatize, impersonate, pose, render ➡ **pretend**
4. *n* deed, action, feat, accomplishment, achievement, exploit, undertaking, step ➡ **work**
5. *n* bill, law, decree, statute, ordinance, legislation ➡ **rule**
6. *n* performance, routine, number, sketch, bit, skit ➡ **pretense**

active *adj* animated, spirited, dynamic, busy, vibrant, bustling, frenetic, hyperactive, strenuous, athletic ➡ **lively, alive** ⇨ *passive*

activity 1. *n* action, motion, liveliness, commotion, bustle ➡ **movement** ⇨ *calm*
2. *n* ➡ **pastime, exercise**

actor *n* actress, performer, player, entertainer, star, thespian, ham ➡ **celebrity, comic, artist**

add 1. *vb* sum, total, calculate, compute, tally, count, score ⇨ *subtract*
2. *vb* combine, include, append, annex, supplement, incorporate, integrate ➡ **join**

addition 1. *n* reckoning, computing, summation, tabulating, counting ⇨ *subtraction*
2. *n* extension, expansion, annex, enlargement, appendix, complement, supplement, amendment, rider, codicil

adhesive 1. *n* glue, paste, mucilage, cement, epoxy, tape, Scotch tape (*trademark*), adhesive tape, masking tape, duct tape
2. *adj* ➡ **sticky**

adjacent 1. *adj* adjoining, neighboring, bordering, abutting, tangent, next, next door ➡ **near**
2. *prep* ➡ **beside**

If the word you want is not a main entry above, look below to find it.

accusation ➡ complaint
accuse ➡ blame
accused ➡ defendant
accustomed ➡ usual
ace ➡ expert
ache ➡ pain, hurt
achieve ➡ do, win
achievement ➡ act, event, success
acid ➡ sour
acidic ➡ sour
acknowledge ➡ admit, answer, believe
acknowledgment ➡ gratitude, apology

acme ➡ top
acquaint ➡ introduce
acquaintance ➡ friend, introduction
acquiesce ➡ surrender
acquiescence ➡ surrender
acquire ➡ get
acquisitive ➡ greedy
acquit ➡ forgive
acrid ➡ smelly
acrobatics ➡ gymnastics
acronym ➡ abbreviation
across from ➡ opposite
acting ➡ temporary

action ➡ act, activity, fight, suit
action figure ➡ doll
activate ➡ start
actress ➡ actor
actual ➡ real
actuality ➡ certainty, event
actually ➡ really
acute ➡ sharp, smart, urgent
ad ➡ advertisement
adage ➡ saying
adamant ➡ resolute, hard
adapt ➡ adjust, prepare
adaptation ➡ translation

added ➡ more
addict ➡ fan
addiction ➡ habit
additional ➡ more
additionally ➡ more, besides
address ➡ approach, welcome, speech, destination
adept ➡ able
adequate ➡ enough, fair
adequately ➡ well
adhere ➡ stick, obey
adhesive tape ➡ adhesive
adieu ➡ good-bye
adios ➡ good-bye

---

adjust *vb* alter, modify, regulate, adapt, tailor, accommodate, conform, acclimatize, orient ➡ **change, fix, arrange**

admit 1. *vb* acknowledge, confess, own, concede, confirm, allow ➡ **reveal**
2. *vb* ➡ **receive**

adopt 1. *vb* embrace, appropriate, assume, espouse ➡ **approve, choose, use**
2. *vb* foster, take in, raise, rear

adult 1. *adj* grown-up, mature, full-grown, ripe
2. *n* grown-up, man, woman ⇨ *child, baby*

advantage *n* benefit, profit, superiority, convenience, vantage, upper hand, asset, virtue, plus, avail

adventure *n* exploit, escapade, venture, enterprise, spree, lark, fling ➡ **event**

advertise *vb* publicize, announce, promote, proclaim, declare, broadcast, pitch, parade, flaunt, plug ➡ **tell, show**

advertisement *n* commercial, ad, notice, circular, flier, billboard, poster, promotion, pitch, plug ➡ **announcement**

advertising *n* promotion, publicity, hype, propaganda ➡ **advertisement**

advice *n* guidance, counsel, recommendation, suggestion, caution, admonition ➡ **tip, warning**

adviser *n* advisor, counselor, counsel, consultant, attorney, lawyer, advocate ➡ **teacher**

affect 1. *vb* influence, impress, move, sway
2. *vb* ➡ **act, pretend**
3. *n* ➡ **emotion**
In the most common or frequent uses of **affect** *and* **effect,** **affect** *is a verb and* **effect** *is a noun. There is also a verb* **effect,** *which you should be careful not to confuse with the verb* **affect.** *See* **effect.**

If the word you want is not a main entry above, look below to find it.

adjoin ➡ border

adjoining ➡ adjacent, beside

adjudge ➡ decide

adjudicate ➡ try

adjustment ➡ repair, correction

ad-lib ➡ invent

administer ➡ lead, govern

administration ➡ government, leadership

administrator ➡ official, principal

admirable ➡ good

admiration ➡ respect

admire ➡ love, respect

admission ➡ ticket

admonish ➡ scold, warn

admonition ➡ warning, advice

adolescence ➡ childhood

adolescent ➡ teenager, young

adorable ➡ cute

adoration ➡ love

adore ➡ love, worship

adoring ➡ loving

adorn ➡ decorate

adornment ➡ decoration

adroit ➡ expert

adroitness ➡ talent, agility

adulate ➡ flatter

adulation ➡ praise, worship

adulterate ➡ weaken

adulthood ➡ maturity

advance ➡ approach, go, promote, lend, progress, loan, forward

advanced ➡ gifted

advancement ➡ progress, promotion

advantageous ➡ useful

advent ➡ approach

adventuresome ➡ brave

adventurous ➡ brave

adversary ➡ enemy, opponent

adverse ➡ unfortunate, destructive

adversity ➡ hardship

advise ➡ suggest, warn

advisor ➡ adviser

advocate ➡ prefer, adviser

aerate ➡ fan

aerialist ➡ acrobat

aerobatics ➡ gymnastics

aerobics ➡ gymnastics

aeronaut ➡ pilot

aeronautics ➡ flight

affable ➡ nice

affair ➡ business

affectation ➡ pretense, habit

affection ➡ love

affectionate ➡ loving

affidavit ➡ document

affiliate ➡ member, department

affiliation ➡ link

n = noun • *vb* = verb • *adj* = adjective • *adv* = adverb • *prep* = preposition • *conj* = conjunction

afford *vb* pay for, support, bear, manage

afraid *adj* scared, frightened, alarmed, terrified, petrified, aghast, scared, timorous ➡ **anxious, nervous, cowardly** ⇨ *brave*

afternoon *n* p.m., midday, lunchtime, teatime ➡ **day, evening**

again *adv* once more, anew, afresh, over ➡ **encore**

agent 1. *n* representative, intermediary, middleman, broker, executor, liaison, delegate, spokesperson, go-between, handler ➡ **seller**
2. *n* ➡ **spy**

agile *adj* nimble, spry, quick, sprightly, dexterous, supple, limber ➡ **active**

agility *n* dexterity, nimbleness, adroitness, spryness ➡ **talent**

agree 1. *vb* consent, assent, concur, accept, accede ⇨ *argue, object*

2. *vb* match, correspond, coincide, harmonize, accord, jibe ➡ **suit**

agreement 1. *n* bargain, deal, contract, lease, treaty, pact, accord, covenant, compact, arrangement, compromise, understanding
2. *n* consent, assent, consensus, concurrence, compliance, conformity, sympathy, harmony ➡ **unity**

air 1. *n* sky, heaven, atmosphere, stratosphere, troposphere ➡ **space**
2. *n* breath, ventilation, oxygen ➡ **wind**
3. *n* ➡ **quality, appearance**
4. *vb* ➡ **broadcast, play, say**

airplane *n* aircraft, plane, flying machine ➡ **vehicle**

alert 1. *adj* attentive, wide-awake, watchful, vigilant, aware, conscious ➡ **awake**
2. *adj* ➡ **smart**
3. *vb* ➡ **warn**

If the word you want is not a main entry above, look below to find it.

affinity ➡ link, similarity, relationship

affirm ➡ believe, testify, approve

affirmative ➡ yes

afflict ➡ hurt, trouble

affliction ➡ hardship, illness, disability

affluence ➡ wealth

affluent ➡ rich

affordable ➡ cheap

affront ➡ insult

aficionado ➡ fan

afire ➡ burning

afresh ➡ again

aft ➡ back

after ➡ past

aftermath ➡ effect

aftershock ➡ earthquake

afterword ➡ conclusion

against ➡ beside, opposite

age ➡ period, weather

aged ➡ old

agency ➡ department

agenda ➡ list

aggravate ➡ bother

aggravated ➡ angry

aggregate ➡ total

aggression ➡ violence, anger

aggressive ➡ belligerent, ambitious

aghast ➡ afraid

agitate ➡ disturb, fan, excite

agitated ➡ tense

agitation ➡ excitement

agnostic ➡ atheist

agonizing ➡ uncomfortable

agony ➡ misery

agrarian ➡ farming

agreeable ➡ nice, pleasant, compatible

agricultural ➡ farming

agriculture ➡ farming

ahead ➡ forward

ahead of ➡ before

aid ➡ help, back

aide ➡ helper

ail ➡ trouble

ailing ➡ sick

ailment ➡ illness

aim ➡ object, plan, intend

aimless ➡ indiscriminate

aircraft ➡ airplane

airfield ➡ field

airless ➡ stuffy

airman ➡ pilot

airport ➡ field

airtight ➡ tight

airy ➡ windy

ajar ➡ open

akin ➡ alike

alarm ➡ fear, scare, warning

alarmed ➡ afraid

alcohol ➡ drink

alcoholic ➡ drunkard

alcove ➡ bay

alertness ➡ attention

➡ = synonym cross-reference • ⇨ = *antonym cross-reference*

alibi *n* defense, excuse, cover story

alike 1. *adj* similar, like, analogous, comparable, equivalent, parallel, close, akin ➡ **same**
⇨ *different*
2. *adv* similarly, likewise, comparably, analogously

alive *adj* living, live, animate, animated, vital, viable, quick, organic ➡ **lively, active**
⇨ *dead*

all 1. *n, pron* everything, everyone, everybody, sum, whole, totality ➡ **total**
2. *adj* every, entire, each, complete, whole, total
3. *adv* ➡ **completely**

alone *adj* lone, solitary, isolated, unaccompanied, unattended, solo, single-handed ➡ **lonely, single**

alternate 1. *vb* reciprocate, oscillate, fluctuate, switch
2. *adj* alternating, every other ➡ **periodic**
3. *n* substitute, replacement, backup, surrogate, double

amateur 1. *n* nonprofessional, novice, beginner, dilettante, apprentice, neophyte
2. *adj* amateurish, unskilled, inexperienced, untrained, inexpert, unpaid, green ➡ **clumsy, incompetent, naive**

ambition 1. *n* aspiration, drive, enterprise, eagerness, desire, will, get-up-and-go, initiative ➡ **hope, enthusiasm, energy**
2. *n* ➡ **object**

ambitious 1. *adj* eager, zealous, enterprising, determined, aggressive, industrious, resourceful ➡ **competitive** ⇨ *lazy*
2. *adj* ➡ **hard**

If the word you want is not a main entry above, look below to find it.

alfalfa ➡ hay
alfresco ➡ outside
alias ➡ pseudonym
alien ➡ foreign, foreigner
alight ➡ descend
align ➡ straighten
aligned ➡ parallel
alignment ➡ order
all around ➡ about
allay ➡ relieve
allegation ➡ complaint
allege ➡ argue
allegiance ➡ loyalty
alleviate ➡ relieve
alley ➡ road
alliance ➡ union
allocate ➡ budget
allot ➡ budget
allotment ➡ share, budget

allow ➡ let, admit
allowable ➡ legal
allowance ➡ share, wage, budget, loan
all right ➡ cool
allude ➡ mention
allure ➡ attraction, enchantment, personality
alluring ➡ attractive
ally ➡ friend
almighty ➡ strong
almost ➡ about
alms ➡ gift
aloft ➡ above
alongside ➡ beside, parallel
aloof ➡ cool
alphabetical ➡ consecutive
already ➡ before
also ➡ besides

alter ➡ change, adjust
alteration ➡ change
altercation ➡ fight
alternately ➡ instead
alternating ➡ alternate
alternative ➡ choice
alternatively ➡ instead
although ➡ but
altitude ➡ height
altogether ➡ completely
altruistic ➡ generous
always ➡ forever, regularly
a.m. ➡ morning
amalgam ➡ mixture
amalgamation ➡ union, mixture
amass ➡ gather
amateurish ➡ amateur
amaze ➡ surprise

amazed ➡ dumbfounded
amazement ➡ surprise
amazing ➡ awesome
ambassador ➡ diplomat, messenger
ambiance ➡ setting
ambiguity ➡ problem
ambiguous ➡ obscure
ambivalent ➡ doubtful
amble ➡ walk
ambush ➡ attack
amen ➡ yes
amend ➡ perfect, correct
amendment ➡ addition
amiability ➡ hospitality
amiable ➡ friendly
amicable ➡ peaceful
amid ➡ between
amidst ➡ between

n = noun • *vb* = verb • *adj* = adjective • *adv* = adverb • *pron* = pronoun • *conj* = conjunction

ammunition *n* munitions, matériel, ammo (*informal*), bullets, shells

ancestor *n* forebear, forefather, progenitor, forerunner, predecessor, antecedent, patriarch, matriarch, elder ➡ **parent**

ancestry *n* lineage, birth, descent, extraction, blood ➡ **family**

anchor 1. *n* mooring, grapnel, stay, mainstay ➡ **support, protection**
2. *n* ➡ **reporter**
3. *vb* ➡ **dock, join**

angel *n* spirit, sprite, archangel, seraph, cherub

anger 1. *n* rage, fury, wrath, temper, indignation, hostility, animosity, annoyance, ire, aggression, belligerence
2. *vb* infuriate, enrage, madden, incense, exasperate, outrage, upset, provoke, rile, antagonize, embitter ➡ **bother**

angry *adj* mad, furious, upset, annoyed, irritated, aggravated, exasperated, indignant, irate, infuriated, livid, bitter, sore ➡ **cross, belligerent, violent**

animal 1. *n* creature, beast, brute, being, organism ➡ **monster**
2. *adj* bestial, beastly, brutish

announcement *n* declaration, notice, notification, proclamation, report, statement, pronouncement, news, revelation, bulletin, message, tidings
➡ **advertisement**

anonymous *adj* unsigned, unnamed, unknown, pseudonymous, nameless, secret

---

If the word you want is not a main entry above, look below to find it.

amigo ➡ friend

amiss ➡ wrong

amity ➡ friendship, peace

ammo ➡ ammunition

amnesty ➡ forgiveness

among ➡ between, through

amongst ➡ between

amorous ➡ loving

amount ➡ number, total, price, measure

amphibian ➡ reptile

amphitheater ➡ hall

ample ➡ enough, abundant

amplify ➡ strengthen, lengthen, grow

amputate ➡ cut

amuse ➡ entertain

amusement ➡ entertainment, pleasure, humor, toy

amusement park ➡ carnival

amusing ➡ funny

analogous ➡ alike

analogously ➡ alike

analogue ➡ duplicate

analogy ➡ similarity

analysis ➡ study, reason

analyze ➡ study

anarchy ➡ confusion

anatomy ➡ body

anchorage ➡ harbor

ancient ➡ old

anecdote ➡ story

anesthetic ➡ drug

anew ➡ again

angelic ➡ innocent

angle ➡ corner, perspective

angleworm ➡ worm

anguish ➡ misery, sorrow

animal farm ➡ zoo

animals ➡ livestock

animate ➡ alive

animated ➡ alive, active

animation ➡ life

animosity ➡ anger, hatred

annex ➡ add, addition

annihilate ➡ destroy, kill

annihilation ➡ murder

announce ➡ tell, advertise

annoy ➡ bother

annoyance ➡ anger, nuisance

annoyed ➡ angry

annoying ➡ inconvenient

annual ➡ flower

annuity ➡ pension

annul ➡ abolish

anoint ➡ rub, bless

anomaly ➡ oddity

anon ➡ soon

➡ = synonym cross-reference • ⇨ = antonym cross-reference

answer 1. *n* reply, response, retort, rejoinder, riposte, reaction, reciprocation ⇨ *question*
2. *n* solution, key, result, explanation, resolution, product ⇨ *problem, question*
3. *vb* reply, respond, retort, acknowledge, echo, counter, react, reciprocate ⇨ *question*
4. *vb* ➡ **solve**
5. *vb* ➡ **satisfy**

anticipate 1. *vb* foresee, expect, look forward to ➡ **predict**
2. *vb* ➡ **hope**

antique 1. *n* heirloom, relic, curio, artifact, antiquity
2. *adj* ➡ **old**

anxious 1. *adj* worried, apprehensive, uneasy, disturbed, insecure ➡ **afraid, nervous, tense**
2. *adj* ➡ **eager**

any *pron* each, some, every, either ➡ **few**

anyway *adv* anyhow, nevertheless, nonetheless, however, regardless, notwithstanding, still

apart *adv* asunder, separately, independently ⇨ *together*

apathetic *adj* indifferent, unconcerned, unresponsive, uncaring, disinterested, nonchalant ➡ **listless, lazy, cool** ⇨ *eager*

apathy *n* indifference, unconcern, nonchalance, disinterest ➡ **boredom** ⇨ *enthusiasm*

apology *n* excuse, acknowledgment, regrets, explanation

apparently 1. *adv* evidently, seemingly, presumably, supposedly, reputedly ➡ **probably**
2. *adv* clearly, obviously, plainly, patently

appeal 1. *vb* petition, pray, supplicate, sue, invoke ➡ **beg, ask**
2. *vb* ➡ **fascinate**
3. *n* request, plea, claim, petition, application ➡ **invitation**
4. *n* ➡ **attraction**

appear 1. *vb* emerge, arise, rise, surface, materialize, come into view, show up, turn up, form ➡ **come**
2. *vb* ➡ **act**
3. *vb* ➡ **look**

If the word you want is not a main entry above, look below to find it.

another ➡ **more, different**

antagonism ➡ **opposition, competition**

antagonist ➡ **enemy, opponent**

antagonistic ➡ **unfriendly, competitive**

antagonize ➡ **anger**

antarctic ➡ **cold**

ante ➡ **bet**

antecedent ➡ **ancestor, past**

antedate ➡ **precede**

anteroom ➡ **hall**

anthem ➡ **hymn**

antibiotic ➡ **drug**

antic ➡ **joke, funny**

anticipated ➡ **due**

anticipation ➡ **foresight, suspense**

antidepressant ➡ **drug**

antidote ➡ **cure**

antipathy ➡ **opposition, hatred**

antiquated ➡ **old**

antiquity ➡ **antique, past**

antiseptic ➡ **sterile**

antisocial ➡ **unfriendly**

antithesis ➡ **opposite**

antithetical ➡ **opposite**

anxiety ➡ **worry, fear**

anyhow ➡ **anyway**

apartment ➡ **home, room**

ape ➡ **boor, imitate**

aperture ➡ **hole**

apex ➡ **top**

aphorism ➡ **saying**

apocryphal ➡ **legendary**

apogee ➡ **top**

apologetic ➡ **sorry**

apologize ➡ **regret**

appall ➡ **shock, disgust**

appalling ➡ **awful, scary**

apparatus ➡ **equipment, tool**

apparel ➡ **clothes**

apparent ➡ **obvious, likely**

apparition ➡ **ghost, illusion**

appealing ➡ **pleasant, attractive**

appearance 1. *n* look, looks, aspect, features, countenance, demeanor, air, atmosphere, bearing, mien, visage
2. *n* ➡ **approach**

appetite *n* hunger, thirst, craving ➡ **desire**

appointment 1. *n* selection, nomination, election, designation, assignment, delegation, installation, investiture, ordination ➡ **choice**
2. *n* ➡ **meeting, visit**
3. *n* ➡ **profession**

appreciate 1. *vb* value, prize, cherish, treasure, relish, savor ➡ **respect**
2. *vb* thank, enjoy ➡ **welcome**
3. *vb* ➡ **understand**

approach 1. *vb* come near, draw near, near, advance, loom, gravitate toward ➡ **come**
2. *vb* address, accost, speak to ➡ **talk**
⇨ *avoid*
3. *n* coming, arrival, appearance, advent, entry
4. *n* ➡ **method, treatment**

approval 1. *n* acceptance, passage, ratification, enactment ➡ **support, praise**
2. *n* ➡ **permission**

approve 1. *vb* endorse, support, authorize, sanction, certify, ratify, validate, legalize, affirm ➡ **agree, back**
2. *vb* accept, favor, applaud, recommend, acclaim, commend ➡ **appreciate**

approximate 1. *adj* rough, inexact, estimated, close, near, ballpark, general
2. *vb* ➡ **estimate**
3. *vb* ➡ **resemble**

arbitrary 1. *adj* chance, random, subjective, unpredictable, unscientific, haphazard, unplanned, careless, stray ➡ **indiscriminate**
2. *adj* capricious, frivolous, impulsive, whimsical ➡ **illogical**
3. *adj* willful, unreasonable ➡ **dictatorial**

If the word you want is not a main entry above, look below to find it.

appease ➡ pacify, soften, satisfy

appellation ➡ name

append ➡ add

appendage ➡ limb

appendix ➡ addition, table

appertain ➡ concern

appetizing ➡ delicious

applaud ➡ approve, clap

applause ➡ praise

appliance ➡ tool

applicable ➡ fit[1], relevant

applicant ➡ candidate

application ➡ use, diligence, appeal

apply ➡ belong, use, ask

appoint ➡ name, hire

apportion ➡ share, divide

apposite ➡ relevant, fit[1]

appraisal ➡ estimate

appreciation ➡ gratitude, wisdom

appreciative ➡ grateful

apprehend ➡ arrest, know

apprehension ➡ worry, fear, suspense, arrest

apprehensive ➡ anxious, suspicious

apprentice ➡ amateur

apprise ➡ introduce

approaching ➡ future

appropriate ➡ fit[1], correct, take, adopt

appropriately ➡ correctly

appropriation ➡ acquisition

approved ➡ official

approvingly ➡ well

approximately ➡ about

approximation ➡ estimate

apricot ➡ orange

apropos ➡ relevant

apt ➡ likely, fit[1], smart

aptitude ➡ talent, ability

aquarium ➡ zoo

aqueduct ➡ channel

aqueous ➡ liquid

arbiter ➡ judge

arbitrate ➡ negotiate, decide

arboretum ➡ greenhouse

arc ➡ curve

arcane ➡ secret

arch ➡ bend, curve

archaic ➡ old, early

archangel ➡ angel

archetypal ➡ model

archetype ➡ model

archfiend ➡ devil

archipelago ➡ island

architect ➡ creator

arctic ➡ cold

---

argue 1. *vb* quarrel, debate, dispute, disagree, bicker, squabble, quibble, wrangle ➡ **fight**
⇨ *agree*
2. *vb* claim, maintain, plead, assert, contend, allege, charge, protest

argument *n* quarrel, dispute, debate, controversy, discussion, squabble, row, fuss, falling-out, disagreement, misunderstanding, spat, tiff ➡ **fight, disagreement**

aristocracy *n* nobility, gentry, elite, upper class, society, high society, haut monde (*French*), jet set, rich

arm 1. *n* forelimb, forearm ➡ **limb**
2. *n* ➡ **branch**
3. *n* ➡ **bay**

arms *n* weapons, weaponry, armament, ordnance, artillery, matériel, armor ➡ **gun**

army 1. *n* force, armed force, troops, military, service, militia, legion ➡ **troop, soldier**
2. *n* ➡ **crowd**

arrange 1. *vb* organize, sort, classify, order, file, systematize, categorize, determine, array, structure, place, rank, orient, orientate ➡ **adjust, straighten**
2. *vb* plan, devise, set up, schedule

arrest 1. *vb* apprehend, detain, take prisoner, bust (*informal*), collar (*informal*), nab (*informal*) ➡ **catch, seize**
2. *vb* ➡ **stop**
3. *n* capture, seizure, detention, apprehension

art *n* skill, craft, technique, artistry, craftsmanship, creativity, artifice ➡ **talent**

articulate 1. *adj* intelligible, understandable, eloquent, lucid, fluent, clear, coherent
2. *vb* ➡ **pronounce**

artist *n* painter, sculptor, artisan, craftsman ➡ **musician, actor, photographer, writer, creator**

If the word you want is not a main entry above, look below to find it.

ardent ➡ eager, loving
ardor ➡ enthusiasm
arduous ➡ hard
area ➡ space, zone, field
arena ➡ field, hall
argot ➡ dialect
arid ➡ dry, sterile
arise ➡ ascend, descend, appear, happen
aristocrat ➡ noble
aristocratic ➡ noble
armada ➡ navy
armament ➡ arms

armed ➡ military
armed force ➡ army
armistice ➡ truce
armoire ➡ closet
armor ➡ arms
armory ➡ warehouse
aroma ➡ smell
aromatic ➡ fragrant
around ➡ about, through
arouse ➡ wake, excite, fan
arraign ➡ try
arrangement ➡ order, structure, display, bouquet, agreement, score

array ➡ assortment, display, arrange, deploy, dress
arrears ➡ debt
arrival ➡ approach, return
arrive ➡ come
arrivederci ➡ good-bye
arrogance ➡ pride
arrogant ➡ proud, dogmatic
arrow ➡ missile
arroyo ➡ canyon
arsenal ➡ warehouse
artery ➡ blood vessel, channel, road

artful ➡ sly
art gallery ➡ gallery
article ➡ object, report
articulation ➡ speech, word
artifact ➡ antique
artifice ➡ art, trick
artificial ➡ fake, manufactured
artillery ➡ arms
artisan ➡ artist
artistic ➡ talented
artistry ➡ art
artless ➡ naive

n = noun • *vb* = verb • *adj* = adjective • *adv* = adverb • *prep* = preposition • *conj* = conjunction

ascend *vb* climb, rise, mount, arise ⇨ *descend*

ashamed *adj* humiliated, mortified, chagrined, embarrassed, shamed, abashed ➡ **sorry**

ask *vb* inquire, request, question, interrogate, query, quiz, examine, interview, grill, petition, apply ➡ **beg**

asleep *adj* sleeping, dozing, napping, resting, dreaming, somnolent, slumbering, dormant, hibernating ➡ **unconscious** ⇨ *awake*

assembly 1. *n* ➡ **meeting, committee, government**
2. *n* construction, building, creation, erection, fabrication, production, manufacture, formation

assortment *n* variety, mix, selection, collection, compilation, array, miscellany, range, series, gamut, medley, potpourri, hash ➡ **pile, mess**

assume 1. *vb* presume, postulate, presuppose, surmise, gather ➡ **guess, believe, pretend**
2. *vb* ➡ **adopt, bear**

atheist *n* agnostic, deist, freethinker, unbeliever, nonbeliever, infidel, heathen ➡ **skeptic**

athlete *n* player, competitor, contender, sportsman, sportswoman, jock (*informal*) ➡ **contestant**

atom *n* molecule

If the word you want is not a main entry above, look below to find it.

as ➡ because

ascendancy ➡ victory

ascension ➡ climb

ascent ➡ slant, climb

ascertain ➡ learn, verify, infer

ascetic ➡ hermit

ascot ➡ tie, scarf

ascribe ➡ attribute

ashen ➡ pale

ashram ➡ monastery

asinine ➡ foolish

askance ➡ sideways

askew ➡ zigzag

aspect ➡ appearance, part

asphyxiate ➡ choke

aspirant ➡ candidate

aspiration ➡ ambition, hope

aspire ➡ hope

assail ➡ attack

assailant ➡ enemy

assassin ➡ killer

assassinate ➡ kill

assassination ➡ murder

assault ➡ attack

assemble ➡ build, gather

assembly plant ➡ factory

assent ➡ agree, agreement

assert ➡ insist, argue

assertion ➡ boast

assertive ➡ certain

assess ➡ estimate, charge

assessment ➡ estimate, tax

asset ➡ advantage

assets ➡ property, wealth

assiduous ➡ patient, diligent

assign ➡ name, attribute, place

assignment ➡ appointment, job, lesson

assimilate ➡ learn

assist ➡ help

assistance ➡ support, help

assistant ➡ helper

associate ➡ friend, partner, join, mix

association ➡ organization, union, link

assonant ➡ musical

assorted ➡ different

assuage ➡ soften

assumption ➡ theory, conclusion

assurance ➡ promise, certainty

assure ➡ guarantee, promise, verify

assured ➡ certain, resolute

asteroid ➡ meteor

astonish ➡ surprise

astonished ➡ dumbfounded

astonishing ➡ awesome

astonishment ➡ surprise

astound ➡ shock

astounding ➡ great

astray ➡ absent

astrologer ➡ prophet

astute ➡ smart

asunder ➡ apart

asylum ➡ protection

at ➡ about

athletic ➡ strong, active

athletic field ➡ field

atmosphere ➡ air, appearance, quality

atoll ➡ island

atone ➡ pay

atrium ➡ court

atrocious ➡ awful

attach ➡ join, attribute

attaché ➡ diplomat

attached ➡ married

attachment ➡ link, love

attack 1. *vb* invade, assault, charge, ambush, waylay, mug, storm, raid, beseige, harry, assail, ravage, bombard, ravage, strike ➡ **fight, argue, pillage** ⇨ *protect*
2. *n* assault, raid, invasion, charge, offensive, offense, incursion, strike, sally, sortie, foray, onset, onslaught, counterattack, operation, sack
3. *n* ➡ **fit²**

attention 1. *n* concentration, awareness, alertness, thought, consideration ➡ **diligence**
2. *n* ➡ **notice**

attic *n* loft, garret, dormer ➡ **room**

attraction *n* allure, appeal, charm, draw, fascination, enticement, temptation, lure, seduction ➡ **pull, personality**

attractive *adj* appealing, fascinating, captivating, magnetic, alluring, inviting, desirable, intriguing, charming, charismatic, winning ➡ **pretty, pleasant**

attribute 1. *n* ➡ **quality**
2. *vb* ascribe, assign, attach, credit ➡ **join**

audacity 1. *n* ➡ **courage**
2. *n* nerve, cheek, impertinence, insolence, temerity, gall

audible *adj* perceptible, discernible, distinct, clear ➡ **loud** ⇨ *quiet*

audience *n* spectators, viewers, onlookers, readers, listeners, patrons, congregation, gallery ➡ **meeting, patron**

automatic 1. *adj* automated, mechanical, mechanized, motorized, self-starting, self-acting, computerized
2. *adj* habitual, involuntary, instinctive, mechanical, spontaneous, reflex, unintentional

---

If the word you want is not a main entry above, look below to find it.

attacker ➡ **enemy**

attain ➡ **finish, come**

attainment ➡ **acquisition, success**

attempt ➡ **try**

attend ➡ **accompany, frequent, concentrate, listen**

attendance ➡ **presence**

attendant ➡ **servant, doorman**

attendants ➡ **court**

attentive ➡ **alert, loving**

attentiveness ➡ **diligence**

attenuate ➡ **weaken**

attest ➡ **testify**

attire ➡ **clothes, dress**

attitude ➡ **belief, perspective, posture**

attorney ➡ **adviser**

attract ➡ **pull, fascinate**

attractiveness ➡ **beauty**

auction ➡ **sale**

audacious ➡ **brave, rude**

audiobook ➡ **book**

audition ➡ **tryout**

auditorium ➡ **hall**

auf Wiedersehen ➡ **good-bye**

augment ➡ **strengthen, grow**

augur ➡ **predict**

augury ➡ **prediction**

august ➡ **grand, dignified**

au revoir ➡ **good-bye**

aurora ➡ **halo**

auspicious ➡ **lucky, successful**

austere ➡ **empty, hard, plain, strict**

austerity ➡ **abstinence, economy**

authentic ➡ **real, correct, official**

authenticate ➡ **verify**

authentication ➡ **proof**

authenticity ➡ **truth**

author ➡ **writer, creator, write**

authoritarian ➡ **dictator, dictatorial**

authoritative ➡ **infallible,**

model

authorities ➡ **police**

authority ➡ **basis, right, expert, permission, rule**

authorization ➡ **permission**

authorize ➡ **approve, let**

authorized ➡ **official, able**

autocrat ➡ **dictator**

autocratic ➡ **dictatorial**

autograph ➡ **signature, sign**

automated ➡ **automatic**

automobile ➡ **vehicle**

autonomous ➡ **free**

autonomy ➡ **freedom**

auxiliary ➡ **subordinate**

avail ➡ **help, advantage**

available *adj* accessible, usable, convenient, handy ➡ **ready**

avalanche *n* slide, landslide, mudslide, rockslide

average 1. *adj* unexceptional, mediocre, unremarkable, standard, routine, medium, modest ➡ **common, normal**
2. *n* mean, median, midpoint, standard, medium, par, norm

avoid *vb* shun, dodge, evade, shirk, duck, sidestep, elude, avert, bypass, circumvent ➡ **escape**

awake 1. *adj* conscious, up, sleepless, wakeful ➡ **alert** ⇨ *asleep*
2. *vb* ➡ **wake**

award 1. *n* honor, decoration, medal, ribbon, citation ➡ **prize**
2. *n* grant, scholarship, fellowship ➡ **prize**
3. *vb* ➡ **give**

awesome 1. *adj* amazing, impressive, astonishing, miraculous, terrific, sensational ➡ **grand, great**
2. *adj* ➡ **scary**

awful *adj* terrible, horrible, dreadful, dire, ghastly, appalling, wretched, grievous, disagreeable, atrocious, outrageous, disgraceful, hateful, odious ➡ **bad, gruesome**

ax, axe *n* hatchet, tomahawk, broadax, pickax, poleax

axis *n* pivot, fulcrum, swivel, hinge ➡ **middle**

If the word you want is not a main entry above, look below to find it.

avarice ➡ **greed**

avaricious ➡ **greedy**

avenge ➡ **revenge**

avenging ➡ **revengeful**

avenue ➡ **road**

averse ➡ **reluctant**

aversion ➡ **opposition, hatred**

avert ➡ **prevent, avoid**

aviary ➡ **zoo**

aviation ➡ **flight**

aviator ➡ **pilot**

avid ➡ **eager**

avocation ➡ **pastime, profession**

await ➡ **wait**

awaken ➡ **wake**

aware ➡ **alert**

awareness ➡ **attention, knowledge**

away ➡ **absent, abroad**

awe ➡ **respect, shock**

awe-inspiring ➡ **grand**

awfully ➡ **very**

awkward ➡ **clumsy, inconvenient**

AWOL ➡ **absent**

awry ➡ **wrong**

axiom ➡ **saying, rule**

aye ➡ **yes**

azure ➡ **blue**

B

baby 1. *n* infant, newborn, toddler, babe, tot ➡ **child** ⇨ *adult*
2. *vb* ➡ **pamper**

back 1. *n* rear, posterior, end, rear end, backside, stern (*of a boat or ship*), aft (*of a boat or ship*), tail (*of an animal or plane*), hindquarters (*of an animal*), rump (*of an animal*), haunch (*of an animal*), reverse (*of a coin or page*) ⇨ *front*
2. *vb* aid, finance, sponsor, fund, promote ➡ **approve, support, help**
3. *vb* back up, reverse ➡ **retreat**
4. *adj, adv* ➡ **backward**

background 1. *n* backdrop, distance, landscape ➡ **setting**
2. *n* ➡ **experience**

backward 1. *adj* backwards, rearward, reversed, behind, retrograde, regressive ➡ **underdeveloped** ⇨ *forward*
2. *adv* backwards, back, rearward, behind, regressively, reversed

bad 1. *adj* evil, sinful, naughty, infamous, villainous, nefarious, incorrigible, disreputable ➡ **wicked, improper, mischievous, dishonest, immoral** ⇨ *good*
2. *adj* unpleasant, disagreeable, undesirable, objectionable, miserable, lousy, nasty, offensive, abominable, repulsive, detestable, despicable, vile, nauseating, sickening, unsavory, disgusting, obnoxious, distasteful ➡ **awful**
3. *adj* rotten, spoiled, rancid, decayed, putrid, moldy ➡ **stale**
4. *adj* ➡ **sad**
5. *adj* ➡ **unhealthy**
6. *adj* ➡ **wrong**

badge *n* insignia, emblem, shield, medallion, escutcheon

bag 1. *n* sack, pouch, purse, handbag, pocketbook, satchel, tote bag, tote, backpack, pack, knapsack, fanny pack ➡ **container, luggage, wallet**
2. *n* ➡ **base**
3. *vb* ➡ **catch**

balance 1. *n* stability, equilibrium, footing, poise
2. *n* symmetry, harmony, counterbalance, proportion, equilibrium
3. *n* ➡ **remainder**
4. *vb* stabilize, counterbalance, steady, poise, counterpoise, neutralize, equalize, redeem, compensate, coordinate, offset

---

If the word you want is not a main entry above, look below to find it.

babble ➡ chatter	backer ➡ support	backwoods ➡ country, rural	baggage ➡ luggage
babe ➡ baby	backing ➡ support	backwoodsman ➡ pioneer	baggage carrier ➡ porter
baby blue ➡ blue	back out ➡ retreat	badger ➡ bother	baguette ➡ bread
baby doll ➡ doll	backpack ➡ bag	badlands ➡ desert	bailiwick ➡ field
babyhood ➡ childhood	backside ➡ back	bad-tempered ➡ cross	bait ➡ tempt
back down ➡ retreat	backslide ➡ relapse	baffle ➡ confuse	bake ➡ cook
backdrop ➡ background, setting	backup ➡ alternate	bafflement ➡ confusion	baked goods ➡ pastry
	backwards ➡ backward	baffling ➡ mysterious	baker ➡ cook

n = noun • *vb* = verb • *adj* = adjective • *adv* = adverb • *prep* = preposition • *conj* = conjunction

bald 1. *adj* hairless, bald-headed, bare
➡ **naked**
2. *adj* flagrant, outright, unadorned, blunt, forthright ➡ **obvious**

ball 1. *n* globe, sphere, orb, globule, drop, pellet, bead, pearl
2. *n* ➡ **dance**
3. *n* ➡ **foot**

ballot *n* slate, ticket, lineup ➡ **vote, choice**

ban 1. *vb* ➡ **forbid**
2. *n* prohibition, embargo, proscription, restriction, injunction, boycott, sanction

band 1. *n* ➡ **group**
2. *n* group, orchestra, ensemble, combo
3. *n* stripe, ribbon, belt, girdle, sash, tape, border, strip, streak, seam, vein ➡ **row, zone, ring**

bandage 1. *n* dressing, compress, Band-Aid (*trademark*), gauze
2. *vb* dress, bind, wrap, swathe

bang 1. *n* crash, crack, pop, boom, blast, explosion, report, thud, detonation, clang, rumble, clap, thunder ➡ **noise, knock**
2. *vb* rattle, clatter, clash, clank, bump ➡ **knock, hit, collide**

banish *vb* deport, exile, expel, expatriate, drive out, drive away, dispel, evict, ostracize ➡ **exclude, oust**

bank 1. *n* ➡ **hill, shore, cliff**
2. *n* savings bank, credit union, trust company, savings and loan, treasury, exchequer, repository, depository
3. *vb* save, deposit, invest
4. *vb* ➡ **slant**

bar 1. *n* rod, shaft, pole, crossbar, boom, rib, rail, stake, stripe, strip ➡ **stick**
2. *n* tavern, saloon, barroom, pub, cocktail lounge, lounge, nightclub, cabaret, brewery
3. *n* ➡ **block**
4. *n* ➡ **table**
5. *n* ➡ **court**
6. *vb* ➡ **lock**
7. *vb* block, obstruct, impede, thwart, hinder, restrict, handicap ➡ **prevent, exclude, forbid, delay**

bargain 1. *n* ➡ **agreement**
2. *n* discount, deal, good deal, buy, reduction, steal (*informal*) ➡ **sale**
3. *vb* ➡ **negotiate**

bark 1. *vb, n* yelp, yap, yip, howl, snarl, growl, woof ➡ **cry**
2. *n* ➡ **boat**
3. *n* ➡ **peel**

If the word you want is not a main entry above, look below to find it.

balanced ➡ **sane**
balderdash ➡ **nonsense**
bald-headed ➡ **bald**
baleful ➡ **ominous**
balk ➡ **hesitate**
ballad ➡ **song**
balloon ➡ **swell**
ballpark ➡ **approximate**

ball-peen hammer ➡ **hammer**
ballpoint ➡ **pen**
baloney ➡ **nonsense**
banal ➡ **trite, common**
banality ➡ **cliché**
Band-Aid® ➡ **bandage**
bandanna ➡ **scarf**
bandit ➡ **criminal**

bane ➡ **poison**
banishment ➡ **exile, suspension**
bankrupt ➡ **ruin**
banner ➡ **flag**
banquet ➡ **feast, meal**
banter ➡ **joke**
baptize ➡ **bless**
barb ➡ **thorn**

barbarian ➡ **vandal**
barbecue ➡ **cook, fireplace**
bard ➡ **musician**
bare ➡ **empty, naked, bald, reveal**
barely ➡ **only, seldom**
barf ➡ **vomit**
baritone ➡ **low**
barkeep ➡ **host**

---

barn *n* stable, stall, cow barn, cowshed, byre ➡ **shed, pen, building**

barrel *n* keg, vat, drum, cask, tub, hogshead, tun ➡ **container**

barrier *n* obstacle, obstruction, hindrance, hurdle, difficulty, impediment, barricade, roadblock, blockade, palisade, clog ➡ **divider**

base 1. *n* foundation, bottom, support, footing, foot, root ➡ **floor** ⇨ *top*
2. *n* ➡ **basis**
3. *n* headquarters, home, home base, base camp, camp, station, terminal
4. *n* plate, goal, bag, sack
5. *vb* found, ground, predicate, establish
6. *vb* locate, station, post, situate

basement *n* cellar, crypt, bunker, storm cellar, crawl space ➡ **room**

basic *adj* elemental, elementary, fundamental, staple, rudimentary, primitive, introductory, primary ➡ **necessary**

basis *n* foundation, support, justification, grounds, authority, underpinning, raison d'être, cornerstone, rudiment ➡ **base, cause**

bat 1. *n* club, stick, pole, mallet
2. *vb* ➡ **hit**

bathrobe *n* robe, dressing gown, negligee, peignoir

bathroom *n* washroom, rest room, lavatory, toilet, bath, women's room, men's room, latrine, head, facilities ➡ **room**

bay 1. *n* inlet, cove, bayou, lagoon, estuary, gulf, arm ➡ **harbor**
2. *n* alcove, niche, nook, recess
3. *vb* ➡ **cry**
4. *adj* ➡ **brown**

beam 1. *n* timber, rafter, stud, joist ➡ **bar, board**
2. *n* ➡ **light**[1]
3. *vb* ➡ **shine**
4. *vb* ➡ **smile**
5. *vb* ➡ **broadcast**

bear 1. *vb* endure, stand, tolerate, abide, stomach, suffer, accept, brook, take, shoulder, assume, undertake ➡ **experience**
2. *vb* ➡ **carry**
3. *vb* ➡ **support, afford**
4. *vb* ➡ **give**

beard *n* whiskers, goatee, Vandyke, stubble, five o'clock shadow, sideburns ➡ **hair**

bearing 1. *n* carriage, demeanor, manner, deportment, presence, mien ➡ **behavior, personality**
2. *n* ➡ **relevance**
3. *n* ➡ **course**
4. *n* ➡ **appearance, posture**

If the word you want is not a main entry above, look below to find it.

barrage ➡ flood	bash ➡ hit	bathing ➡ swim	bazaar ➡ market
barren ➡ sterile	bashful ➡ shy	baton ➡ stick	be ➡ live[1]
barrens ➡ desert	basically ➡ chiefly, practically	batter ➡ hit	beach ➡ shore
barricade ➡ barrier, wall	basin ➡ bowl, sink, valley	battle ➡ fight	beacon ➡ light[1]
barring ➡ but	bass ➡ low	battlefield ➡ field	bead ➡ trinket, drop, ball
barroom ➡ bar	bassinet ➡ bed	battleground ➡ field	beak ➡ nose
barrow ➡ grave	baste ➡ sew	bauble ➡ trinket	beaker ➡ glass
bartender ➡ host	batch ➡ number	bawdy ➡ dirty	bear on ➡ concern
barter ➡ trade, buy, sell	bath ➡ bathroom, cleaning	bawl ➡ cry	beast ➡ animal, monster
base camp ➡ base	bathe ➡ clean, swim	bayou ➡ bay, swamp	beastly ➡ animal

n = noun • *vb* = verb • *adj* = adjective • *adv* = adverb • *prep* = preposition • *conj* = conjunction

beautiful *adj* gorgeous, glamorous, exquisite, beauteous, elegant, stunning, ravishing, dazzling, magnificent ➡ **pretty** ⇨ *ugly*

beauty *n* attractiveness, loveliness, prettiness, elegance, winsomeness, pulchritude, grace, charm, good looks

because *conj* since, due to, for, as, on account of

bed 1. *n* couch, cot, futon, mattress, bedstead, bunk, berth, crib, cradle, bassinet, gurney, stretcher, litter
2. *n* ➡ **floor**

bedroom *n* bedchamber, boudoir, dormitory, guest room, nursery ➡ **room**

before 1. *adv* previously, formerly, earlier, already, beforehand, yet
2. *prep* prior to, ahead of, preceding ➡ **until**

beg *vb* implore, entreat, beseech, plead, urge, solicit, importune ➡ **ask**

beggar 1. *n* panhandler, tramp, bum, hobo, pauper, wretch, derelict, vagrant
2. *vb* ➡ **ruin**

beginning *n* origin, source, outset, onset, commencement, initiation, inauguration, start, birth, conception, genesis, infancy, threshold ➡ **front** ⇨ *finish, conclusion*

behavior 1. *n* conduct, manners, etiquette, decorum ➡ **bearing**
2. *n* performance, function, operation, execution

belief 1. *n* conviction, opinion, view, notion, mind, instinct, hunch, suspicion, attitude, sentiment ➡ **theory, idea, feeling, perspective**
2. *n* faith, trust, confidence, credit, credence, understanding ➡ **certainty**
3. *n* creed, doctrine, dogma, credo, principle ➡ **religion, philosophy, superstition**

believe 1. *vb* accept, think, hold, deem, trust, acknowledge, affirm, view ⇨ *deny*
2. *vb* ➡ **guess**

bell *n* chime, gong, carillon, buzzer, signal

belligerent *adj* hostile, aggressive, combative, contentious, bellicose, pugnacious, militant ➡ **angry, violent, unfriendly**

If the word you want is not a main entry above, look below to find it.

beat ➡ hit, defeat, mix, tick, accent, rhythm, round
beatify ➡ bless
beating ➡ defeat
beauteous ➡ beautiful
beautification ➡ decoration
beautify ➡ decorate
beckon ➡ call, wave
become ➡ suit
becoming ➡ pretty, correct
bed-and-breakfast ➡ hotel
bedazzle ➡ surprise
bedchamber ➡ bedroom
bedeck ➡ decorate

bedraggled ➡ messy
bedspread ➡ blanket
bedstead ➡ bed
bedtime ➡ night
befall ➡ happen
befit ➡ suit
be fond of ➡ like
beforehand ➡ before
befoul ➡ dirty
befuddle ➡ confuse
beget ➡ reproduce
begin ➡ start
beginner ➡ amateur
begrudge ➡ envy

begrudging ➡ jealous
beguile ➡ cheat, entertain, enchant
behave ➡ obey, act
behemoth ➡ giant
behest ➡ order
behind ➡ backward, late, past
behindhand ➡ late
behold ➡ see
beholden ➡ grateful
beige ➡ brown
being ➡ life, existence, animal, human being

belated ➡ late
belatedly ➡ late
belfry ➡ tower
believable ➡ possible
belittle ➡ ridicule, underestimate
bellboy ➡ porter
belles lettres ➡ literature
bellhop ➡ porter
bellicose ➡ belligerent, military
belligerence ➡ anger
bellow ➡ yell, cry
belly ➡ stomach

➡ = synonym cross-reference • ⇨ = antonym cross-reference

belong *vb* fit, go, fit in, pertain, apply, relate, concern

bend 1. *vb* twist, curve, wind, arch, warp, flex, buckle, bow, droop, veer, meander, thread, contort, distort ➡ **turn, slant**
⇨ *straighten*
2. *vb* bow, curtsy, genuflect, stoop, kneel, crouch, squat, duck, hunch, slouch, slump
3. *n* twist, kink, crimp, curl, tangle
➡ **curve, corner**

bent *adj* curved, twisted, warped, bowed, crooked, contorted, misshapen, gnarled
⇨ *straight*

beside *prep* next to, alongside, adjoining, adjacent to, against, near, with

besides 1. *adv* moreover, furthermore, plus, also, too, additionally
2. *prep* ➡ **but**

best 1. *adj* finest, choicest, first, prime, premium, optimum, preeminent, leading, unparalleled, unsurpassed, superlative, foremost, ultimate, supreme, prime, top, upper ➡ **good**
⇨ *worst*
2. *adv* most, above all ⇨ *least*
3. *vb* ➡ **defeat, exceed**

bet *n, vb* wager, venture, gamble, risk, stake, ante

betray 1. *vb* deceive, trick, tell on, inform on, double-cross, abandon ➡ **cheat**
2. *vb* ➡ **reveal**

better 1. *adj* finer, greater, preferable, improved, superior ➡ **good, best**
2. *adj* improved, improving, convalescent, convalescing ➡ **healthy**
3. *adv* ➡ **more**
4. *vb* ➡ **exceed**
5. *vb* ➡ **defeat**

between *prep* among, amid, amongst, amidst, betwixt ➡ **through**
Note that **among** refers to more than two people or things, and **between** most often refers to two, but sometimes more than two.

big *adj* large, generous, substantial, considerable, giant, stout, stocky, great
➡ **huge, heavy, fat, infinite, abundant, high**
⇨ *small*

If the word you want is not a main entry above, look below to find it.

belongings ➡ property
beloved ➡ love
beloved ➡ valuable
below ➡ under
belowground ➡ underground
belt ➡ band, zone, punch
bemoan ➡ regret
bench ➡ seat, court
benchmark ➡ measure
bendable ➡ flexible
beneath ➡ under
benefactor ➡ patron
beneficial ➡ useful

benefit ➡ worth, advantage, pension, help, prosper
benevolence ➡ generosity
benevolent ➡ kind
benign ➡ kind
bequeath ➡ leave, give
bequest ➡ inheritance, will
berate ➡ scold
berry ➡ fruit
berserk ➡ violent, insane
berth ➡ dock, bed
beseech ➡ beg
beseige ➡ attack
beset ➡ infest

besotted ➡ drunk
bestial ➡ animal
best-liked ➡ favorite
bestow ➡ give, leave
betrayal ➡ treason
betrothed ➡ married
betting ➡ gambling
betwixt ➡ between
beverage ➡ drink
bevy ➡ herd
bewail ➡ grieve, regret
bewilder ➡ confuse
bewildered ➡ dumbfounded
bewilderment ➡ confusion

bewitch ➡ enchant
bewitching ➡ magic
beyond ➡ above, past
bias ➡ prejudice, tendency
biased ➡ prejudiced
bicker ➡ argue
bicyclist ➡ rider
bid ➡ order, offer, try, estimate
bidding ➡ invitation
bifocals ➡ glasses
big house ➡ jail
bigoted ➡ prejudiced
bigotry ➡ prejudice

---

n = noun • *vb* = verb • *adj* = adjective • *adv* = adverb • *prep* = preposition • *conj* = conjunction

bill 1. *n* check, tab, invoice, charge, tally, statement ➡ **price, debt**
2. *n* ➡ **act**
3. *n* ➡ **nose**
4. *n* visor, peak, brim
5. *vb* ➡ **charge**

binge *n* spree, bout, fling

bird *n* fowl, songbird, seagull, waterfowl, wader, chick, fledgling ➡ **animal**

birth 1. *n* childbirth, delivery, nativity ⇨ *death*
2. *n* ➡ **beginning**
3. *n* ➡ **ancestry**

bit 1. *n* piece, fragment, particle, scrap, shred, chip, flake, fleck, trifle, snippet, snatch ➡ **bite, block, part**
2. *n* trace, hint, suggestion, shade, touch, lick, glimmer, dash, pinch, tang, modicum, jot, iota, shred
3. *n* ➡ **role, act**

bite 1. *vb* chew, gnaw, nibble, munch, taste, chomp, nip, snap
2. *n* morsel, taste, mouthful, nibble, scrap ➡ **bit, meal**

black *adj, n* ebony, jet, sable, raven, inky, pitch-black, coal-black ➡ **dark** ⇨ *white*

blame 1. *vb* censure, criticize, condemn, denounce, accuse, implicate, charge ➡ **try, scold** ⇨ *forgive*
2. *n* ➡ **guilt**

blank 1. *adj* ➡ **empty, clean**
2. *adj* expressionless, vacuous, impassive, vacant, deadpan, poker-faced

blanket 1. *n* cover, quilt, comforter, duvet, featherbed, bedspread, sheet, shroud
2. *n* ➡ **coat**
3. *adj* ➡ **comprehensive**
4. *vb* ➡ **cover**

bleach *vb* fade, whiten, blanch, lighten, pale

bleak *adj* dreary, desolate, somber, grim, depressing, drear, hopeless, cheerless, gloomy, oppressive, dismal, dour ➡ **sad, sterile, pessimistic**

bless *vb* consecrate, sanctify, dedicate, exalt, hallow, beatify, glorify, anoint, baptize, ordain

blind 1. *adj* sightless, visually impaired, visionless, eyeless, unseeing
2. *adj* ➡ **unaware**

If the word you want is not a main entry above, look below to find it.

billboard ➡ advertisement
billet ➡ house
billfold ➡ wallet
billow ➡ wave, cloud
bind ➡ tie, wrap, bandage
binocular ➡ glass
biographer ➡ writer
birthplace ➡ source
biscuit ➡ bread
bishop ➡ priest

bistro ➡ restaurant
biting ➡ sharp
bitter ➡ sour, sharp, hard, angry
bizarre ➡ strange
blackfly ➡ fly
blackness ➡ dark
blade ➡ knife
blameless ➡ innocent
blameworthy ➡ guilty

blanch ➡ bleach
bland ➡ insipid
blasé ➡ bored
blaspheme ➡ curse
blasphemy ➡ curse
blast ➡ bang, blow¹, wind, shoot
blatant ➡ obvious
blather ➡ chatter
blaze ➡ burn, fire

blazer ➡ coat
blazing ➡ bright, burning
bleached ➡ fair
bleachers ➡ seat
bleeding ➡ bloody
blemish ➡ spot, defect, scar
blend ➡ mix, mixture
blessed ➡ holy
blight ➡ disease, fungus, destroy

blink *vb* wink, flicker, flash, twinkle
➡ **shine**

block 1. *n* piece, chunk, cube, cake, slice, slab, bar, hunk, wedge ➡ **bit, part**
2. *n* ➡ **neighborhood, building**
3. *vb* ➡ **hide**
4. *vb* ➡ **bar**

blood vessel *n* artery, vein, capillary, duct

bloody *adj* bleeding, gory, bloodstained

blossom 1. *n* ➡ **flower**
2. *vb* bloom, flower, bud ➡ **grow, prosper**

blow[1] 1. *n* hit, stroke, strike, punch, slap, jab, lick, swat, kick, stab, poke, whack, thwack, smack ➡ **push**
2. *n* blast, impact, concussion, shock, wallop, jolt
3. *n* ➡ **shock**

blow[2] 1. *vb* waft, float, sail, drift ➡ **wave**
2. *vb* honk, toot, sound ➡ **play**
3. *vb* ➡ **breathe**
4. *n* ➡ **wind**

blue 1. *adj, n* navy, azure, turquoise, royal blue, powder blue, baby blue, sky blue
2. *adj* ➡ **sad**

blush *vb* flush, redden, color, glow

board 1. *n* plank, beam, slat, timber, lumber, rafter, joist, two-by-four
2. *n* meals, fare, keep ➡ **food**
3. *n* ➡ **committee**
4. *vb* ➡ **enter**
5. *vb* ➡ **house**

boast 1. *vb* brag, gloat, crow, show off, vaunt, swagger, exult
2. *n* brag, bragging, vaunt, claim, assertion, bluster, swagger, bravado

boat *n* ship, vessel, craft, bark

body 1. *n* build, physique, frame, anatomy, figure, form, torso, trunk
2. *n* corpse, carcass, cadaver, remains, skeleton, bones
3. *n* ➡ **human being**
4. *n* ➡ **group**
5. *n* ➡ **matter**
6. *n* ➡ **density**

bogeyman *n* bogey, bugaboo, goblin, hobgoblin, bugbear

boil 1. *vb* simmer, stew, seethe, parboil, bubble, poach ➡ **cook**
2. *n* ➡ **sore**

If the word you want is not a main entry above, look below to find it.

bliss ➡ heaven, pleasure

blissful ➡ ecstatic

blizzard ➡ storm, snow

blob ➡ lump

bloc ➡ group, party

blockade ➡ barrier

blockhead ➡ fool

blond, blonde ➡ fair, yellow

blood ➡ ancestry

bloodshed ➡ murder

bloodstained ➡ bloody

bloodthirsty ➡ predatory

bloom ➡ flower, blossom

blooper ➡ mistake

blot ➡ spot

blotch ➡ spot

blow up ➡ explode

blue-blooded ➡ noble

bluebottle ➡ fly

blueprint ➡ pattern

bluff ➡ cheat, cliff

blunder ➡ mistake

blunderbuss ➡ gun

blunt ➡ dull, bald, abrupt, straightforward

blurry ➡ dim

blushing ➡ red

bluster ➡ boast

blustery ➡ stormy, windy

B.O. ➡ sweat

boards ➡ stage

boating ➡ nautical

boatman ➡ sailor

bobby pin ➡ pin

bodily ➡ physical

body odor ➡ sweat

bog ➡ swamp

bogey ➡ bogeyman

bogus ➡ fake

boiler ➡ furnace

boiling ➡ hot

boisterous ➡ loud

bold ➡ brave, rude

boldness ➡ courage

bolster ➡ cushion, support

bolt ➡ lock, nail, missile, run, escape, eat

bombard ➡ attack

bombardment ➡ fire

bombastic ➡ pompous

bond 1. *n* shackle, chain, fetter, manacle, handcuff, restraint
2. *n* ➡ **link**

book *n* volume, publication, text, paperback, hardcover, work, tome, manual, handbook, audiobook, manuscript, script, libretto ➡ **pamphlet**

boor *n* lout, oaf, churl, bumpkin, yahoo, Philistine, ape, lummox, dullard

booth *n* stall, counter, kiosk, stand, cubicle, compartment, enclosure

booty *n* loot, plunder, spoils, winnings, contraband, pillage ➡ **prize**

border 1. *n* frontier, boundary, march, borderland ➡ **edge, circumference, band**
2. *vb* abut, adjoin, neighbor, bound, skirt, flank ➡ **join**

bored *adj* uninterested, jaded, blasé ➡ **tired**

boredom *n* ennui, apathy, tedium, monotony

borrow *vb* rent, hire, bum (*informal*), scrounge (*informal*), mooch (*informal*) ➡ **adopt, get, use**

boss 1. *n* chief, leader, head, director, employer, foreman, manager, supervisor, superior, captain, commander, skipper ➡ **principal, chairperson**
2. *vb* ➡ **lead, control**

bother 1. *vb* annoy, vex, tease, plague, pester, needle, aggravate, irk, nag, hound, badger, harass, bug, irritate, chafe, rankle ➡ **disturb, worry**
2. *n* ➡ **nuisance**

bottle *n* jug, pitcher, flask, canteen, carafe, ewer, crock, cruet ➡ **container**

bouquet 1. *n* bunch, posy, nosegay, arrangement, spray, garland
2. *n* ➡ **smell**

bowl *n* dish, vessel, basin, tureen, crock ➡ **container, kettle, plate**

If the word you want is not a main entry above, look below to find it.

bona fide ➡ real
bondage ➡ slavery
bones ➡ body
bonfire ➡ fire
bong ➡ ring
bonjour ➡ hello
bon mot ➡ joke
bonnet ➡ hat
bonus ➡ prize, tip
boo ➡ yell
boo-boo ➡ mistake
bookish ➡ educated
booklet ➡ pamphlet
boom ➡ bang, bar
boon ➡ gift
boondocks ➡ country

boorishness ➡ rudeness
boost ➡ lift, strengthen
boot ➡ shoe, kick
bordering ➡ adjacent
borderland ➡ border
bore ➡ dig, well, tire
boring ➡ dull
borough ➡ town, neighborhood
bosom ➡ chest
botch ➡ fumble
bothersome ➡ inconvenient
bottom ➡ base, floor, essence
bottomland ➡ swamp
boudoir ➡ bedroom

bough ➡ limb
boulder ➡ rock
boulevard ➡ road
bounce ➡ jump, reflect
bound ➡ jump, border
boundary ➡ edge, border, hedge
boundless ➡ infinite
bounteous ➡ abundant
bountiful ➡ abundant
bounty ➡ generosity
bourgeoisie ➡ people
bout ➡ game, period, binge
bow ➡ bend, curve, play, surrender, front
bowed ➡ bent

bow tie ➡ tie
box ➡ container, square, punch
boy ➡ child, man
boycott ➡ ban, forbid
boyfriend ➡ friend, love
boyhood ➡ childhood
boyish ➡ young
brace ➡ support, strengthen, pair
bracing ➡ brisk, cool
brackish ➡ salty
brad ➡ nail
brag ➡ boast
bragging ➡ boast

---

braid 1. *n* plait, pigtail, queue, twist
2. *vb* ➡ **weave**

branch 1. *n* limb, arm, wing, offshoot, fork, projection, tributary ➡ **stick, department**
2. *vb* ➡ **divide**

brave 1. *adj* courageous, heroic, fearless, valiant, valorous, gallant, bold, stalwart, daring, audacious, intrepid, dauntless, undaunted, adventurous, adventuresome, plucky, dashing ⇨ *afraid*
2. *vb* ➡ **face**

bread *n* loaf, biscuit, roll, baguette, tortilla ➡ **cake, pastry**

break 1. *vb* crack, shatter, smash, fracture, split, snap, crash, splinter, burst, rupture, crush, squash, chip ➡ **destroy, explode, separate**
2. *n* fracture, split, crack, rift, breach, gap, opening, chip, schism
3. *n* pause, recess, intermission, breather, respite, delay, interlude, interruption, lull, hiatus, suspension, disruption ➡ **vacation, rest, truce**
4. *vb* ➡ **disobey**

5. *vb* ➡ **defeat**
6. *n* ➡ **luck**

breakable *adj* fragile, delicate, dainty, brittle, flimsy, friable, crumbly ➡ **weak** ⇨ *unbreakable*

breath 1. *n* respiration, inhalation, exhalation, breathing
2. *n* ➡ **life**
3. *n* ➡ **air, wind**

breathe 1. *vb* inhale, exhale, respire, expire, pant, gasp, wheeze, puff, huff, gulp ➡ **mumble**
2. *vb* ➡ **live¹**

brevity *n* conciseness, concision, succinctness, economy, terseness

bridge 1. *n* span, overpass, catwalk, gangway, gangplank, viaduct
2. *n* ➡ **link**
3. *vb* cross, connect, span ➡ **join**

bright 1. *adj* brilliant, glowing, radiant, sunny, dazzling, glaring, blazing, intense, luminous, colorful, gay, vivid, flashy ➡ **fair, shiny** ⇨ *dim, dull*
2. *adj* ➡ **happy**
3. *adj* ➡ **smart**

If the word you want is not a main entry above, look below to find it.

brain ➡ mind, genius
brake ➡ stop
bramble ➡ thorn
brand ➡ make, label
brandish ➡ swing
brand name ➡ make
brand-new ➡ new
brash ➡ rude
brat ➡ urchin
brava ➡ encore
bravado ➡ boast
bravery ➡ courage

bravissimo ➡ encore
bravo ➡ encore
brawl ➡ fight
brawny ➡ fat
breach ➡ break
breadth ➡ width
breadwinner ➡ worker
breaker ➡ wave
breakfast nook ➡ dining room
break out ➡ escape
breakthrough ➡ event, invention

break up ➡ separate
breakwater ➡ jetty
breast ➡ chest
breather ➡ break
breathing ➡ breath
breathtaking ➡ exciting
breed ➡ reproduce, grow, type
breeder ➡ farmer
breeding ➡ class, civilization
breeze ➡ wind

breezeway ➡ porch
breezy ➡ windy
brew ➡ cook
brewery ➡ bar
briar ➡ thorn
bride ➡ spouse
brief ➡ short
brier ➡ thorn
brig ➡ jail
brighten ➡ light¹
brightness ➡ light¹

bring *vb* fetch, deliver, lead, conduct, escort
➡ **take, lead, carry, pull**

brisk 1. *adj* crisp, bracing, invigorating
➡ **cold, cool**
2. *adj* ➡ **lively**

broach *vb* mention, bring up, introduce,
raise ➡ **say**

broad *adj* wide, thick, deep, expansive,
extensive, capacious ➡ **big** ⇨ *narrow*
   Note that **broad** and **wide** are close synonyms in
   that both refer to the distance across something, as
   in "a **broad** street" or "a **wide** street." However,
   broad suggests the whole area or expanse of the
   surface itself and **wide** stresses more the distance
   from one side to the other. If you want to give
   the actual distance, use **wide**: three feet **wide,**
   a yard **wide.**

broadcast 1. *vb* transmit, beam, air, televise,
telecast, relay ➡ **send, play**
2. *vb* ➡ **advertise**
3. *vb* ➡ **plant**
4. *n* ➡ **program**

broken 1. *adj* cracked, shattered, fractured,
damaged, defective, faulty, malfunctioning,
disabled, broken-down, down, unusable,
out of order ➡ **useless**
2. *adj* ➡ **tame**

brown *adj, n* tan, chestnut, beige, fawn, tawny,
khaki, bay, bronze, chocolate, taupe, umber
➡ **dark**

brush 1. *n* underbrush, undergrowth, shrubbery,
scrub, thicket, bushes ➡ **hedge**
2. *n* ➡ **meeting**
3. *vb* ➡ **clean, sweep, rub**
4. *vb* ➡ **comb**

budget 1. *n* finances, expenses, allotment,
allowance, resources
2. *vb* allot, allocate, ration, estimate ➡ **share**
3. *adj* ➡ **cheap**

bug 1. *n* insect, beetle, spider, vermin, pest
2. *n* ➡ **disease, germ**
3. *vb* ➡ **bother**

If the word you want is not a main entry above, look below to find it.

brilliance ➡ light[1]

brilliant ➡ bright, smart, jewel

brim ➡ bill, edge

brimful ➡ full

bring up ➡ broach

brink ➡ edge

briny ➡ salty

brittle ➡ breakable

broadax ➡ ax, axe

broad-minded ➡ liberal

broadside ➡ sideways

broadsword ➡ sword

brochure ➡ pamphlet

broil ➡ cook

broiling ➡ hot

broke ➡ poor

broken-down ➡ broken, shabby

broker ➡ agent

bromide ➡ cliché

bronze ➡ brown, statue

brooch ➡ pin

brood ➡ worry, mope, herd

brook ➡ river, bear

brother ➡ religious

brotherhood ➡ friendship

brownie ➡ fairy

browse ➡ read, eat

bruise ➡ hurt

bruised ➡ sore

brunette ➡ dark

brusque ➡ abrupt

brutal ➡ sharp, mean

brutality ➡ violence

brute ➡ animal, monster

brutish ➡ animal

bubble ➡ boil

bubbles ➡ foam

buccaneer ➡ pirate

bucket ➡ container

buckle ➡ clasp, join, bend

bud ➡ flower, blossom, shoot

buddy ➡ friend

budge ➡ move

budgetary ➡ financial

buff ➡ shine

buffer ➡ cushion, protection

buffet ➡ hit, cupboard

buffoon ➡ fool

bugaboo ➡ bogeyman

bugbear ➡ bogeyman

buggy ➡ wagon

---

build 1. *vb* construct, erect, assemble, raise, fabricate, fashion ➡ **form, invent, make**
⇨ *destroy*
2. *vb* ➡ **strengthen**
3. *n* ➡ **body**

building 1. *n* structure, edifice, block, shelter ➡ **house, hall**
2. *n* ➡ **assembly**

bulge 1. *n* bump, lump, hump, knob, swelling, protrusion, protuberance
2. *vb* ➡ **swell**

bully 1. *n* ruffian, troublemaker, tyrant, tormentor, tough, rowdy, hooligan
➡ **rascal, criminal**
2. *vb* ➡ **threaten**

burn 1. *vb* blaze, flare, incinerate, scorch, singe, sear, char, glow ➡ **smoke, cook**
2. *vb* ➡ **hurt**

burning *adj* flaming, fiery, blazing, ablaze, afire, inflamed, smoldering ➡ **hot**

bury *vb* inter, entomb, lay to rest, enshrine, mummify, cremate ➡ **hide**

business 1. *n* industry, commerce, trade, traffic, manufacturing, finance, economics
2. *n* affair, matter, concern, transaction ➡ **job**
3. *n* company, firm, establishment, corporation, enterprise, outfit, partnership, concern ➡ **factory**

but 1. *conj* however, although, though, yet, except, nevertheless
2. *prep* except, besides, save, excluding, barring

buy 1. *vb* purchase, pay for, barter, shop ➡ **get, hire**
2. *n* ➡ **bargain**

If the word you want is not a main entry above, look below to find it.

bulb ➡ seed, flower, light[1]

bulk ➡ size, density, most

bulky ➡ clumsy, heavy

bulldoze ➡ dig

bullet ➡ missile

bulletin ➡ announcement

bullets ➡ ammunition

bullfrog ➡ frog

bullish ➡ optimistic

bullwhip ➡ whip

bulwark ➡ jetty

bum ➡ beggar, borrow

bumbling ➡ clumsy

bump ➡ hit, bang, bulge

bumpkin ➡ boor

bumpy ➡ rough

bunch ➡ group, number, bouquet

buncombe ➡ nonsense

bundle ➡ package, number

bung ➡ top

bungalow ➡ home

bungle ➡ fumble

bunk ➡ bed, nonsense

bunker ➡ basement

buoyant ➡ light[2]

burden ➡ load, worry

bureau ➡ chest, department

bureaucrat ➡ official

burglar ➡ criminal

burglarize ➡ steal

burglary ➡ theft

burial ground ➡ cemetery

buried ➡ underground

burlesque ➡ parody

burly ➡ strong

burnable ➡ inflammable

burner ➡ furnace

burnish ➡ shine

burr ➡ accent

burro ➡ donkey

burrow ➡ dig, den

burst ➡ break, explode

bush ➡ country, plant

bushes ➡ brush, hedge

businessman, businessperson, businesswoman ➡ tycoon

buss ➡ kiss

bust ➡ chest, statue, arrest

bustle ➡ activity

bustling ➡ active

busy ➡ active, employed

C

cake 1. *n* layer cake, coffee cake, fruitcake, cupcake, torte ➡ **pastry, bread**
2. *n* ➡ **block**
3. *vb* ➡ **harden**

call 1. *vb* summon, beckon, invite, page, accost ➡ **welcome, visit**
2. *vb, n* ➡ **yell**
3. *vb* phone, telephone, ring, dial, buzz
4. *vb* ➡ **name**
5. *n* ➡ **attraction**
6. *n* ➡ **reason**

calm 1. *adj* peaceful, serene, tranquil, placid, undisturbed, untroubled, composed, self-possessed, relaxed, poised ➡ **quiet, gentle**
2. *n* quiet, tranquility, peacefulness, serenity, stillness, composure, silence, hush ➡ **peace** ⇨ *activity*
3. *vb* quiet, relax, soothe, ease, comfort, compose, lull ➡ **pacify** ⇨ *excite*

candidate *n* nominee, aspirant, applicant, office-seeker, front-runner, dark horse, favorite son ➡ **contestant**

canyon *n* ravine, gorge, gully, arroyo, crevasse, crevice, chasm, gulch ➡ **valley**

cape 1. *n* peninsula, promontory, point, headland, neck, spit
2. *n* ➡ **wrap**

If the word you want is not a main entry above, look below to find it.

cab ➡ taxi
cabal ➡ party
cabaret ➡ bar
cabin ➡ shack, home
cabinet ➡ cupboard, committee
cable ➡ rope
cache ➡ supply
cackle ➡ laugh
cacophonous ➡ loud
cadaver ➡ body
cadence ➡ rhythm, accent
cadet ➡ soldier
café ➡ restaurant
cafeteria ➡ restaurant
cage ➡ pen
cajole ➡ persuade
calamitous ➡ destructive
calamity ➡ disaster
calcify ➡ harden

calculate ➡ add, estimate
calculation ➡ mathematics
calendar ➡ diary
caliber ➡ class
caliph ➡ emperor
caller ➡ visitor
calligraphy ➡ handwriting
calling ➡ profession
callous ➡ insensitive
camaraderie ➡ friendship
Camelot ➡ utopia
camerman ➡ photographer
camouflage ➡ hide, disguise
camp ➡ base
campaign ➡ movement
campanile ➡ tower
campfire ➡ fire
can ➡ container, fire
canal ➡ channel
canard ➡ lie

cancel ➡ abolish
cancer ➡ growth
candid ➡ straightforward
candor ➡ truth, honesty
cane ➡ stick, whip
canine ➡ dog
cannon ➡ gun
canny ➡ smart
canon ➡ rule
canopy ➡ tent
cant ➡ slant, dialect
cantankerous ➡ cross
cantata ➡ hymn
canteen ➡ restaurant, bottle
canter ➡ run
canto ➡ stanza
cantor ➡ singer
canvass ➡ study
cap ➡ top, hat, climax
capability ➡ ability, sense

capable ➡ able
capacious ➡ broad
capacity ➡ function, ability, size, measure
caper ➡ joke, dance
capillary ➡ blood vessel
capital ➡ property, money, good
capitalist ➡ tycoon
capitulate ➡ surrender
capitulation ➡ surrender
caprice ➡ fancy, impulse
capricious ➡ arbitrary
capsize ➡ upset
capsule ➡ medicine
captain ➡ boss, control
caption ➡ headline
captivate ➡ fascinate
captivating ➡ attractive
captive ➡ prisoner
capture ➡ catch, arrest

---

carefree *adj* lighthearted, easygoing, nonchalant, casual, informal, untroubled, devil-may-care, laid-back, mellow ➡ **happy, calm**

careful 1. *adj* painstaking, thorough, exact, accurate, particular, precise, meticulous, conscientious, studious, scrupulous, nice
2. *adj* cautious, wary, prudent, concerned, circumspect, politic, discreet, judicious, guarded ➡ **alert, suspicious** ⇨ *thoughtless*

carefully 1. *adv* precisely, meticulously, deliberately, faithfully, thoroughly
2. *adv* cautiously, warily, prudently, discreetly, mindfully, gingerly, delicately

carnival *n* fair, circus, festival, amusement park, theme park

carry 1. *vb* move, transport, convey, bear, cart, pack, haul, transfer, tote, lug (*informal*) ➡ **take**
2. *vb* ➡ **sell**
3. *vb* ➡ **support**

carve *vb* sculpt, sculpture, whittle, etch, inscribe, engrave, incise, hew, chisel ➡ **cut**

cash register *n* register, till, cash box ➡ **safe**

castle *n* fortress, fort, garrison, fortification, stronghold, citadel, keep, donjon, palace

casualty 1. *n* victim, death, injury, fatality, dead
2. *n* ➡ **disaster**

catch 1. *vb* capture, trap, grasp, take, bag, snag, clasp, snare, ensnare, entangle, mire, enslave ➡ **seize, arrest** ⇨ *free*
2. *vb* pass, overtake, outrun, outstrip
3. *vb* contract, develop, come down with, incur ➡ **get**
4. *n* grab, snag, scoop
5. *n* ➡ **clasp, lock**
6. *n* ➡ **trap**

If the word you want is not a main entry above, look below to find it.

car ➡ vehicle

carafe ➡ bottle

carapace ➡ shell

carbine ➡ gun

carcass ➡ body

card ➡ letter

cardinal ➡ important, priest

care ➡ worry, diligence, protection, treatment

career ➡ profession, life

care for ➡ like

carefulness ➡ diligence

careless ➡ thoughtless, arbitrary

caress ➡ pet, embrace, touch

caretaker ➡ guardian, doorman

cargo ➡ load

caricature ➡ parody, imitate

carillon ➡ bell

caring ➡ loving

carjack ➡ seize

carmine ➡ red

carnage ➡ murder

carnivorous ➡ predatory

carol ➡ hymn

carouse ➡ celebrate

carpet ➡ rug, cover

carpeting ➡ rug

carport ➡ garage

carriage ➡ wagon, posture, bearing, gait

carrier ➡ messenger

carry on ➡ continue

carry out ➡ do, act, commit

cart ➡ carry, wagon

cartel ➡ monopoly

carton ➡ container

cartoon ➡ picture

cascade ➡ flood, flow

case ➡ container, example, suit

cash ➡ money

cash box ➡ cash register

casing ➡ shell

cask ➡ barrel

cast ➡ throw, form

castigate ➡ scold

cast off ➡ shed

castrate ➡ sterilize

casual ➡ carefree, spontaneous

cataclysm ➡ disaster

catacomb ➡ grave, cemetery

catalog ➡ list, table

catalogue ➡ list

catapult ➡ throw

catastrophe ➡ disaster

catastrophic ➡ destructive, unfortunate

catching ➡ contagious

categorization ➡ stereotype

categorize ➡ arrange, stereotype

category ➡ type

caterpillar ➡ larva

cathedral ➡ church

catholic ➡ universal

catnap ➡ sleep

cat-o'-nine-tails ➡ whip

cattle ➡ livestock

catwalk ➡ bridge

cauldron ➡ pot

n = noun • *vb* = verb • *adj* = adjective • *adv* = adverb • *prep* = preposition • *interj* = interjection

cause 1. *vb* produce, create, effect, generate, prompt, inspire, motivate, engender ➡ **start, make, do**
2. *n* origin, source, stimulus, basis ➡ **reason**
3. *n* principle, conviction ➡ **movement**

cave *n* cavern, tunnel, grotto, chamber ➡ **hole, den**

celebrate 1. *vb* observe, commemorate, keep, solemnize, honor ➡ **praise**
2. *vb* rejoice, carouse, revel, party

celebrity 1. *n* ➡ **fame**
2. *n* notable, luminary, personage, personality, name, star, superstar, dignitary, VIP ➡ **actor**

celibate *adj* abstinent, chaste, virginal, unmarried

cemetery *n* graveyard, burial ground, memorial park, churchyard, crypt, sepulcher, catacomb ➡ **grave, monument**

ceremony 1. *n* service, ritual, rite, celebration, tradition, commemoration, festival
2. *n* formality, pomp, solemnity, protocol

certain 1. *adj* sure, positive, confident, definite, assertive, forceful, vehement, self-confident, assured, convinced
2. *adj* undeniable, unquestionable, definite, absolute, inevitable, inescapable, unavoidable ➡ **reliable, conclusive, infallible**
3. *adj* ➡ **special**
4. *adj* ➡ **reliable**

certainly *adv, interj* absolutely, positively, definitely, perfectly, completely, surely, truly, undoubtedly, unquestionably, indeed, really ➡ **finally**

certainty 1. *n* certitude, assurance, conviction, confidence, self-confidence ➡ **belief**
2. *n* fact, reality, truth, actuality, truth, foregone conclusion, sure thing

chairperson *n* chair, chairman, chairwoman, head ➡ **boss, host**

chance 1. *n* fate, fortune, luck, destiny, lot, accident, coincidence, happenstance, serendipity
2. *n* ➡ **possibility**
3. *n* ➡ **opportunity**
4. *adj* ➡ **arbitrary, accidental**
5. *vb* ➡ **happen**

If the word you want is not a main entry above, look below to find it.

caustic ➡ **sharp, sarcastic**

caution ➡ **warn, warning, advice, protection**

cautious ➡ **careful**

cautiously ➡ **carefully**

cavalcade ➡ **parade**

caveat ➡ **warning**

cavern ➡ **cave**

cavity ➡ **hole**

cavort ➡ **dance**

cay ➡ **island**

cease ➡ **stop, abandon**

cease-fire ➡ **truce**

celebrated ➡ **famous**

celebration ➡ **party, ceremony**

celerity ➡ **speed**

celestial ➡ **heavenly**

celestial body ➡ **planet**

celibacy ➡ **abstinence**

cell ➡ **jail**

cellar ➡ **basement**

cement ➡ **adhesive, join**

censor ➡ **forbid**

censure ➡ **blame**

census ➡ **study**

center ➡ **middle**

central ➡ **middle**

ceramics ➡ **pottery**

cerebral ➡ **intellectual, profound**

ceremonious ➡ **dignified**

certificate ➡ **document**

certification ➡ **proof**

certify ➡ **guarantee, approve, testify**

certitude ➡ **certainty**

chafe ➡ **rub, bother**

chagrin ➡ **embarrass, shame**

chagrined ➡ **ashamed**

chain ➡ **bond, row**

chair ➡ **seat, chairperson, lead**

chairman ➡ **chairperson**

chairwoman ➡ **chairperson**

chalet ➡ **home**

chalky ➡ **pale**

challenge ➡ **contradict, face, dare**

challenger ➡ **opponent**

chamber ➡ **room, cave**

chamois ➡ **hide, cloth**

champ ➡ **winner**

champion ➡ **winner, savior, support**

chandelier ➡ **light[1]**

---

change 1. *vb* alter, vary, modify, transform, convert, mutate, shift, innovate ➡ **correct, adjust, distort, tinker**

2. *vb* switch, exchange, replace, interchange, substitute, swap, reverse, invert, transpose ➡ **trade**

3. *n* alteration, variation, shift, deviation, evolution, mutation, transformation, revolution, modification, metamorphosis, transition, vicissitude

channel *n* trough, chute, gutter, sluice, shaft, ramp, slide, groove, furrow, trench, rut, ditch, moat, aqueduct, canal, waterway, artery ➡ **pipe, course**

charge 1. *vb* bill, assess, invoice
2. *vb* ➡ **attack**
3. *vb* ➡ **argue, blame, try**
4. *n* ➡ **bill, price**
5. *n* ➡ **duty**
6. *n* ➡ **rule, order**
7. *n* ➡ **complaint**

chatter *vb* prattle, babble, gibber, jabber, gossip, tattle, ramble, prate, blather ➡ **talk**

cheap 1. *adj* inexpensive, reasonable, affordable, economical, low-priced, cut-rate, budget ⇨ *expensive*

2. *adj* inferior, shoddy, mediocre, second-rate, chintzy

3. *adj* thrifty, frugal, prudent, stingy, miserly, niggardly, tight-fisted, penny-pinching, cheeseparing, penurious, tight

cheat 1. *vb* trick, deceive, swindle, chisel, hoodwink, beguile, bluff, defraud, dupe, con, gyp, prey on ➡ **fool**

2. *n* cheater, swindler, quack, charlatan, fraud, shyster, imposter, fake, humbug ➡ **criminal, hypocrite**

chest 1. *n* trunk, footlocker, locker, bureau, dresser, chiffonier ➡ **container, safe**

2. *n* breast, bosom, bust, ribcage, ribs, trunk, thorax

If the word you want is not a main entry above, look below to find it.

changeable ➡ **variable, fickle**

change purse ➡ **wallet**

chant ➡ **sing, hymn**

chaos ➡ **confusion**

chaotic ➡ **frantic**

chap ➡ **man**

chapeau ➡ **hat**

chapel ➡ **church**

chaperon, chaperone ➡ **accompany, host**

chaplain ➡ **minister**

chaplet ➡ **crown**

chapter ➡ **division, department**

char ➡ **burn**

character ➡ **personality, reputation, quality, role**

characteristic ➡ **quality**

characterization ➡ **description, stereotype**

characterize ➡ **describe, stereotype**

chargé d'affaires ➡ **diplomat**

charisma ➡ **personality**

charismatic ➡ **attractive**

charitable ➡ **generous, kind**

charitableness ➡ **generosity**

charity ➡ **kindness, generosity**

charlatan ➡ **cheat, rascal**

charm ➡ **beauty, attraction, personality, curse, enchantment, enchant, fascinate**

charmed ➡ **magic**

charming ➡ **nice, attractive, cute, suave**

chart ➡ **table, plan**

charter ➡ **hire, license**

chartreuse ➡ **green**

chase ➡ **follow, hunt**

chasm ➡ **canyon, hole**

chassis ➡ **framework**

chaste ➡ **innocent, celibate**

chastise ➡ **scold**

chastity ➡ **virtue**

chat ➡ **talk**

chateau ➡ **home**

chatty ➡ **talkative**

chauvinistic ➡ **patriotic**

cheapskate ➡ **miser**

cheater ➡ **cheat**

check ➡ **prevent, stop, try, bill, tick**

check mark ➡ **tick**

cheek ➡ **audacity**

cheeky ➡ **rude**

cheep ➡ **peep**

cheer ➡ **clap, entertain**

cheerful ➡ **happy, optimistic**

cheerio ➡ **good-bye**

cheerless ➡ **bleak**

cheeseparing ➡ **cheap**

chef ➡ **cook**

cherish ➡ **love, appreciate, respect**

cherished ➡ **valuable**

cherub ➡ **angel**

chestnut ➡ **brown**

chew ➡ **bite**

n = noun • *vb* = verb • *adj* = adjective • *adv* = adverb • *prep* = preposition • *conj* = conjunction

chiefly *adv* mainly, primarily, essentially, principally, particularly, substantially, especially, notably, importantly, fundamentally, predominantly, basically, generally, mostly

child 1. *n* juvenile, youngster, minor, kid (*informal*), youth, boy, girl ➡ **baby, teenager, urchin** ➪ *adult*
2. *n* daughter, son, offspring, progeny, descendant

childhood *n* infancy, babyhood, youth, minority, boyhood, girlhood, adolescence, puberty, immaturity

childish *adj* childlike, infantile, immature, juvenile, puerile, sophomoric ➡ **young**

choice 1. *n* alternative, option, selection, pick, preference, way, recourse, vote, voice ➡ **preference**
2. *adj* ➡ **good, favorite, special**

choir *n* chorus, chorale, glee club, ensemble ➡ **singer**

choke *vb* strangle, suffocate, asphyxiate, stifle, smother, drown ➡ **die, kill**

choose *vb* select, pick, elect, opt, name, take, designate, vote ➡ **decide, prefer** ➪ *exclude*

choosy *adj* finicky, fussy, particular, picky, dainty, fastidious

chorus 1. *n* ➡ **choir**
2. *n* refrain, theme, strain, motif, leitmotif

church 1. *n* cathedral, temple, synagogue, mosque, chapel, mission ➡ **building**
2. *n* congregation, parish, parishioners, flock

circle 1. *n* ring, loop, hoop, disk, coil, circuit, circumference, perimeter, periphery, revolution, orbit ➡ **round**
2. *vb* ➡ **ring**

circumference *n* perimeter, periphery, circuit, outline, contour, silhouette ➡ **edge, border, circle**

If the word you want is not a main entry above, look below to find it.

chic ➡ fashionable
chick ➡ bird
chicken ➡ cowardly
chide ➡ scold
chief ➡ boss, important
chiffonier ➡ chest
childbirth ➡ birth
childless ➡ sterile
childlike ➡ childish
chill ➡ cool
chilly ➡ cool
chime ➡ bell, ring
chimney ➡ fireplace
china ➡ plate, pottery
chintzy ➡ cheap

chip ➡ bit, break
chirp ➡ peep, sing
chisel ➡ carve, cheat
chitchat ➡ talk
chivalric ➡ noble
chivalrous ➡ polite, noble
chocolate ➡ brown
choicest ➡ best
chomp ➡ bite
chop ➡ cut
choppy ➡ rough
chorale ➡ choir
chore ➡ job
chorister ➡ singer
christen ➡ name

chronic ➡ continual, frequent
chronicle ➡ diary, story
chronograph ➡ clock
chronometer ➡ clock
chubby ➡ fat
chuck ➡ throw
chuckle ➡ laugh
chum ➡ friend
chunk ➡ block, lump
church-going ➡ religious
churchyard ➡ cemetery
churl ➡ boor
churn ➡ mix
chute ➡ channel
ciao ➡ good-bye, hello

cicatrix ➡ scar
cinema ➡ movies
cinematographer ➡ photographer
cipher ➡ zero, number
circlet ➡ crown, ring
circuit ➡ circle, circumference, round
circuitous ➡ indirect
circular ➡ round, advertisement
circulate ➡ spread
circulation ➡ flow
circumspect ➡ careful
circumspection ➡ tact
circumstance ➡ event, state

circumstantial *adj* indirect, inferential, inconclusive, incidental

citizen *n* inhabitant, subject, native, resident, national, denizen ➡ **occupant**

civilization 1. *n* cultivation, culture, enlightenment, refinement, breeding, polish ➡ **progress**
2. *n* ➡ **people**

clap 1. *vb* applaud, cheer, root ➡ **praise**
2. *n* ➡ **bang**

clarity *n* clearness, lucidity, simplicity, transparency, definition, focus, sharpness, resolution

clasp 1. *n* fastener, clamp, buckle, zipper, button, catch, snap, clip ➡ **lock**
2. *vb* ➡ **join, squeeze, embrace, catch**

class 1. *n* ➡ **type, group, grade**
2. *n* refinement, polish, quality, panache, grace, style, breeding, cultivation, caliber ➡ **elegance**
3. *n* ➡ **lesson, course**

clean 1. *vb* wash, cleanse, rinse, scrub, scrape, scour, launder, bathe, brush, tidy, purify, sterilize, filter ➡ **shine, sweep**
2. *adj* spotless, washed, unblemished, unused, unsoiled, fresh, blank, pristine, immaculate ➡ **neat, sterile** ⇨ *dirty*

cleaning *n* washing, wash, bath, shower, rinse, soak, scrub ➡ **laundry**

cliché *n* platitude, truism, commonplace, bromide, banality ➡ **saying, stereotype**

cliff *n* bluff, crag, precipice, escarpment, bank, promontory, palisade ➡ **hill, mountain**

climax 1. *n* ➡ **top**
2. *vb* crest, peak, culminate, cap, consummate, crown ➡ **finish**

climb 1. *vb* scale, clamber, scramble, crawl ➡ **ascend**
2. *n* ascent, ascension, rise ➡ **growth, slant**

If the word you want is not a main entry above, look below to find it.

circumvent ➡ avoid
circus ➡ carnival
cistern ➡ well
citadel ➡ castle
citation ➡ award, document
cite ➡ quote
citizenry ➡ people
city ➡ town, urban
civic ➡ public, urban
civil ➡ polite, public
civil servant ➡ official
clack ➡ tick
claim ➡ boast, argue, appeal, interest
clairvoyant ➡ prophet
clamber ➡ climb
clammy ➡ damp
clamor ➡ noise

clamorous ➡ loud
clamp ➡ clasp
clan ➡ family
clandestine ➡ secret
clang ➡ bang, ring
clank ➡ bang
claptrap ➡ nonsense
clarify ➡ explain
clash ➡ bang, fight
classic ➡ masterpiece, model
classified ➡ secret
classify ➡ arrange
clatter ➡ bang
clause ➡ term, excerpt
claustrophic ➡ stuffy
claw ➡ foot
clawhammer ➡ hammer

clean out ➡ empty
cleanse ➡ clean
clear ➡ transparent, fair, legible, obvious, articulate, audible, open, forgive
clearance ➡ sale
clearing ➡ field
clearly ➡ apparently
clearness ➡ clarity
cleave ➡ cut, separate, stick
cleaver ➡ knife
cleft ➡ cut, hole
clemency ➡ pity, forgiveness
clementine ➡ orange
clench ➡ tighten, embrace
clergy ➡ minister
clergyman ➡ minister
clergywoman ➡ minister

cleric ➡ minister
clerical ➡ religious
clever ➡ able, smart
clichéd ➡ trite
click ➡ peep, tick
client ➡ patron
climate ➡ weather, setting
clime ➡ weather
clinch ➡ finish, join
cling ➡ stick
clinic ➡ hospital
clink ➡ peep, jail
clip ➡ cut, pin, clasp
clique ➡ group
cloak ➡ wrap, hide
cloakroom ➡ closet
clobber ➡ hit

clock *n* timepiece, watch, wristwatch, stopwatch, chronometer, chronograph, timer, hourglass, egg timer, sundial

close 1. *vb* shut, fasten, slam ➡ **lock**
2. *vb* plug, seal, stop, clog, obstruct, fill
3. *adj* ➡ **near**
4. *adj* ➡ **alike, approximate**
5. *adj* ➡ **narrow**
6. *adj* ➡ **friendly**
7. *adj* ➡ **thick**
8. *adj* ➡ **stuffy**
   In general, **shut** *is a stronger or more forceful word than* **close,** *and it suggests the action of moving the door, lid, cover, etc., to a closed and fastened position.*

closet *n* armoire, wardrobe, cloakroom, locker, storeroom, pantry, larder ➡ **cupboard**

cloth 1. *n* fabric, material, textile, weave
2. *n* dustcloth, dishrag, dishcloth, washcloth, chamois, rag, remnant

clothes *n* clothing, dress, apparel, wardrobe, garments, attire, garb, vestments, finery, habit
   Note that **clothes** *is a plural noun and always takes a plural verb:* "My **clothes** are on fire!" **Clothing** *is a collective noun; it may refer to clothes in general or to all of the clothes you are wearing, but it always takes a singular verb:* "Warm **clothing** is necessary in the winter."

cloud 1. *n* haze, mist, billow, vapor ➡ **fog, smoke**
2. *n* shadow, pall, gloom

cloudy 1. *adj* overcast, hazy, lowering ➡ **dim** ⇨ *fair*
2. *adj* ➡ **obscure**

clumsy 1. *adj* (in reference to people) awkward, ungraceful, ungainly, inept, fumbling, bumbling, uncoordinated, gauche ➡ **amateur**
2. *adj* (in reference to objects) awkward, bulky, cumbersome, unwieldy, unmanageable

coat 1. *n* overcoat, jacket, blazer, sport coat, sport jacket, raincoat, windbreaker, parka, trench coat
2. *n* fur, wool, fleece ➡ **hair, hide**
3. *n* coating, film, covering, blanket, mantle, veneer, crust, scale ➡ **layer**
4. *vb* ➡ **cover**

If the word you want is not a main entry above, look below to find it.

clog ➡ close, barrier
clogged ➡ stuffy
cloister ➡ court, monastery
clone ➡ reproduce
closed ➡ impassable
close-fitting ➡ tight
closeness ➡ presence
closeout ➡ sale
closing ➡ last
clot ➡ lump, harden
clothe ➡ dress, wrap
clothing ➡ clothes

cloudburst ➡ rain
clown ➡ comic, fool
clowning ➡ play
cloying ➡ rich
club ➡ bat, stick, organization
clue ➡ sign
clump ➡ lump, pile
cluster ➡ group, flower
clutch ➡ seize, touch
clutter ➡ mess
coach ➡ teach, teacher, wagon

coagulate ➡ harden
coal-black ➡ black
coarse ➡ rough, common, rude, dirty
coarseness ➡ rudeness
coast ➡ shore, slide
coating ➡ coat
coax ➡ persuade, urge
cobblestone ➡ rock
cocktail lounge ➡ bar
coda ➡ conclusion
coddle ➡ pamper

code ➡ rule
codicil ➡ addition
coerce ➡ force
coffee cake ➡ cake
coffeehouse ➡ restaurant
coffeepot ➡ pot
coffer ➡ safe
cogent ➡ valid
cogitate ➡ think
cohere ➡ stick
coherent ➡ articulate

---

cold *adj* frosty, icy, freezing, frigid, arctic, polar, antarctic, raw ➡ **cool** ⇨ *hot*

college *n* university, institute, institution, community college, junior college ➡ **school**

collide *vb* crash, smash, impact, sideswipe, rear-end ➡ **hit, knock**

collision *n* crash, impact, wreck, fender-bender (*informal*) ➡ **accident**

colony 1. *n* possession, dependency, settlement, satellite ➡ **state, country**
2. *n* ➡ **herd**

color 1. *n* shade, hue, tinge, tone, tint
2. *vb* ➡ **draw**
3. *vb* ➡ **blush**

comb 1. *vb* brush, untangle, disentangle, straighten, groom, tease, curry

2. *vb* ➡ **hunt**

come *vb* arrive, reach, appear, attain ➡ **approach, descend** ⇨ *go*

comfort 1. *n* contentment, ease, relaxation, repose ➡ **pleasure**
2. *n* succor, consolation, solace ➡ **pity, help, support, kindness**
3. *vb* console, solace, condole, reassure ➡ **calm, support**
4. *vb* ➡ **pity**

comfortable 1. *adj* cozy, snug, comfy, restful, homey, roomy, spacious ⇨ *uncomfortable*
2. *adj* ➡ **rich**

comic 1. *n* comedian, comedienne, joker, humorist, clown ➡ **actor**
2. *adj* ➡ **funny**

If the word you want is not a main entry above, look below to find it.

coil ➡ turn, circle
coin ➡ money
coincide ➡ agree
coincidence ➡ chance
coincident ➡ simultaneous
coincidental ➡ accidental
coinciding ➡ simultaneous
Coke® ➡ soda
cola ➡ soda
cold-blooded ➡ mean, insensitive
coldhearted ➡ insensitive
coliseum ➡ field
collaborate ➡ help
collaborative ➡ common
collapse ➡ fall
collar ➡ arrest
collateral ➡ parallel
colleague ➡ member, worker
collect ➡ gather, earn
collection ➡ assortment

collective ➡ common
collectively ➡ together
colloquium ➡ course
colonist ➡ pioneer
colonizer ➡ pioneer
colorful ➡ bright
colors ➡ flag
colossal ➡ huge
colossus ➡ giant
colt ➡ horse
column ➡ post, row
comatose ➡ unconscious
combat ➡ fight
combatant ➡ soldier
combative ➡ belligerent, unfriendly, military
comber ➡ wave
combination ➡ mixture, union
combine ➡ mix, add
combo ➡ band

combustible ➡ inflammable
combustion ➡ fire
come across ➡ find
come back ➡ return
comedian ➡ comic
comedienne ➡ comic
come down with ➡ catch
comedy ➡ humor, play
come into view ➡ appear
comely ➡ pretty
come near ➡ approach
comet ➡ meteor
comforter ➡ blanket
comfy ➡ comfortable
comical ➡ funny
coming ➡ approach
command ➡ control, order, rule
commandeer ➡ take
commander ➡ boss

commanding ➡ grand
commandment ➡ order
commemorate ➡ celebrate, remember
commemoration ➡ ceremony
commence ➡ start
commencement ➡ beginning
commend ➡ praise, approve
commendable ➡ praiseworthy
comment ➡ remark
commentary ➡ remark
commerce ➡ business
commercial ➡ advertisement, financial
commiserate ➡ pity
commiseration ➡ pity
commission ➡ committee

n = noun • *vb* = verb • *adj* = adjective • *adv* = adverb • *prep* = preposition • *conj* = conjunction

commit 1. *vb* perpetrate, enact, carry out
➡ **act, do**
2. *vb* ➡ **entrust**
3. *vb* ➡ **dedicate**
4. *vb* ➡ **jail**

committee *n* board, council, panel, commission, subcommittee, delegation, mission, cabinet, assembly

common 1. *adj* ordinary, typical, familiar, everyday, widespread, average, unpretentious, humble, commonplace, pedestrian, popular, prevalent ➡ **general, normal, usual, plain**
⇨ *strange*
2. *adj* vulgar, coarse, commonplace, crass, crude, banal, plebeian ➡ **cheap, dirty**
3. *adj* communal, mutual, joint, collective, collaborative, shared ➡ **unanimous, public**
4. *n* ➡ **park**

compare *vb* contrast, juxtapose, parallel, liken, match, correlate ➡ **study, distinguish**

compatible *adj* similar, harmonious, agreeable, congruous ➡ **friendly**

compete *vb* contend, rival, play, contest, vie
➡ **fight, face**

competition 1. *n* rivalry, contention, antagonism ➡ **fight, game**
2. *n* ➡ **opponent**

competitive *adj* rival, contentious, antagonistic, vying ➡ **ambitious**

complain *vb* protest, gripe, grouch, grumble, whine, nag, fuss, moan, groan, squawk (*informal*) ➡ **mumble, object**

complaint 1. *n* objection, grievance, criticism, lament, charge, accusation, allegation, indictment, denunciation, reproach, outcry, grudge ➡ **protest**
2. *n* ➡ **illness, hardship**

complete 1. *adj* entire, full, total, whole, absolute, utter, uncut, intact, unbroken, exhaustive, thorough, unabridged, uncensored
➡ **all, comprehensive, perfect**
2. *vb* ➡ **finish**

If the word you want is not a main entry above, look below to find it.

commitment ➡ promise

committed ➡ faithful

commodity ➡ product

commonplace ➡ common, cliché

common sense ➡ wisdom

commonwealth ➡ country, state

commotion ➡ disturbance, noise, activity

communal ➡ common, public

communicable ➡ contagious

communicate ➡ talk, tell

communication ➡ speech, mail

communications ➡ media

community ➡ town, neighborhood, people

community college ➡ college

commute ➡ travel

commuter ➡ traveler

compact ➡ firm, small, short, thick, agreement

companion ➡ friend

companionship ➡ friendship

company ➡ business, friendship, visitor, team, troop

comparable ➡ alike

comparably ➡ alike

comparison ➡ similarity, estimate

compartment ➡ booth

compass ➡ range

compassion ➡ pity, kindness

compassionate ➡ kind

compatibility ➡ relationship

compeer ➡ equal

compel ➡ force

compelling ➡ interesting, urgent

compensate ➡ pay, balance, refund

compensation ➡ wage, refund, revenge

competence ➡ ability

competent ➡ able, efficient

competently ➡ well

competitor ➡ athlete, contestant, opponent

compilation ➡ assortment

compile ➡ gather, write

complacent ➡ satisfied

complement ➡ suit, addition

completely 1. *adv* fully, totally, entirely, utterly, wholly, altogether, quite, thoroughly, stark
2. *adv* ➡ **certainly**

complicated *adj* complex, intricate, elaborate, sophisticated, involved, subtle ➡ **hard**

comprehensive *adj* thorough, inclusive, exhaustive, blanket ➡ **complete, general**

concentrate 1. *vb* focus, devote, attend ➡ **meditate, think, study**
2. *vb* focus, converge, consolidate, condense, compress, intensify, thicken, distill ➡ **gather**

concern 1. *vb* involve, touch, pertain, appertain, regard, bear on, refer to, encompass ➡ **affect, belong**
2. *vb* ➡ **worry**

3. *n* ➡ **worry, interest**
4. *n* ➡ **business**

conclusion 1. *n* inference, assumption, deduction ➡ **decision** ⇨ *beginning*
2. *n* afterword, epilogue, postscript, postlude, coda ⇨ *introduction*
3. *n* ➡ **finish**

conclusive *adj* decisive, definitive, undeniable ➡ **certain**

condense *vb* shorten, contract, abbreviate, abridge, compress, telescope, cut, prune ➡ **decrease, shrink, concentrate** ⇨ *lengthen*

condescend *vb* stoop, deign, vouchsafe, demean, degrade, humble, accommodate, patronize

---

If the word you want is not a main entry above, look below to find it.

completion ➡ finish

complex ➡ complicated

compliance ➡ agreement

compliant ➡ passive

complicate ➡ confuse

compliment ➡ praise

complimentary ➡ free

comply ➡ obey

component ➡ part, division

compose ➡ calm, make, write

composed ➡ calm

composer ➡ musician

composite ➡ mixture

composition ➡ structure, work, report, score

composure ➡ calm

compound ➡ mix, mixture

comprehend ➡ know, read

comprehension ➡ wisdom

compress ➡ concentrate, condense, squeeze, bandage

comprise ➡ contain

compromise ➡ agreement

compulsion ➡ obsession

compulsory ➡ necessary

compunction ➡ regret

computation ➡ mathematics

compute ➡ add

computerized ➡ automatic

computing ➡ addition

comrade ➡ friend

comradeship ➡ friendship

con ➡ cheat

con artist ➡ hypocrite

conceal ➡ hide

concealed ➡ invisible

concede ➡ admit, surrender, abandon

conceit ➡ pride

conceited ➡ proud

conceivable ➡ possible

conceivably ➡ maybe

conceive ➡ imagine, invent

concentration ➡ attention

concept ➡ idea

conception ➡ beginning

concerned ➡ careful

concerning ➡ about

concert ➡ program

concerted ➡ unanimous

concession ➡ surrender

conciliatory ➡ peaceful

concise ➡ short

conciseness ➡ brevity

concision ➡ brevity

conclude ➡ finish, decide, infer

concluding ➡ last

conclusively ➡ finally

concoct ➡ invent

concoction ➡ mixture, lie

concord ➡ peace, unity

concordance ➡ dictionary

concrete ➡ real

concur ➡ agree

concurrence ➡ agreement

concurrent ➡ simultaneous

concurrently ➡ together

concussion ➡ blow[1]

condemn ➡ blame

condensation ➡ summary

condensed ➡ thick

n = noun • *vb* = verb • *adj* = adjective • *adv* = adverb • *prep* = preposition • *conj* = conjunction

confuse *vb* perplex, puzzle, bewilder, confound, complicate, baffle, disconcert, disorient, befuddle, abash, stymie, mystify, throw, stump

confusion 1. *n* disorder, chaos, anarchy, turmoil, discord, mayhem, lawlessness
➡ **excitement, hysteria, violence**
2. *n* perplexity, bewilderment, bafflement, puzzlement, consternation, nervousness
➡ **misunderstanding**

consecutive *adj* successive, continuous, progressive, ensuing, numerical, alphabetical, sequential, serial

conservative *adj* conventional, traditional, orthodox, moderate, reactionary, right-wing, illiberal ➡ **stuffy** ⇨ *liberal*

consider *vb* reflect, weigh, entertain, contemplate ➡ **study, think**

If the word you want is not a main entry above, look below to find it.

condescending ➡ **pompous**

condition ➡ **state, health, exercise, term**

conditioning ➡ **exercise**

conditions ➡ **weather**

condo ➡ **home**

condole ➡ **comfort**

condolence ➡ **pity**

condominium ➡ **home**

condone ➡ **forgive**

conduct ➡ **behavior, lead, bring**

conductor ➡ **guide**

conduit ➡ **pipe**

confederate ➡ **partner**

confer ➡ **talk, negotiate, give**

conference ➡ **meeting**

confess ➡ **admit, reveal**

confide ➡ **entrust**

confidence ➡ **certainty, secrecy, secret, belief**

confident ➡ **certain, optimistic**

confidential ➡ **secret**

configuration ➡ **pattern**

confine ➡ **jail**

confinement ➡ **privacy**

confirm ➡ **verify, admit**

confirmation ➡ **proof**

confiscate ➡ **take**

conflagration ➡ **fire**

conflict ➡ **fight**

conflicting ➡ **opposite**

confluence ➡ **union**

conform ➡ **adjust**

conformity ➡ **agreement**

confound ➡ **confuse**

confront ➡ **face**

confrontation ➡ **fight, meeting**

confronting ➡ **opposite**

confused ➡ **delirious**

congeal ➡ **harden, cool**

congenial ➡ **pleasant**

congenital ➡ **natural**

congested ➡ **stuffy**

congratulate ➡ **praise**

congratulations ➡ **praise**

congregate ➡ **gather**

congregation ➡ **audience, church**

congress ➡ **government**

congruity ➡ **similarity**

congruous ➡ **compatible**

conifer ➡ **tree**

conjectural ➡ **theoretical**

conjecture ➡ **theory**

conjurer ➡ **magician**

connect ➡ **join, bridge**

connection ➡ **link, junction, relevance**

conniption ➡ **fit²**

connive ➡ **plan**

connoisseur ➡ **expert**

connotation ➡ **meaning**

connote ➡ **mean**

conquer ➡ **defeat**

conqueror ➡ **winner**

conquest ➡ **defeat, victory**

conscientious ➡ **reliable, careful**

conscious ➡ **alert, awake**

consciously ➡ **purposely**

consciousness ➡ **life, mind**

conscript ➡ **soldier**

consecrate ➡ **bless**

consecrated ➡ **holy**

consensus ➡ **agreement**

consent ➡ **agree, agreement, permission**

consequence ➡ **effect, importance, punishment**

consequently ➡ **therefore**

conservation ➡ **economy**

conservatory ➡ **greenhouse**

conserve ➡ **save**

considerable ➡ **big**

considerably ➡ **far**

considerate ➡ **kind, thoughtful**

consideration ➡ **kindness, attention, price**

consign ➡ **entrust**

consistency ➡ **density**

consistent ➡ **same, continual**

consist of ➡ **contain**

consolation ➡ **comfort**

console ➡ **comfort**

consolidate ➡ **concentrate, mix, unify**

consolidation ➡ **union**

consort ➡ **mix, spouse**

consortium ➡ **monopoly**

conspicuous ➡ **obvious, striking**

conspiracy ➡ **plan**

conspire ➡ **plan**

constable ➡ **police officer**

constant ➡ **continual, faithful**

constantly ➡ **regularly**

consternation ➡ **confusion, fear**

constituent ➡ **matter, member**

constitute ➡ **make**

constitutional ➡ **legal**

➡ = synonym cross-reference • ⇨ = antonym cross-reference

contagious *adj* infectious, catching, communicable, transmissible, transmittable, spreadable, epidemic

contain 1. *vb* hold, include, consist of, comprise, accommodate ➡ **carry, embody**
2. *vb* restrain, limit, suppress, curb, quell, quash, quench, control, repress, swallow
➡ **stop, extinguish, prevent**

container *n* receptacle, box, carton, case, crate, can, jar, cup, glass, bucket, pail, tank, tub, tube
➡ **bag, bowl, barrel, chest, package, bottle, wrapper**

contestant *n* competitor, participant, contender, player, entry ➡ **athlete, opponent, candidate**

continual *adj* continuous, incessant, unceasing, constant, persistent, relentless, steady, chronic, unvarying, invariable, unchanging, ongoing, consistent, nonstop, unbroken ➡ **frequent, permanent**

continue 1. *vb* last, endure, remain, persist, persevere, carry on, proceed
2. *vb* resume, recommence, renew, pick up
➡ **start**

contradict *vb* deny, refute, challenge, dispute
➡ **object, discredit**

contradiction *n* disagreement, discrepancy, inconsistency, incongruity, paradox, oxymoron
➡ **problem, disagreement**

control 1. *vb* command, direct, manage, dominate, subject, regulate, engineer, tame, captain, cope, handle, harness
➡ **govern, lead, contain**
2. *vb* ➡ **contain**
3. *n* ➡ **rule, discipline**

If the word you want is not a main entry above, look below to find it.

constrain ➡ force

constrict ➡ shrink

constricted ➡ narrow

constricting ➡ tight

construct ➡ build

construction ➡ assembly

consul ➡ diplomat

consult ➡ talk

consultant ➡ adviser

consultation ➡ talk

consume ➡ eat, use

consummate ➡ climax

consumption ➡ use

contact ➡ touch, link

contact lenses ➡ glasses

contacts ➡ glasses

contagion ➡ disease

contaminate ➡ dirty

contaminated ➡ dirty

contemplate ➡ consider, meditate

contemplative ➡ thoughtful

contemporaneous ➡ simultaneous

contemporaneously ➡ together

contemporary ➡ modern, fashionable, simultaneous

contempt ➡ hatred

contemptible ➡ shameful

contend ➡ argue, compete

contender ➡ athlete, contestant

content ➡ part, pleasure, please, satisfied

contented ➡ satisfied

contention ➡ competition, disagreement

contentious ➡ belligerent, competitive

contentment ➡ satisfaction, comfort

contest ➡ game, compete

context ➡ setting

continually ➡ regularly

continuous ➡ continual, consecutive

contort ➡ bend

contorted ➡ bent

contour ➡ circumference

contraband ➡ booty

contract ➡ agreement, catch, condense, shrink, tighten

contraction ➡ abbreviation

contradictory ➡ opposite

contrary ➡ opposite

contrast ➡ compare, differ, difference

contrasting ➡ opposite

contribute ➡ give

contribution ➡ gift

contributor ➡ patron

contrite ➡ sorry

contrition ➡ shame

contrivance ➡ invention

contrive ➡ invent, plan

controls ➡ wheel

controversy ➡ argument

controvert ➡ disprove

conundrum ➡ problem

convalescence ➡ cure

convalescent ➡ better, patient

convalescing ➡ better

convene ➡ gather

convenience ➡ advantage

convenient ➡ available

convent ➡ monastery

convention ➡ meeting

conventional ➡ normal, conservative, stuffy

converge ➡ concentrate

convergence ➡ junction

cook 1. *vb* fry, bake, broil, roast, grill, stew, sauté, steam, barbecue, microwave, brew
➡ **boil, prepare**
2. *n* chef, sous-chef, pastry chef, baker
➡ **servant**

cool 1. *adj* chilly, chill, brisk, fresh, bracing, nippy ➡ **cold**
2. *adj* remote, aloof, distant, reserved, chilly, impersonal ➡ **calm, apathetic, unfriendly**
3. *adj* excellent, all right, fashionable ➡ **good**
4. *vb* chill, refrigerate, freeze, congeal ➡ **fan**

copy 1. *n* reproduction, facsimile, photocopy, likeness ➡ **duplicate**
2. *vb* ➡ **reproduce, imitate**

corner 1. *n* angle, turn ➡ **bend, curve**
2. *n* intersection, turn, junction, juncture, crossroad
2. *n* ➡ **monopoly**
3. *vb* ➡ **catch**

correct 1. *adj* accurate, right, exact, precise, true, faultless, flawless, authentic, faithful, factual ➡ **perfect** ⇨ *wrong*
2. *adj* respectable, decent, proper, fitting, appropriate, seemly, decorous, becoming
➡ **fit, prim**
3. *vb* remedy, rectify, revise, edit, amend, emend, reconcile, improve, reform, redress
➡ **fix, adjust, perfect, change**
4. *vb* ➡ **punish**

correction *n* revision, remedy, adjustment, emendation, reparation, rectification ➡ **repair**

correctly *adv* properly, accurately, appropriately, right, satisfactorily ➡ **precisely**

corrode *vb* erode, rust, rot, oxidize, tarnish
➡ **decay, melt**

cosmopolitan 1. *adj* ➡ **urban**
2. *adj* sophisticated, worldly, experienced
➡ **suave**

If the word you want is not a main entry above, look below to find it.

conversation ➡ **talk**

converse ➡ **talk, opposite**

convert ➡ **change, translate**

convey ➡ **carry, give, send, take, tell**

conveyance ➡ **movement**

convict ➡ **criminal, decide**

conviction ➡ **belief, cause, certainty, will**

convince ➡ **persuade**

convinced ➡ **certain**

convincing ➡ **valid**

convivial ➡ **friendly**

convoy ➡ **accompany**

convulsion ➡ **fit²**

cookhouse ➡ **kitchen**

cookie ➡ **pastry**

cooler ➡ **refrigerator**

coop ➡ **pen**

cooperate ➡ **help**

cooperation ➡ **help**

cooperatively ➡ **together**

coordinate ➡ **balance**

cop ➡ **police officer**

cope ➡ **control**

copious ➡ **abundant**

copse ➡ **forest**

copyright ➡ **license**

coral ➡ **orange**

cord ➡ **string**

cordial ➡ **friendly**

cordiality ➡ **hospitality**

core ➡ **middle, essence**

cork ➡ **top**

cornerstone ➡ **basis**

cornfield ➡ **field**

corona ➡ **halo**

coronet ➡ **crown**

corporal ➡ **physical**

corporation ➡ **business, organization**

corporeal ➡ **physical**

corps ➡ **troop**

corpse ➡ **body**

corpulent ➡ **fat**

corral ➡ **pen**

correctional facility ➡ **jail**

correctness ➡ **accuracy**

correlate ➡ **compare**

correlation ➡ **link**

correspond ➡ **agree, resemble**

correspondence ➡ **mail, similarity**

correspondent ➡ **reporter**

corresponding ➡ **same**

corridor ➡ **hall**

corroborate ➡ **verify**

corroboration ➡ **proof**

corroded ➡ **rusty**

corrosion ➡ **decay**

corrupt ➡ **dishonest, wrong**

corruption ➡ **dishonesty**

corsair ➡ **pirate**

cortege ➡ **court**

cosmetic ➡ **superficial**

cosmic ➡ **universal**

cosmos ➡ **space**

cost ➡ **price**

cost-effective ➡ **efficient**

costly ➡ **expensive**

costume ➡ **disguise, dress, suit**

cot ➡ **bed**

coterie ➡ **following**

country 1. *n* nation, republic, kingdom, dominion, realm, commonwealth, land, domain, homeland, fatherland, motherland ➡ **state, colony**
2. *n* countryside, landscape, hinterland, wilderness, wild, backwoods, frontier, bush, boondocks (*informal*), sticks (*informal*)
3. *n* ➡ **music**

courage *n* bravery, valor, fortitude, boldness, spirit, gallantry, heroism, daring, audacity, nerve, mettle, grit, stomach, guts (*informal*)

course 1. *n* path, route, direction, heading, bearing, way, itinerary
2. *n* track, racetrack, trail ➡ **road**
3. *n* class, subject, seminar, program, major, minor, colloquium, elective

court 1. *n* courtyard, square, quadrangle, quad, atrium, patio, plaza, piazza, cloister

2. *n* ➡ **field**
3. *n* tribunal, law court, bench, bar, judiciary, forum
4. *n* courthouse, courtroom
5. *n* retinue, entourage, cortege, royal household, attendants
6. *vb* woo, date, romance, flirt ➡ **love**

cover 1. *vb* cover up, blanket, carpet, spread, coat, overspread, surface, pave, flag ➡ **wrap, protect, plate**
2. *vb* ➡ **hide**
3. *n* ➡ **top**
4. *n* ➡ **blanket, wrapper**
5. *n* ➡ **protection**

cowardly *adj* timid, timorous, fearful, cowering, fainthearted, yellow (*informal*), chicken (*informal*) ➡ **afraid** ⇨ *brave*

If the word you want is not a main entry above, look below to find it.

cottage ➡ **home**

cotter pin ➡ **pin**

couch ➡ **seat, bed**

council ➡ **committee, meeting**

counsel ➡ **advice, adviser, suggest, warn**

counselor ➡ **adviser**

count ➡ **add, matter, score**

countenance ➡ **appearance, face**

counter ➡ **answer, booth, shelf, table, opposite**

counterattack ➡ **attack**

counterbalance ➡ **balance**

counterespionage ➡ **spying**

counterfeit ➡ **fake, invent**

counterintelligence ➡ **spying**

countermand ➡ **abolish**

counterpart ➡ **duplicate**

counterpoise ➡ **balance**

counterproductive ➡ **useless**

countersign ➡ **sign**

counterspy ➡ **spy**

counting ➡ **addition**

countless ➡ **infinite, many**

count on ➡ **depend**

countryside ➡ **country**

coup ➡ **revolution**

coup d'état ➡ **revolution**

couple ➡ **pair, few, join**

coupling ➡ **union**

courageous ➡ **brave**

courier ➡ **messenger**

courteous ➡ **polite**

courtesy ➡ **kindness, respect, hospitality**

courthouse ➡ **court**

courtly ➡ **noble**

courtroom ➡ **court**

courtyard ➡ **court**

cove ➡ **bay**

covenant ➡ **agreement, promise**

covered ➡ **underground**

covering ➡ **coat, wrapper**

cover story ➡ **alibi**

covert ➡ **secret, den**

covet ➡ **envy**

covetous ➡ **greedy**

covetousness ➡ **envy**

cow ➡ **scare**

cow barn ➡ **barn**

cower ➡ **fear, jump**

cowering ➡ **cowardly**

co-worker ➡ **partner**

cowshed ➡ **barn**

coxswain ➡ **pilot**

cozy ➡ **comfortable**

crack ➡ **hole, bang, break**

cracked ➡ **broken**

crackle ➡ **rustle**

cradle ➡ **bed, source**

craft ➡ **art, profession, boat**

craftsman ➡ **artist**

craftsmanship ➡ **art**

crafty ➡ **sly**

crag ➡ **cliff**

cram ➡ **load**

crammed ➡ **full**

cramp ➡ **pain**

cramped ➡ **uncomfortable**

cranky ➡ **cross**

crash ➡ **bang, break, collide, collision, depression**

crawl 1. *vb* creep, squirm, wiggle, wriggle, slither, grovel, drag, inch ➡ **walk, climb**
2. *n* ➡ **swim**

creator *n* author, originator, architect, framer, designer, engineer, inventor, pioneer, innovator, founder ➡ **artist**

crime *n* offense, violation, sin, evil, wrong, wrongdoing, misdeed, trespass, transgression, infraction, felony, misdemeanor ➡ **theft, treason, murder**

criminal 1. *n* crook, thief, bandit, outlaw, desperado, convict, felon, offender, robber, burglar, perpetrator, wrongdoer, malefactor, lawbreaker, culprit ➡ **cheat, vandal, pirate**
2. *adj* ➡ **illegal**

cross 1. *adj* grouchy, irritable, disagreeable, cranky, fussy, peevish, cantankerous, ill-tempered, bad-tempered, ill-natured, petulant, grumpy, testy, sullen, surly ➡ **angry, rude, abrupt** ⇨ *happy*
2. *n* ➡ **tick**
3. *n* ➡ **hybrid**
4. *vb* ➡ **bridge**

crowd *n* mob, multitude, host, throng, army, legion, horde, swarm, flock ➡ **band, group, troop**

crown 1. *n* diadem, coronet, tiara, circlet, garland, chaplet, wreath
2. *vb* enthrone, invest, install, induct, inaugurate ➡ **bless**
3. *vb* ➡ **climax**

If the word you want is not a main entry above, look below to find it.

crass ➡ **rude, common**

crate ➡ **container**

crater ➡ **hole**

cravat ➡ **tie**

crave ➡ **want**

craving ➡ **appetite**

crawl space ➡ **basement**

craze ➡ **fashion**

crazed ➡ **insane**

crazy ➡ **insane, foolish**

creak ➡ **squeak**

creamy ➡ **rich, fair, white**

crease ➡ **fold, wrinkle**

create ➡ **cause, make**

creation ➡ **invention, work, assembly, earth**

creative ➡ **talented**

creativity ➡ **art, imagination**

creature ➡ **animal**

credence ➡ **belief**

credentials ➡ **document**

credible ➡ **possible**

credit ➡ **loan, belief, attribute**

credit union ➡ **bank**

creditable ➡ **praiseworthy**

credo ➡ **belief**

credulous ➡ **naive, superstitious**

creed ➡ **belief**

creek ➡ **river**

creep ➡ **crawl, sneak, tingle**

cremate ➡ **bury**

creole ➡ **dialect**

crepe paper ➡ **paper**

crescent ➡ **curve**

crest ➡ **climax, top**

crevasse ➡ **canyon, hole**

crevice ➡ **hole, canyon**

crew ➡ **group, team**

crib ➡ **bed**

crimp ➡ **bend, wrinkle**

crimson ➡ **red**

cringe ➡ **jump**

crinkle ➡ **wrinkle**

cripple ➡ **paralyze, weaken**

crippled ➡ **lame**

crisis ➡ **emergency**

crisp ➡ **brisk**

criterion ➡ **measure**

critic ➡ **judge**

critical ➡ **important**

criticism ➡ **complaint**

criticize ➡ **blame, study**

croak ➡ **grunt**

crock ➡ **bottle, bowl**

crook ➡ **criminal, curve**

crooked ➡ **bent, zigzag, dishonest**

crookedness ➡ **dishonesty**

croon ➡ **sing**

crop ➡ **growth, whip**

crossbar ➡ **bar**

crossbreed ➡ **hybrid**

crossroad ➡ **corner**

crouch ➡ **bend**

crow ➡ **boast**

crowded ➡ **full**

crucial ➡ **urgent**

crude ➡ **primitive, common, rude**

crudeness ➡ **rudeness**

crude oil ➡ **oil**

crudity ➡ **rudeness**

cruel ➡ **mean**

cruet ➡ **bottle**

cruise ➡ **patrol, travel, trip**

---

cry 1. *vb* weep, sob, wail, bawl, whimper, whine, moan, groan
2. *n, vb* shout, scream, howl, screech, bellow, shriek, roar, whoop, squeal, bay, yowl, wail, squawk ➡ **noise, yell, bark**

cupboard *n* cabinet, sideboard, buffet, locker ➡ **closet**

cure 1. *n* remedy, treatment, antidote, curative, therapy ➡ **medicine**
2. *n* recovery, recuperation, healing, rehabilitation, convalescence
3. *vb* ➡ **heal**

curious 1. *adj* inquisitive, prying, nosy, inquiring ➡ **meddlesome**
2. *adj* ➡ **strange**

curse 1. *n* oath, profanity, blasphemy, expletive
2. *n* hex, charm, spell, jinx
3. *vb* swear, blaspheme, damn, revile, vilify, cuss (*informal*)

curve 1. *n* bow, bend, turn, arch, arc, crook, trajectory, curvature, crescent, horseshoe, oxbow
2. *vb* ➡ **bend**

cushion 1. *n* pad, mat, pillow, bolster, pallet
2. *n* padding, buffer, shock absorber ➡ **protection**
3. *vb* ➡ **protect**

cut 1. *vb* chop, slice, dice, mince, shred, grate, carve, cleave, gouge, hew, hack, lacerate, amputate ➡ **rip, peel, carve**
2. *vb* trim, shave, clip, snip, shear, prune, mow, reap
3. *vb* ➡ **condense, decrease**
4. *n* gash, slash, wound, injury, incision, laceration, scrape, scratch, nick, gouge, cleft, notch, slit ➡ **rip, hole, sore**

cute *adj* adorable, charming, quaint, cutesy ➡ **pretty**

If the word you want is not a main entry above, look below to find it.

crumble ➡ decay, grind
crumbly ➡ breakable
crumple ➡ fall, wrinkle
crumpled ➡ rough
crusade ➡ movement
crush ➡ break, grind, trample, defeat
crust ➡ coat
crypt ➡ cemetery, grave, basement
cryptic ➡ obscure, secret
crystalline ➡ transparent
cube ➡ block
cubicle ➡ booth
cuddle ➡ embrace, snuggle
cue ➡ reminder
cuisine ➡ food
culminate ➡ climax
culmination ➡ finish

culpability ➡ guilt
culpable ➡ guilty
culprit ➡ criminal, defendant
cult ➡ religion
cultivate ➡ dig, grow
cultivation ➡ farming, civilization, class
culture ➡ civilization
cultured ➡ suave
cumbersome ➡ clumsy, heavy
cunning ➡ sly, dishonesty
cup ➡ container, glass
cupcake ➡ cake
cur ➡ dog
curative ➡ medicinal, cure
curator ➡ guardian
curb ➡ contain
curio ➡ novelty, antique

curiosity ➡ interest, novelty
curious ➡ strange
curl ➡ bend, lock
currency ➡ money
current ➡ energy, flood, modern
curry ➡ comb
cursive ➡ handwriting
cursory ➡ superficial, fast
curt ➡ abrupt
curtail ➡ decrease
curtain ➡ divider
curtsy ➡ bend
curvature ➡ curve
curved ➡ bent
cuss ➡ curse
custodian ➡ guardian
custody ➡ possession
custom ➡ habit, rule

customarily ➡ usually
customary ➡ usual
customer ➡ patron
cutesy ➡ cute
cutlass ➡ sword
cut-rate ➡ cheap
cutting ➡ sharp
cycle ➡ period, round, periodic
cyclical ➡ periodic
cyclist ➡ rider
cyclone ➡ storm
cylindrical ➡ round
cynic ➡ skeptic
cynical ➡ pessimistic
cyst ➡ growth
czar ➡ emperor
czarina ➡ empress

D

dam *n* embankment, dike, levee, weir ➡ **wall**

damage 1. *n* destruction, wreckage, wear, devastation, desolation, ruin, havoc, mayhem, injury, sabotage ➡ **decay, harm**
2. *vb* impair, mar, deface, scratch, scrape, scar, disfigure, deform, distort ➡ **hurt, break, destroy**

damp *adj* moist, humid, clammy, dank, muggy, sultry, sticky ➡ **wet, liquid**

dance 1. *n* ball, prom, social, mixer, gala ➡ **party**
2. *vb* step, trip, glide, pirouette, whirl
3. *vb* gambol, frolic, scamper, caper, cavort, romp ➡ **jump**

danger *n* risk, threat, peril, hazard, menace, jeopardy

dangerous *adj* harmful, perilous, hazardous, unsafe, risky, treacherous, precarious, explosive ➡ **deadly, destructive** ⇨ *safe*

dare 1. *vb* hazard, presume, risk ➡ **try**
2. *vb* defy, challenge, provoke ➡ **face**

dark 1. *adj* gloomy, murky, dusky, shady, unlit, somber, overcast, pitch-black, black, opaque ➡ **dim**
2. *adj* brunette, brown, tan, black, swarthy, sable, ebony
3. *n* darkness, dusk, gloom, blackness, shade, shadow ➡ **night**

day *n* daylight, daytime, light, midday, date ➡ **morning, afternoon** ⇨ *night*

dead 1. *adj* deceased, departed, late, lifeless, extinct, defunct, inanimate ⇨ *alive*
2. *adj* inert, still, stagnant, motionless ➡ **calm**
3. *adj* ➡ **tired**
4. *adv* ➡ **completely**
5. *n* ➡ **casualty**

deadly 1. *adj* fatal, mortal, lethal, deathly, murderous, homicidal, terminal, incurable
2. *adj* poisonous, venomous, virulent, malignant, toxic, noxious ➡ **dangerous**
3. *adj* ➡ **dull**
4. *adv* terminally ➡ **completely**

If the word you want is not a main entry above, look below to find it.

dab ➡ rub
dabble ➡ tinker
dagger ➡ knife
daily ➡ paper
dainty ➡ breakable, choosy
dais ➡ platform
dale ➡ valley
dally ➡ wait
damaged ➡ broken
damaging ➡ destructive
damn ➡ curse
dampen ➡ wet

dampness ➡ humidity
dangle ➡ hang
Danish ➡ pastry
dank ➡ damp
dapper ➡ fashionable
dappled ➡ speckled
daring ➡ brave, courage
dark horse ➡ candidate
darkness ➡ dark
darling ➡ favorite, love
dart ➡ run, missile
dash ➡ bit, race, hurry, run

dashing ➡ fashionable, brave
data ➡ knowledge, proof
date ➡ day, period, meeting, court
datebook ➡ diary
daub ➡ rub
daughter ➡ child
daunt ➡ discourage
dauntless ➡ brave
dawdle ➡ lag
dawn ➡ morning
daybook ➡ diary

daybreak ➡ morning
daydream ➡ dream
daylight ➡ day
daytime ➡ day
daze ➡ dream, surprise
dazed ➡ dizzy
dazzle ➡ surprise
dazzling ➡ bright, beautiful, striking
deadbeat ➡ loafer
deadlock ➡ tie
deadpan ➡ blank, dry

➡ = synonym cross-reference • ⇨ = antonym cross-reference

deaf 1. *adj* hearing-impaired, unhearing, hard of hearing ➡ **disabled**
2. *adj* ➡ **unaware**

death *n* decease, demise, dying, passing, expiration, loss ➡ **casualty, fate, finish** ⇨ *birth*

debt *n* liability, obligation, debit, arrears, deficit, indebtedness ➡ **bill**

decay 1. *vb* deteriorate, disintegrate, crumble, decompose, wear, rot, molder, spoil, putrefy ➡ **corrode, destroy**
2. *n* deterioration, degeneration, decomposition, spoilage, disrepair, disintegration, corrosion ➡ **damage**

decide *vb* settle, resolve, determine, rule, conclude, reconcile, negotiate, mediate, arbitrate, judge, adjudge, convict ➡ **choose**

decision *n* judgment, determination, resolution, ruling, finding, verdict, sentence, decree, declaration ➡ **choice, conclusion**

decorate 1. *vb* adorn, beautify, ornament, embellish, trim, garnish, bedeck, redecorate, refurbish, festoon
2. *vb* ➡ **praise**

decoration 1. *n* adornment, ornamentation, embellishment, redecoration, beautification
2. *n* ornament, garnish, trim, accent, flourish
3. *n* ➡ **prize, award**

decrease 1. *vb* lessen, diminish, abate, decline, wane, subside, ebb, dwindle, taper, shrink, shrivel, reduce, depress, lower, slash, curtail, cut ➡ **condense, weaken, shrink**
2. *n* ➡ **drop**

dedicate *vb* devote, commit, set apart, pledge ➡ **bless**

If the word you want is not a main entry above, look below to find it.

deafening ➡ loud
deal ➡ agreement, bargain, sale
dealer ➡ seller
deal out ➡ share
dean ➡ principal
dear ➡ expensive, valuable, love
dearly ➡ much
dearth ➡ absence, want
deathless ➡ eternal
deathly ➡ deadly
debacle ➡ disappointment
debase ➡ shame
debate ➡ argue, argument
debit ➡ debt
debonair ➡ suave
debris ➡ trash

debunk ➡ disprove
debut ➡ introduction
decayed ➡ rusty, shabby, bad
decease ➡ death, die
deceased ➡ dead
deceit ➡ dishonesty, pretense
deceitful ➡ dishonest
deceive ➡ betray, cheat, lie
deceiver ➡ liar, hypocrite
decency ➡ kindness, virtue
decent ➡ correct, fair, kind
deception ➡ lie, pretense, trick
deceptive ➡ dishonest, unreliable
decipher ➡ solve, translate, read

decipherable ➡ legible
decisive ➡ conclusive, resolute
decisively ➡ finally
deck ➡ floor, dress
declaim ➡ quote
declaration ➡ announcement, decision
declare ➡ tell, advertise
decline ➡ decrease, drop, refuse, depression
declivity ➡ slant
decode ➡ solve, translate, read
decompose ➡ decay
decomposition ➡ decay
decorative ➡ fancy

decorous ➡ correct, dignified, prim
decorum ➡ behavior
decoy ➡ tempt
decree ➡ act, decision, order
decrepit ➡ old
dedication ➡ loyalty, inscription
deduce ➡ infer
deduct ➡ subtract
deduction ➡ conclusion, reason, subtraction
deed ➡ act, document
deem ➡ believe
deep ➡ broad, profound, ocean
deepness ➡ depth
deface ➡ damage

n = noun • *vb* = verb • *adj* = adjective • *adv* = adverb • *prep* = preposition • *conj* = conjunction

defeat 1. *vb* conquer, beat, overcome, surmount, overpower, vanquish, best, better, top, break, overthrow, throw, upset, down, whip, crush ➡ **subdue, win**
2. *n* loss, downfall, failure, conquest, destruction, rout, upset, beating, thrashing ⇨ *victory*

defect 1. *n* imperfection, flaw, blemish, shortcoming, drawback, minus ➡ **fault, mistake, spot**
2. *vb* ➡ **leave**

defendant *n* accused, suspect, culprit ➡ **prisoner**

delay 1. *vb* postpone, defer, put off, deter, stall, procrastinate ➡ **wait, hesitate**
2. *vb* hamper, detain, impede, hinder, retard ➡ **prevent**
3. *n* ➡ **break**

delicate 1. *adj* ➡ **breakable, weak**
2. *adj* ➡ **thin**
3. *adj* sensitive, touchy, ticklish, tricky, sticky ➡ **dangerous, doubtful**

delicious *adj* tasty, delectable, appetizing, luscious, savory, mouth-watering, flavorful, scrumptious ➡ **rich**

delirious *adj* incoherent, hysterical, confused, hallucinating ➡ **frantic, insane**

delivery 1. *n* shipment, transfer, transmission, dispatch, distribution, transportation ➡ **flow**
2. *n* ➡ **birth**
3. *n* ➡ **salvation**
4. *n* enunciation, pronunciation, elocution, diction, presentation, performance

---

If the word you want is not a main entry above, look below to find it.

defame ➡ insult

defective ➡ broken

defector ➡ runaway

defend ➡ protect, verify

defense ➡ protection, justification, alibi

defenseless ➡ vulnerable

defer ➡ delay, surrender

deference ➡ respect

deferential ➡ shy, passive

defiance ➡ disobedience, fight

defiant ➡ rebellious

deficiency ➡ absence, want

deficient ➡ inadequate, partial, poor

deficit ➡ debt

defile ➡ dirty

define ➡ describe, specify

definite ➡ certain

definitely ➡ certainly

definition ➡ meaning, clarity

definitive ➡ conclusive, model

deflate ➡ empty, shrink

deflect ➡ distract

deform ➡ damage

defraud ➡ cheat

deft ➡ able

defunct ➡ dead

defy ➡ disobey, rebel, face, dare

degenerate ➡ immoral

degeneration ➡ decay

degrade ➡ condescend

degree ➡ grade

dehydrate ➡ dry

dehydrated ➡ dry

deign ➡ condescend

deist ➡ atheist

deity ➡ god

déjà vu ➡ memory

dejected ➡ sad

dejection ➡ depression

delayed ➡ late

delectable ➡ delicious

delegate ➡ agent, entrust, name

delegation ➡ appointment, committee

delete ➡ erase

deli ➡ restaurant

deliberate ➡ slow, voluntary, think

deliberately ➡ carefully, purposely

delicacy ➡ tact, pastry

delicately ➡ carefully

delight ➡ please, pleasure

delighted ➡ happy

delightful ➡ pleasant, nice

delight in ➡ like

delineate ➡ draw

delinquent ➡ late, negligent, vandal

delirium ➡ hysteria

deliver ➡ bring, take, give, free, save

deliverance ➡ escape, salvation

deliverer ➡ savior

dell ➡ valley

delude ➡ fool

deluge ➡ flood

delusion ➡ illusion

delve ➡ dig, hunt

demand ➡ insist, order

demanding ➡ hard

demean ➡ condescend, shame

demeanor ➡ appearance, bearing

demented ➡ insane

demigod ➡ god

demise ➡ death

---

den 1. *n* lair, burrow, nest, hole, warren, covert ➡ **cave**
2. *n* study, office, library, family room, recreation room, rec room, playroom ➡ **room**

density *n* substance, bulk, body, consistency, mass ➡ **weight**

dent 1. *n* indentation, depression, impression, dimple, pit, nick, notch ➡ **hole**
2. *vb* indent, pit, nick, notch ➡ **bend**

department *n* section, division, branch, bureau, agency, chapter, subsidiary, affiliate ➡ **field, business, job, arm**

departure 1. *n* exit, going, leaving, withdrawal, farewell, embarkation, exodus ➡ **escape**
2. *n* deviation, divergence, digression, aberration, irregularity ➡ **change, difference**

depend 1. *vb* trust, rely, count on ➡ **believe**
2. *vb* hang, hinge, rest ➡ **turn**

deploy *vb* position, array, marshal ➡ **arrange**

depression 1. *n* ➡ **dent**
2. *n* desolation, despair, despondency, dejection ➡ **sorrow, misery**
3. *n* recession, slump, decline, downturn, crash

deprive *vb* withhold, divest, rob ➡ **refuse**

depth 1. *n* deepness, lowness, extent ➡ **measure** ⇨ *height*
2. *n* ➡ **middle**
3. *n* profundity, gravity, insight, profoundness ➡ **wisdom**

descend 1. *vb* swoop, stoop, dip ➡ **fall, decline, sink** ⇨ *ascend*
2. *vb* dismount, land, light, alight, settle, perch
3. *vb* issue, derive, come, spring, arise

describe *vb* characterize, define, depict, represent, recount, detail ➡ **explain, draw**

If the word you want is not a main entry above, look below to find it.

demolish ➡ destroy

demon ➡ devil

demonic ➡ wicked

demonstrate ➡ explain, verify, protest

demonstration ➡ experiment, protest, parade, movement

demonstrative ➡ emotional, loving

demoralize ➡ discourage

demur ➡ hesitate

demure ➡ shy

denial ➡ abstinence, rejection

denizen ➡ citizen

denomination ➡ religion

denotation ➡ meaning

denote ➡ mean

denounce ➡ blame

dense ➡ dull, firm, thick

denseness ➡ ignorance

denunciation ➡ complaint

deny ➡ refuse, contradict

depart ➡ leave, die

departed ➡ dead

dependability ➡ loyalty

dependable ➡ reliable

dependency ➡ habit, colony

depict ➡ draw, describe

depiction ➡ description

deplane ➡ leave

deplete ➡ use

deplorable ➡ shameful, unfortunate

deplore ➡ hate, regret

deport ➡ banish

deportation ➡ exile

deportee ➡ exile

deportment ➡ bearing

depose ➡ oust

deposit ➡ put, bank

depository ➡ warehouse, bank

depot ➡ warehouse

depraved ➡ immoral

depravity ➡ immorality

deprecate ➡ ridicule, underestimate

depress ➡ sadden, decrease

depressed ➡ sad, underdeveloped

depressing ➡ bleak, sorry

deprived ➡ poor, underdeveloped

deputy ➡ helper

deranged ➡ insane

derby ➡ race

derelict ➡ abandoned, negligent, guilty, homeless, beggar

deride ➡ ridicule

derision ➡ ridicule

derisive ➡ sarcastic

derivation ➡ source, product

derivative ➡ product

derive ➡ descend, extract

descendant ➡ child

descending ➡ down

descent ➡ drop, slant, ancestry

n = noun • *vb* = verb • *adj* = adjective • *adv* = adverb • *prep* = preposition • *conj* = conjunction

description *n* portrayal, characterization, account, depiction, portrait, profile
➡ **picture, story**

desert 1. *n* wasteland, wilderness, waste, barrens, badlands ➡ **country, plain**
2. *adj* ➡ **sterile**
3. *vb* ➡ **leave**

deserve *vb* merit, earn, warrant, justify, rate

desire 1. *n* ➡ **ambition**
2. *n* ➡ **hope**
3. *n* passion, lust, infatuation, appetite, urge, hunger, longing, nostalgia, wistfulness, yearning, yen, itch ➡ **love, greed, envy**
4. *vb* ➡ **want, envy**

destination *n* end, terminus, terminal, station, address, target

destroy *vb* wreck, spoil, demolish, ruin, annihilate, damage, devastate, ravage, raze, level, blight ➡ **abolish, break, mutilate**
⇨ *build*

destructive 1. *adj* ruinous, calamitous, catastrophic, devastating ➡ **violent, dangerous**
2. *adj* harmful, injurious, adverse, unfavorable, damaging

detail 1. *n* particular, trait, feature, factor, specific, peculiarity, fact, point
2. *vb* ➡ **specify, describe**

detour 1. *n* bypass, diversion, byway, digression, deviation ➡ **departure**
2. *vb* divert, redirect, skirt, bypass

development 1. *n* ➡ **growth**
2. *n* ➡ **invention**
3. *n* subdivision, project, housing estate

If the word you want is not a main entry above, look below to find it.

descry ➡ discover

deserted ➡ abandoned, open

deserter ➡ runaway

desertion ➡ escape

deserts ➡ punishment

deserving ➡ praiseworthy

design ➡ pattern, plan, intend, invent

designate ➡ choose, name

designation ➡ name, appointment

designer ➡ creator

desirable ➡ attractive, pleasant, useful

desk ➡ table

desolate ➡ abandoned, bleak, sadden

desolation ➡ damage, depression

despair ➡ depression

desperado ➡ criminal

desperate ➡ frantic, urgent, useless

despicable ➡ bad

despise ➡ hate

despised ➡ unpopular

despondency ➡ depression

despondent ➡ sad

despot ➡ dictator

despotic ➡ dictatorial

despotism ➡ tyranny

dessicated ➡ dry

destiny ➡ chance, fate, future

destitute ➡ poor

destitution ➡ poverty

destruction ➡ damage, violence, defeat

destructiveness ➡ violence

detach ➡ separate

detached ➡ fair

detachment ➡ division

detain ➡ delay, arrest, jail

detainee ➡ prisoner

detect ➡ discover

detection ➡ discovery

detective ➡ police officer

detention ➡ arrest

deter ➡ delay, prevent

deteriorate ➡ decay, relapse

deteriorated ➡ shabby

deterioration ➡ decay

determination ➡ will, decision

determine ➡ decide, arrange, verify, learn

determined ➡ ambitious, resolute

deterred ➡ disabled

detest ➡ hate

detestable ➡ bad

dethrone ➡ oust

detonate ➡ explode

detonation ➡ bang

detrain ➡ leave

detriment ➡ harm

devastate ➡ destroy, shock

devastating ➡ destructive

devastation ➡ damage

develop ➡ grow, invent, prepare, catch

developing ➡ early

developmental ➡ experimental

deviate ➡ differ, swerve, wander

deviation ➡ change, departure, detour

device ➡ equipment, tool, object, trick

---

devil *n* demon, fiend, archfiend

dialect *n* idiom, vernacular, patois, slang, lingo, argot, jargon, cant, creole, pidgin ➡ **accent, language**

diary *n* journal, chronicle, memoir, datebook, daybook, calendar

dictator *n* despot, tyrant, autocrat, fascist, totalitarian, authoritarian ➡ **ruler**

dictatorial *adj* despotic, tyrannical, autocratic, fascist, totalitarian, authoritarian, absolute, arbitrary ➡ **dogmatic**

dictionary *n* glossary, lexicon, vocabulary, concordance, thesaurus, encyclopedia ➡ **book**

die 1. *vb* decease, expire, pass away, pass on, perish, succumb, depart, starve ⇨ *live*
2. *n* ➡ **form**

differ *vb* vary, contrast, deviate, diverge, disagree ➡ **change**

difference *n* dissimilarity, contrast, distinction, disparity, variation, variance, discrepancy, irregularity, inequality, nuance, gulf
➡ **departure** ⇨ *similarity*

different 1. *adj* distinct, other, else, another, separate, dissimilar, unlike, irregular, uneven, unequal ➡ **unique** ⇨ *same, similar*
2. *adj* diverse, various, assorted, miscellaneous, disparate, eclectic, assorted, varied, heterogeneous, motley ➡ **many**
3. *adj* ➡ **strange**

differently *adv* variously, diversely, separately, else, otherwise

dig *vb* shovel, delve, scoop, excavate, burrow, tunnel, drill, bore, bulldoze, plow, hoe, cultivate, harrow, rake, grub

dignified *adj* formal, stately, solemn, decorous, ceremonious, lofty, imperious, august ➡ **serious, grand**

diligence *n* perseverance, industry, persistence, application, care, carefulness, thoroughness, attentiveness

---

If the word you want is not a main entry above, look below to find it.

devilish ➡ wicked

devil-may-care ➡ carefree

devilment ➡ mischief

devious ➡ indirect, sly

devise ➡ arrange, invent

devoid ➡ empty

devote ➡ dedicate, concentrate

devoted ➡ faithful, loving

devotee ➡ fan

devotion ➡ love, loyalty, worship

devour ➡ eat

devout ➡ religious

dew ➡ humidity

dexterity ➡ agility

dexterous ➡ able, agile

diabolical ➡ wicked

diacritic ➡ accent

diadem ➡ crown

diagram ➡ pattern, picture, draw

dial ➡ call

dialogue ➡ talk

diameter ➡ width

diamond ➡ field

diaphanous ➡ thin, transparent

dice ➡ cut

dictate ➡ say, order

dictatorship ➡ tyranny

diction ➡ speech, delivery

diet ➡ food

differentiate ➡ distinguish

differently abled ➡ disabled

difficult ➡ hard, intolerable, stubborn

difficulty ➡ trouble, barrier

diffident ➡ shy, reluctant

digest ➡ absorb, learn, summary

digit ➡ number

dignitary ➡ celebrity

dignity ➡ pride, respect, importance

digress ➡ wander

digression ➡ detour, departure

dike ➡ dam, jetty

dilapidated ➡ shabby

dilate ➡ swell

dilatory ➡ slow, negligent

dilemma ➡ problem

dilettante ➡ amateur

diligent *adj* industrious, hardworking, assiduous, tireless, inexhaustible, unflagging, dogged ➡ **patient, careful**

dim *adj* faint, indistinct, obscure, hazy, blurry, shadowy, murky, foggy ➡ **dark, dull** ⇨ *bright*

dining room *n* dining hall, eating area, breakfast nook ➡ **room, restaurant**

diplomat *n* ambassador, consul, emissary, statesman, attaché, envoy, minister, chargé d'affaires ➡ **official**

dirge *n* lament, requiem, funeral march, elegy, threnody ➡ **hymn**

dirt 1. *n* earth, soil, loam, humus, turf, topsoil, sand, gravel, grit, land, ground
2. *n* filth, grime, dust, mud, muck, slime, ooze, slop, sludge, mire ➡ **trash**

dirty 1. *adj* filthy, grimy, soiled, dingy, grubby, unclean, impure, unsanitary, contaminated, polluted, foul, dusty, squalid ➡ **messy** ⇨ *clean*
2. *adj* obscene, lewd, pornographic, ribald, vulgar, bawdy, coarse, earthy, salty, risqué, racy ➡ **common**
3. *vb* soil, stain, sully, pollute, contaminate, infect, defile, tarnish, taint, foul, befoul, smudge, muddy, mess ⇨ *clean*

disability *n* handicap, disadvantage, impairment, impediment, affliction, hindrance ➡ **defect**

disabled 1. *adj* handicapped, physically challenged, differently abled, impaired, incapacitated
2. *adj* hampered, thwarted, encumbered, deterred, handicapped, disadvantaged, stymied
3. *adj* ➡ **broken**

disagreement *n* contention, friction, discord, strife, dissent, dissension, heresy ➡ **argument, contradiction, fight, opposition**

disappear *vb* vanish, fade, lift, dissipate, dissolve, evaporate, fizzle, disperse, thin ➡ **melt, stop**

disappoint *vb* let down, fail, discourage, dishearten, dissatisfy, disillusion, frustrate ➡ **sadden**

disappointment 1. *n* failure, discouragement, dissatisfaction, frustration, disillusionment ➡ **regret**
2. *n* letdown, failure, disaster, debacle, fiasco, flop, dud (*informal*)

If the word you want is not a main entry above, look below to find it.

dilute ➡ **weaken**

dimension ➡ **measure**

diminish ➡ **decrease, subtract**

diminished ➡ **less**

diminished by ➡ **minus**

diminution ➡ **subtraction**

diminutive ➡ **small**

dimple ➡ **dent**

din ➡ **noise**

dine ➡ **eat**

diner ➡ **restaurant**

ding ➡ **ring**

dingy ➡ **dirty, dull**

dining hall ➡ **dining room**

dinnerware ➡ **plate**

dip ➡ **descend, drop, sink, swim**

diploma ➡ **document**

diplomacy ➡ **tact**

diplomatic ➡ **suave**

dipper ➡ **spoon**

dire ➡ **awful, urgent**

direct ➡ **control, lead, order, straight**

direction ➡ **course, perspective, leadership, order**

directions ➡ **recipe**

directive ➡ **order**

directly ➡ **now, precisely**

director ➡ **boss**

disable ➡ **mutilate, paralyze**

disadvantage ➡ **harm, disability**

disadvantaged ➡ **disabled, underdeveloped**

disagree ➡ **argue, differ, object**

disagreeable ➡ **cross, awful, bad, thankless, uncomfortable**

disallow ➡ **abolish, forbid**

---

disaster 1. *n* catastrophe, calamity, tragedy, casualty, cataclysm, misfortune, pity, evil ➡ **accident, emergency**
2. *n* ➡ **disappointment**

discard *vb* throw away, dispose, reject, dump, scrap, junk, jettison ➡ **abandon, shed** ⇨ *save*

discipline 1. *n* self-control, self-restraint, willpower, control ➡ **will**
2. *n* training, regimen, regimentation ➡ **practice, science**
3. *n* ➡ **field**
4. *n* ➡ **punishment**
5. *vb* ➡ **punish**

discourage 1. *vb* dispirit, dismay, demoralize, intimidate, unnerve, daunt ➡ **disappoint**
2. *vb* dissuade ➡ **prevent** ⇨ *persuade, urge*

discover 1. *vb* detect, unearth, uncover, strike, descry, ferret out ➡ **find, notice**
2. *vb* ➡ **learn**

discovery *n* finding, detection, unearthing, identification, sighting, disclosure ➡ **invention**

disease *n* infection, virus, fever, contagion, blight, syndrome, bug (*informal*), blight ➡ **illness, epidemic**

disguise 1. *n* mask, camouflage, guise, costume, masquerade, makeup ➡ **pretense**
2. *vb* ➡ **hide**

disgust 1. *vb* repel, revolt, offend, nauseate, sicken, appall
2. *n* loathing, revulsion, repugnance, distaste ➡ **hatred**

dishonest *adj* untruthful, untrustworthy, deceitful, crooked, lying, deceptive, corrupt, unprincipled, unscrupulous ➡ **fake, sly, bad**

dishonesty *n* deceit, corruption, fraudulence, vice, crookedness, duplicity, cunning, guile, hypocrisy ➡ **lie, trick**

If the word you want is not a main entry above, look below to find it.

disapproval ➡ opposition

disapprove ➡ object, refuse

disarrange ➡ disturb

disastrous ➡ unfortunate

disband ➡ finish

disbelief ➡ doubt

disbelieve ➡ doubt

disburse ➡ pay

discern ➡ see

discernible ➡ audible, visible

discerning ➡ smart, profound

discernment ➡ wisdom

discharge ➡ fire, explode, shoot, free, relieve, suspension

disciple ➡ student

disclose ➡ reveal, tell

disclosure ➡ discovery

discoloration ➡ scar

discomfit ➡ embarrass

discomfited ➡ uncomfortable

discomfort ➡ pain

disconcert ➡ confuse, disturb, embarrass

discontinue ➡ stop, abandon

discord ➡ disagreement, confusion

discount ➡ bargain, sale, subtraction

discouragement ➡ disappointment

discourse ➡ speech

discourteous ➡ rude

discourtesy ➡ rudeness

discredit ➡ disprove, shame

discreet ➡ careful

discreetly ➡ carefully

discrepancy ➡ contradiction, difference

discretion ➡ tact

discriminate ➡ distinguish, separate

discrimination ➡ prejudice

discriminatory ➡ prejudiced

discuss ➡ talk

discussion ➡ talk, argument

disdain ➡ hatred, ridicule, hate

disembark ➡ leave

disentangle ➡ comb

disfigure ➡ damage, mutilate

disfigurement ➡ scar

disgrace ➡ shame

disgraceful ➡ awful, shameful

disgusting ➡ bad

dish ➡ bowl, plate, meal

dishcloth ➡ cloth

dishearten ➡ sadden, disappoint

dishevel ➡ disturb

disheveled ➡ messy

dishonor ➡ shame

dishonorable ➡ shameful

dish out ➡ give

dishrag ➡ cloth

disillusion ➡ disappoint

disillusionment ➡ disappointment

disinclined ➡ reluctant

disinfected ➡ sterile

disinformation ➡ lie

disintegrate ➡ decay

disintegration ➡ decay

disinterest ➡ apathy

disinterested ➡ apathetic

disk ➡ circle

dislike ➡ hate, hatred, opposition

n = noun • *vb* = verb • *adj* = adjective • *adv* = adverb • *prep* = preposition • *conj* = conjunction

disobedience *n* defiance, rebellion, insubordination, transgression, waywardness ➡ **revolution**

disobey *vb* defy, disregard, violate, break, misbehave, transgress ➡ **rebel, refuse, fight, sin** ⇨ *obey*

display 1. *n* exhibit, exhibition, presentation, arrangement, array ➡ **show**
2. *n* ➡ **show**
3. *vb* ➡ **show**

disprove *vb* discredit, refute, rebut, invalidate, controvert, expose, debunk ➡ **contradict**

distance 1. *n* stretch, length, interval, gap, way, expanse, extent ➡ **measure**
2. *n* ➡ **background**

distinguish *vb* differentiate, discriminate, identify, recognize ➡ **separate, compare**

distort 1. *vb* ➡ **bend, damage**
2. *vb* misrepresent, pervert, misconstrue, stretch ➡ **change, lie**

distract *vb* divert, sidetrack, deflect ➡ **bother, disturb**

disturb 1. *vb* disarrange, displace, dislocate, disorder, mess, muss, dishevel, rumple, garble ➡ **move**
2. *vb* interrupt, disrupt, intrude, interfere, impose ➡ **bother, distract**
3. *vb* agitate, upset, perturb, unnerve, unsettle, disconcert, ruffle, jar ➡ **worry, bother**

If the word you want is not a main entry above, look below to find it.

disliked ➡ unpopular
dislocate ➡ disturb, hurt
dislodge ➡ move
disloyal ➡ unfaithful
disloyalty ➡ treason
dismal ➡ bleak, sad
dismay ➡ discourage, fear, shock
dismember ➡ mutilate
dismiss ➡ refuse, fire, relieve
dismissal ➡ rejection
dismount ➡ descend
disobedient ➡ mischievous, rebellious
disorder ➡ confusion, illness, disturb
disorderly ➡ messy, wild
disorient ➡ confuse
disparage ➡ ridicule
disparate ➡ different
disparity ➡ difference
dispatch ➡ delivery, letter, speed, send, kill
dispel ➡ banish

dispense ➡ give, inflict
dispersal ➡ flow
disperse ➡ spread, disappear
dispirit ➡ discourage
displace ➡ disturb
displaced ➡ homeless
displacement ➡ movement
disport ➡ play
dispose ➡ discard, persuade
disposed ➡ likely, ready, vulnerable
disposition ➡ mood, personality, tendency, order
dispossessed ➡ homeless
dispute ➡ argument, argue, contradict, object
disregard ➡ disobey, forget, neglect
disregarded ➡ unnoticed
disrepair ➡ decay
disreputable ➡ shameful, bad
disrespect ➡ rudeness, neglect
disrespectful ➡ rude

disrobe ➡ undress
disrupt ➡ disturb
disruption ➡ disturbance, break
dissatisfaction ➡ disappointment
dissatisfy ➡ disappoint
dissemble ➡ lie
dissembler ➡ hypocrite
dissembling ➡ hypocritical
disseminate ➡ spread
dissemination ➡ flow
dissension ➡ disagreement
dissent ➡ disagreement, object
dissertation ➡ report
dissident ➡ rebel
dissimilar ➡ different
dissimilarity ➡ difference
dissipate ➡ disappear, waste
dissolute ➡ immoral
dissolve ➡ melt, disappear, finish
dissuade ➡ discourage

distant ➡ far, foreign, cool
distaste ➡ disgust
distasteful ➡ thankless, bad
distend ➡ swell, lengthen
distill ➡ concentrate
distinct ➡ different, special, obvious, audible, legible
distinction ➡ difference, excellence
distinctive ➡ special
distinguished ➡ famous
distracted ➡ absentminded
distraught ➡ frantic
distress ➡ misery, sorrow, trouble
distressful ➡ uncomfortable
distressing ➡ pitiful
distribute ➡ spread, share, give
distribution ➡ delivery, division, flow
district ➡ zone
distrust ➡ doubt
distrustful ➡ suspicious

➡ = synonym cross-reference • ⇨ = antonym cross-reference

disturbance n commotion, uproar, riot, disruption, fracas, upheaval, turbulence, unrest, rampage ➡ **noise, confusion, protest, violence, fight**

divide 1. vb part, split, partition, segment, subdivide, portion, apportion, halve, quarter, zone ➡ **cut, separate, share**
2. vb diverge, branch, fork
3. vb ➡ **arrange**

divider n partition, barrier, screen, curtain, veil ➡ **wall**

division 1. n separation, detachment, partition, distribution, divorce, severance, subdivision
2. n section, component, chapter, passage, paragraph, scene, episode ➡ **part, share, department**

dizzy adj light-headed, giddy, woozy, faint, dazed, tipsy

do 1. vb accomplish, achieve, carry out, render ➡ **act, cause, work**
2. vb ➡ **solve**
3. vb ➡ **satisfy**

dock 1. n pier, wharf, quay, landing, slip ➡ **harbor**
2. vb moor, land, anchor, berth ➡ **descend** ⇨ *leave*

doctor 1. n physician, M.D., GP, professor, Ph.D.
2. vb ➡ **heal**

document n record, certificate, form, file, diploma, citation, affidavit, passport, deed, credentials, manuscript ➡ **report, agreement, license, ticket**

dog n hound, mongrel, mutt, cur, puppy, canine, whelp

dogmatic adj opinionated, doctrinaire, dictatorial, arrogant, overbearing, imperious ➡ **stubborn**

doll n dolly, baby doll, figurine, mannequin, action figure ➡ **puppet, toy**

door n doorway, entrance, entry, exit, gate, gateway, access, portal, passage, outlet, opening, mouth ➡ **threshold**

If the word you want is not a main entry above, look below to find it.

disturbed ➡ **anxious**

ditch ➡ **channel**

ditty ➡ **song**

dive ➡ **fall, jump**

diverge ➡ **differ, divide, swerve, wander**

divergence ➡ **departure**

diverse ➡ **different, many**

diversely ➡ **differently**

diversion ➡ **detour, entertainment**

divert ➡ **distract, entertain, detour**

divertissement ➡ **entertainment**

divest ➡ **deprive, undress**

divination ➡ **prediction**

divine ➡ **holy, heavenly, religious, predict**

diviner ➡ **prophet**

divinity ➡ **god**

divorce ➡ **separate, division**

divorced ➡ **single**

divulge ➡ **reveal**

docile ➡ **gentle, passive, tame**

doctrinaire ➡ **dogmatic**

doctrine ➡ **belief**

documentation ➡ **proof**

dodder ➡ **limp**

dodge ➡ **avoid, escape, swerve, trick**

dogged ➡ **diligent, stubborn**

dogma ➡ **belief**

doleful ➡ **sad**

dolly ➡ **doll**

dolt ➡ **fool**

domain ➡ **country, field**

domestic ➡ **native, family, tame, servant**

domesticated ➡ **tame**

domicile ➡ **home**

dominant ➡ **predominant**

dominate ➡ **control, excel**

dominion ➡ **country, state, rule**

don ➡ **dress, teacher**

donate ➡ **give**

donation ➡ **gift**

done ➡ **past**

donjon ➡ **castle**

donor ➡ **patron**

doom ➡ **fate**

doorkeeper ➡ **doorman**

doorman *n* doorkeeper, porter, gatekeeper, caretaker, watchman, attendant ➡ **porter, servant**

dose *n* dosage, treatment, teaspoonful ➡ **measure**

doubt 1. *vb* suspect, mistrust, distrust, disbelieve, wonder ➡ **question**
2. *n* uncertainty, suspicion, skepticism, distrust, misgiving, disbelief, doubtfulness, reservation, question, qualm ➡ **suspense**

doubtful *adj* dubious, questionable, uncertain, indefinite, unclear, unsure, skeptical, ambivalent, perplexed, incredulous, vague, tentative ➡ **suspicious, unbelievable, unresolved**

down 1. *adv* downward, downhill, descending
2. *adj* ➡ **sad**
3. *adj* ➡ **broken**

4. *n* ➡ **hill**
5. *vb* ➡ **defeat**
6. *vb* ➡ **drink**

draw 1. *vb* ➡ **pull**
2. *vb* ➡ **earn**
3. *vb* sketch, paint, color, portray, depict, illustrate, picture, trace, delineate, draft, diagram ➡ **describe**
4. *n* ➡ **attraction**
5. *n* ➡ **tie**

dream *n* reverie, daydream, trance, daze, spell, stupor, study, swoon ➡ **hope**

dress 1. *vb* wear, clothe, don, robe, attire, costume, outfit, deck
2. *vb* trim, groom, array ➡ **decorate**
3. *vb* ➡ **bandage**
4. *n* gown, frock, jumper, sheath, skirt, shift, shirtwaist, pinafore, smock, sari, sarong, muumuu ➡ **clothes**

If the word you want is not a main entry above, look below to find it.

doorsill ➡ threshold
doorstep ➡ threshold
doorway ➡ door
do-rag ➡ scarf
dormant ➡ asleep, latent
dormer ➡ attic
dormitory ➡ bedroom
dosage ➡ dose
dot ➡ spot
dote on ➡ love, pamper
double ➡ duplicate, alternate, fold
double agent ➡ spy
double-cross ➡ betray
doubter ➡ skeptic
doubtfulness ➡ doubt

doubting Thomas ➡ skeptic
dour ➡ bleak
douse ➡ extinguish, wet
dowel ➡ nail
downcast ➡ sad
downfall ➡ defeat, fate
downhearted ➡ sad
downhill ➡ down
downpour ➡ rain
downs ➡ plain
down-to-earth ➡ practical
downturn ➡ drop, depression
downward ➡ down
downy ➡ fuzzy
doze ➡ sleep

dozing ➡ asleep
drab ➡ dull, plain, gray
draft ➡ draw, hire, write, drink, wind
draftee ➡ soldier
drafty ➡ windy
drag ➡ pull, crawl
drain ➡ dry, empty
drained ➡ tired
drainpipe ➡ pipe
dram ➡ drink
drama ➡ emotion, play
dramatic ➡ sensational
dramatization ➡ play
dramatize ➡ exaggerate, act
drape ➡ hang

drastic ➡ excessive
drawback ➡ defect
drawing ➡ picture
drawing room ➡ living room
drawl ➡ accent
drawn ➡ tense
draw near ➡ approach
dread ➡ fear
dreadful ➡ awful, scary
dreamer ➡ idealist
dreaming ➡ asleep
drear ➡ bleak
dreary ➡ bleak, dull
drench ➡ wet
drenched ➡ wet

drink 1. *n* beverage, refreshment, alcohol, liquor, spirits ➡ **soda, liquid**

2. *n* sip, glass, swallow, taste, drop, dram, nip, swig, gulp, draft

3. *vb* swallow, gulp, guzzle, quaff, sip, swig, imbibe, down

drive 1. *vb* steer, maneuver, navigate, pilot, ride, propel, jockey ➡ **operate, control**

2. *vb* ➡ **banish**

3. *n* ➡ **trip**

4. *n* ➡ **ambition, energy**

drop 1. *n* droplet, raindrop, teardrop, tear, bead, drip, glob, trickle, dribble ➡ **ball**

2. *n* ➡ **drink**

3. *n* plunge, reduction, decrease, descent, decline, slump, downturn, dip ➡ **fall**

4. *vb* drip, trickle, leak, seep, ooze ➡ **splash**

5. *vb* ➡ **descend, fall, lose, shed**

drug *n* antibiotic, narcotic, sedative, tranquilizer, painkiller, anesthetic, opiate, hallucinogen, antidepressant ➡ **medicine**

drunk *adj* drunken, intoxicated, inebriated, tipsy, besotted

drunkard *n* alcoholic, drinker, inebriate, sot, souse, tippler, lush (*informal*), wino (*informal*)

dry 1. *adj* arid, parched, dehydrated, dessicated, dusty, thirsty ➡ **stale** ⇨ *wet*

2. *adj* ➡ **dull**

3. *adj* droll, wry, deadpan, sardonic ➡ **funny**

4. *adj* ➡ **sour**

5. *vb* wipe, drain

6. *vb* evaporate, dehydrate, wilt, wither, shrivel ➡ **harden**

due 1. *adj* unpaid, payable, outstanding, overdue, receivable

2. *adj* expected, scheduled, anticipated

3. *adv* ➡ **precisely**

dull 1. *adj* uninteresting, boring, tedious, dreary, monotonous, tiresome, prosaic, humdrum, shallow, deadly, dry, drab ➡ **insipid** ⇨ *interesting, lively*

2. *adj* slow, stolid, obtuse, dense, unimaginative, square ➡ **stupid**

3. *adj* blunt, unsharpened ⇨ *sharp*

4. *adj* drab, dim, dingy, faded, lackluster, flat ➡ **bleak, dark, dim** ⇨ *bright*

If the word you want is not a main entry above, look below to find it.

dresser ➡ chest, table

dressing ➡ bandage

dressing gown ➡ bathrobe

dribble ➡ drop

drift ➡ blow², fly, wander

drifter ➡ loafer

drill ➡ dig, teach, practice, lesson

drinker ➡ drunkard

drip ➡ drop

dripping ➡ wet

drivel ➡ nonsense

drive out, drive away ➡ banish

driver's seat ➡ wheel

drizzle ➡ rain

drizzly ➡ wet

droll ➡ dry

drone ➡ hum

droop ➡ bend, weaken

droopy ➡ limp

drop by, drop in ➡ visit

drop-kick ➡ kick

droplet ➡ drop

drown ➡ choke, flood

drowsy ➡ listless

drudgery ➡ work

drum ➡ barrel, knock

drunken ➡ drunk

dry cleaning ➡ laundry

dub ➡ name

dubious ➡ doubtful, suspicious

duck ➡ avoid, bend, sink

duct ➡ pipe, blood vessel

duct tape ➡ adhesive

dud ➡ disappointment

due to ➡ because

duel ➡ fight

due process ➡ justice

duffel bag ➡ luggage

dumb *adj* mute, speechless, silent, inarticulate, voiceless, wordless, tongue-tied ➡ **quiet**
  For the informal use of **dumb** *meaning "not very smart," see* **stupid**.

dumbfounded *adj* astonished, amazed, bewildered, thunderstruck, flabbergasted, surprised

dump 1. *n* landfill, recycling center, trash heap, junkyard
  2. *vb* ➡ **discard, empty**

duplicate 1. *n* double, twin, replica, counterpart, equivalent, analogue, parallel
  ➡ **copy, model**
  2. *vb* ➡ **repeat, reproduce**

during *prep* throughout, through

duty 1. *n* responsibility, obligation, trust, charge
  2. *n* ➡ **job**
  3. *n* ➡ **tax**

If the word you want is not a main entry above, look below to find it.

dullard ➡ **boor**
dummy ➡ **fake, fool, puppet**
dunce ➡ **fool**
dune ➡ **hill**
dungeon ➡ **jail**
dunk ➡ **sink**
duo ➡ **pair**

dupe ➡ **cheat, tool**
duplicity ➡ **dishonesty**
durable ➡ **strong, tough, unbreakable, permanent**
duration ➡ **period**
duress ➡ **stress**
dusk ➡ **dark, evening**
dusky ➡ **dark, gray**

dust ➡ **dirt, sweep**
dustcloth ➡ **cloth**
dust jacket ➡ **wrapper**
dusty ➡ **dirty, dry**
dutiful ➡ **good**
duvet ➡ **blanket**
dwarf ➡ **midget**

dwell ➡ **live**[1]
dwelling ➡ **home**
dwindle ➡ **decrease**
dye ➡ **paint**
dying ➡ **death**
dynamic ➡ **active**
dynamo ➡ **engine**

➡ = synonym cross-reference • ▷ = antonym cross-reference

E

eager *adj* enthusiastic, keen, avid, anxious, ardent, passionate, fervent, exuberant, impatient ➡ **ready, ambitious**

early 1. *adj* initial, original, first, earliest, pioneering, pioneer, primary, inaugural, introductory, preliminary, incipient, embryonic, developing, nascent ⇨ *late*
2. *adj* premature, untimely, precocious, hasty, prompt ➡ **sudden** ⇨ *late*
3. *adj* primitive, primeval, prehistoric, primal, archaic, primordial ➡ **old** ⇨ *modern*

earn 1. *vb* make, collect, realize, profit, net, gross, draw, take (in) ➡ **get, receive, win pay**
2. *vb* ➡ **deserve**

earth 1. *n* world, globe, nature, creation ➡ **planet, space**
2. *n* ➡ **dirt**

earthquake *n* quake, tremor, tremblor, shock, aftershock ➡ **vibration**

easy *adj* effortless, light, simple, moderate, straightforward ➡ **obvious, plain** ⇨ *hard*

eat 1. *vb* consume, devour, dine, feast, feed, graze, browse, gulp, gobble, wolf, gorge, bolt, prey on
2. *vb* ➡ **corrode**
The words **breakfast** *and* **lunch**, *but not* dinner *or* supper, *can also be used as verbs meaning "to eat breakfast or lunch."*

economy 1. *n* thrift, thriftiness, frugality, austerity, prudence, conservation
2. *n* ➡ **brevity**

ecstatic *adj* elated, overjoyed, thrilled, blissful, jubilant, exultant, triumphant ➡ **happy**

edge *n* rim, margin, fringe, brink, boundary, verge, brim, lip, hem, periphery ➡ **border, circumference, side, shore**

educated *adj* literate, learned, knowledgeable, informed, studious, scholarly, erudite, lettered, well-read, well-informed, well-versed, schooled, bookish ➡ **smart** ⇨ *ignorant*

education *n* learning, schooling, instruction, teaching, tuition, training, scholarship, erudition ➡ **study, lesson, knowledge**

If the word you want is not a main entry above, look below to find it.

each ➡ **all, any**

eagerness ➡ **enthusiasm, ambition**

earlier ➡ **before, older**

earliest ➡ **early**

earnest ➡ **serious**

earnestly ➡ **sincerely**

earnings ➡ **wage**

earsplitting ➡ **loud**

earthenware ➡ **pottery**

earthworm ➡ **worm**

earthy ➡ **dirty**

ease ➡ **calm, facilitate, relieve, rest, comfort, freedom, leisure**

easygoing ➡ **carefree, tolerant**

eating area ➡ **dining room**

eavesdrop ➡ **listen, spy**

ebb ➡ **retreat, decrease**

ebony ➡ **black, dark**

eccentric ➡ **strange**

eccentricity ➡ **oddity**

ecclesiastical ➡ **religious**

echo ➡ **answer, reflect, repeat**

eclectic ➡ **different**

eclipse ➡ **hide, exceed**

economic ➡ **financial**

economical ➡ **efficient, cheap**

economics ➡ **business**

ecosystem ➡ **habitat**

ecstasy ➡ **pleasure**

Eden ➡ **utopia**

edgy ➡ **nervous**

edibles ➡ **food**

edict ➡ **order**

edifice ➡ **building**

edit ➡ **correct, write**

educate ➡ **teach**

educational ➡ **intellectual**

educator ➡ **teacher**

eerie ➡ **strange**

efface ➡ **erase**

---

n = noun • *vb* = verb • *adj* = adjective • *adv* = adverb • *prep* = preposition • *conj* = conjunction

effect 1. *n* result, outcome, consequence, upshot, aftermath, issue ➡ **product**
2. *n* impact, impression, influence
3. *vb* ➡ **cause**
Be careful not to confuse the verb **effect** *with the verb* **affect**. *See the note at* **affect**.

efficiency *n* productivity, effectiveness, efficacy, proficiency

efficient *adj* proficient, productive, competent, effective, economical, expedient, cost-effective, practical ➡ **able, useful**

egg 1. *n* ovum, embryo, germ, roe, spawn ➡ **seed**
2. *vb* ➡ **urge**

elapse *vb* pass, lapse, slip by, expire

elegance *n* class, taste, polish, style, grace, splendor, glory, grandeur, sophistication, opulence, luxury ➡ **beauty**

embalm *vb* preserve, mummify ➡ **keep**

embarrass *vb* abash, disconcert, rattle, faze, discomfit, fluster, mortify, chagrin ➡ **shame**

embed *vb* imbed, enclose, insert, inset, wedge, implant, lodge, inlay ➡ **put**

embody *vb* represent, typify, incorporate, exemplify ➡ **contain**

If the word you want is not a main entry above, look below to find it.

effective ➡ efficient, successful
effectively ➡ practically
effectiveness ➡ efficiency
effects ➡ property, luggage
effeminite ➡ feminine
efficacy ➡ efficiency, ability
effigy ➡ statue, god
effort ➡ work, try
effortless ➡ easy
effusive ➡ talkative
eggshell ➡ shell
egg timer ➡ clock
ego ➡ mind, soul
egocentric ➡ proud
egotism ➡ pride
egotistic ➡ proud
Einstein ➡ genius
either ➡ any
eject ➡ exclude, oust
elaborate ➡ complicated, fancy, exaggerate
elaboration ➡ exaggeration

elastic ➡ flexible, rubber band
elastic band ➡ rubber band
elated ➡ ecstatic
elbow ➡ push
elbow grease ➡ work
elbowroom ➡ space
elder ➡ ancestor, older
elderly ➡ old
elect ➡ choose
election ➡ vote, appointment
elective ➡ course
electric ➡ exciting
electricity ➡ energy
electrify ➡ shock
electrifying ➡ exciting
electroplate ➡ plate
elegant ➡ beautiful, grand, fashionable
elegy ➡ dirge
element ➡ matter, part

elemental ➡ basic
elementary ➡ basic
elevate ➡ lift, promote
elevation ➡ height, promotion
elf ➡ fairy
elfin ➡ mischievous
elfish ➡ mischievous
elicit ➡ extract
eligible ➡ able, single
eliminate ➡ abolish, exclude
elite ➡ noble, aristocracy
elocution ➡ delivery
elongate ➡ lengthen
elongated ➡ long
elope ➡ escape
eloquent ➡ articulate
else ➡ different, differently
elsewhere ➡ absent
elucidate ➡ explain
elude ➡ avoid, escape
elusive ➡ inaccessible, sly

elysian fields, Elysium ➡ heaven
emaciated ➡ thin, hungry
e-mail ➡ send
emancipate ➡ free
emancipated ➡ free
emancipation ➡ salvation
embankment ➡ dam
embargo ➡ ban
embark ➡ leave, enter
embarkation ➡ departure
embarrassed ➡ ashamed
embarrassment ➡ shame
embellish ➡ decorate, exaggerate
embellished ➡ fancy
embellishment ➡ decoration, exaggeration
embezzle ➡ steal
embezzlement ➡ theft
embitter ➡ anger
emblem ➡ badge
emboss ➡ print

embrace 1. *vb* hug, clasp, cuddle, enfold, envelop, squeeze, hold, grip, grasp, clench
2. *vb* ➡ **adopt**
3. *n* hug, clasp, handshake, caress, squeeze

emergency *n* crisis, exigency, extremity ➡ **disaster, trouble, accident**

emotion *n* sentiment, passion, drama, affect ➡ **feeling**

emotional 1. *adj* moving, poignant, touching, tearful, passionate, impassioned ➡ **pitiful, sad**
2. *adj* sentimental, demonstrative, sensitive, impetuous, overemotional, maudlin ➡ **temperamental, excited, loving**

emperor *n* czar, tzar, tsar (*Russian*), kaiser (*German*), caliph (*Islamic*), pharaoh (*Egyptian*), mikado (*Japanese*) ➡ **ruler, king**

emphasize *vb* highlight, feature, stress, accent, accentuate, underscore, underline

employed *adj* working, occupied, busy, engaged ⇨ *unemployed*

empress *n* czarina, tzarina, tsarina (*Russian*), kaiserin (*German*) ➡ **ruler, queen**

empty 1. *adj* vacant, unoccupied, uninhabited, bare, austere, blank, void, devoid, hollow, open ➡ **abandoned** ⇨ *full*
2. *adj* idle, vain, meaningless, hollow
3. *vb* unload, unpack, unwrap, remove, dump out, pour out, clean out, evacuate, vacate, deflate, drain

enchant *vb* beguile, entrance, charm, bewitch, hypnotize, mesmerize, spellbind, snow ➡ **fascinate, tempt**

enchantment *n* charm, spell, allure ➡ **attraction, magic**

encore *interj* bravo, brava, bravissimo, hurrah ➡ **again**

enemy *n* rival, adversary, antagonist, foe, attacker, assailant ➡ **opponent**

If the word you want is not a main entry above, look below to find it.

embroider ➡ **sew, exaggerate**

embroidery ➡ **exaggeration**

embryo ➡ **egg**

embryonic ➡ **early**

emcee ➡ **host**

emend ➡ **correct**

emendation ➡ **correction**

emerald ➡ **green**

emerge ➡ **appear**

emigrant ➡ **exile, foreigner**

emigrate ➡ **move**

emigration ➡ **movement**

emigré ➡ **exile, foreigner**

eminence ➡ **excellence, fame**

eminent ➡ **famous**

emissary ➡ **messenger, diplomat**

emit ➡ **throw**

empathy ➡ **pity**

emphasis ➡ **accent**

employ ➡ **hire, use**

employee ➡ **servant, worker**

employer ➡ **boss**

employment ➡ **profession, use**

emporium ➡ **market**

empower ➡ **let**

emulate ➡ **imitate**

enable ➡ **let**

enact ➡ **act, commit**

enactment ➡ **approval**

encephalogram ➡ **X ray**

enchanted ➡ **magic**

enchanter ➡ **magician**

encircle ➡ **ring**

enclose ➡ **ring, embed**

enclosure ➡ **booth, pen**

encompass ➡ **ring, concern**

encounter ➡ **face, fight, meeting, experience**

encourage ➡ **urge**

encouragement ➡ **incentive, support**

encroach ➡ **intrude**

encumber ➡ **load**

encumbered ➡ **disabled**

encyclopedia ➡ **dictionary**

end ➡ **abolish, finish, back, destination, fate, point, side**

endanger ➡ **jeopardize**

endeavor ➡ **try, work**

ended ➡ **past**

endemic ➡ **native**

ending ➡ **finish**

endless ➡ **eternal, infinite**

endlessly ➡ **forever**

endorse ➡ **approve, prefer, sign**

endow ➡ **give**

endowment ➡ **gift, inheritance**

endurance ➡ **energy, patience**

endure ➡ **bear, weather, continue, experience**

enduring ➡ **permanent**

energy 1. *n* vigor, vitality, life, liveliness, pep, stamina, endurance, vim, drive, get-up-and-go, zip, steam ➡ **strength, excitement**
2. *n* power, horsepower, pressure, thrust, propulsion, voltage, current, electricity, heat, fuel

engine *n* motor, machine, generator, turbine, dynamo

enough *adj* ample, sufficient, adequate, abundant, plentiful, plenty, much
  Note that **enough, plenty,** *and* **much** *cannot be used after an or before a singular noun such as supply, amount, quantity, or number. The other words in this list can be used in this way:* "an **ample** supply," "a **sufficient** amount," "an **abundant** quantity," "an **adequate** number of items," "a **plentiful** supply."

enter 1. *vb* penetrate, invade, infiltrate ➡ **go, approach, intrude** ⇨ *leave*
2. *vb* board, mount, embark, entrain, enplane ⇨ *leave*
3. *vb* ➡ **join**

entertain 1. *vb* amuse, divert, cheer (up), beguile, regale, enthrall, humor ➡ **please**
2. *vb* host, receive, treat, invite ➡ **welcome**
3. *vb* ➡ **consider**

entertainment *n* diversion, recreation, amusement, divertissement ➡ **pleasure, play, game, program**

enthusiasm *n* passion, zeal, fervor, zest, ardor, eagerness, exuberance, gusto ➡ **pleasure, excitement, ambition**

If the word you want is not a main entry above, look below to find it.

energetic ➡ **lively**

energize ➡ **excite**

enfold ➡ **embrace**

enforce ➡ **support**

engage ➡ **interest, hire**

engaged ➡ **absorbed, employed, married**

engagement ➡ **meeting, fight**

engaging ➡ **interesting**

engender ➡ **cause**

engineer ➡ **control, creator**

engrave ➡ **carve, print**

engraving ➡ **inscription, print**

engross ➡ **interest**

engrossed ➡ **absorbed**

engrossing ➡ **interesting**

engulf ➡ **flood, sink**

enhance ➡ **strengthen, suit**

enigma ➡ **problem**

enigmatic ➡ **mysterious, obscure**

enjoy ➡ **appreciate, like, own**

enjoyable ➡ **pleasant**

enjoyment ➡ **pleasure**

enlarge ➡ **grow, strengthen**

enlargement ➡ **addition, growth**

enlighten ➡ **teach**

enlightenment ➡ **civilization**

enlist ➡ **join, hire, mobilize**

enliven ➡ **excite**

en masse ➡ **together**

enmity ➡ **opposition**

ennui ➡ **boredom**

enormous ➡ **huge**

enormously ➡ **much**

enplane ➡ **enter**

enrage ➡ **anger**

enraged ➡ **violent**

enrich ➡ **help**

enroll ➡ **join, hire**

enrollee ➡ **member**

ensemble ➡ **band, choir, suit**

enshrine ➡ **bury**

ensign ➡ **flag**

enslave ➡ **catch**

enslavement ➡ **slavery**

ensnare ➡ **catch**

ensue ➡ **follow, happen**

ensuing ➡ **consecutive, following**

ensure ➡ **guarantee, verify**

entangle ➡ **catch**

enterprise ➡ **ambition, adventure, business**

enterprising ➡ **ambitious**

entertainer ➡ **actor, musician, host**

entertaining ➡ **interesting**

enthrall ➡ **fascinate, entertain**

enthrone ➡ **crown**

enthusiast ➡ **fan**

enthusiastic ➡ **eager**

entice ➡ **tempt, persuade**

enticement ➡ **attraction**

entire ➡ **all, complete**

entirely ➡ **completely**

entirety ➡ **total**

entitle ➡ **name, let**

entomb ➡ **bury**

entourage ➡ **court, following**

entrain ➡ **enter**

entrance ➡ **door, enchant**

entranceway ➡ **threshold**

entrancing ➡ **magic**

entreat ➡ **beg**

entrepreneur ➡ **tycoon**

---

entrust *vb* commit, confide, consign, delegate, relegate

envy 1. *vb* desire, covet, resent, grudge, begrudge ➡ **want**
2. *n* jealousy, covetousness, resentment, spite, desire, malice ➡ **greed**

epidemic 1. *n* plague, pestilence, outbreak, eruption, rash, pandemic ➡ **disease**
2. *adj* ➡ **contagious**

equal 1. *adj* ➡ **same, fair**
2. *n* peer, fellow, mate, match, compeer ➡ **duplicate**

equipment *n* machinery, apparatus, paraphernalia, device, implement, fixture, gear, tackle, harness, kit, accoutrement, facilities ➡ **tool**

erase *vb* obliterate, delete, scratch, eradicate, expunge, efface ➡ **abolish**

escape 1. *vb* flee, elude, evade, dodge, break out, bolt, elope ➡ **avoid, leave**
2. *n* flight, getaway, evasion, desertion, deliverance, rescue ➡ **departure**

essence *n* core, heart, substance, quintessence, bottom, marrow, root, gist ➡ **basis, middle, soul**

If the word you want is not a main entry above, look below to find it.

entry ➡ approach, door, contestant

entryway ➡ hall, threshold

enumerate ➡ list

enunciate ➡ pronounce

enunciation ➡ speech, delivery

envelop ➡ embrace, wrap

envelope ➡ wrapper

envious ➡ jealous

environment ➡ habitat, setting, terrain, nature

envisage ➡ imagine

envision ➡ imagine

envoy ➡ messenger, diplomat

eon ➡ period

épée ➡ sword

ephemeral ➡ temporary

epic ➡ myth

epicure ➡ glutton

epilogue ➡ conclusion

episode ➡ division, event

epistle ➡ letter

epitaph ➡ inscription

epithet ➡ name

epoch ➡ period

epoxy ➡ adhesive

equalize ➡ balance

equatorial ➡ tropical

equestrian ➡ rider

equidistant ➡ parallel

equilibrium ➡ balance

equip ➡ supply

equipped ➡ ready

equitable ➡ fair

equity ➡ justice

equivalent ➡ alike, same, duplicate

equivocate ➡ hesitate, lie

equivocator ➡ liar

era ➡ period

eradicate ➡ abolish, erase, kill

erect ➡ build, lift, vertical

erection ➡ assembly

ergo ➡ therefore

erode ➡ corrode, weaken

err ➡ misunderstand, sin

errand ➡ job

erratic ➡ fickle, periodic, variable, zigzag

erroneous ➡ wrong

error ➡ mistake

ersatz ➡ fake

erudite ➡ educated, profound

erudition ➡ education, knowledge

erupt ➡ explode

eruption ➡ epidemic

escalation ➡ growth

escapade ➡ adventure

escape artist ➡ magician

escapee ➡ runaway

escarpment ➡ cliff

eschew ➡ abstain

escort ➡ accompany, bring, guide, patrol

escutcheon ➡ badge

esoteric ➡ secret

especial ➡ special

especially ➡ chiefly

espionage ➡ spying

espousal ➡ marriage

espouse ➡ adopt, marry

espoused ➡ married

essay ➡ report, try

essayist ➡ writer

essential ➡ necessary, important, necessity

essentially ➡ chiefly, practically

establish ➡ base, verify

establishment ➡ business

estate ➡ property

esteem ➡ respect

esthetics ➡ philosophy

estimable ➡ praiseworthy

n = noun • *vb* = verb • *adj* = adjective • *adv* = adverb • *prep* = preposition • *conj* = conjunction

estimate 1. *vb* calculate, evaluate, approximate, reckon, figure, gauge, assess, judge, appraise
➡ **guess**
2. *n* approximation, evaluation, appraisal, assessment, estimation, bid, quotation, quote, comparison ➡ **budget**

eternal *adj* everlasting, endless, unending, perpetual, interminable, infinite, immortal, deathless, undying ➡ **continual, permanent**

evening *n* nightfall, twilight, dusk, eventide, sundown, sunset ➡ **afternoon, night**
⇨ *morning*

event 1. *n* incident, occurrence, episode, circumstance, occasion, happening, phenomenon, actuality, fact
2. *n* milestone, landmark, breakthrough, achievement, experience, adventure
➡ **ceremony, disaster**
3. *n* ➡ **game**

exaggerate *vb* overstate, overdo, inflate, embellish, embroider, elaborate, gild, magnify, dramatize

exaggeration *n* overstatement, hyperbole, embroidery, embellishment, elaboration

examination 1. *n* exam, test, quiz, final, midterm, take-home, inquest, trial
2. *n* ➡ **study**

examine 1. *vb* investigate, scrutinize, inspect, probe, scan ➡ **study, look**
2. *vb* test, quiz, interrogate ➡ **ask**

example *n* instance, case, illustration, specimen, sample, representation, representative
➡ **model**

exceed *vb* outdo, surpass, pass, top, better, best, transcend, outshine, eclipse, outnumber, overstep ➡ **excel**

excel *vb* dominate, prevail ➡ **exceed**

excellence *n* perfection, faultlessness, superiority, greatness, distinction, eminence, majesty

If the word you want is not a main entry above, look below to find it.

estimated ➡ approximate

estimation ➡ estimate, reputation, respect, worth

estuary ➡ bay, river

etch ➡ carve

etching ➡ print

eternally ➡ forever

eternity ➡ future

ethereal ➡ invisible

ethics ➡ philosophy

etiquette ➡ behavior

euphonious ➡ musical

evacuate ➡ empty, leave

evade ➡ avoid, escape

evaluate ➡ estimate, study

evaluation ➡ estimate

evaluator ➡ judge

evaporate ➡ disappear, dry, melt

evasion ➡ escape

even ➡ level, parallel, straight

evenhandedness ➡ justice

eventide ➡ evening

eventuality ➡ possibility

eventually ➡ finally

ever ➡ regularly

evergreen ➡ pine, tree

everlasting ➡ eternal

evermore ➡ forever

every ➡ all, any

everybody ➡ all

everyday ➡ common

everyone ➡ all

every other ➡ alternate

everything ➡ all

everywhere ➡ about

evict ➡ banish

evidence ➡ proof, knowledge

evident ➡ obvious

evidently ➡ apparently

evil ➡ bad, wicked, crime, disaster, immorality

evoke ➡ extract

evolution ➡ change

evolve ➡ grow

ewer ➡ bottle

exact ➡ careful, correct, literal, extract, inflict

exacting ➡ strict

exactitude ➡ accuracy

exactly ➡ precisely

exactness ➡ accuracy

exaggerated ➡ sensational

exalt ➡ bless, worship

exalted ➡ grand

exam ➡ examination

exasperate ➡ anger

exasperated ➡ angry

excavate ➡ dig

excavation ➡ mine

exceeding ➡ above

excellent ➡ good, model, cool

excerpt *n* clause, section, provision, passage, portion, quotation, selection, extract

excessive *adj* extreme, drastic, radical, inordinate, immoderate, intemperate, exorbitant, overabundant ➡ **unnecessary**

excite *vb* stimulate, exhilarate, agitate, thrill, energize, arouse, galvanize, enliven ➡ **fan** ⇨ *calm*

excited *adj* thrilled, exhilarated, hysterical, stimulated ➡ **eager, nervous, frantic, angry, emotional**

excitement *n* agitation, tumult, exhilaration, stimulation, thrill, zest, fever, fireworks ➡ **enthusiasm, energy, confusion, hysteria**

exciting *adj* riveting, gripping, breathtaking, sensational, electric, electrifying, rousing, thrilling, exhilarating ➡ **interesting**

exclude *vb* eliminate, suspend, reject, omit, eject, skip, neglect, ignore, overlook, miss, remove, rid ➡ **banish, bar, forbid, forget**

exercise 1. *n* exertion, training, workout, activity, conditioning
2. *n* ➡ **use**
3. *n* ➡ **lesson**
4. *vb* train, work out, condition
5. *vb* ➡ **use**

exhaustion *n* fatigue, weariness, tiredness, listlessness, prostration

exile 1. *n* expulsion, banishment, deportation, transportation, ostracism
2. *n* refugee, fugitive, emigré, emigrant, deportee, expatriate, outcast, pariah ➡ **foreigner**
3. *vb* ➡ **banish**

existence *n* being, reality, substance, materiality

If the word you want is not a main entry above, look below to find it.

excellently ➡ well

except ➡ but

exceptional ➡ special

excess ➡ abundance

exchange ➡ trade, change

exchequer ➡ bank

exclaim ➡ say

excluding ➡ but

exclusive ➡ private

exclusively ➡ only

excursion ➡ trip

excuse ➡ apology, alibi, opportunity, pretense, forgive, relieve

execrate ➡ hate

execute ➡ act, kill, hang

execution ➡ behavior

executioner ➡ killer

executive ➡ official

executor ➡ agent

exemplar ➡ model

exemplary ➡ perfect

exemplify ➡ embody, explain

exempt ➡ free

exert ➡ use

exertion ➡ exercise, work

exhalation ➡ breath

exhale ➡ breathe

exhaust ➡ tire, use

exhausted ➡ tired

exhaustive ➡ complete, comprehensive

exhibit ➡ display, show

exhibition ➡ display

exhibition hall ➡ gallery

exhilarate ➡ excite

exhilarated ➡ excited

exhilarating ➡ exciting

exhilaration ➡ excitement

exhort ➡ preach, warn

exigency ➡ emergency

exist ➡ happen, live[1]

exit ➡ departure, door, leave

exodus ➡ departure

exonerate ➡ forgive

exoneration ➡ forgiveness

exorbitant ➡ excessive

exotic ➡ foreign

expand ➡ grow, spread, swell, strengthen

expanse ➡ distance, space

expansion ➡ addition, growth

expansive ➡ broad

expatriate ➡ banish, exile

expect ➡ anticipate, hope

expectant ➡ optimistic, pregnant

expectation ➡ possibility

expected ➡ due

expecting ➡ pregnant

expedient ➡ efficient

expedite ➡ facilitate

expedition ➡ trip

expeditious ➡ punctual

expeditiously ➡ quickly

expel ➡ banish, oust

expend ➡ pay, use

expenditure ➡ use

expense ➡ price

expenses ➡ budget

expensive *adj* costly, invaluable, precious, dear, high-priced, overpriced, extravagant, upscale ➡ **valuable, rich** ⇨ *cheap*

experience 1. *n* background, training, knowledge, skill, know-how, expertise ➡ **knowledge, wisdom, event** 2. *vb* undergo, encounter, endure, live through ➡ **bear**

experiment 1. *n* trial, test, experimentation, demonstration ➡ **examination, study** 2. *vb* ➡ **try, study**

experimental *adj* test, trial, innovative, developmental, provisional

expert 1. *n* authority, specialist, master, virtuoso, ace, connoisseur 2. *adj* proficient, skilled, masterly, adroit, ace, versed, well-versed ➡ **able, smart**

explain *vb* clarify, interpret, justify, demonstrate, elucidate, illustrate, illuminate, exemplify, expound, show, treat ➡ **solve, describe**

explicit *adj* vivid, realistic, graphic, precise ➡ **straightforward** ⇨ *obscure*

explode *vb* erupt, discharge, detonate, blow up, burst ➡ **break**

extinguish *vb* put out, quench, douse, smother, stifle ➡ **contain, kill**

extract 1. *vb* remove, withdraw, retract, pluck, extricate, leach ➡ **gather, pull** 2. *vb* elicit, evoke, extort, exact, derive ➡ **get, pull** 3. *n* ➡ **excerpt**

extremist *n* zealot, fanatic, maniac, radical ➡ **rebel**

If the word you want is not a main entry above, look below to find it.

experienced ➡ cosmopolitan

experimentation ➡ experiment

expertise ➡ experience, talent

expiate ➡ pay

expiration ➡ death

expire ➡ breathe, die, finish, elapse

explanation ➡ answer, reason, apology

expletive ➡ curse

exploit ➡ adventure, act, use

exploration ➡ hunt, study

explore ➡ hunt, travel

explosion ➡ bang

explosive ➡ dangerous, inflammable

export ➡ send

expose ➡ disprove, reveal, weather

exposed ➡ naked

expound ➡ explain

express ➡ say

expression ➡ face, saying, speech, word, sign

expressionless ➡ blank

expressive ➡ meaningful

expressway ➡ highway

expropriate ➡ take

expulsion ➡ exile, suspension

expunge ➡ erase

exquisite ➡ beautiful, perfect

extemporaneous ➡ spontaneous

extend ➡ lengthen, spread, offer, lend

extended ➡ long

extension ➡ addition

extensive ➡ broad, long, general

extent ➡ depth, distance, range, period

exterior ➡ outside

exterminate ➡ abolish, kill

external ➡ outside

extinct ➡ dead

extol ➡ praise

extort ➡ extract

extortion ➡ theft

extra ➡ more, unnecessary

extraction ➡ ancestry

extraneous ➡ unnecessary

extraordinary ➡ special

extravagant ➡ expensive, wasteful

extreme ➡ excessive, last

extremely ➡ much, very

extremity ➡ emergency, limb, foot

extricate ➡ extract, free

exuberance ➡ enthusiasm

exuberant ➡ eager

exude ➡ sweat

exult ➡ boast

exultant ➡ ecstatic

eye ➡ look

eyeglasses ➡ glasses

eyeless ➡ blind

eyesight ➡ sight

eyewitness ➡ observer

F

face 1. *n* features, visage, countenance, expression, profile ➡ **appearance**
2. *n* ➡ **side**
3. *vb* oppose, confront, defy, brave, challenge, encounter ➡ **bear, compete, fight** ⇨ *retreat*

facilitate *vb* ease, expedite, simplify, foster ➡ **help**

factory *n* plant, shop, workshop, mill, assembly plant ➡ **business**

faculty 1. *n* staff, personnel ➡ **teacher**
2. *adj* ➡ **ability**

fair 1. *adj* just, impartial, equal, unbiased, equitable, objective, unprejudiced, neutral nonpartisan, detached, impersonal ➡ **right**
2. *adj* satisfactory, acceptable, adequate, mediocre, decent
3. *adj* clear, sunny, bright, pleasant, mild ➡ **bright** ⇨ *cloudy*
4. *adj* blond, blonde, light, white, ivory, creamy, bleached ➡ **pale**
5. *adj* ➡ **pretty**
6. *n* ➡ **carnival**

fairy *n* elf, pixie, sprite, spirit, brownie, leprechaun

faithful 1. *adj* loyal, true, devoted, steadfast, constant, trusty, trustworthy, resolute, staunch, fast, unfailing, unshaken, committed, tenacious ➡ **reliable, religious** ⇨ *unfaithful*
2. *adj* ➡ **correct**

fake 1. *adj* false, artificial, imitation, dummy, ersatz, counterfeit, spurious, phony, bogus, sham, mock ➡ **dishonest** ⇨ *real*
2. *n* phony, counterfeit, forgery, imitation, dummy ➡ **copy**
3. *n* ➡ **cheat**
4. *vb* forge, counterfeit, falsify ➡ **imitate, pretend**

fall 1. *vb* drop, collapse, plunge, topple, tumble, plummet, slump, plump, crumple, subside, slip, lapse, sink, set ➡ **descend, trip, lose**
2. *n* tumble, spill, dive, nosedive ➡ **drop**
3. *n* ➡ **wig**

fame *n* renown, celebrity, glory, eminence, standing, notoriety, popularity, prestige ➡ **reputation, respect**

If the word you want is not a main entry above, look below to find it.

fable ➡ myth, superstition

fabled ➡ legendary

fabric ➡ cloth

fabricate ➡ build, invent, lie

fabrication ➡ pretense, lie, assembly

fabulous ➡ legendary, great

façade ➡ outside

facet ➡ side, part

facetious ➡ funny

facile ➡ suave

facilities ➡ equipment, bathroom

facility ➡ talent

facing ➡ opposite

facsimile ➡ copy

fact ➡ knowledge, detail, event, certainty

faction ➡ party, movement

factor ➡ detail

factual ➡ correct

fad ➡ fashion

fade ➡ disappear, tire, bleach

faded ➡ dull

fail ➡ lose, disappoint

failing ➡ fault

failure ➡ defeat, disappointment, inability

faint ➡ dim, dizzy

fainthearted ➡ cowardly

fairness ➡ justice

fair-skinned ➡ white

faith ➡ belief, religion, hope

faithfully ➡ carefully

faithfulness ➡ loyalty

faker ➡ hypocrite

fallacious ➡ illogical

fallacy ➡ mistake

falling-out ➡ argument

falling star ➡ meteor

false ➡ fake, wrong, unfaithful

false-hearted ➡ unfaithful

falsehood ➡ lie

falsifier ➡ liar

falsify ➡ lie, fake

falter ➡ hesitate, limp

famed ➡ famous

family 1. *n* relative, relation, kin, people, kindred, lineage, clan, tribe, stock, strain
➡ **ancestry**
2. *adj* familial, domestic, home, homey, household, residential

famous *adj* famed, noted, prominent, renowned, eminent, notorious, celebrated, illustrious, distinguished, well-known, popular, important, great

fan 1. *n* enthusiast, supporter, devotee, aficionado, fanatic, addict, partisan, lover
2. *vb* ventilate, aerate, cool
3. *vb* inflame, incite, excite, stir up, arouse, agitate

fancy 1. *adj* elaborate, ornate, embellished, decorative, ostentatious, flamboyant
➡ **loud, rich**
2. *n* whim, caprice, fantasy, notion, fiction, figment ➡ **illusion, imagination, impulse**
3. *vb* ➡ **imagine**
4. *vb* ➡ **like**

far 1. *adj* distant, remote, faraway, far-flung, removed, outlying, yonder
2. *adv* considerably, incomparably, notably, greatly ➡ **much**
   As adverbs, **far** *and its synonyms are used with comparative adjectives:* "I'm feeling **far** better

today." "This hill is **considerably** steeper than I remembered it!"

farm 1. *n* ranch, homestead, plantation, spread, farmstead
2. *vb* till, harvest, garden ➡ **grow**

farmer *n* planter, grower, breeder, rancher, husbandman, sharecropper, farmhand, peasant, yeoman, serf ➡ **worker**

farming 1. *n* agriculture, cultivation, husbandry, horticulture, sharecropping, homesteading, ranching ➡ **rural**
2. *adj* agricultural, agrarian

fascinate *vb* attract, intrigue, captivate, enthrall, charm, appeal ➡ **interest, enchant**

fashion 1. *n* style, trend, fad, craze, rage, mode, vogue, thing
2. *vb* ➡ **make, form, build**

fashionable *adj* stylish, chic, elegant, dapper, dashing, popular, trendy, hot, contemporary, sharp, with-it, smart, in (*informal*) ➡ **suave, cool**

fast 1. *adj* rapid, quick, speedy, swift, fleet, hasty, hurried, prompt, cursory, perfunctory, snap ➡ **sudden** ⇨ *slow*
2. *adj* ➡ **faithful**
3. *adj* ➡ **tight**
4. *adv* ➡ **quickly**

I f   t h e   w o r d   y o u   w a n t   i s   n o t   a   m a i n   e n t r y   a b o v e ,   l o o k   b e l o w   t o   f i n d   i t .

familial ➡ **family**

familiar ➡ **common**

familiarize ➡ **introduce**

family room ➡ **den**

famine ➡ **hunger**

famished ➡ **hungry**

fanatic ➡ **fan, extremist**

fanciful ➡ **imaginary**

fanny pack ➡ **bag**

fantasize ➡ **imagine**

fantastic ➡ **nice**

fantasy ➡ **fancy**

faraway ➡ **far**

farce ➡ **play**

farcical ➡ **funny**

fare ➡ **board, food, price, traveler**

far-flung ➡ **far**

farewell ➡ **departure, good-bye**

farmhand ➡ **farmer, field**

farmstead ➡ **farm**

fascinating ➡ **interesting, attractive**

fascination ➡ **attraction, obsession**

fascism ➡ **tyranny**

fascist ➡ **dictator, dictatorial**

fashion model ➡ **model**

fasten ➡ **join, close, lock, tie**

fastener ➡ **clasp**

fastidious ➡ **choosy**

fat 1. *adj* plump, obese, stout, overweight, corpulent, portly, chubby, brawny, husky, heavyset, stocky, pudgy, squat ➡ **big, heavy**
2. *n* oil, lard, shortening, tallow, suet, grease

fate 1. *n* destiny, lot, doom, death, end, ruin, downfall ➡ **future**
2. *n* ➡ **chance**

fatherly *adj* paternal, parental, protective ➡ **masculine** ⇨ *motherly*

faucet *n* spigot, tap, spout, nozzle, valve, petcock

fault *n* failing, weakness, vice ➡ **defect, guilt, mistake**

favorite 1. *adj* preferred, favored, pet, choice, best-liked, popular
2. *n* darling, pet, precious, ideal ➡ **lover**
3. *n* ➡ **preference**

fear 1. *n* alarm, fright, dread, terror, panic, horror, phobia, anxiety, apprehension, foreboding, dismay, consternation, scare ➡ **worry**
2. *vb* flinch, cower, tremble, quail, quake, dread

feast 1. *n* banquet, fiesta, repast, spread (*informal*) ➡ **meal, party**
2. *vb* ➡ **eat**

feeling 1. *n* sense, sensation, perception, feel, touch ➡ **quality**
2. *n* sensitivity, sentimentality, intuition, instinct, heart, soul, warmth ➡ **emotion, impulse**
3. *n* ➡ **belief**

feminine *adj* female, ladylike, womanly, matronly, effeminate, motherly ⇨ *masculine*

fertile 1. *adj* fruitful, productive, prolific, teeming, fecund, gravid ⇨ *sterile*
2. *adj* ➡ **talented**

If the word you want is not a main entry above, look below to find it.

fatal ➡ deadly
fatalistic ➡ pessimistic
fatality ➡ casualty
father ➡ parent
fatherland ➡ country
fathom ➡ know
fatigue ➡ tire, exhaustion
fatigued ➡ tired
fattening ➡ rich
faultless ➡ correct, perfect, infallible, innocent
faultlessness ➡ excellence
faulty ➡ broken
faux pas ➡ mistake
favor ➡ approve, resemble, prefer, gift
favorable ➡ good, successful
favorably ➡ well

favored ➡ favorite
favorite son ➡ candidate
favoritism ➡ prejudice
fawn ➡ flatter, brown
fawning ➡ servile
faze ➡ embarrass
fealty ➡ loyalty
fearful ➡ cowardly, scary, superstitious
fearless ➡ brave
feasible ➡ possible
feasibly ➡ maybe
feat ➡ act
featherbed ➡ blanket
feature ➡ emphasize, detail
features ➡ appearance, face
fecund ➡ fertile
federal ➡ public

federation ➡ union
fee ➡ wage, tax, price
feeble ➡ weak
feed ➡ eat, support, hay
feel ➡ touch, feeling
feign ➡ pretend
feint ➡ tactic
felicity ➡ pleasure
fell ➡ hide
fellow ➡ man, equal, member
fellowship ➡ friendship, award
felon ➡ criminal
felony ➡ crime
female ➡ woman, feminine
fen ➡ swamp
fence ➡ wall

fender-bender ➡ collision
fend off ➡ repel
ferocious ➡ wild
ferret out ➡ discover
fervent ➡ eager
fervor ➡ enthusiasm
festival ➡ carnival, ceremony
festive ➡ happy
festivity ➡ party, mirth
festoon ➡ decorate
fetch ➡ bring
fete ➡ party
fetish ➡ obsession
fetter ➡ bond
feud ➡ fight
fever ➡ disease, excitement
feverish ➡ frantic

n = noun • *vb* = verb • *adj* = adjective • *adv* = adverb • *prep* = preposition • *conj* = conjunction

few *adj* several, couple, scant, scanty, negligible, sporadic ⇨ **many**
Note that **few** and **couple** are used with a, but **several** is not.

fickle *adj* changeable, untrustworthy, inconstant, mercurial, irresolute, flighty, erratic ➡ **variable, arbitrary, unreliable, unfaithful**

fidget 1. *vb* squirm, twitch, wiggle, wriggle, writhe, stir
2. *vb* ➡ **tinker**

field 1. *n* meadow, pasture, clearing, glade, plot, hayfield, cornfield, wheatfield, farmland ➡ **pen**
2. *n* playing field, athletic field, diamond, gridiron, arena, track, court, stadium, coliseum ➡ **gymnasium**
3. *n* airfield, airport, battlefield, battleground
4. *n* subject, area, sphere, realm, discipline, province, arena, bailiwick, domain, orbit ➡ **department, profession, specialty**

fight 1. *vb* battle, struggle, wrestle, grapple, combat, clash, conflict, war, brawl, feud, duel, skirmish, scrap, strive, resist ➡ **argue, attack, compete, face**
All the terms at **fight 1** are used as nouns as well as verbs, except for **wrestle, grapple, strive,** and **resist.**
2. *n* battle, engagement, struggle, war, action, strife, conflict, hostilities, warfare, combat, skirmish, confrontation, encounter ➡ **violence, competition, game**
3. *n* altercation, clash, scuffle, tussle, scrap, melee, brawl, feud, duel, showdown, fray, rumble ➡ **argument, disturbance**
4. *n* defiance, resistance, opposition, struggle

finally 1. *adv* conclusively, decisively, irrevocably, permanently ➡ **certainly**
2. *adv* eventually, ultimately, lastly

financial *adj* monetary, fiscal, economic, pecuniary, commercial, budgetary ➡ **business**

find *vb* locate, come across, spot, retrieve, stumble across ➡ **discover, recover, learn, notice, get** ⇨ **lose**

If the word you want is not a main entry above, look below to find it.

fewer ➡ less
fiancé ➡ love
fiancée ➡ love
fiasco ➡ disappointment
fib ➡ lie
fibber ➡ liar
fiber ➡ string
fiction ➡ lie, fancy
fictional ➡ imaginary
fictitious ➡ imaginary
fiddle ➡ tinker
fidelity ➡ loyalty
fidgety ➡ nervous

field house ➡ gymnasium
fiend ➡ devil
fiendish ➡ wicked
fierce ➡ wild, sharp, violent, stormy
fiery ➡ burning, wild
fiesta ➡ feast
fighter ➡ soldier
figment ➡ fancy
figure ➡ number, estimate, body, statue
figure out ➡ solve
figurine ➡ doll, statue
filament ➡ string

filch ➡ steal
file ➡ document, row, arrange, walk, sharpen
fill ➡ load, close, occupy
filled ➡ full
filly ➡ horse
film ➡ movie, coat, layer
filter ➡ net, clean, sift
filth ➡ dirt
filthy ➡ dirty
fin ➡ limb
final ➡ last, latter, examination
finale ➡ finish

finalize ➡ finish
finance ➡ back, business
finances ➡ budget
financier ➡ tycoon
finding ➡ decision, discovery
find out ➡ learn
fine ➡ good, punish
finer ➡ better
finery ➡ clothes
finesse ➡ tact
finest ➡ best
finger ➡ play
fingerprint ➡ print
finicky ➡ choosy

finish 1. *vb* complete, end, terminate, conclude, attain, expire, wind up, finalize, clinch, use up, dissolve, disband ➡ **stop, use, climax** ⇨ *start*

2. *n* end, conclusion, ending, finale, completion, termination, culmination, death, fulfillment

3. *n* shine, polish, paint, varnish, shellac, lacquer, stain, wax

finite *adj* limited, measurable, restricted ⇨ *infinite*

fire 1. *n* flame, blaze, conflagration, combustion, campfire, bonfire, pyre, inferno, holocaust ➡ **fireplace**

2. *n* gunfire, shooting, firing, shelling, bombardment

3. *vb* ➡ **shoot**

4. *vb* dismiss, discharge, terminate, lay off, let go, sack (*informal*), can (*informal*) ➡ **oust** ⇨ *hire*

fireplace *n* hearth, chimney, fireside, barbecue ➡ **fire**

fireworks *n* pyrotechnics, illuminations ➡ **excitement**

firm 1. *adj* rigid, hard, solid, stiff, inflexible, steady, compact, dense ➡ **tough, hard, thick**

2. *n* ➡ **business**

fit[1] 1. *adj* suitable, proper, appropriate, fitting, apt, applicable, pertinent, apposite ➡ **correct, relevant**

2. *adj* ➡ **healthy, able**

3. *vb* ➡ **suit, belong**

fit[2] 1. *n* seizure, attack, convulsion, spasm, paroxysm, spell ➡ **illness**

2. *n* outburst, tantrum, frenzy, huff, snit, conniption (*informal*) ➡ **hysteria**

fix 1. *vb* repair, mend, patch, restore, renovate, renew, rebuild, overhaul, recondition, service ➡ **adjust, correct, tinker**

2. *vb* ➡ **sterilize**

3. *n* ➡ **trouble**

flag 1. *n* banner, standard, pennant, colors, ensign, jack

2. *vb* ➡ **wave**

3. *vb* ➡ **weaken**

4. *vb* ➡ **cover**

flatter *vb* adulate, fawn, pander, butter up, kowtow to ➡ **praise, suit**

flavor *n* taste, savor, tang, flavoring ➡ **spice**

If the word you want is not a main entry above, look below to find it.

finished ➡ past

fir ➡ pine

firearm ➡ gun

fireside ➡ fireplace

firewood ➡ wood

firing ➡ fire

firn ➡ snow

first ➡ early, best

first-rate ➡ model

fiscal ➡ financial

fish ➡ hunt

fishpond ➡ lake

fissure ➡ hole

fitful ➡ periodic

fitness ➡ health

fitting ➡ fit[1], correct

five o'clock shadow ➡ beard

fixation ➡ obsession

fixed ➡ stationary, tight

fixture ➡ equipment

fizz ➡ foam

fizzle ➡ disappear

flabbergast ➡ surprise

flabbergasted

➡ dumbfounded

flabby ➡ limp

flaccid ➡ limp

flagrant ➡ bald

flair ➡ talent

flake ➡ bit

flamboyant ➡ fancy

flame ➡ fire

flaming ➡ burning

flammable ➡ inflammable

flank ➡ border

flap ➡ wave

flare ➡ burn, light[1]

flash ➡ light[1], moment, blink

flashlight ➡ light[1]

flashy ➡ loud, bright

flask ➡ bottle

flat ➡ level, prone, dull, insipid, stale, room

flatten ➡ level, iron, trample

flattery ➡ praise

flaunt ➡ advertise

flavorful ➡ delicious

flavoring ➡ herb, flavor

n = noun • *vb* = verb • *adj* = adjective • *adv* = adverb • *prep* = preposition • *conj* = conjunction

flexible *adj* bendable, limber, supple, lithe, malleable, elastic, pliable, plastic, soft, resilient, pliant ➡ **limp**

flight 1. *n* flying, gliding, soaring
2. *n* aviation, aeronautics, flying, space flight
3. *n* ➡ **escape**
4. *n* ➡ **floor**

flood 1. *n* deluge, torrent, inundation, cascade ➡ **rain, storm**
2. *n* river, surge, current, rush, flow, stream, tide ➡ **wave, fountain**
3. *n* barrage, hail, volley, spate, deluge, torrent, storm
4. *vb* inundate, overflow, submerge, drown, engulf, swamp, overwhelm ➡ **flow**

floor 1. *n* flooring, ground, deck, bed, bottom ➡ **base**
2. *n* story, flight, stage, tier, level
3. *vb* ➡ **surprise**

flow 1. *vb* pour, cascade, stream, run, spill, gush, spurt, squirt ➡ **flood**
2. *n* ➡ **flood**
3. *n* distribution, circulation, dissemination, dispersal, spread ➡ **delivery**

flower 1. *n* blossom, bloom, bud, floret, cluster, posy
2. *n* wildflower, perennial, annual, bulb, vine, houseplant ➡ **plant**
3. *vb* ➡ **blossom, prosper**

fly 1. *vb* soar, glide, float, drift, wing, hover, sail, flutter
2. *vb* ➡ **hurry**
3. *n* housefly, horsefly, bluebottle, blackfly, fruit fly ➡ **bug**
4. *n* ➡ **tent**

If the word you want is not a main entry above, look below to find it.

flaw ➡ defect
flawless ➡ perfect, correct
flaxen ➡ yellow
flay ➡ peel
flea market ➡ market
fleck ➡ bit
fledgling ➡ bird
flee ➡ escape, leave
fleece ➡ hide, coat
fleecy ➡ fuzzy
fleet ➡ fast, navy
fleeting ➡ temporary, short
fleshly ➡ physical
flex ➡ bend

flick ➡ lick, movie
flicker ➡ blink
flier ➡ advertisement, pilot
flighty ➡ fickle
flimsy ➡ breakable, thin, unreliable, weak
flinch ➡ jump, fear
fling ➡ throw, binge, adventure
flintlock ➡ gun
flip ➡ turn, rude
flipper ➡ limb
flirt ➡ court
float ➡ fly, blow², swim
flock ➡ herd, crowd, church

floe ➡ glacier
flog ➡ whip
flooring ➡ floor
flop ➡ disappointment
floppy ➡ limp
flora ➡ plant
floret ➡ flower
florid ➡ red
flotilla ➡ navy
flotsam ➡ trash
flounce ➡ strut
flounder ➡ fumble
flourish ➡ prosper, swing, decoration

flout ➡ refuse
flowery ➡ pompous
flowing ➡ liquid
fluctuate ➡ alternate, swing
fluent ➡ articulate
fluffy ➡ fuzzy
fluid ➡ liquid
flurry ➡ snow
flush ➡ blush, level
flushed ➡ red
fluster ➡ embarrass
flutter ➡ wave, fly, shake, rustle
flying ➡ flight
flying machine ➡ airplane

foam *n* froth, lather, bubbles, suds, head, fizz, spume, scum, spray

fog *n* mist, smog, haze, murk ➡ **cloud, smoke**

fold 1. *n* crease, pleat, tuck, lap, overlap ➡ **wrinkle**
2. *n* ➡ **pen**
3. *vb* crease, pleat, tuck, double, lap, overlap ➡ **wrinkle**

follow 1. *vb* succeed, ensue, supplant, supersede, replace ⇨ *lead, precede*
2. *vb* pursue, chase, trail, track, shadow, hunt, stalk, hound, tail
3. *vb* ➡ **obey**
4. *vb* ➡ **know**

following 1. *adj* succeeding, next, ensuing, subsequent, later, latter ➡ **adjacent**
2. *n* entourage, retinue, coterie, public ➡ **audience, fan**

food *n* nourishment, diet, sustenance, edibles, victuals, refreshment, rations, provisions, cuisine, fare, nutrition, fuel ➡ **board, meal**

fool 1. *n* simpleton, nitwit, idiot, dunce, imbecile, nincompoop, blockhead, moron, oaf, clown, ignoramus, buffoon, dolt, dummy, half-wit, ninny
2. *vb* outsmart, outwit, outfox, delude ➡ **cheat**

foolish *adj* silly, ridiculous, absurd, preposterous, ludicrous, idiotic, crazy, nonsensical, asinine, imbecilic ➡ **funny, stupid** ⇨ *smart*

foot 1. *n* paw, hoof, pad, extremity, claw, talon
2. *n* ➡ **base**
3. *n* ➡ **measure**

forbid *vb* prohibit, ban, disallow, outlaw, censor, gag, boycott, proscribe, sanction ➡ **bar, exclude** ⇨ *let*

force 1. *vb* require, compel, coerce, make, oblige, obligate, impel, constrain, pressure ➡ **insist, order**
2. *n* ➡ **strength**
3. *n* ➡ **army**

foreign *adj* alien, imported, exotic, remote, distant, nonnative, immigrant ➡ **strange**

foreigner *n* alien, immigrant, émigré, emigrant ➡ **stranger, exile**

If the word you want is not a main entry above, look below to find it.

foal ➡ horse

focus ➡ middle, concentrate, clarity

fodder ➡ hay

foe ➡ enemy, opponent

foggy ➡ dim, obscure

foil ➡ sword, prevent, repel

folder ➡ wrapper

foliage ➡ plant

folio ➡ page

folk ➡ people

folklore ➡ myth

folly ➡ nonsense

fond ➡ loving

fondle ➡ pet

fondness ➡ love

font ➡ source

foolhardy ➡ thoughtless

foolishness ➡ nonsense

footfall ➡ step

foothill ➡ hill

footing ➡ balance, base

footlocker ➡ chest

footpath ➡ path

footprint ➡ print, track

footrace ➡ race

footstep ➡ step

footwear ➡ shoe

for ➡ because, therefore

forage ➡ hunt

foray ➡ attack

forbear ➡ abstain

forbearance ➡ abstinence, pity

forbearing ➡ patient

forceful ➡ certain, strong

fore ➡ front

forearm ➡ arm

forebear ➡ ancestor

foreboding ➡ ominous, fear

forecast ➡ prediction, predict

forefather ➡ ancestor

foregoing ➡ past

foregone conclusion ➡ certainty

foreground ➡ front

n = noun • *vb* = verb • *adj* = adjective • *adv* = adverb • *prep* = preposition • *conj* = conjunction

foresight 1. *n* foreknowledge, prescience, vision
2. *n* forethought, prudence, anticipation

forest *n* woods, wood, woodland, rainforest, jungle, timberland, grove, thicket, copse

forever *adv* always, eternally, permanently, perpetually, interminably, endlessly, evermore ➡ **regularly**

forget *vb* neglect, omit, overlook, disregard, misremember ➡ **exclude** ⇨ *remember*

forgive *vb* excuse, pardon, absolve, acquit, exonerate, clear, vindicate, condone ⇨ *blame*

forgiveness *n* absolution, pardon, remission, reprieve, exoneration, amnesty, mercy, clemency ➡ **salvation**

form 1. *vb* shape, mold, fashion, pattern ➡ **build, invent, make**

2. *vb* ➡ **appear**
3. *n* mold, die, cast, frame ➡ **structure**
4. *n* ➡ **body**
5. *n* ➡ **document**

forward 1. *adj* front, advance, foremost, progressive
2. *adj* ➡ **rude**
3. *adv* forwards, forth, ahead, onward, onwards ⇨ *backward*
4. *vb* ➡ **send**

fountain 1. *n* spout, geyser, spray, stream, jet, squirt ➡ **well, flood**
2. *n* ➡ **source**

fragrant *adj* pungent, aromatic, savory, perfumed, scented, redolent ➡ **smelly, spicy**

framework 1. *n* frame, shell, hull, skeleton, chassis
2. *n* ➡ **setting**

If the word you want is not a main entry above, look below to find it.

foreknowledge ➡ foresight
forelimb ➡ arm
foreman ➡ boss
foremost ➡ forward, best, important
forerunner ➡ ancestor
foresee ➡ anticipate, predict
forestall ➡ prevent
foretell ➡ predict
forethought ➡ foresight
forewarn ➡ warn
forewarning ➡ warning
foreword ➡ introduction
forfeit ➡ abandon, surrender
forge ➡ make, fake, furnace
forge ahead ➡ go
forgery ➡ fake
forgetful ➡ absentminded
forgo ➡ abstain

fork ➡ divide, branch
forlorn ➡ sorry, sad
formal ➡ official, dignified, prim
formality ➡ ceremony
formation ➡ order, assembly
former ➡ past
formerly ➡ once, before
formfitting ➡ tight
formidable ➡ strong
formula ➡ recipe
formulate ➡ invent
forsake ➡ leave
forsaken ➡ abandoned
fort ➡ castle
forte ➡ specialty
forth ➡ forward
forthcoming ➡ future
forthright ➡ straightforward, bald

forthwith ➡ soon
fortification ➡ castle
fortify ➡ protect, strengthen
fortitude ➡ courage, strength, patience
fortress ➡ castle
fortuitous ➡ accidental, successful
fortuitously ➡ accidentally
fortunate ➡ lucky, successful
fortune ➡ chance, wealth
fortune telling ➡ prediction
fortune-teller ➡ prophet
forum ➡ court
forwards ➡ forward
fossil fuel ➡ oil
fossilize ➡ harden
foster ➡ adopt, facilitate, support
foster parent ➡ parent

foul ➡ smelly, dirty
found ➡ base
foundation ➡ base, basis, organization
founder ➡ creator
fount ➡ source
fountain pen ➡ pen
fountainhead ➡ source
four-sided ➡ square
foursquare ➡ square
fowl ➡ bird
foyer ➡ hall
fracas ➡ disturbance
fraction ➡ part, number, share
fracture ➡ break
fractured ➡ broken
fragile ➡ breakable, weak
fragment ➡ part, bit

---

frantic 1. *adj* frenzied, distraught, overwrought, frenetic, desperate, delirious, feverish ⇨ *calm*
2. *adj* hectic, chaotic, furious ⇨ *calm*

free 1. *vb* release, liberate, emancipate, deliver, discharge, extricate, exempt, loose, loosen, unloose, unloosen
➡ **forgive, open**
2. *adj* independent, liberated, sovereign, self-governing, autonomous, emancipated, unconfined, unrestrained, unfettered, unshackled, loose, exempt
3. *adj* complimentary, gratis, gratuitous
4. *adj* ➡ **generous**

freedom 1. *n* liberty, independence, autonomy, liberation, sovereignty ⇨ *slavery*
2. *n* license, liberty, immunity, frankness, openness, ease, spontaneity ➡ **right**
3. *n* ➡ **leisure**

frequent 1. *adj* regular, recurrent, habitual, incessant, chronic ➡ **continual, usual, many**
2. *vb* visit, haunt, patronize, attend

friction 1. *n* rubbing, abrasion, scraping, resistance, traction, grating, grinding
2. *n* ➡ **fight, disagreement**

friend *n* girlfriend, boyfriend, companion, associate, partner, acquaintance, ally, comrade, pal, chum, playmate, buddy, *amigo (Spanish)* ⇨ *enemy, opponent*

friendly *adj* sociable, social, cordial, neighborly, amiable, genial, intimate, close, sweet, warm, convivial, hearty, hospitable
➡ **kind, nice, loving, peaceful** ⇨ *unfriendly*

friendship *n* companionship, amity, company, society, camaraderie, comradeship, fellowship, brotherhood, sisterhood, fraternity
➡ **relationship, link, kindness**

frog *n* bullfrog, spring peeper, tadpole, polliwog

front 1. *n* fore, lead, head, van, vanguard, foreground, bow *(of a boat)*, prow *(of a boat)*, obverse *(of a coin)* ➡ **beginning** ⇨ *back*
2. *adj* ➡ **forward**

If the word you want is not a main entry above, look below to find it.

fragmentary ➡ partial

fragrance ➡ smell

frail ➡ weak, mortal

frame ➡ body, form, framework

framer ➡ creator

franchise ➡ license

frank ➡ straightforward

frankly ➡ sincerely

frankness ➡ freedom, honesty

fraternity ➡ organization, friendship

fraternize ➡ mix

fraud ➡ cheat, rascal, theft, pretense

fraudulence ➡ dishonesty

fray ➡ fight

frayed ➡ ragged

freak ➡ monster

freebooter ➡ pirate

freedom fighter ➡ rebel

freely ➡ voluntary

freethinker ➡ atheist

freeway ➡ highway

freeze ➡ harden, cool

freezer ➡ refrigerator

freezing ➡ cold

freight ➡ load

frenetic ➡ active, frantic

frenzied ➡ frantic

frenzy ➡ fit²

frequently ➡ often

fresh ➡ new, rude, clean, cool

freshman ➡ student

freshness ➡ novelty

fret ➡ worry, grieve

friable ➡ breakable

friar ➡ religious

friary ➡ monastery

fridge ➡ refrigerator

friendless ➡ lonely, unpopular

friendliness ➡ kindness

fright ➡ fear

frighten ➡ scare

frightened ➡ afraid

frightening ➡ scary

frightful ➡ scary

frigid ➡ cold

fringe ➡ edge

frippery ➡ trinket

frisk ➡ play

fritter away ➡ waste

frivolity ➡ nonsense

frivolous ➡ arbitrary, trivial

frock ➡ dress

frolic ➡ play, dance

front ➡ forward

frontier ➡ border, country

frontiersman ➡ pioneer

fronting ➡ opposite

n = noun • *vb* = verb • *adj* = adjective • *adv* = adverb • *prep* = preposition • *conj* = conjunction

frown 1. *vb, n* scowl, grimace, glare, pout, glower, lower ⇨ *smile*
2. *vb* ➡ **object**

fruit *n* seed, grain, nut, legume, berry ➡ **plant, vegetable**

full 1. *adj* packed, loaded, laden, filled, crowded, stuffed, replete, sated, brimful, crammed, jammed ⇨ *empty*
2. *adj* ➡ **complete**

fumble *vb* bungle, flounder, stumble, wallow, muddle, muff, botch, goof, louse ➡ **try**

function 1. *n* capacity, office, role, part ➡ **duty, job, object, use**
2. *n* ➡ **party**
3. *n* ➡ **behavior**
4. *n* ➡ **sense**
5. *vb* ➡ **operate, act**

fungus 1. *n* mold, mildew, rot, rust, blight
2. *n* mushroom, toadstool, lichen, truffle

funny 1. *adj* laughable, amusing, humorous, witty, hilarious, comical, comic, ridiculous, whimsical, facetious, antic, farcical, zany, ludicrous ➡ **dry, foolish, strange**
2. *adj* ➡ **sick**

furnace *n* heater, boiler, burner, stove, incinerator, kiln, forge

future 1. *n* hereafter, eternity, futurity, *mañana (Spanish)*, tomorrow, morrow, destiny, fate
2. *adj* imminent, impending, pending, forthcoming, upcoming, approaching, prospective, projected

fuzzy *adj* furry, downy, hairy, woolly, shaggy, fluffy, fleecy, velvety, soft

---

If the word you want is not a main entry above, look below to find it.

front-runner ➡ **candidate**

frost ➡ **ice**

frosting ➡ **icing**

frosty ➡ **cold, white**

froth ➡ **foam**

frugal ➡ **cheap, plain**

frugality ➡ **economy**

fruitcake ➡ **cake**

fruit fly ➡ **fly**

fruitful ➡ **fertile**

fruitless ➡ **useless**

frustrate ➡ **prevent, disappoint**

frustration ➡ **disappointment**

fry ➡ **cook**

fuel ➡ **light[1], energy, food**

fugitive ➡ **runaway, exile**

fulcrum ➡ **axis**

fulfill ➡ **keep, satisfy**

fulfillment ➡ **satisfaction, finish**

full-grown ➡ **adult**

fully ➡ **completely**

fumbling ➡ **clumsy**

fume ➡ **smoke**

fumes ➡ **smoke**

fuming ➡ **violent**

fun ➡ **pleasure**

fund ➡ **supply, back**

fundamental ➡ **necessary, basic**

fundamentally ➡ **chiefly, practically**

funeral march ➡ **dirge**

funnel ➡ **pipe, lead**

fur ➡ **hair, coat**

furious ➡ **angry, violent, frantic**

furlough ➡ **vacation**

furnish ➡ **give, supply, lend**

furrow ➡ **channel**

furry ➡ **fuzzy**

further ➡ **more**

furthermore ➡ **more, besides**

furtive ➡ **sly**

furtiveness ➡ **secrecy**

fury ➡ **anger**

fuse ➡ **melt, unify**

fusion ➡ **union**

fuss ➡ **argument, complain**

fussy ➡ **choosy, cross**

futile ➡ **useless**

futon ➡ **bed**

futurity ➡ **future**

➡ = synonym cross-reference • ⇨ = *antonym cross-reference*

G

gait *n* pace, stride, tread, step, walk, carriage, movement, swagger, strut

gallery 1. *n* art gallery, exhibition hall, salon, showroom, studio, museum
2. *n* ➡ **room, porch**
3. *n* ➡ **audience**

gallows *n* scaffold, gibbet, yardarm

gambling *n* betting, gaming, wagering ➡ **lottery**

game *n* sport, pastime, recreation, contest, match, competition, bout, event, meet, tournament, series ➡ **fight**

garage 1. *n* carport, parking garage
2. *n* service station, gas station, repair shop

gargoyle *n* grotesque, rainspout, waterspout

gasoline *n* gas, petrol (*British*) ➡ **oil**

gather 1. *vb* collect, assemble, accumulate, amass, compile, congregate, convene, meet, rendezvous ➡ **save, pile**
2. *vb* pick, harvest, reap, pluck, garner, glean
3. *vb* ➡ **assume, infer**

general 1. *adj* widespread, extensive, comprehensive ➡ **common, usual, universal**
2. *adj* ➡ **approximate**

generosity *n* liberality, bounty, benevolence, philanthropy, charitableness, charity, unselfishness, munificence, largess ➡ **help** ⇨ *greed*

If the word you want is not a main entry above, look below to find it.

gadget ➡ object, tool

gag ➡ joke, forbid, quiet, vomit

gaggle ➡ herd

gaiety ➡ mirth

gain ➡ get, take, growth

gal ➡ woman

gala ➡ party, dance

gale ➡ wind, storm

gall ➡ audacity

gallant ➡ brave

gallantry ➡ courage

galley ➡ kitchen

gallop ➡ run

galvanize ➡ excite

gambit ➡ tactic

gamble ➡ bet

gambol ➡ play, dance

game farm, game preserve ➡ zoo

gamin ➡ urchin

gaming ➡ gambling

gamma ray ➡ X ray

gamut ➡ assortment

gang ➡ group

gangplank ➡ bridge

gangway ➡ bridge

gap ➡ hole, break, valley, distance

gape ➡ stare, spread

garb ➡ clothes

garbage ➡ trash

garble ➡ disturb

garden ➡ farm

gargantuan ➡ huge

garish ➡ loud

garland ➡ bouquet, crown, prize

garment bag ➡ luggage

garments ➡ clothes

garner ➡ gather

garnish ➡ decorate, decoration

garret ➡ attic

garrison ➡ castle, troop

garrulous ➡ talkative

gas ➡ smoke, gasoline

gash ➡ cut

gasp ➡ breathe

gas station ➡ garage

gate ➡ door

gatekeeper ➡ doorman

gateway ➡ door

gathering ➡ party, meeting

gauche ➡ clumsy

gaudy ➡ loud

gauge ➡ estimate, measure

gaunt ➡ thin

gauntlet ➡ glove

gauze ➡ bandage

gavel ➡ hammer

gawk ➡ stare

gay ➡ happy, bright

gaze ➡ stare, look

gazette ➡ paper

gear ➡ luggage, equipment

gelatinous ➡ thick

geld ➡ sterilize

gelding ➡ horse

gem ➡ jewel

gemstone ➡ jewel

general store ➡ market

generalize ➡ stereotype

generally ➡ chiefly, usually

generate ➡ cause, reproduce

generator ➡ engine

n = noun • *vb* = verb • *adj* = adjective • *adv* = adverb • *prep* = preposition • *conj* = conjunction

generous 1. *adj* unselfish, charitable, liberal, unsparing, altruistic, kind, free ➡ **noble** ⇨ *selfish*
2. *adj* liberal, handsome, lavish ➡ **abundant, big**

genius 1. *n* prodigy, virtuoso, mastermind, wizard, Einstein (*informal*), wunderkind (*German*), brain (*informal*), whiz (*informal*), rocket scientist (*informal*)
2. *n* ➡ **talent**
3. *n* ➡ **soul**

gentle 1. *adj* light, mild, soft, tender, moderate, temperate ➡ **calm**
2. *adj* ➡ **friendly, kind**
3. *adj* docile, meek, tractable ➡ **tame**

get 1. *vb* obtain, acquire, gain, win, take, procure, earn, score ➡ **catch, receive, seize, find**
2. *vb* ➡ **know**
3. *vb* ➡ **persuade**

ghost *n* spirit, apparition, shade, specter, wraith, spook, phantom ➡ **soul**

giant 1. *n* behemoth, mammoth, titan, leviathan, colossus, Goliath ➡ **monster**
2. *adj* ➡ **big**

gift 1. *n* present, donation, grant, contribution, endowment, offering, alms, sacrifice, favor, surprise, boon ➡ **inheritance, prize**
2. *n* ➡ **talent**

gifted *adj* precocious, advanced, progressive, mature ➡ **talented, smart**

give 1. *vb* present, donate, grant, endow, bestow, impart, award, confer, bequeath, contribute ➡ **supply** ⇨ *receive*
2. *vb* pass, hand, deliver, convey, render, serve, dish out, hand over, hand in, submit, dispense, distribute, inflict ➡ **offer**
3. *vb* have, hold, stage ➡ **act, play**
4. *vb* ➡ **surrender**
5. *vb* yield, bear, produce, furnish ➡ **make**

glacier *n* iceberg, floe, ice floe, icecap

glass 1. *n* cup, mug, tumbler, goblet, beaker ➡ **container, drink**
2. *n* ➡ **mirror**
3. *n* telescope, binocular, spyglass, magnifying glass, lens, microscope

If the word you want is not a main entry above, look below to find it.

genesis ➡ **beginning**
genetic ➡ **natural**
genial ➡ **friendly**
geniality ➡ **hospitality**
genre ➡ **type**
gentleman ➡ **man**
gentlemanly ➡ **masculine**
gentlewoman ➡ **woman**
gentry ➡ **aristocracy**
genuflect ➡ **bend**
genuine ➡ **real, sincere**
genuinely ➡ **really, sincerely**
germ ➡ **poison, egg**

germane ➡ **relevant**
germ-free ➡ **sterile**
germinate ➡ **grow**
gesture ➡ **wave, sign**
getaway ➡ **escape**
get-together ➡ **visit**
get-up-and-go ➡ **ambition, energy**
gewgaw ➡ **trinket**
geyser ➡ **fountain**
ghastly ➡ **awful**
ghoul ➡ **monster**
gibber ➡ **chatter**
gibberish ➡ **talk**

gibbet ➡ **gallows**
gibe ➡ **ridicule**
giddy ➡ **dizzy**
gift wrap ➡ **wrap**
gigantic ➡ **huge**
giggle ➡ **laugh**
gild ➡ **plate, exaggerate**
gimp ➡ **limp**
gingerly ➡ **carefully**
gird ➡ **ring**
girdle ➡ **band**
girl ➡ **woman, child**
girlfriend ➡ **friend, love**

girlhood ➡ **childhood**
girlish ➡ **young**
girth ➡ **width**
gist ➡ **subject, essence**
give off ➡ **throw**
giver ➡ **patron**
glad ➡ **happy**
gladden ➡ **please**
glade ➡ **field**
gladiator ➡ **soldier**
glamorous ➡ **beautiful**
glance ➡ **look**
glare ➡ **light[1], frown**
glaring ➡ **bright, obvious**

glasses *n* eyeglasses, spectacles, sunglasses, goggles, bifocals, trifocals, shades, contact lenses, contacts

glove *n* mitten, mitt, gauntlet

glutton *n* gourmand, epicure, pig *(informal)*, hog *(informal)*

go 1. *vb* progress, proceed, pass, head, advance, forge ahead ➡ **leave, move, travel** ⇨ *come*
2. *vb* ➡ **act**
3. *vb* ➡ **belong**
4. *vb* ➡ **happen**
5. *n* ➡ **try**

god *n* goddess, deity, divinity, demigod, immortal, idol, icon, effigy

good 1. *adj* fine, excellent, outstanding, choice, admirable, splendid, rave, favorable, hopeful, positive, suitable, proper, capital, tiptop ➡ **fair, great, nice, cool** ⇨ *bad*
2. *adj* honest, honorable, virtuous, worthy, respectable, reputable, moral, righteous, scrupulous ➡ **kind**
3. *adj* obedient, well-behaved, dutiful, well-mannered, respectful, obliging ➡ **polite** ⇨ *rude*
4. *n* ➡ **welfare**

good-bye *interj* farewell, so long, adieu, *adios (Spanish)*, *au revoir (French)*, *ciao (Italian)*, *arrivederci (Italian)*, *auf Wiedersehen (German)*, *shalom (Hebrew)*, *salaam (Arabic)*, toodle-oo *(informal)*, cheerio *(informal)* ⇨ **hello**

If the word you want is not a main entry above, look below to find it.

glasshouse ➡ greenhouse
glassy ➡ slippery
glaze ➡ icing
gleam ➡ shine, light[1]
gleaming ➡ shiny
glean ➡ gather
glee ➡ pleasure
glee club ➡ choir
gleeful ➡ happy
glen ➡ valley
glib ➡ superficial, suave
glide ➡ fly, slide, dance
gliding ➡ flight
glimmer ➡ light[1], bit
glimpse ➡ view, look, see
glint ➡ light[1]
glisten ➡ shine
glistening ➡ shiny
glitter ➡ light[1]
gloat ➡ boast

glob ➡ drop, lump
global ➡ universal
globe ➡ earth, ball
globular ➡ round
globule ➡ ball
glockenspiel ➡ xylophone
gloom ➡ cloud, dark, sorrow
gloomy ➡ dark, bleak, sad
glorify ➡ worship, bless
glorious ➡ grand
glory ➡ elegance, fame
gloss ➡ light[1]
glossary ➡ dictionary
glossy ➡ shiny
glow ➡ light[1], shine, blush, burn
glower ➡ frown
glowing ➡ bright
glue ➡ adhesive, stick
glut ➡ abundance, load
glutinous ➡ thick

gluttonous ➡ greedy
gluttony ➡ greed
gnarled ➡ bent
gnash ➡ grind
gnaw ➡ bite
go back ➡ return
goad ➡ urge
goal ➡ object, base, plan
goatee ➡ beard
gobble ➡ eat
gobbledygook ➡ nonsense
go-between ➡ agent
goblet ➡ glass
goblin ➡ bogeyman
goddess ➡ god
God-fearing ➡ religious
godly ➡ religious
godsend ➡ luck
goggles ➡ glasses
going ➡ departure

gold ➡ yellow
Goliath ➡ giant
gong ➡ bell
good day ➡ hello
good deal ➡ bargain
good-for-nothing ➡ loafer
good-humored ➡ nice
good-looking ➡ pretty
good looks ➡ beauty
good-natured ➡ nice
goodness ➡ virtue
goods ➡ property, product
goodwill ➡ kindness
goof ➡ fumble
goose egg ➡ zero
gore ➡ stick
gorge ➡ canyon, eat
gorgeous ➡ beautiful
gory ➡ bloody
gossamer ➡ thin
gossip ➡ rumor, chatter

n = noun • *vb* = verb • *adj* = adjective • *adv* = adverb • *prep* = preposition • *interj* = interjection

govern *vb* rule, reign, administer, legislate ➡ **control, lead**

government *n* administration, legislature, congress, senate, parliament, assembly, regime ➡ **rule**

grade *n* class, rank, step, score, standing, position, degree, plateau ➡ **level, state, slant**

grand *adj* magnificent, superb, majestic, splendid, stately, glorious, grandiose, august, regal, imposing, sumptuous, elegant, exalted, commanding, awe-inspiring, proud ➡ **great, good, rich, dignified**

grateful *adj* thankful, pleased, appreciative, indebted, obliged, gratified, beholden

gratitude *n* appreciation, thankfulness, thanks, gratefulness, recognition, acknowledgment

grave 1. *n* tomb, sepulcher, mausoleum, crypt, vault, catacomb, barrow, pit ➡ **cemetery, monument**
2. *adj* ➡ **serious**

gray *adj, n* grey, drab, leaden, dusky, slate, smoky

great 1. *adj, interj* wonderful, terrific, superb, remarkable, astounding, incredible, spectacular, tremendous, marvelous, fabulous, super, heavenly ➡ **good, grand, nice**
2. *adj* ➡ **famous**
3. *adj* ➡ **big**

greed *n* greediness, selfishness, avarice, gluttony ➡ **desire, envy** ⇨ *generosity*

greedy *adj* selfish, possessive, covetous, acquisitive, avaricious, stingy, rapacious, grasping, voracious, insatiable, gluttonous ➡ **jealous, predatory**

green 1. *adj, n* emerald, chartreuse, lime, olive, kelly, pea green, verdant, veridian
2. *adj* ➡ **naive, amateur**
3. *n* ➡ **park**
4. *n* ➡ **vegetable**

greenhouse *n* nursery, conservatory, hothouse, glasshouse, arboretum

---

If the word you want is not a main entry above, look below to find it.

gouge ➡ cut

gourmand ➡ glutton

governmental ➡ public

governor ➡ ruler

gown ➡ dress

GP ➡ doctor

grab ➡ seize, catch

grace ➡ beauty, class, elegance

gracious ➡ polite

gradual ➡ slow

graduate ➡ promote

graft ➡ join

grain ➡ seed, fruit

grain elevator ➡ warehouse

granary ➡ warehouse

grandeur ➡ elegance

grandiloquent ➡ pompous

grandiose ➡ pompous, grand

grandstand ➡ seat

grant ➡ gift, license, award, give

graph ➡ table

graphic ➡ visible, explicit

grapnel ➡ anchor

grapple ➡ fight

grasp ➡ catch, know, embrace

grasping ➡ greedy

grass ➡ hay, plant

grassland ➡ plain

grate ➡ cut, grind, squeak

gratefulness ➡ gratitude

gratification ➡ satisfaction

gratified ➡ grateful

gratify ➡ please

gratifying ➡ pleasant

grating ➡ hoarse, friction

gratis ➡ free

gratuitous ➡ free, unnecessary

gratuity ➡ tip

graupel ➡ snow

gravel ➡ dirt, rock

gravelly ➡ hoarse

graveyard ➡ cemetery

gravid ➡ pregnant, fertile

gravitate toward ➡ approach

gravity ➡ importance, depth

graze ➡ eat, rub

grease ➡ fat, oil

grease monkey ➡ mechanic

greater ➡ better

greatest ➡ most

greatly ➡ very, far, much

greatness ➡ excellence

greediness ➡ greed

---

grieve *vb* mourn, lament, fret, rue, languish, bewail, pine ➡ **sadden, mope**

grind 1. *vb* crush, pulverize, crumble, powder, mash
2. *vb* ➡ **sharpen**
3. *vb* grate, grit, gnash ➡ **rub**

group 1. *n* gang, bunch, crew, pack, set, class, band, body, cluster, ring, bloc, clique, syndicate, junta ➡ **troop**
2. *n* ➡ **band**

grow 1. *vb* sprout, germinate, develop, expand, increase, mature, ripen, evolve, enlarge, wax, magnify, amplify, heighten, augment, mushroom, multiply ➡ **prosper, blossom, strengthen**
2. *vb* raise, breed, cultivate, nurture, rear ➡ **plant**

growth 1. *n* development, spread, enlargement, expansion, proliferation, escalation, rise, inflation, gain, hike, increment, increase ➡ **progress**

2. *n* lump, tumor, cancer, swelling, cyst, mole, polyp, sarcoma
3. *n* crop, harvest, yield

gruesome *adj* morbid, gross, sick, sadistic, grisly, macabre, grim ➡ **awful, bad, mean**

grunt *vb, n* groan, snort, oink, croak ➡ **cry**

guarantee 1. *vb* insure, assure, secure, ensure, warrant, certify ➡ **promise**
2. *n* ➡ **promise**

guardian *n* guard, custodian, caretaker, overseer, curator, trustee, keeper, monitor, watchdog ➡ **parent, patrol, guide, boss, savior**

guess *vb* suppose, think, believe, imagine, suspect, reckon, speculate, surmise ➡ **estimate, assume**

guide 1. *n* conductor, escort, leader, usher, shepherd, pilot
2. *n* ➡ **pattern**
3. *vb* ➡ **lead**

If the word you want is not a main entry above, look below to find it.

greet ➡ welcome, receive
greeting ➡ welcome
greetings ➡ hello
grey ➡ gray
gridiron ➡ field
grief ➡ sorrow, misery
grievance ➡ complaint
grievous ➡ awful
grill ➡ cook, ask
grim ➡ bleak, gruesome
grimace ➡ frown
grime ➡ dirt
grimy ➡ dirty
grin ➡ smile

grinding ➡ friction
grip ➡ embrace
gripe ➡ complain
gripping ➡ exciting
grisly ➡ gruesome, ugly
grit ➡ dirt, courage, grind
groan ➡ cry, complain, grunt
grocery ➡ market
groom ➡ spouse, comb, dress
groove ➡ channel
grope ➡ touch
gross ➡ obvious, huge, gruesome, earn
grotesque ➡ ugly, gargoyle

grotto ➡ cave
grouch ➡ complain
grouchy ➡ cross
ground ➡ base, floor, dirt, terrain
groundless ➡ superstitious
grounds ➡ basis, property, reason
grove ➡ forest
grovel ➡ crawl
grower ➡ farmer
growl ➡ bark
grown-up ➡ adult
grub ➡ larva, dig
grubby ➡ dirty

grudge ➡ complaint, envy
grudging ➡ reluctant
gruff ➡ hoarse, abrupt
grumble ➡ complain
grumpy ➡ cross
guard ➡ protect, watch, guardian
guarded ➡ safe, careful
guest ➡ visitor, occupant
guest room ➡ bedroom
guffaw ➡ laugh
guidance ➡ advice, leadership
guideline ➡ rule

guilt *n* fault, blame, responsibility, culpability, liability ➡ **shame**

guilty *adj* culpable, blameworthy, responsible, liable, derelict ⇨ *innocent*

gun *n* firearm, weapon, pistol, revolver, sidearm, handgun, rifle, carbine, shotgun, machine gun, musket, flintlock, muzzle loader, blunderbuss, cannon ➡ **arms**

gymnasium *n* gym, sports center, recreation center, field house

gymnastics *n* acrobatics, tumbling, vaulting, aerobatics, aerobics ➡ **exercise**

If the word you want is not a main entry above, look below to find it.

guild ➡ union

guile ➡ dishonesty

guiltless ➡ innocent

guise ➡ disguise

gulch ➡ canyon

gulf ➡ bay, difference

gullible ➡ naive

gully ➡ canyon

gulp ➡ drink, eat, breathe

gum band ➡ rubber band

gummy ➡ sticky

gun down ➡ shoot

gunfire ➡ fire

gurney ➡ bed

guru ➡ teacher

gush ➡ flow

gust ➡ wind

gusto ➡ enthusiasm

gut ➡ stomach

guts ➡ courage

gutter ➡ channel

guttural ➡ hoarse

guy ➡ man, rope

guzzle ➡ drink

gym ➡ gymnasium

gymnast ➡ acrobat

gyp ➡ cheat

gypsy ➡ traveler

gyrate ➡ turn

➡ = synonym cross-reference • ⇨ = antonym cross-reference

H

habit 1. *n* custom, practice, routine, institution, usage, rule
2. *n* dependency, addiction, instinct, reflex, wont ➡ **tendency**
3. *n* mannerism, affectation, quirk, trait ➡ **oddity**
4. *n* ➡ **clothes**

habitat *n* environment, habitation, ecosystem ➡ **den, house**

hair *n* locks, tresses, mane, fur ➡ **braid, lock, wig, beard, coat**

hall 1. *n* corridor, hallway, passage, passageway, entryway, foyer, vestibule, lobby, lounge, anteroom
2. *n* auditorium, theater, arena, amphitheater ➡ **room, building**

halo *n* nimbus, corona, aurora

hammer 1. *n* clawhammer, mallet, maul, sledgehammer, sledge, ball-peen hammer, gavel ➡ **tool**
2. *vb* ➡ **hit**

handwriting *n* writing, penmanship, script, cursive, longhand, printing, calligraphy ➡ **print**

hang 1. *vb* dangle, drape, suspend, swing, hover ➡ **depend**
2. *vb* lynch, execute ➡ **kill**

happen *vb* occur, transpire, chance, go, befall, ensue, arise, recur, exist

happy *adj* glad, cheerful, joyful, joyous, merry, gay, jolly, delighted, gleeful, proud, jovial, high, festive, bright ➡ **ecstatic, satisfied, lucky** ⇨ *sad*
   Note that **happy**, **glad**, *and* **delighted** *are often used in statements simply to be polite:* "*I'm* **happy**/**glad**/**delighted** *to meet you.*"

If the word you want is not a main entry above, look below to find it.

habitation ➡ home, habitat

habitual ➡ usual, automatic, frequent

habitually ➡ regularly

hack ➡ taxi, cut

hackneyed ➡ trite

haggard ➡ thin

haggle ➡ negotiate

hail ➡ flood, welcome, snow, ice

hailstorm ➡ storm

hairless ➡ bald

hairpiece ➡ wig

hairpin ➡ pin

hairy ➡ fuzzy

hale ➡ healthy

haleness ➡ health

half-wit ➡ fool

hallow ➡ bless

hallowed ➡ holy

hallucinating ➡ delirious

hallucination ➡ illusion

hallucinatory ➡ imaginary

hallucinogen ➡ drug

hallway ➡ hall

halt ➡ stop, limp

halve ➡ divide

ham ➡ actor

hamlet ➡ town

hamper ➡ delay

hampered ➡ disabled

hand ➡ worker, lift, give

handbag ➡ bag

handbook ➡ book

handcuff ➡ bond

hand down ➡ leave

handgun ➡ gun

handicap ➡ disability, bar

handicapped ➡ disabled

hand in ➡ give

handkerchief ➡ scarf

hand over ➡ give

handle ➡ touch, sell, control

handler ➡ agent

handling ➡ treatment

handshake ➡ embrace

handsome ➡ pretty, generous

handy ➡ useful, available, able

hanging ➡ gallows

hanker ➡ want

haphazard ➡ arbitrary

hapless ➡ unfortunate

happening ➡ event

happenstance ➡ chance

happiness ➡ pleasure

harangue ➡ yell

harass ➡ bother, abuse

n = noun • *vb* = verb • *adj* = adjective • *adv* = adverb • *prep* = preposition • *conj* = conjunction

harbor *n* port, haven, anchorage ➡ **dock, bay, protection**

hard 1. *adj* stony, rocky, adamant ➡ **firm, tough**
2. *adj* difficult, tough, demanding, strenuous, arduous, rigorous, heavy, rough, trying ⇨ *easy*
3. *adj* harsh, severe, bitter, austere, stark, stern

harden *vb* solidify, freeze, petrify, fossilize, set, temper, dry, calcify, toughen, clot, congeal, jell, thicken, coagulate, congeal, cake ➡ **strengthen**

hardship *n* misfortune, adversity, affliction, need, tribulation, want, complaint, injustice ➡ **trouble, misery, poverty**

harm 1. *n* injury, hurt, loss, impairment, detriment, disadvantage ➡ **abuse, damage**
2. *vb* ➡ **hurt, damage**

harmless 1. *adj* innocuous, inoffensive, unobjectionable ➡ **naive, kind**
2. *adj* ➡ **safe**

hat *n* cap, helmet, headgear, chapeau, bonnet

hate 1. *vb* detest, abhor, despise, deplore, loathe, disdain, dislike, abominate, scorn, execrate ⇨ *love*
2. *n* ➡ **hatred**

hatred *n* hate, abhorrence, aversion, revulsion, loathing, contempt, scorn, malice, hostility, dislike, disdain, antipathy, animosity, malevolence ➡ **prejudice** ⇨ *love*

hay *n* fodder, feed, grass, timothy, alfalfa

headline *n* head, heading, leader, title, header, caption, screamer *(informal)*

heal *vb* cure, remedy, mend, knit, treat, medicate, nurse, doctor
*In general, **heal** refers to the making better or getting better of a sore, wound, or injury. **Cure** usually refers to getting rid of a disease or illness.*

If the word you want is not a main entry above, look below to find it.

hard of hearing ➡ **deaf**
hardcover ➡ **book**
hardhearted ➡ **insensitive**
hardly ➡ **only, seldom**
hardwood ➡ **tree**
hardworking ➡ **diligent**
hardy ➡ **strong, healthy**
hark ➡ **listen**
harmful ➡ **dangerous, destructive, unhealthy**
harmonious ➡ **musical, compatible, unanimous**
harmonize ➡ **sing, agree**
harmony ➡ **music, peace, unity, balance, agreement**
harness ➡ **equipment, control**

harrow ➡ **dig**
harry ➡ **attack, trouble**
harsh ➡ **sharp, hard, rough**
harvest ➡ **gather, farm, growth**
hash ➡ **assortment, mess**
haste ➡ **hurry**
hasten ➡ **hurry**
hastily ➡ **quickly**
hasty ➡ **fast, early**
hat pin ➡ **pin**
hatch ➡ **reproduce, invent**
hatchet ➡ **ax, axe**
hateful ➡ **awful**
haughtiness ➡ **pride**

haughty ➡ **proud**
haul ➡ **pull, carry**
haunch ➡ **back**
haunt ➡ **frequent**
haut monde ➡ **aristocracy**
have ➡ **keep, own, give, need**
haven ➡ **harbor, protection**
havoc ➡ **damage**
hawk ➡ **sell**
hayfield ➡ **field**
hazard ➡ **danger, dare, jeopardize**
hazardous ➡ **dangerous**
haze ➡ **fog, cloud**
hazy ➡ **cloudy, dim**

head ➡ **front, boss, chairperson, bathroom, foam, headline, go**
headache ➡ **nuisance**
header ➡ **headline**
headgear ➡ **hat**
heading ➡ **headline, name, course**
headland ➡ **cape**
headlong ➡ **quickly**
headmaster ➡ **principal**
head-over-heels ➡ **upside down**
headquarters ➡ **base, office**
headstrong ➡ **stubborn**
headway ➡ **progress**
healing ➡ **cure, medicinal**

---

health *n* fitness, condition, shape, vigor, vitality, haleness, wellness, healthfulness
➡ **welfare**

healthy 1. *adj* well, fit, sound, hale, hardy, hearty, vigorous, whole ➡ **better, strong**
⇨ *sick*
2. *adj* healthful, nourishing, nutritious, wholesome

heaven 1. *n* paradise, bliss, nirvana, elysian fields, Elysium, Valhalla ➡ **utopia, pleasure**
2. *n* ➡ **air**

heavenly 1. *adj* divine, sublime, celestial, spiritual ➡ **supernatural**
2. *adj* ➡ **great**

heavy 1. *adj* cumbersome, hefty, ponderous, massive, weighty, bulky ➡ **big** ⇨ *light*
2. *adj* ➡ **serious**
3. *adj* ➡ **hard**

hedge *n* hedgerow, shrubbery, bushes,

height 1. *n* altitude, elevation, stature, loftiness, tallness ⇨ *depth*
2. *n* ➡ **top**

hello *interj* good day, how do you do?, greetings, hi, *hola (Spanish)*, *bonjour (French)*, *ciao (Italian)*, *shalom (Hebrew)*, howdy *(informal)*, yo *(informal)* ⇨ **good-bye**

help 1. *vb* assist, aid, serve, wait on, cooperate, collaborate, team up, succor, benefit, improve, enrich, avail
➡ **relieve, support**
2. *n* aid, assistance, cooperation, relief, service ➡ **support, comfort, generosity, welfare**
3. *n* ➡ **worker**

helper *n* assistant, aide, deputy, lieutenant, subordinate ➡ **partner, worker**

herb *n* seasoning, flavoring ➡ **plant, spice**

herd *n* flock, pack, swarm, hive, colony, bevy, brood, school, gaggle, pod ➡ **group, crowd**

hermit *n* recluse, shut-in, ascetic

hesitate *vb* falter, vacillate, balk, pause, demur, equivocate, waver ➡ **stop, delay, wait**

If the word you want is not a main entry above, look below to find it.

healthful ➡ **healthy**	heartily ➡ **sincerely**	heed ➡ **obey, notice**	hem ➡ **edge**
healthfulness ➡ **health**	heartless ➡ **insensitive**	heedless ➡ **unaware, thoughtless**	hem and haw ➡ **stammer**
heap ➡ **pile**	hearty ➡ **friendly, healthy**	heft ➡ **weight**	hence ➡ **therefore**
hear ➡ **listen**	heat ➡ **energy**	hefty ➡ **heavy**	herald ➡ **welcome, precede**
hearing ➡ **tryout, suit**	heated ➡ **warm**	heighten ➡ **grow**	here ➡ **present**
hearing-impaired ➡ **deaf**	heater ➡ **furnace**	heinous ➡ **wicked**	hereafter ➡ **future**
hearken ➡ **listen**	heath ➡ **plain**	heirloom ➡ **antique**	hereditary ➡ **natural**
hearsay ➡ **rumor**	heathen ➡ **atheist**	helm ➡ **wheel**	heresy ➡ **disagreement**
heart ➡ **essence, feeling**	heave ➡ **lift, throw, vomit**	helmet ➡ **hat**	heritage ➡ **inheritance**
heartache ➡ **sorrow, misery**	heavens ➡ **space**	helmsman ➡ **pilot**	hero ➡ **winner, savior**
heartbreaking ➡ **pitiful**	heaviness ➡ **weight**	helpful ➡ **useful**	heroic ➡ **brave**
hearten ➡ **please**	heavyset ➡ **fat**	helpless ➡ **weak**	heroism ➡ **courage**
heartfelt ➡ **sincere**	hectic ➡ **frantic**	helpmate ➡ **spouse**	hesitant ➡ **reluctant**
hearth ➡ **fireplace**	hedgerow ➡ **hedge**		

hide 1. *vb* conceal, disguise, secrete, bury, withhold, hoard, squirrel (away) ⇨ *reveal*
2. *vb* cover (up), camouflage, obscure, eclipse, mask, block, screen, shade, shroud, veil, cloak ➡ **cover**
3. *n* pelt, skin, fleece, fell, rawhide, chamois ➡ **coat**

high 1. *adj* tall, lofty, towering, soaring ➡ **big**
2. *adj* high-pitched, shrill, treble, piping ➡ **loud** ⇨ *low*
3. *adj* ➡ **important**
4. *adj* ➡ **happy**

highway *n* interstate, expressway, freeway, thruway, turnpike, parkway ➡ **road**

hill 1. *n* knoll, mound, hillock, foothill, down, dune, bank, ridge ➡ **pile, mountain, cliff** ⇨ *valley*
2. *n* ➡ **slant**

hire 1. *vb* (*in reference to people*) engage, employ, appoint, enlist, draft, recruit, enroll ⇨ *fire*
2. *vb* (*in reference to things or property*) rent, charter, lease, let, sublet ➡ **lend, borrow**

hit 1. *vb* strike, pound, batter, beat, maul, bash, bump, pelt, smash, smack, swat, hammer, buffet, pat, clobber (*informal*), slug (*informal*), whack (*informal*) ➡ **punch, knock, collide, whip**
2. *n* ➡ **blow**[1]

hoarse *adj* raspy, gruff, grating, throaty, guttural, husky, gravelly ➡ **rough**

hole 1. *n* hollow, cavity, pit, crater, abyss, chasm, crevasse ➡ **cave, den, well**
2. *n* puncture, perforation, opening, aperture, vent, crack, cleft, fissure, crevice, split, gap, rupture, leak, pore

---

If the word you want is not a main entry above, look below to find it.

heterogeneous ➡ different
hew ➡ cut, carve
hex ➡ curse
hi ➡ hello
hiatus ➡ break
hibernate ➡ sleep
hidden ➡ secret, invisible
hidebound ➡ provincial
hideous ➡ ugly
hiding ➡ secrecy
highborn ➡ noble
higher than ➡ above
highland ➡ plateau
highlight ➡ emphasize
highly ➡ well
high-pitched ➡ high
high-priced ➡ expensive
high seas ➡ ocean

high society ➡ aristocracy
high-strung ➡ tense, nervous
hijack ➡ seize
hike ➡ walk, growth
hiker ➡ pedestrian
hilarious ➡ funny
hilarity ➡ laughter
hillock ➡ hill
hinder ➡ prevent, bar, delay
hindmost ➡ last
hindquarters ➡ back
hindrance ➡ barrier, disability
hinge ➡ depend, turn, axis
hint ➡ suggest, bit, reminder, tip
hinterland ➡ country
'

hiss ➡ yell
historian ➡ writer
historic ➡ memorable
history ➡ past, story
hitch ➡ knot, trap, tie
hitchhiker ➡ rider
hive ➡ herd
hoard ➡ save, hide, wealth, supply
hoarder ➡ miser
hoary ➡ old
hoax ➡ trick
hobble ➡ limp, prevent
hobby ➡ pastime
hobgoblin ➡ bogeyman
hobnob ➡ mix
hobo ➡ beggar
hock ➡ pawn

hocus-pocus ➡ magic
hodgepodge ➡ mess
hoe ➡ dig
hog ➡ glutton
hogshead ➡ barrel
hogwash ➡ nonsense
hoi polloi ➡ people
hoist ➡ lift
hola ➡ hello
hold ➡ contain, own, support, embrace, believe, give
holder ➡ owner
holding ➡ supply
holdings ➡ property
holiday ➡ vacation
holier-than-thou ➡ self-righteous

---

holy *adj* sacred, divine, hallowed, blessed, consecrated, sacramental ➡ **holy**

home 1. *n* house, apartment, condominium, condo (*informal*), dwelling, residence, abode, domicile, habitation, cabin, cottage, bungalow, chalet, mansion, palace, manor, villa, chateau ➡ **den, shack**
2. *n* ➡ **family**
3. *n* ➡ **base**
4. *n* ➡ **hospital**

homeless *adj* vagrant, vagabond, derelict, outcast, stray, lost, displaced, dispossessed

homonym *n* homograph, homophone

honesty *n* candor, frankness, veracity ➡ **truth, virtue**

hope 1. *vb* wish, expect, anticipate, aspire ➡ **believe, want, intend**
2. *n* desire, faith, longing, aspiration, dream ➡ **ambition**
3. *n* ➡ **virtue**

horizon *n* skyline, limit, range ➡ **border**

horse *n* pony, foal, colt, filly, stallion, mare, steed, mount, gelding

hospital *n* infirmary, clinic, medical center, rehabilitation center, sanatorium, sanitarium, nursing home, home

hospitality *n* geniality, cordiality, warmth, amiability, courtesy, welcome ➡ **generosity, kindness**

host 1. *n* hostess, entertainer, presenter, moderator, master of ceremonies, MC, emcee, chaperon, chaperone
2. *n* hostess, innkeeper, bartender, barkeep, maitre d'
3. *n* ➡ **crowd**
4. *vb* ➡ **entertain**

hot 1. *adj* scalding, boiling, broiling, roasting, sizzling, sweltering, torrid ➡ **warm, burning, tropical** ⇨ *cold*
2. *adj* ➡ **spicy**
3. *adj* ➡ **fashionable**

If the word you want is not a main entry above, look below to find it.

hollow ➡ empty, hole, valley
holm ➡ island
holocaust ➡ fire
homage ➡ respect
home base ➡ base
homecoming ➡ return
homegrown ➡ native
homeland ➡ country
homely ➡ plain
homesick ➡ lonely
homestead ➡ farm
homesteader ➡ pioneer
homesteading ➡ farming
homework ➡ lesson
homey ➡ comfortable, family
homicidal ➡ deadly

homicide ➡ murder
hominid ➡ human being
homogeneity ➡ unity
homograph ➡ homonym
homophone ➡ homonym
hone ➡ sharpen, perfect
honed ➡ sharp
honest ➡ good, sincere
honestly ➡ sincerely
honeyed ➡ rich
honk ➡ blow²
honor ➡ respect, virtue, award, praise, celebrate, keep
honorable ➡ good
hood ➡ top, vandal
hoodlum ➡ vandal

hoodwink ➡ cheat
hoof ➡ foot
hook ➡ lock
hooligan ➡ bully, vandal
hoop ➡ circle, ring
hoot ➡ yell
hop ➡ jump
hopeful ➡ good, optimistic
hopeless ➡ bleak, useless
horde ➡ crowd
horizontal ➡ level, prone
horrible ➡ awful
horrid ➡ ugly
horrify ➡ scare, shock
horrifying ➡ scary
horror ➡ fear

horsefly ➡ fly
horseman ➡ rider
horseplay ➡ play
horsepower ➡ energy
horse race ➡ race
horseshoe ➡ curve
horsewoman ➡ rider
horticulture ➡ farming
hose ➡ pipe
hospitable ➡ friendly
hostage ➡ prisoner
hostel ➡ hotel
hostess ➡ host
hostile ➡ belligerent
hostilities ➡ fight
hostility ➡ opposition, anger, hatred

n = noun • *vb* = verb • *adj* = adjective • *adv* = adverb • *prep* = preposition • *conj* = conjunction

hotel *n* inn, motel, hostel, lodge, bed-and-breakfast, resort, spa, retreat

house 1. *n* ➡ **home**
2. *vb* accommodate, board, lodge, put up, shelter, quarter, billet

huge *adj* enormous, immense, gigantic, prodigious, colossal, tremendous, mighty, vast, gross, gargantuan, monstrous, jumbo, mammoth, massive, titanic, humongous (*informal*) ➡ **big**

hum *vb* buzz, drone, murmur, whir, purr ➡ **sing**

human being *n* human, person, individual, being, soul, body, mortal, hominid ➡ **humanity, man, woman, people**

humanity 1. *n* humankind, mankind, man, society, human race ➡ **people, human being, man, woman**
2. *n* ➡ **kindness**

Many people object to the words **man** (*when used without* the *or* a), *and* **mankind** *in the sense of "humanity," because the word* **man** *is more frequently used to mean "an adult male person." Because this more common sense (a man, the young man) refers to males and not to females, they feel that the "humanity" sense of* **man** *and* **mankind** *also excludes women. It may be more thoughtful to use* **humanity**, **humankind**, *the phrase the* **human race**, *or the plural compound* **human beings** *when you want to refer to humans in general. The "humanity" sense of* **man** *is very common in the writing of earlier periods.*

humble 1. *adj* meek, modest, unassuming, unpretentious, self-deprecating, self-effacing ➡ **shy** ⇨ *proud*
2. *adj* ➡ **common**
3. *vb* ➡ **condescend**

humidity *n* moisture, dampness, mugginess, wetness, dew ➡ **liquid**

humor 1. *n* wit, comedy, levity, amusement, jest, jocularity, whimsicality ➡ **irony**
2. *n* ➡ **mood**
3. *vb* ➡ **entertain, pamper**

hunger 1. *n* starvation, famine ➡ **poverty**
2. *n* ➡ **appetite, desire**

hungry *adj* starving, starved, famished, ravenous, underfed, malnourished, undernourished, emaciated, wasted

---

If the word you want is not a main entry above, look below to find it.

hothouse ➡ greenhouse
Houdini ➡ magician
hound ➡ dog, bother, follow
hourglass ➡ clock
housebroken ➡ tame
housefly ➡ fly
houseguest ➡ visitor
household ➡ family
householder ➡ occupant
houseplant ➡ flower
house-trained ➡ tame
housing estate ➡ development

hovel ➡ shack
hover ➡ hang, fly
how do you do? ➡ hello
howdy ➡ hello
however ➡ but, anyway
howl ➡ cry, bark, laugh
hub ➡ middle
hubbub ➡ noise
hubris ➡ pride
huddle ➡ snuggle
hue ➡ color
huff ➡ breathe, fit²

hug ➡ embrace
hull ➡ framework
hullabaloo ➡ noise
human ➡ human being, mortal
humane ➡ kind
humanistic ➡ liberal
humankind ➡ humanity
human-made ➡ manufactured
human race ➡ humanity
humbug ➡ cheat
humdrum ➡ dull

humid ➡ damp, tropical
humiliate ➡ insult, shame
humiliated ➡ ashamed
humiliation ➡ shame
humongous ➡ huge
humorist ➡ writer, comic
humorous ➡ funny
hump ➡ bulge
humus ➡ dirt
hunch ➡ impulse, belief, bend
hunk ➡ block, lump

---

hunt 1. *vb* fish, shoot, poach, track ➡ **follow**
2. *vb* search, seek, look, investigate, scour, forage, probe, ransack, rummage, delve, explore, prospect, comb, sift
3. *n* search, investigation, pursuit, chase, quest, exploration ➡ **study**

hurry 1. *vb* rush, hasten, hustle, speed, race, hurtle, accelerate, quicken, scurry, sally, dash, zip, whiz, zoom, scamper, scuttle, surge, swarm, pour, stampede, storm
2. *n* rush, haste, scramble, stampede ➡ **speed**

hurt 1. *vb* injure, afflict, damage, wound, bruise, tear, wrench, twist, dislocate ➡ **harm, abuse, hit, insult, punish, break, pull**

2. *vb* smart, sting, burn, irritate, ache, throb ➡ **tingle**

hybrid *n* cross, crossbreed, mongrel ➡ **mixture**

hymn *n* carol, anthem, psalm, chant, motet, oratorio, cantata ➡ **song, dirge**

hypocrite *n* deceiver, faker, dissembler, quack, con artist ➡ **cheat**

hypocritical *adj* insincere, two-faced, dissembling ➡ **self-righteous, dishonest, sly**

hysteria *n* delirium, rage, mania, madness, panic, hysterics ➡ **excitement, confusion, fit**

If the word you want is not a main entry above, look below to find it.

hurdle ➡ barrier, jump
hurl ➡ throw
hurrah ➡ encore
hurricane ➡ storm
hurried ➡ abrupt, fast
hurriedly ➡ quickly
hurtful ➡ sore
hurtle ➡ hurry

husband ➡ man, spouse
husbandman ➡ farmer
husbandry ➡ farming
hush ➡ calm, quiet
hushed ➡ quiet
husk ➡ shell, peel
husky ➡ fat, hoarse

hustle ➡ hurry
hut ➡ shack
hybernating ➡ asleep
hygienic ➡ sterile
hype ➡ advertising
hyperactive ➡ active
hyperbole ➡ exaggeration

hypnotize ➡ enchant
hypocrisy ➡ dishonesty
hypothesis ➡ theory
hypothetical ➡ theoretical, imaginary
hysterical ➡ excited, delirious
hysterics ➡ hysteria

n = noun • *vb* = verb • *adj* = adjective • *adv* = adverb • *prep* = preposition • *conj* = conjunction

ice *n* frost, hail, sleet, icicle, ice cube, permafrost

ice cream *n* ice milk, sherbet, sorbet, sundae, spumoni, parfait

icing *n* frosting, glaze, topping, meringue

idea *n* thought, concept, impression, inspiration, notion, inkling ➡ **belief, theory, plan, suggestion**

idealist *n* optimist, romantic, perfectionist, dreamer, visionary

idealistic *adj* utopian, romantic, visionary ➡ **optimistic, impractical**

ignorance *n* illiteracy, innocence, simplicity, inexperience, denseness, stupidity, unawareness

ignorant *adj* illiterate, uneducated, unlearned, unlettered, unschooled, unread ➡ **naive, stupid, unaware** ➪ *educated*

illegal *adj* unlawful, illegitimate, illicit, criminal, outlawed, wrongful, prohibited, taboo

illegible *adj* indecipherable, unreadable, unintelligible ➡ **dim**

illness *n* sickness, ailment, malady, affliction, disorder, infirmity, complaint ➡ **disease, nausea**

illogical *adj* irrational, unreasonable, absurd, fallacious, inconsistent, incoherent ➡ **wrong**

illusion *n* mirage, hallucination, delusion, apparition ➡ **fancy, trick**

imaginary *adj* unreal, nonexistent, fictional, fictitious, illusory, hypothetical, fanciful, hallucinatory ➡ **legendary** ➪ *real*

imagination *n* fancy, ingenuity, creativity, originality, vision, inspiration

---

If the word you want is not a main entry above, look below to find it.

ICBM ➡ missile
iceberg ➡ glacier
icebox ➡ refrigerator
icecap ➡ glacier
ice cube ➡ ice
ice floe ➡ glacier
ice milk ➡ ice cream
ice storm ➡ storm
icicle ➡ ice
icon ➡ god
icy ➡ cold, slippery
ideal ➡ perfect, model, favorite
identical ➡ same
identification ➡ discovery
identify ➡ name, distinguish

identity ➡ personality, unity
ideology ➡ philosophy
idiom ➡ dialect
idiosyncrasy ➡ oddity
idiosyncratic ➡ unique
idiot ➡ fool
idiotic ➡ foolish
idle ➡ passive, lazy, unemployed, empty, rest
idleness ➡ laziness
idler ➡ loafer
idol ➡ god, statue
idolize ➡ love
ignite ➡ light[1]
ignoble ➡ shameful

ignoramus ➡ fool
ignore ➡ exclude
ill ➡ sick
ill-advised ➡ imprudent
ill-at-ease ➡ uncomfortable
ill-behaved ➡ mischievous
illegitimate ➡ illegal
illiberal ➡ conservative
illicit ➡ illegal
illiteracy ➡ ignorance
illiterate ➡ ignorant
ill-natured ➡ cross
ill-tempered ➡ cross
ill-treat ➡ abuse
ill-treatment ➡ abuse

illuminate ➡ light[1], explain
illumination ➡ light[1]
illuminations ➡ fireworks
illumine ➡ light[1]
illusionist ➡ magician
illusory ➡ imaginary
illustrate ➡ draw, explain
illustration ➡ picture, example
illustrative ➡ visible
illustrious ➡ famous
image ➡ picture, statue, photograph
imaginable ➡ possible
imaginative ➡ talented

---

imagine 1. *vb* conceive, picture, see, envision, envisage, visualize, fancy, fantasize ➡ **pretend**
2. *vb* ➡ **guess, think**

imitate *vb* copy, mimic, emulate, simulate, parrot, ape, parody, mock, lampoon, satirize, impersonate, caricature

immoral *adj* unethical, unprincipled, shameless, dissolute, degenerate, depraved, perverted ➡ **bad, wrong**

immorality *n* sin, depravity, wickedness, evil, iniquity, perversion, perversity

impassable *adj* closed, obstructed, trackless, pathless, untrodden, impenetrable ➡ **inaccessible**

importance *n* significance, consequence, import, moment, value, gravity, weight, stature, dignity ➡ **relevance, worth**

important 1. *adj* significant, principal, chief, major, main, essential, primary, critical, key, paramount, prime, cardinal, foremost, high, weighty ➡ **urgent, necessary, valuable, meaningful, memorable, predominant**
2. *adj* influential, prominent, powerful ➡ **famous**

impossible 1. *adj* inconceivable, unattainable, unthinkable, incomprehensible ➡ **useless, illogical, unbelievable**
2. *adj* insoluble, unsolvable, inexplicable, unexplainable, unaccountable
3. *adj* ➡ **intolerable**

If the word you want is not a main entry above, look below to find it.

imbecile ➡ fool
imbecilic ➡ foolish
imbed ➡ embed
imbibe ➡ drink
imbue ➡ instill
imitation ➡ fake, parody
immaculate ➡ perfect, clean
immature ➡ young, childish
immaturity ➡ childhood
immeasurable ➡ infinite
immediate ➡ sudden, near
immediately ➡ now
immense ➡ huge
immensely ➡ very
immerse ➡ sink, wet
immersed ➡ absorbed
immigrant ➡ foreign, foreigner, pioneer
immigrate ➡ move
immigration ➡ movement
imminent ➡ near, future
immobile ➡ stationary
immobilize ➡ paralyze

immoderate ➡ excessive
immortal ➡ eternal, god
immovable ➡ tight
immune ➡ safe
immunity ➡ freedom
immunize ➡ vaccinate
imp ➡ rascal, urchin
impact ➡ collision, blow[1], effect, collide
impair ➡ damage, weaken
impaired ➡ disabled
impairment ➡ disability, harm
impalpable ➡ invisible
impart ➡ give
impartial ➡ fair
impartiality ➡ justice
impassioned ➡ emotional
impassive ➡ blank
impatient ➡ eager
impeach ➡ try
impeccable ➡ perfect, innocent
impede ➡ bar, delay

impediment ➡ barrier, disability
impel ➡ push, force
impending ➡ ominous, future
impenetrable ➡ impassable, thick
imperative ➡ necessary, urgent
imperceptible ➡ invisible
imperfect ➡ partial
imperfection ➡ defect
imperial ➡ noble
imperil ➡ jeopardize
imperious ➡ dignified, dogmatic
impermanent ➡ mortal
impermeable ➡ tight
impersonal ➡ cool, fair
impersonate ➡ act, imitate
impertinence ➡ audacity
impertinent ➡ rude
impetuous ➡ abrupt, emotional

impetus ➡ impulse
impinge ➡ intrude
impish ➡ mischievous
implant ➡ instill, embed, put
implausible ➡ unbelievable
implement ➡ tool, equipment
implicate ➡ blame
implication ➡ meaning
implicit ➡ virtual
implied ➡ virtual
implore ➡ beg
imply ➡ suggest, matter, mean
impolite ➡ rude
import ➡ importance, meaning
importantly ➡ chiefly
imported ➡ foreign
importune ➡ beg
impose ➡ order, inflict, disturb
imposing ➡ grand
imposter ➡ cheat

impractical *adj* unrealistic, quixotic, unfeasible ➡ **illogical, idealistic** ⇨ *practical*

improper *adj* inappropriate, unseemly, unbecoming, indecent, indelicate, indecorous, unsuitable, unbefitting, impure ➡ **wrong, bad, shameful**

imprudent *adj* ill-advised, inadvisable, unwise, rash, indiscreet, overconfident, unsound

impulse 1. *n* whim, fancy, caprice, whimsy, hunch
2. *n* thrust, surge, pulse, pulsation, impetus, shove, momentum

inability *n* incapability, ineptitude, incompetence, incapacity, inefficacy, impotence, powerlessness, failure

inaccessible *adj* unobtainable, unattainable, unreachable, out-of-the-way, elusive, unavailable ➡ **impassable**

inadequate *adj* lacking, deficient, short, sparse, insufficient ➡ **poor**

incentive *n* motivation, motive, encouragement, inspiration, inducement, stimulus, spur, spark ➡ **reason, support**

incompetent *adj* incapable, inept, ineffectual, unqualified, unfit, inefficient, unable ➡ **amateur, clumsy**

If the word you want is not a main entry above, look below to find it.

impotence ➡ **inability**

impotent ➡ **weak, sterile**

impound ➡ **jail**

impoverish ➡ **ruin**

impoverished ➡ **poor, underdeveloped**

impoverishment ➡ **poverty**

impregnable ➡ **safe**

impress ➡ **affect, print**

impression ➡ **idea, effect, print, track, dent**

impressive ➡ **awesome, striking**

imprint ➡ **print, track, signature**

imprison ➡ **jail**

improbable ➡ **unbelievable**

impromptu ➡ **spontaneous**

improve ➡ **correct, help**

improved ➡ **better**

improvement ➡ **repair, progress**

improving ➡ **better**

improvise ➡ **invent**

impudence ➡ **rudeness**

impudent ➡ **rude**

impulsive ➡ **spontaneous, arbitrary**

impure ➡ **improper, dirty**

in ➡ **fashionable**

inaccuracy ➡ **mistake**

inaccurate ➡ **wrong**

inactive ➡ **passive, unemployed**

inadequacy ➡ **mediocrity**

inadvertent ➡ **accidental**

inadvertently ➡ **accidentally**

inadvisable ➡ **imprudent**

inane ➡ **trite**

inanimate ➡ **dead, unconscious**

inappropriate ➡ **improper**

inarticulate ➡ **dumb**

inattentive ➡ **absentminded, negligent**

inaudible ➡ **quiet**

inaugural ➡ **early**

inaugurate ➡ **start, crown**

inauguration ➡ **beginning**

inauspicious ➡ **ominous**

inborn ➡ **natural**

incapability ➡ **inability**

incapable ➡ **incompetent**

incapacitate ➡ **weaken**

incapacitated ➡ **disabled**

incapacity ➡ **inability**

incarcerate ➡ **jail**

incense ➡ **anger, smell**

incessant ➡ **continual, frequent**

inch ➡ **crawl**

inchworm ➡ **worm**

incident ➡ **event**

incidental ➡ **accidental, circumstantial**

incidentally ➡ **accidentally**

incinerate ➡ **burn**

incinerator ➡ **furnace**

incipient ➡ **early**

incise ➡ **carve**

incision ➡ **cut**

incisive ➡ **smart**

incite ➡ **urge, fan**

inclement ➡ **wet, stormy**

inclination ➡ **preference, tendency**

incline ➡ **slant**

inclined ➡ **likely**

include ➡ **contain, add**

inclusive ➡ **comprehensive**

incoherent ➡ **illogical, delirious**

income ➡ **wage**

incomparable ➡ **unique**

incomparably ➡ **far**

incompetence ➡ **inability**

incomplete ➡ **partial, unresolved**

incompletely ➡ **partly**

incomprehensible ➡ **obscure, impossible**

inconceivable ➡ **impossible**

inconclusive ➡ **circumstantial**

incongruity ➡ **contradiction, irony**

inconsiderate ➡ **thoughtless**

inconsistency ➡ **contradiction**

---

inconspicuous *adj* unnoticeable, unobtrusive, unapparent ➡ **invisible** ⇨ *obvious*

inconvenient *adj* awkward, bothersome, troublesome, onerous, irksome, annoying, untimely

indirect *adj* circuitous, roundabout, twisting, meandering, tortuous, rambling, devious ➡ **circumstantial**

indiscriminate *adj* aimless, uncritical,

promiscuous ➡ **thoughtless, carefree, arbitrary**

inexcusable *adj* unforgiveable, unpardonable, unjustifiable, indefensible

infallible *adj* unerring, faultless, irrefutable, authoritative, incontrovertible ➡ **perfect, certain, reliable**

infer *vb* deduce, conclude, gather, judge, reason, ascertain ➡ **assume, mention**

If the word you want is not a main entry above, look below to find it.

inconsistent ➡ illogical, variable

inconstant ➡ fickle

incontrovertible ➡ infallible

inconvenience ➡ nuisance, trouble

incorporate ➡ add, embody

incorrect ➡ wrong

incorrigible ➡ bad

increase ➡ more, growth, strengthen, grow

incredible ➡ great, unbelievable

incredulity ➡ surprise

incredulous ➡ doubtful

increment ➡ growth

inculcate ➡ instill

incur ➡ catch

incurable ➡ deadly

incursion ➡ attack

indebted ➡ grateful

indebtedness ➡ debt

indecent ➡ improper

indecipherable ➡ illegible

indecorous ➡ improper

indeed ➡ certainly, really

indefensible ➡ inexcusable

indefinite ➡ doubtful

indelible ➡ permanent

indelicate ➡ improper

indent ➡ dent

indentation ➡ dent, print

independence ➡ freedom

independent ➡ free

independently ➡ apart

indescribable ➡ unbelievable

indestructible ➡ unbreakable

indeterminate ➡ unresolved

index ➡ sign

indicate ➡ read, mean

indication ➡ sign

indict ➡ try

indictment ➡ complaint

indifference ➡ apathy, neglect

indifferent ➡ apathetic

indigence ➡ poverty

indigenous ➡ native

indigent ➡ poor

indigestion ➡ nausea

indignant ➡ angry

indignation ➡ anger

indignity ➡ insult

indirectly ➡ sideways

indiscernible ➡ invisible

indiscreet ➡ imprudent

indispensable ➡ necessary

indisposed ➡ sick

indistinct ➡ dim

indite ➡ write

individual ➡ human being, private

indivisible ➡ inseparable

indolence ➡ laziness

indolent ➡ lazy

indomitable ➡ invincible

indoor ➡ inside

induce ➡ persuade

inducement ➡ incentive

induct ➡ crown

induction ➡ reason

indulge ➡ pamper

indulgent ➡ tolerant

industrialist ➡ tycoon

industrious ➡ lively, ambitious, diligent

industry ➡ diligence, work, business

inebriate ➡ drunkard

inebriated ➡ drunk

ineffective ➡ useless

ineffectual ➡ incompetent, useless

inefficacy ➡ inability

inefficient ➡ incompetent

inept ➡ clumsy, incompetent

ineptitude ➡ inability

inequality ➡ difference

inert ➡ passive, stationary, dead

inescapable ➡ certain

inestimable ➡ valuable

inevitable ➡ certain

inexact ➡ approximate

inexhaustible ➡ infinite, diligent

inexpensive ➡ cheap

inexperience ➡ ignorance

inexperienced ➡ naive, amateur, unprepared

inexpert ➡ amateur

inexplicable ➡ mysterious, obscure, impossible

infamous ➡ bad

infancy ➡ childhood, beginning

infant ➡ baby

infantile ➡ childish

infatuation ➡ love, desire

infect ➡ dirty

infection ➡ disease, poison

infectious ➡ contagious

n = noun • *vb* = verb • *adj* = adjective • *adv* = adverb • *prep* = preposition • *conj* = conjunction

infest *vb* overrun, plague, swarm, beset

infinite *adj* boundless, unbounded, endless, limitless, unlimited, interminable, countless, immeasurable, inexhaustible ➡ **eternal, big** ⇨ *finite*

inflammable *adj* flammable, combustible, burnable, volatile, explosive

inflict *vb* impose, exact, dispense, wreak, mete out ➡ **give**

inheritance *n* bequest, legacy, heritage, patrimony, endowment, trust ➡ **gift, acquisition**

innocent 1. *adj* blameless, guiltless, faultless, sinless, pure, chaste, angelic, impeccable ⇨ *guilty*
2. *adj* ➡ **naive**

insane *adj* crazy, mad, crazed, lunatic, psychotic, maniacal, demented, deranged, berserk, paranoid, unbalanced, unhinged, mental (*informal*) ⇨ *sane*

If the word you want is not a main entry above, look below to find it.

inference ➡ conclusion

inferential ➡ circumstantial

inferior ➡ cheap, poor, subordinate

inferiority ➡ mediocrity

inferior to ➡ under

inferno ➡ fire

infertile ➡ sterile

infidel ➡ atheist

infiltrate ➡ enter

infinity ➡ space

infirm ➡ weak, sick

infirmary ➡ hospital

infirmity ➡ illness

inflame ➡ fan

inflamed ➡ sore, burning

inflammation ➡ sore

inflate ➡ swell, exaggerate

inflation ➡ growth

inflection ➡ accent

inflexible ➡ firm

influence ➡ affect, effect, persuade

influential ➡ important

inform ➡ tell, introduce, teach

informal ➡ carefree

information ➡ knowledge

informed ➡ educated

inform on ➡ betray

infraction ➡ crime

infrequent ➡ rare

infrequently ➡ seldom

infringe ➡ intrude

infuriate ➡ anger

infuriated ➡ angry

infuse ➡ instill

ingenious ➡ talented

ingenuity ➡ ability, imagination

ingenuous ➡ naive, straightforward

ingest ➡ take

ingredient ➡ part

inhabit ➡ live[1]

inhabitant ➡ citizen, occupant

inhalation ➡ breath

inhale ➡ breathe, smoke

inherent ➡ natural

inherit ➡ receive

inherited ➡ natural

inhibit ➡ prevent

inhospitable ➡ unfriendly

inhuman ➡ mean

iniquity ➡ immorality

initial ➡ early, sign

initialism ➡ abbreviation

initiate ➡ start

initiation ➡ beginning, introduction

initiative ➡ ambition

inject ➡ instill

injection ➡ medicine

injunction ➡ ban

injure ➡ hurt

injurious ➡ destructive, unhealthy

injury ➡ cut, damage, scar, harm, abuse, casualty

injustice ➡ hardship

inkling ➡ idea

inky ➡ black

inlay ➡ embed

inlet ➡ bay

inmate ➡ prisoner

inn ➡ hotel, restaurant

innate ➡ natural

inner ➡ inside, middle

innermost ➡ inside

innkeeper ➡ host

innocence ➡ virtue, ignorance

innocuous ➡ harmless

innovate ➡ start, change

innovation ➡ invention

innovative ➡ experimental

innovator ➡ creator

innumerable ➡ many

inoculate ➡ vaccinate

inoffensive ➡ harmless

inordinate ➡ excessive

inpatient ➡ patient

inquest ➡ examination

inquire ➡ ask

inquiring ➡ curious

inquiry ➡ question, study

inquisitive ➡ curious

inquisitiveness ➡ interest

---

inscription *n* engraving, dedication, epitaph, legend, lettering ➡ **signature**

insensitive *adj* unfeeling, uncaring, tactless, heartless, hardhearted, coldhearted, callous, unsympathetic, cold-blooded ➡ **thoughtless, apathetic, stubborn** ⇨ *thoughtful*

inseparable *adj* indivisible, unified, united, integrated, integral, joined

inside 1. *adj* interior, internal, inner, indoor, innermost ➡ **middle**
2. *n* ➡ **middle**
Note that **inside** *and* **interior** *are often used as nouns:* "The **inside** of the house is as beautiful as the outside." "We grew up in the **interior** of the country." **Inside** may also be used as a preposition ("I put your things **inside** the suitcase") or an adverb ("Greg went **inside** when it started raining").

insipid 1. *adj* bland, tasteless, flat, mild
2. *adj* ➡ **trite, dull**

insist *vb* demand, require, assert ➡ **argue, order, force**

instead *adv* rather, alternatively, alternately, preferably

instill *vb* infuse, suffuse, imbue, inject, interject, implant, inculcate ➡ **teach, give, put**

insult 1. *vb* offend, humiliate, slander, defame, malign, smear, slight, snub, outrage, tease, taunt, scorn ➡ **abuse, hurt, ridicule**
2. *n* affront, offense, indignity, outrage, slander, libel, smear, jeer, put-down (*informal*)

intellectual *adj* scholarly, scholastic, educational, academic, cerebral, mental ➡ **profound, thoughtful**

If the word you want is not a main entry above, look below to find it.

insatiable ➡ greedy

inscribe ➡ write, print, carve, sign

inscrutable ➡ obscure

insect ➡ bug

insecure ➡ anxious, unsteady

insensate ➡ unconscious

insensible ➡ unconscious

insert ➡ put, embed

inset ➡ embed

insight ➡ depth

insightful ➡ smart

insignia ➡ badge, label

insignificant ➡ trivial

insincere ➡ hypocritical

insinuate ➡ suggest

insolence ➡ audacity, rudeness

insolent ➡ rude

insoluble ➡ impossible

inspect ➡ examine, patrol

inspection ➡ look

inspiration ➡ imagination, idea, incentive

inspire ➡ cause, urge

install ➡ put, crown

installation ➡ appointment

instance ➡ example

instant ➡ moment

instantaneous ➡ sudden

instantaneously ➡ quickly

instantly ➡ now

instigate ➡ urge

instinct ➡ habit, feeling, belief

instinctive ➡ automatic, natural

institute ➡ school, college

institution ➡ organization, college, habit

institutionalize ➡ jail

instruct ➡ teach, order

instruction ➡ education

instructions ➡ recipe

instructor ➡ teacher

instrument ➡ tool

instrumentalist ➡ musician

insubordinate ➡ rebellious

insubordination ➡ disobedience

insubstantial ➡ light^2, thin

insufferable ➡ intolerable

insufficient ➡ inadequate

insular ➡ private, provincial

insulate ➡ separate

insure ➡ guarantee

insurgence ➡ revolution

insurgent ➡ rebel

insurrection ➡ revolution

intact ➡ complete

intake ➡ wage

integer ➡ number

integral ➡ inseparable

integrate ➡ unify, add

integrated ➡ inseparable

integrity ➡ virtue, unity

intellect ➡ mind, wisdom

intelligence ➡ mind, wisdom, spying

intelligent ➡ smart

intelligible ➡ articulate

intemperate ➡ excessive

---

n = noun • *vb* = verb • *adj* = adjective • *adv* = adverb • *prep* = preposition • *conj* = conjunction

intend *vb* mean, propose, plan, aim, design, purpose ➡ **hope, prepare**

interest 1. *n* curiosity, concern, inquisitiveness ➡ **attention**
2. *n* claim, stake, investment ➡ **share**
3. *n* ➡ **pastime**
4. *vb* engage, absorb, preoccupy, engross ➡ **appeal, entertain**

interesting *adj* fascinating, intriguing, stimulating, engrossing, absorbing, engaging, entertaining, provocative, stirring, compelling ➡ **exciting** ⇨ *dull*

interference *n* intervention, intrusion, interruption, prying, meddling

intolerable *adj* unbearable, insufferable, difficult, impossible

introduce 1. *vb* present, acquaint, familiarize, inform, apprise ➡ **broach**
2. *vb* preface ➡ **precede, start**

introduction 1. *n* meeting, presentation, debut, initiation, acquaintance ➡ **beginning**
2. *n* preface, foreword, prologue, preamble, prelude, overture, intro (*informal*) ⇨ *conclusion*

intrude *vb* trespass, encroach, infringe, invade, impinge ➡ **enter, meddle, disturb**

invent 1. *vb* devise, design, develop, conceive, formulate, originate, contrive, hatch, improvise, ad-lib ➡ **build, discover, form, make, start**
2. *vb* fabricate, concoct, make up, counterfeit ➡ **lie**

If the word you want is not a main entry above, look below to find it.

intense ➡ **bright, strong**

intensify ➡ **strengthen, concentrate**

intensity ➡ **strength**

intent ➡ **absorbed, plan, object**

intention ➡ **object**

intentional ➡ **voluntary**

intentionally ➡ **purposely**

inter ➡ **bury**

intercede ➡ **negotiate**

intercept ➡ **seize**

interchange ➡ **change, trade**

intercourse ➡ **speech**

interfere ➡ **meddle, disturb**

interfering ➡ **meddlesome**

interim ➡ **temporary**

interior ➡ **inside, middle**

interject ➡ **instill**

interlace ➡ **weave**

interlock ➡ **join**

interlude ➡ **break**

intermediary ➡ **agent**

intermediate ➡ **middle**

interminable ➡ **infinite, eternal**

interminably ➡ **forever**

intermingle ➡ **mix**

intermission ➡ **break**

intermittent ➡ **periodic**

intern ➡ **page**

internal ➡ **inside**

international ➡ **universal**

internee ➡ **prisoner**

interpret ➡ **translate, explain**

interpretation ➡ **translation**

interrogate ➡ **ask, examine**

interrogation ➡ **question**

interrogative ➡ **question**

interrupt ➡ **disturb**

interruption ➡ **break, interference**

intersection ➡ **corner**

interstate ➡ **highway**

intertwine ➡ **weave**

interval ➡ **period, distance**

intervene ➡ **meddle**

intervention ➡ **interference**

interview ➡ **ask, meeting**

intimate ➡ **friendly, private, near, suggest**

intimidate ➡ **threaten, discourage**

intolerance ➡ **prejudice**

intolerant ➡ **prejudiced, mean, provincial**

intoxicated ➡ **drunk**

intractable ➡ **stubborn**

intrepid ➡ **brave**

intricate ➡ **complicated**

intrigue ➡ **fascinate, secret**

intriguing ➡ **interesting, attractive**

intrinsic ➡ **natural**

intro ➡ **introduction**

introductory ➡ **basic, early**

intrusion ➡ **interference**

intrusive ➡ **meddlesome**

intuition ➡ **feeling**

inundate ➡ **flood**

inundation ➡ **flood**

invade ➡ **attack, enter, intrude**

invalid ➡ **weak, patient, wrong**

invalidate ➡ **disprove**

invaluable ➡ **expensive**

invariable ➡ **continual**

invariably ➡ **regularly**

invasion ➡ **attack**

➡ = *synonym cross-reference* • ⇨ = *antonym cross-reference*

invention 1. *n* creation, contrivance, innovation, development, breakthrough
➡ **discovery, novelty**
2. *n* ➡ **lie**

invincible *adj* unbeatable, unconquerable, invulnerable, indomitable, unmanageable
➡ **strong, safe**

invisible *adj* imperceptible, indiscernible, undetectable, concealed, hidden, unseen, microscopic, impalpable, ethereal
➡ **supernatural, inconspicuous**

invitation *n* request, bidding, offer, summons
➡ **appeal, suggestion**

iron *vb* press, steam, mangle, flatten

irony *n* sarcasm, satire, incongruity
➡ **parody, humor**

island *n* isle, islet, atoll, key, cay, archipelago, holm

If the word you want is not a main entry above, look below to find it.

inventive ➡ **talented**

inventor ➡ **creator**

inventory ➡ **supply, list**

inverse ➡ **opposite**

invert ➡ **upset, change**

inverted ➡ **upside down**

invest ➡ **bank, crown**

investigate ➡ **examine, hunt**

investigation ➡ **study, hunt**

investiture ➡ **appointment**

investment ➡ **interest**

invigorate ➡ **renew**

invigorating ➡ **brisk**

invite ➡ **call, entertain**

inviting ➡ **attractive**

invoice ➡ **bill, charge**

invoke ➡ **appeal**

involuntary ➡ **automatic**

involve ➡ **concern**

involved ➡ **absorbed, complicated**

invulnerable ➡ **invincible, safe**

iota ➡ **bit**

irate ➡ **angry**

ire ➡ **anger**

irk ➡ **bother**

irksome ➡ **inconvenient**

ironic ➡ **sarcastic**

ironical ➡ **sarcastic**

irrational ➡ **illogical**

irrationality ➡ **nonsense**

irrefutable ➡ **infallible**

irregular ➡ **rough, different, strange, periodic**

irregularity ➡ **oddity, difference, departure**

irrelevant ➡ **unnecessary**

irresolute ➡ **fickle**

irresponsible ➡ **unreliable, negligent**

irreverent ➡ **rude**

irrevocably ➡ **finally**

irritable ➡ **cross**

irritate ➡ **hurt, bother**

irritated ➡ **angry, sore**

irritation ➡ **nuisance**

isle ➡ **island**

islet ➡ **island**

isolate ➡ **separate**

isolated ➡ **alone, private**

isolation ➡ **privacy**

issue ➡ **subject, effect, descend, print**

itch ➡ **tingle, desire, want**

item ➡ **object**

itemize ➡ **list**

itinerant ➡ **traveler**

itinerary ➡ **course**

ivory ➡ **white, fair**

n = noun • *vb* = verb • *adj* = adjective • *adv* = adverb • *prep* = preposition • *conj* = conjunction

J

jail 1. *n* prison, penitentiary, correctional facility, jailhouse, reformatory, cell, dungeon, brig, stockade, pen (*informal*), slammer (*informal*), clink (*informal*), stir (*informal*), big house (*informal*)
2. *vb* imprison, confine, detain, incarcerate, impound, remand, institutionalize, commit

jealous *adj* envious, resentful, possessive, begrudging ➡ **suspicious, greedy**

jelly *n* jam, preserve, marmalade

jeopardize *vb* risk, endanger, imperil, hazard, threaten

jetty *n* breakwater, dike, sea wall, pier, bulwark ➡ **dam**

jewel *n* gem, gemstone, brilliant, ornament, precious stone, stone, rock ➡ **trinket**

job *n* task, chore, work, duty, errand, assignment, project, mission, labor, living ➡ **profession, function**

join 1. *vb* connect, associate, attach, link, fasten, unite, couple, interlock, anchor, bridge, buckle, clasp, clinch, knit, pair, graft, weld, solder, cement, pin ➡ **tie, unify, marry**
2. *vb* enter, enroll, enlist, register, participate

joke 1. *n* prank, practical joke, gag, caper, antic ➡ **trick**
2. *n* jest, wisecrack, pun, witticism, quip, one-liner, bon mot ➡ **story**
3. *vb* jest, quip, banter, spar, kid, tease, josh

If the word you want is not a main entry above, look below to find it.

jab ➡ stick, blow[1]

jabber ➡ chatter

jack ➡ flag

jacket ➡ coat, wrapper

jackknife ➡ knife

jaded ➡ bored

jagged ➡ zigzag, rough

jailbird ➡ prisoner

jailhouse ➡ jail

jam ➡ jelly, trouble, push

jammed ➡ full

jangle ➡ ring

jar ➡ container, shake, disturb

jargon ➡ dialect

jaunt ➡ trip

jaunty ➡ lively

javelin ➡ missile

jealousy ➡ envy

jeer ➡ insult, ridicule, yell

jell ➡ harden

jeopardy ➡ danger

jerk ➡ pull, jump

jest ➡ joke, humor

jet ➡ fountain, black

jet set ➡ aristocracy

jettison ➡ discard

jibe ➡ agree

jiffy ➡ moment

jingle ➡ ring

jinx ➡ curse

jittery ➡ nervous

jobholder ➡ worker

jobless ➡ unemployed

jock ➡ athlete

jockey ➡ drive, rider

jocularity ➡ humor

jog ➡ run

John Hancock ➡ signature

joined ➡ inseparable

joining ➡ junction

joint ➡ link, common

jointly ➡ together

joist ➡ beam, board

joker ➡ comic

jolly ➡ happy

jolt ➡ shock, blow[1], jump

josh ➡ joke

jostle ➡ push

jot ➡ write, bit

jounce ➡ jump

journal ➡ paper, diary

journalist ➡ reporter

journey ➡ trip, travel

jovial ➡ happy

joviality ➡ mirth

---

judge 1. *n* justice, magistrate, jurist
2. *n* referee, umpire, official, evaluator, reviewer, critic, arbiter
3. *vb* ➡ **decide**
4. *vb* ➡ **estimate, infer**

jump 1. *vb, n* leap, spring, bound, vault, hop, pounce, bounce, jounce, jolt, pop, skip, hurdle, dive, plunge, lunge ➡ **dance**
2. *vb, n* start, flinch, wince, recoil, twitch, jerk, cringe, cower

junction *n* juncture, meeting, convergence, connection, joining ➡ **link, corner**

justice 1. *n* fairness, impartiality, equity, due process, evenhandedness ➡ **honesty, truth, virtue**
2. *n* ➡ **judge**

justification *n* vindication, defense, validation ➡ **basis, reason**

If the word you want is not a main entry above, look below to find it.

joy ➡ pleasure
joyful ➡ happy
joyous ➡ happy
jubilant ➡ ecstatic
jubilee ➡ party
judgment ➡ wisdom, tact, decision
judiciary ➡ court

judicious ➡ careful
jug ➡ bottle
juggle ➡ tinker
juice ➡ liquid
jumble ➡ mess, mix
jumbo ➡ huge
jumper ➡ dress
jumpy ➡ nervous

juncture ➡ junction, corner
jungle ➡ forest, maze
junior ➡ subordinate, student
junior college ➡ college
junk ➡ trash, discard
junkyard ➡ dump
junta ➡ group, party

jurisdiction ➡ rule
jurist ➡ judge
just ➡ fair, only, recently
justify ➡ explain, deserve
jut ➡ swell
juvenile ➡ young, childish, teenager, child
juxtapose ➡ compare

K

keep 1. *vb* have, possess, maintain, retain, preserve, sustain ➡ **own**
2. *vb* ➡ **save**
3. *vb* fulfill, honor, respect ➡ **celebrate**
4. *n* ➡ **board**
5. *n* ➡ **castle, tower**

kick 1. *vb* boot, punt, drop-kick, placekick ➡ **hit**
2. *n* ➡ **blow**[1]

kill *vb* murder, slay, assassinate, dispatch, massacre, butcher, execute, slaughter, exterminate, annihilate, eradicate, martyr, sacrifice ➡ **destroy, extinguish, choke**

killer *n* murderer, assassin, slayer, executioner

kind 1. *adj* compassionate, considerate, benevolent, well-meaning, charitable, merciful, kindhearted, tenderhearted, warmhearted, decent, kindly, benign, humane ➡ **friendly, generous, loving, nice, tolerant**
2. *n* ➡ **type**

kindness *n* mercy, charity, compassion, consideration, decency, goodwill, humanity, tenderness, courtesy, thoughtfulness, friendliness ➡ **love, pity**

king *n* monarch, sovereign, maharajah (*India*), rajah (*India*), sultan (*Muslim*), shah (*Iran*), pasha (*Turkey, N. Africa*), khan (*central Asia, China*), sachem (*Native American*) ➡ **ruler, emperor**

kiss *n, vb* peck, buss, smooch, smack

kitchen *n* kitchenette, galley, cookhouse, scullery, pantry, larder ➡ **room**

knife *n* blade, jackknife, penknife, dagger, stiletto, scalpel, razor, cleaver ➡ **sword**

knock 1. *vb* tap, rap, drum, thump, whack ➡ **bang, hit**
2. *n* tap, rap, thump, patter, pitter-patter ➡ **bang, blow**[1]

knot 1. *n* tangle, snarl, snag, hitch, splice
2. *vb* ➡ **tie**

If the word you want is not a main entry above, look below to find it.

kaiser ➡ emperor
kaiserin ➡ empress
keen ➡ sharp, eager, smart
keeper ➡ guardian
keepsake ➡ reminder
keg ➡ barrel
kelly ➡ green
kennel ➡ pen
kernel ➡ seed
kerosene ➡ oil
kettle ➡ pot

key ➡ answer, important, island
khaki ➡ brown
khan ➡ king
kid ➡ joke, child
kidnap ➡ seize
kiln ➡ furnace
kin ➡ family
kindhearted ➡ kind
kindle ➡ light[1]
kindling ➡ wood

kindly ➡ kind, well
kindred ➡ family
kingdom ➡ country
kingly ➡ noble
kink ➡ bend
kinship ➡ relationship
kiosk ➡ booth
kit ➡ equipment
kitchenette ➡ kitchen
knack ➡ talent

knapsack ➡ bag
knave ➡ rascal
knead ➡ rub, mix
kneel ➡ bend
knell ➡ ring
knickknack ➡ novelty
knife-edged ➡ sharp
knit ➡ weave, join, heal
knob ➡ bulge
knock out ➡ paralyze
knoll ➡ hill

---

know *vb* understand, realize, recognize, apprehend, comprehend, see, fathom, grasp, follow, get, penetrate ➡ **remember**

knowledge *n* fact, information, learning, data, evidence, education, awareness, erudition ➡ **experience, wisdom, education**

If the word you want is not a main entry above, look below to find it.

know-how ➡ **experience**

knowingly ➡ **purposely**

knowledgeable ➡ **educated**

kowtow to ➡ **flatter**

kudos ➡ **praise**

n = noun • *vb* = verb • *adj* = adjective • *adv* = adverb • *prep* = preposition • *conj* = conjunction

L

label 1. *n* tag, sticker, ticket, tab, marker, insignia, trademark, logo, service mark, brand ➡ **name**
2. *vb* mark, ticket ➡ **name**
3. *vb* ➡ **stereotype**

lag *vb* dawdle, straggle, saunter, plod, trail ➡ **delay, wait**

lake *n* pond, pool, fishpond, lagoon, loch, reservoir

lame 1. *adj* crippled, limping
2. *adj* ➡ **poor**

language *n* tongue, lingua franca ➡ **accent, dialect, speech**

larva *n* grub, maggot, caterpillar ➡ **worm**

last 1. *adj* latest, final, ultimate, extreme, concluding, closing, terminal, hindmost, outermost ➡ **latter**
2. *vb* ➡ **continue**

late 1. *adj* overdue, tardy, belated, delayed, delinquent ⇨ *early, punctual*
2. *adj* ➡ **new**
3. *adj* ➡ **dead**
4. *adv* behind, behindhand, belatedly, tardily

latent *adj* potential, dormant, undeveloped, unrealized, underlying

latter *adj* second, final ➡ **last, following**

If the word you want is not a main entry above, look below to find it.

labor ➡ work, job
laborer ➡ worker
labyrinth ➡ maze
lace ➡ string, tie
lacerate ➡ cut
laceration ➡ cut
lack ➡ need, want, absence
lackadaisical ➡ slow
lacking ➡ inadequate
lackluster ➡ dull
laconic ➡ short
lacquer ➡ finish
lad ➡ man
laden ➡ full
ladle ➡ spoon
lady ➡ woman, noble
ladylike ➡ feminine
lagoon ➡ bay, lake

laid-back ➡ carefree
lair ➡ den
lamasery ➡ monastery
lameness ➡ limp
lament ➡ grieve, regret, complaint, dirge
lamentable ➡ unfortunate
laminate ➡ plate
lamp ➡ light[1]
lampoon ➡ imitate
lance ➡ stick, missile
land ➡ property, country, dirt, terrain, descend, leave, dock
landfill ➡ dump
landing ➡ dock
landlady ➡ owner
landlord ➡ owner
landmark ➡ event

landowner ➡ owner
landscape ➡ country, nature, terrain, background
landslide ➡ avalanche
lane ➡ road, path
languid ➡ listless
languish ➡ grieve
languor ➡ laziness
languorous ➡ listless
lank ➡ thin
lanky ➡ thin
lantern ➡ light[1]
lap ➡ fold, lick
lapse ➡ relapse, fall, elapse
larceny ➡ theft
lard ➡ fat
larder ➡ closet, kitchen
large ➡ big

largess ➡ generosity
lariat ➡ rope
lark ➡ adventure
lash ➡ tie, whip
lass ➡ woman
lassitude ➡ laziness
lasso ➡ rope
lasting ➡ permanent
lastly ➡ finally
latch ➡ lock
lately ➡ recently
later ➡ following
latest ➡ last, new
lather ➡ foam
latrine ➡ bathroom
latter-day ➡ modern
latterly ➡ recently

---

laugh *vb, n* giggle, chuckle, snicker, roar, guffaw, snigger, titter, cackle, howl, shriek ➡ **smile**

laughter *n* hilarity, merriment, levity ➡ **laugh, ridicule, mirth**

laundry *n* wash, washing, cleaning, dry cleaning

layer *n* stratum, tier, sheet, level, film, membrane ➡ **coat**

laziness *n* indolence, sloth, lethargy, listlessness, idleness, torpor, languor, lassitude

lazy *adj* indolent, idle, shiftless, slothful, apathetic ➡ **listless** ⇨ *ambitious*

lead 1. *vb* guide, direct, conduct, usher, steer, take, send, show, funnel ➡ **bring** ⇨ *follow*
2. *vb* direct, manage, supervise, administer, run, preside, oversee, chair, officiate ➡ **control, govern, command** ⇨ *follow*
3. *n* ➡ **front**

leadership *n* supervision, management, guidance, administration, direction ➡ **rule**

learn 1. *vb* ascertain, realize, discover, determine, see, find, find out
2. *vb* memorize, absorb, assimilate, master, digest ➡ **study, remember, practice**

least *adj* smallest, tiniest, minutest, slightest, minimal, minimum, merest ⇨ *best*

leave 1. *vb* depart, exit, embark, withdraw, desert, abandon, vacate, evacuate, forsake, quit, maroon, strand, set out, set off, flee, defect ➡ **go, move** ⇨ *enter, wait*
2. *vb* disembark, detrain, deplane, land ➡ **descend** ⇨ *enter*
3. *vb* will, bequeath, bestow, hand down ➡ **give**
4. *n* ➡ **vacation**

legal *adj* lawful, legitimate, permissible, statutory, prescribed, allowable, licit, constitutional, sanctioned, valid ➡ **official** ⇨ *illegal*

legendary *adj* mythical, mythological, fabulous, fabled, apocryphal, traditional, proverbial ➡ **imaginary**

If the word you want is not a main entry above, look below to find it.

laud ➡ **praise, worship**
laudable ➡ **praiseworthy**
laughable ➡ **funny**
launch ➡ **shoot, throw, start**
launder ➡ **clean**
laurel ➡ **prize**
lavatory ➡ **bathroom, sink**
lavender ➡ **purple**
lavish ➡ **generous, rich, wasteful**
law ➡ **rule, act**
lawbreaker ➡ **criminal**
law court ➡ **court**
lawful ➡ **legal**

lawlessness ➡ **confusion**
lawsuit ➡ **suit**
lawyer ➡ **adviser**
lax ➡ **negligent**
lay ➡ **put**
layabout ➡ **loafer**
layer cake ➡ **cake**
lay off ➡ **fire**
layout ➡ **order**
lay to rest ➡ **bury**
laze ➡ **rest**
lazybones ➡ **loafer**
leach ➡ **extract**
leaden ➡ **gray**

leader ➡ **boss, ruler, official, guide, headline**
leading ➡ **best**
leaf ➡ **page**
leaflet ➡ **pamphlet**
league ➡ **union, party**
leak ➡ **drop, hole**
lean ➡ **slant, thin**
leaning ➡ **tendency**
leap ➡ **jump**
learned ➡ **smart, educated**
learner ➡ **student**
learning ➡ **knowledge, education**
lease ➡ **agreement, hire**

leash ➡ **rope, prevent**
leaving ➡ **departure**
lecher ➡ **rascal**
lecture ➡ **speech, teach**
lecturer ➡ **speaker, teacher**
ledge ➡ **shelf**
leery ➡ **suspicious**
leftover ➡ **unnecessary**
left-wing ➡ **liberal**
leg ➡ **limb**
legacy ➡ **inheritance**
legal pad ➡ **notepad**
legalize ➡ **approve**
legend ➡ **myth, inscription**

---

n = noun • *vb* = verb • *adj* = adjective • *adv* = adverb • *prep* = preposition • *conj* = conjunction

legible *adj* readable, decipherable, distinct, clear, neat

leisure *n* freedom, relaxation, recreation, repose, ease ➡ **vacation**

lend *vb* loan, advance, furnish, extend ➡ **give, hire**

lengthen *vb* stretch, extend, prolong, elongate, protract, distend, amplify ⇨ *shrink, condense*

less 1. *adj* fewer, smaller, diminished, reduced, lower ⇨ *more*
2. *prep* ➡ **minus**

lesson *n* class, teaching, drill, exercise, homework, assignment ➡ **education**

let 1. *vb* allow, permit, authorize, license, tolerate, enable, entitle, qualify, empower ➡ **agree** ⇨ *prevent*
2. *vb* ➡ **hire**

letter *n* message, card, postcard, note, epistle, missive, memorandum, memo, reminder, dispatch ➡ **mail**

letter carrier *n* mail carrier, mailman, postman, postmaster, postmistress ➡ **messenger**

level 1. *adj* flat, smooth, even, flush, parallel, trim ➡ **straight**
2. *adj* plane, horizontal, flat ➡ **low**
3. *n* ➡ **grade, layer, floor**
4. *vb* ➡ **destroy**
5. *vb* even, smooth, flatten, grade, plane ➡ **straighten**

liar *n* fibber, storyteller, deceiver, prevaricator, perjurer, falsifier, equivocator ➡ **cheat**

liberal 1. *adj* ➡ **generous**
2. *adj* progressive, broadminded, radical, left-wing, reformist, humanistic ➡ **tolerant** ⇨ *conservative*

license 1. *n* permit, registration, copyright, franchise, charter, patent, grant ➡ **document**
2. *n* ➡ **permission, freedom, right**
3. *vb* ➡ **let**

lick 1. *vb* lap, tongue, flick
2. *n* ➡ **blow**[1]
3. *n* ➡ **bit**

If the word you want is not a main entry above, look below to find it.

legion ➡ crowd, army

legislate ➡ govern

legislation ➡ act

legislature ➡ government

legitimate ➡ legal, official, real

legume ➡ fruit

leisurely ➡ slow

leitmotif ➡ chorus

lemon ➡ yellow

length ➡ distance

lengthy ➡ long

lenient ➡ tolerant

lens ➡ glass

leprechaun ➡ fairy

lessen ➡ decrease, relieve

less than ➡ under

let down ➡ disappoint

letdown ➡ disappointment

let go ➡ fire

lethal ➡ deadly

lethargic ➡ listless

lethargy ➡ laziness

lettered ➡ educated

lettering ➡ inscription

letters ➡ literature

levee ➡ dam

lever ➡ lift

leviathan ➡ giant

levity ➡ humor, laughter

levy ➡ tax

lewd ➡ dirty

lexicon ➡ dictionary

liability ➡ guilt, debt

liable ➡ likely, guilty

liaison ➡ agent

libel ➡ insult

liberality ➡ generosity

liberate ➡ free

liberated ➡ free

liberation ➡ freedom, salvation

libertine ➡ rascal

liberty ➡ freedom

library ➡ den

libretto ➡ book

licensed ➡ official

lichen ➡ fungus

licit ➡ legal

lid ➡ top

---

lie 1. *n* falsehood, fib, untruth, fiction, story, tale, fabrication, invention, deception, disinformation, misrepresentation, concoction, canard ➡ **pretense, dishonesty** ⇨ *truth*

2. *vb* deceive, fib, prevaricate, falsify, mislead, dissemble, misstate, equivocate, fabricate ➡ **invent, pretend**

3. *vb* rest, recline, repose, sprawl, loll

life 1. *n* being, animation, vitality, breath, sentience, consciousness, living ➡ **existence**

2. *n* lifetime, longevity, span, career

3. *n* ➡ **energy**

lift 1. *vb* raise, elevate, hoist, boost, heave, uplift, rear, erect, pry, lever

2. *vb* ➡ **stop**

3. *vb* ➡ **disappear**

4. *n* boost, hand

light¹ 1. *n* radiance, illumination, luminosity, brilliance, brightness, glare, glow, sheen, glimmer, shine, gleam, luster, gloss, glitter, twinkle, sparkle, glint

2. *n* ➡ **day**

3. *n* lamp, lightbulb, bulb, streetlight, lantern, chandelier, flashlight, torch

4. *n* ray, beam, beacon, flash, flare, signal, spark

5. *adj* ➡ **bright**

6. *adj* ➡ **fair**

7. *vb* illuminate, light up, illumine, brighten, lighten

8. *vb* ignite, kindle, strike, fuel ➡ **burn**

light² 1. *adj* lightweight, underweight, slight, slender, scant, sparse, buoyant, weightless, insubstantial ⇨ *heavy*

2. *adj* ➡ **gentle**

3. *adj* ➡ **easy**

4. *vb* ➡ **descend**

like 1. *vb* enjoy, be fond of, care for, relish, fancy, delight in ➡ **love, appreciate**

2. *adj* ➡ **alike, same**

likely 1. *adj* liable, prone, apt, inclined, disposed

2. *adj* probable, apparent ➡ **possible**

limb 1. *n* bough, offshoot ➡ **branch, stick**

2. *n* member, appendage, extremity, arm, leg, wing, pinion, flipper, fin

limp 1. *vb* shuffle, stagger, hobble, totter, dodder, falter ➡ **walk**

2. *n* falter, halt, lameness, shuffle, gimp

3. *adj* flaccid, droopy, floppy, flabby, limber, slack ➡ **flexible**

link 1. *n* connection, association, contact, bond, correlation, attachment, tie, joint, affinity, affiliation, bridge, junction ➡ **union**

2. *vb* ➡ **join**

If the word you want is not a main entry above, look below to find it.

lieutenant ➡ **helper**

lifeless ➡ **dead, passive**

lifesaver ➡ **savior**

lifetime ➡ **life**

lightbulb ➡ **light¹**

lighten ➡ **light¹, relieve, bleach**

light-headed ➡ **dizzy**

lighthearted ➡ **carefree**

lightweight ➡ **light²**

likelihood ➡ **possibility**

liken ➡ **compare**

likeness ➡ **similarity, photograph, copy, statue**

likewise ➡ **alike**

lilac ➡ **purple**

Lilliputian ➡ **small**

limber ➡ **flexible, agile, limp**

lime ➡ **green**

limit ➡ **contain, horizon**

limitation ➡ **term**

limited ➡ **finite**

limitless ➡ **infinite, universal**

limo ➡ **taxi**

limousine ➡ **taxi**

limpid ➡ **transparent**

limping ➡ **lame**

line ➡ **rope, string, row**

lineage ➡ **ancestry, family**

linear ➡ **straight**

lineup ➡ **ballot**

linger ➡ **wait**

lingo ➡ **dialect**

lingua franca ➡ **language**

lip ➡ **edge**

n = noun • *vb* = verb • *adj* = adjective • *adv* = adverb • *prep* = preposition • *conj* = conjunction

liquid 1. *n* fluid, juice, sap, water, liquor ➡ **humidity**
2. *adj* fluid, flowing, molten, aqueous, watery ➡ **wet, damp**

list 1. *n* catalog, program, schedule, agenda, outline, menu, roster, inventory ➡ **table**
2. *vb* itemize, record, catalogue, inventory, register, tabulate, enumerate ➡ **specify**
3. *vb* ➡ **slant**

listen *vb* hear, hearken, hark, overhear, eavesdrop, attend

listless *adj* lethargic, sluggish, drowsy, languid, languorous ➡ **tired, lazy, passive, dull, slow** ⇨ *active*

literal 1. *adj* word-for-word, verbatim, exact ➡ **correct**
2. *adj* ➡ **real**

literature *n* letters, writing, belles-lettres

live¹ 1. *vb* exist, be, thrive, subsist, breathe ➡ **experience**
2. *vb* survive, outlive, outlast, persevere, persist ➡ **continue** ⇨ *die*
3. *vb* reside, dwell, stay, abide, inhabit, lodge, room, sojourn ➡ **occupy**

live² *adj* ➡ **lively, alive, active**

lively *adj* vital, energetic, vivacious, vigorous, industrious, spry, zestful, playful, spirited, sprightly, jaunty, brisk, zippy ➡ **active, alive** ⇨ *dull*

livestock *n* cattle, animals

living room *n* sitting room, drawing room, parlor, salon, lounge ➡ **room**

load 1. *n* burden, cargo, freight, shipment ➡ **weight**
2. *n* ➡ **abundance**
3. *vb* fill, pack, encumber, burden, stuff, cram, glut, stock, stow

loafer 1. *n* idler, layabout, slacker, sluggard, lazybones (*informal*), malingerer, ne'er-do-well, good-for-nothing (*informal*), drifter, deadbeat
2. *n* ➡ **shoe**

loan 1. *n* credit, advance, mortgage, rental, accommodation, allowance
2. *vb* ➡ **lend**

lock 1. *vb* fasten, latch, bolt, bar, secure ➡ **close**
2. *n* latch, catch, hook, bolt, padlock ➡ **clasp**
3. *n* tuft, ringlet, curl, tress, shock ➡ **braid, hair**

If the word you want is not a main entry above, look below to find it.

liquefy ➡ melt

liquor ➡ drink, liquid

listeners ➡ audience

listlessness ➡ exhaustion, laziness

literally ➡ really

literate ➡ educated

lithe ➡ flexible

lithograph ➡ print

litigant ➡ party

litigation ➡ suit

litter ➡ trash, mess, bed

little ➡ small

liturgical ➡ religious

livelihood ➡ support, profession

liveliness ➡ energy, activity

live through ➡ experience

livid ➡ angry, sore

living ➡ alive, life, job

lizard ➡ reptile

loaded ➡ full

loaf ➡ bread, rest

loam ➡ dirt

loath ➡ reluctant

loathe ➡ hate

loathing ➡ hatred, disgust

loathsome ➡ ugly

lobby ➡ hall, party

local ➡ native, near

locale ➡ place

locality ➡ place

locate ➡ find, base, place

location ➡ place

loch ➡ lake

locker ➡ closet, cupboard, chest

locks ➡ hair

locomotion ➡ movement

locution ➡ speech, word

lodge ➡ house, hotel, live¹, embed

lodging ➡ room

loft ➡ attic

loftiness ➡ height

lofty ➡ high, dignified

log ➡ wood

---

lonely *adj* lonesome, homesick, solitary, friendless, outcast ➡ **alone, sad**

long 1. *adj* lengthy, tall, extended, elongated, outstretched, extensive ➡ **big** ⇨ *short*
2. *adj* lengthy, protracted, unending, long-winded, sustained
3. *vb* ➡ **want**

look 1. *vb* watch, glance, observe, witness, view, regard, spy, sight, eye, survey, peek ➡ **see, stare, examine**
2. *vb* seem, appear ➡ **resemble**
3. *vb* ➡ **hunt**
4. *n* glance, peek, view, gaze, glimpse, scrutiny, inspection
5. *n* ➡ **appearance**

lose 1. *vb* misplace, mislay, drop, miss ➡ **forget** ⇨ *find*
2. *vb* succumb, fall, fail ➡ **surrender** ⇨ *win*

lost 1. *adj* missing, mislaid, misplaced ➡ **absent**
2. *adj* ➡ **homeless**

lottery *n* raffle, pool, sweepstakes, wager ➡ **gambling**

loud 1. *adj* noisy, resounding, deafening, thunderous, earsplitting, piercing, resonant, strident, shrill ➡ **audible, high** ⇨ *quiet*
2. *adj* boisterous, rowdy, rambunctious, raucous, vociferous, clamorous, obstreperous, stentorian, cacophonous, uproarious ➡ **rude**
3. *adj* garish, flashy, gaudy, showy, ostentatious, tacky ➡ **bright, fancy**

love 1. *vb* adore, cherish, admire, worship, idolize, dote on, revere ➡ **like, court** ⇨ *hate*
2. *n* affection, devotion, fondness, passion, tenderness, adoration, attachment, infatuation ➡ **kindness, desire, virtue** ⇨ *hate*
3. *n* ➡ lover, beloved, darling, dear, sweetheart, girlfriend, boyfriend, fiancé, fiancée
4. *n* ➡ **zero** (*in tennis*)

loving *adj* affectionate, caring, devoted, tender, attentive, demonstrative, amorous, romantic, passionate, adoring, ardent, fond ➡ **friendly, eager**

If the word you want is not a main entry above, look below to find it.

logic ➡ reason
logical ➡ valid
logician ➡ philosopher
logo ➡ label
loiter ➡ wait
loll ➡ lie
lone ➡ alone, only
lonesome ➡ lonely
longevity ➡ life
longhand ➡ handwriting

longing ➡ hope, desire
long-suffering ➡ patient
long-winded ➡ long, talkative
look forward to ➡ anticipate
looking glass ➡ mirror
look like ➡ resemble
lookout ➡ patrol, watch
looks ➡ appearance
loom ➡ approach, tower

loop ➡ round, circle, ring
loose ➡ free
loosen ➡ free
loot ➡ booty, pillage
looting ➡ theft
lope ➡ run
loquacious ➡ talkative
lord ➡ ruler, noble
lore ➡ myth, superstition
loss ➡ defeat, death, harm

lot ➡ chance, number, property, abundance, fate
lotion ➡ medicine
lounge ➡ bar, hall, living room, rest
louse ➡ fumble
lousy ➡ bad
lout ➡ boor
loveliness ➡ beauty
lovely ➡ pretty
lover ➡ love

n = noun • *vb* = verb • *adj* = adjective • *adv* = adverb • *prep* = preposition • *conj* = conjunction

low 1. *adj* squat, level, low-lying, low-hanging ➡ **short**
2. *adj* low-pitched, bass, baritone
3. *adj* ➡ **quiet**
4. *adj* ➡ **mean**
5. *adj* ➡ **sad**

loyalty *n* allegiance, fidelity, faithfulness, devotion, fealty, dependability, dedication, patriotism

luck *n* windfall, godsend, opportunity, break, success ➡ **chance**

lucky *adj* fortunate, auspicious, serendipitous, providential ➡ **accidental, magic**

luggage *n* baggage, suitcase, trunk, duffel bag, overnight bag, garment bag, valise, gear, effects ➡ **bag**

lump *n* mass, glob, clot, clump, chunk, hunk, blob, tuft ➡ **bulge, growth, pile**

If the word you want is not a main entry above, look below to find it.

lower ➡ less, subordinate, decrease, frown

lowering ➡ cloudy

lower than ➡ under

lowest ➡ worst

low-hanging ➡ low

lowland ➡ valley

low-lying ➡ low

lowness ➡ depth

low-pitched ➡ low

low-priced ➡ cheap

loyal ➡ faithful, patriotic

LPN ➡ nurse

lube ➡ oil

lubricate ➡ oil

lucid ➡ articulate, sane, transparent

lucidity ➡ reason, clarity

ludicrous ➡ foolish, funny, strange

lug ➡ carry

lukewarm ➡ warm

lull ➡ break, calm

lullaby ➡ song

lumber ➡ board, wood, walk

luminary ➡ celebrity

luminosity ➡ light[1]

luminous ➡ bright

lummox ➡ boor

lunacy ➡ nonsense

lunatic ➡ insane

luncheonette ➡ restaurant

lunchtime ➡ afternoon

lunge ➡ jump

lurch ➡ trip, swing

lure ➡ tempt, attraction

lurid ➡ sensational

lurk ➡ sneak

luscious ➡ delicious, rich

lush ➡ rich, tropical, drunkard

lust ➡ desire

luster ➡ light[1]

lustrous ➡ shiny

luxurious ➡ rich

luxury ➡ wealth, elegance

lying ➡ dishonest

lying (down) ➡ prone

lyric ➡ song, poem

lyrical ➡ musical

---

magic 1. *adj* enchanted, charmed, magical, mystical, occult, bewitching, entrancing, spellbinding ➡ **lucky, mysterious**
2. *n* sorcery, witchcraft, wizardry, enchantment, hocus-pocus, voodoo

magician 1. *n* conjurer, enchanter, sorcerer, wizard, witch, warlock, shaman, medicine man ➡ **prophet**
2. *n* illusionist, prestidigitator, escape artist, Houdini

mail 1. *n* post, correspondence, communication ➡ **letter, package**

2. *vb* ➡ **send**

make 1. *vb* create, make up, manufacture, produce, fashion, model, compose, constitute, forge, strike ➡ **build, form, invent**
2. *vb* ➡ **force**
3. *vb* ➡ **earn**
4. *n* brand, model, brand name ➡ **type**

man *n* gentleman, boy, guy, fellow, husband, male, chap, lad ➡ **human being, humanity, adult**

If the word you want is not a main entry above, look below to find it.

macabre ➡ gruesome
machine ➡ tool, engine
machine gun ➡ gun
machine-made ➡ manufactured
machinery ➡ equipment
machinist ➡ mechanic
macho ➡ masculine
mad ➡ angry, insane
madden ➡ anger
made ➡ manufactured
madness ➡ hysteria, nonsense
madrigal ➡ song
magazine ➡ paper, warehouse
magenta ➡ purple
maggot ➡ larva
magical ➡ magic
magistrate ➡ judge
magnanimous ➡ noble
magnate ➡ tycoon

magnetic ➡ attractive
magnetism ➡ personality
magnificent ➡ grand, beautiful
magnify ➡ strengthen, grow, exaggerate
magnifying glass ➡ glass
magnitude ➡ size
magnum opus ➡ masterpiece
maharajah ➡ king
maharani ➡ queen
maiden ➡ woman
mail carrier ➡ letter carrier
mailman ➡ letter carrier
maim ➡ mutilate
main ➡ important
mainly ➡ chiefly
mainstay ➡ anchor, support
maintain ➡ keep, save, own, support, argue
maintenance ➡ support

maitre d' ➡ host
majestic ➡ grand
majesty ➡ excellence
major ➡ important, course
majority ➡ most, maturity
makeshift ➡ temporary
makeup ➡ disguise
malady ➡ illness
male ➡ man, masculine
malefactor ➡ criminal
malevolence ➡ hatred
malevolent ➡ wicked, ominous
malfunctioning ➡ broken
malice ➡ hatred, envy
malicious ➡ mean
malign ➡ insult
malignant ➡ mean, deadly
malingerer ➡ loafer
mall ➡ market
malleable ➡ flexible

mallet ➡ hammer, bat
malnourished ➡ hungry
maltreat ➡ abuse
mammoth ➡ giant, huge
manacle ➡ bond
manage ➡ control, afford, lead
manageable ➡ tame
management ➡ leadership
manager ➡ boss
mañana ➡ future
mandarin orange ➡ orange
mandate ➡ order
mandatory ➡ necessary
mane ➡ hair
maneuver ➡ movement, tactic, drive
mangle ➡ mutilate, iron
mangy ➡ shabby
manhood ➡ maturity
mania ➡ obsession, hysteria

n = noun • *vb* = verb • *adj* = adjective • *adv* = adverb • *prep* = preposition • *conj* = conjunction

manufactured *vb* made, machine-made, manmade, mass-produced, synthetic, artificial, human-made

many 1. *adj* numerous, various, countless, manifold, diverse, multiple, innumerable, sundry, myriad ➡ **different** ⇨ *few*
2. *n* ➡ **abundance**

market 1. *n* supermarket, store, shop, grocery, mall, shopping mall, marketplace, mart, general store, bazaar, emporium, flea market
2. *vb* ➡ **sell**

marriage 1. *n* wedding, nuptials, espousal ➡ **union**

2. *n* matrimony, wedlock

married *adj* wed, wedded, espoused, attached, betrothed, engaged ⇨ *single*

marry *vb* wed, espouse ➡ **join**

masculine *adj* male, manly, virile, macho, gentlemanly, fatherly ➡ **feminine**

masterpiece *n* masterwork, showpiece, classic, magnum opus (*Latin*), pièce de résistance (*French*), monument

mathematics *n* computation, calculation, math ➡ **science**

If the word you want is not a main entry above, look below to find it.

maniac ➡ extremist
maniacal ➡ insane
manifest ➡ show
manifestation ➡ sign
manifold ➡ many
manikin ➡ midget
manipulate ➡ touch, tinker
mankind ➡ humanity
manly ➡ masculine
manmade ➡ manufactured
mannequin ➡ model, doll, puppet
manner ➡ method, type, bearing
mannerism ➡ habit
manners ➡ behavior
manor ➡ home
mansion ➡ home
manslaughter ➡ murder
mantel ➡ shelf
mantelpiece ➡ shelf
mantle ➡ wrap, coat
manual ➡ book

manufacture ➡ make, assembly
manufacturing ➡ business
manuscript ➡ book, document
map ➡ plan
mar ➡ damage
marathon ➡ race
marauder ➡ pirate
march ➡ walk, parade, movement, border
mare ➡ horse
margin ➡ edge
marimba ➡ xylophone
marine ➡ nautical
mariner ➡ sailor
marionette ➡ puppet
maritime ➡ nautical
mark ➡ spot, signature, tick, label, scar
marked ➡ obvious
marker ➡ pen, monument, label
marketing ➡ sale

marketplace ➡ market
marmalade ➡ jelly
maroon ➡ red, leave
marrow ➡ essence
marsh ➡ swamp
marshal ➡ police officer, mobilize, deploy
marshland ➡ swamp
mart ➡ market
martial ➡ military
martyr ➡ kill
marvel ➡ miracle
marvelous ➡ great
mash ➡ grind
mask ➡ disguise, hide
masking tape ➡ adhesive
masquerade ➡ disguise
mass ➡ size, density, weight, measure, lump, pile
massacre ➡ kill, murder
massage ➡ rub
massive ➡ heavy, huge
mass media ➡ media

mass-produced ➡ manufactured
master ➡ learn, expert, principal, owner
masterly ➡ expert
mastermind ➡ genius
master of ceremonies ➡ host
masterwork ➡ masterpiece
mastery ➡ victory, rule
mat ➡ cushion, rug
match ➡ game, agree, resemble, compare, equal
matching ➡ same
matchless ➡ unique
mate ➡ equal, spouse
material ➡ cloth, matter, real
materiality ➡ existence
materialize ➡ appear
matériel ➡ arms, ammunition
maternal ➡ motherly
math ➡ mathematics
matriarch ➡ ancestor

➡ = synonym cross-reference • ⇨ = antonym cross-reference

matter 1. *n* substance, material, body, element, constituent, stuff
2. *n* ➡ **subject**
3. *n* ➡ **business**
4. *n* ➡ **trouble**
5. *vb* count, signify, imply ➡ **mean**

maturity *n* adulthood, majority, womanhood, manhood

maybe *adv* perhaps, possibly, conceivably, feasibly, perchance ➡ **probably**
All of these words express uncertainty about something. **Maybe** *and* **perhaps** *are very close synonyms and it usually makes no difference which one you use.* **Possibly** *stresses the uncertainty more than* **maybe.** **Conceivably** *and* **feasibly** *suggest even greater uncertainty.* **Perchance** *is a more formal and less common synonym.*

maze *n* labyrinth, network, morass, jungle, tangle ➡ **net, mess, confusion**

meal *n* refreshment, repast, bite, snack, picnic, banquet, dish ➡ **feast, food, board**

mean 1. *adj* cruel, vicious, malicious, merciless, savage, malignant, ruthless, brutal, low, cold-blooded, inhuman, relentless, pitiless, unkind ➡ **violent, revengeful**
2. *adj* small-minded, petty, selfish, intolerant ➡ **prejudiced, greedy** ⇨ *tolerant*
3. *adj* ➡ **middle**
4. *n* ➡ **average**
5. *vb* signify, indicate, symbolize, connote, denote, imply, spell ➡ **matter, intend, suggest**

meaning *n* sense, denotation, connotation, definition, significance, implication, import

meaningful *adj* significant, telling, pregnant, expressive ➡ **important**

measure 1. *n* dimension, distance, capacity, weight, volume, mass, amount ➡ **number, size, speed**
2. *n* rule, gauge, scale, standard, criterion, benchmark, yardstick, touchstone
3. *n* ➡ **rhythm**
4. *vb* weigh, gauge, rule, time

mechanic *n* repairman, machinist, technician, grease monkey (*informal*)

meddle *vb* interfere, intervene, intrude, pry, snoop, tamper

meddlesome *adj* intrusive, obtrusive, interfering, meddling, pushy ➡ **curious**

media *n, pl* mass media, communications

If the word you want is not a main entry above, look below to find it.

matrimony ➡ **marriage**
matron ➡ **woman**
matronly ➡ **feminine**
matter-of-fact ➡ **practical**
mattress ➡ **bed**
mature ➡ **adult, old, gifted, grow**
maudlin ➡ **emotional**
maul ➡ **hit, hammer**
mausoleum ➡ **grave, monument**

mauve ➡ **purple**
maxim ➡ **saying**
maximum ➡ **most**
mayhem ➡ **confusion, mess, damage**
MC ➡ **host**
M.D. ➡ **doctor**
meadow ➡ **field**
meager ➡ **small, trivial**
mealy-mouthed ➡ **servile**
meander ➡ **wander, bend**

meandering ➡ **zigzag, indirect**
meanest ➡ **worst**
meaningless ➡ **empty**
means ➡ **tool, wealth**
measurable ➡ **finite**
mechanical ➡ **automatic**
mechanism ➡ **tool**
mechanized ➡ **automatic**
medal ➡ **award**
medalist ➡ **winner**

medallion ➡ **badge**
meddling ➡ **meddlesome, interference**
median ➡ **average, middle**
mediate ➡ **negotiate, decide**
medic ➡ **nurse**
medical ➡ **medicinal**
medical center ➡ **hospital**
medicate ➡ **heal**
medication ➡ **medicine**

n = noun • *vb* = verb • *adj* = adjective • *adv* = adverb • *prep* = preposition • *conj* = conjunction

medicinal *adj* medical, therapeutic, healing, curative, remedial, pharmaceutical

medicine 1. *n* medication, prescription, pill, tablet, capsule, ointment, lotion, injection, shot, vaccine ➡ **cure, drug**
2. *n* medical science, medical profession, healing ➡ **science**

mediocrity *n* inferiority, inadequacy, ordinariness

meditate *vb* ponder, contemplate, muse, reflect, speculate ➡ **think, consider**

meeting 1. *n* appointment, engagement, date, rendezvous, tryst, encounter, confrontation, run-in, brush
2. *n* conference, assembly, gathering, reunion, convention, council, interview, session ➡ **talk**
3. *n* ➡ **introduction**
4. *n* ➡ **junction**

melt *vb* dissolve, thaw, liquefy, fuse, evaporate, soften ➡ **disappear**

member 1. *n* affiliate, constituent, fellow, enrollee, colleague, participant ➡ **partner**
2. *n* ➡ **limb**

memorable *adj* unforgettable, momentous, historic, notable, monumental ➡ **important**

memory *n* recollection, reminiscence, recall, remembrance, déjà vu

mention 1. *vb* refer to, touch on, infer, allude, state, name, specify ➡ **say, suggest, broach**
2. *n* ➡ **remark**

mess 1. *n* jumble, tangle, litter, clutter, mayhem, hodgepodge, muddle, hash ➡ **confusion**
2. *vb* ➡ **disturb, dirty**
3. *vb* ➡ **tinker**

messenger *n* courier, carrier, runner, envoy, ambassador, emissary

messy *adj* untidy, disorderly, sloppy, slovenly, disheveled, bedraggled, unkempt ➡ **dirty** ⇨ *neat*

If the word you want is not a main entry above, look below to find it.

medicine man ➡ magician

mediocre ➡ cheap, average, fair

meditative ➡ thoughtful

medium ➡ average, setting, tool, prophet

medley ➡ assortment

meek ➡ humble, shy, gentle

meet ➡ touch, gather, obey, game

megalopolis ➡ town

melancholy ➡ sad, sorrow

melee ➡ fight

mellow ➡ carefree

melodious ➡ musical

melodrama ➡ play

melodramatic ➡ sensational

melody ➡ song, music

membrane ➡ layer

memento ➡ reminder

memo ➡ letter

memoir ➡ diary

memo pad ➡ notepad

memorandum ➡ letter

memorial ➡ reminder, monument

memorial park ➡ cemetery

memorialize ➡ remember

memorize ➡ learn

menace ➡ danger, threaten

menacing ➡ ominous

menagerie ➡ zoo

mend ➡ fix, repair, heal, sew

men's room ➡ bathroom

mental ➡ insane, intellectual

mental health ➡ reason

mentor ➡ teacher

menu ➡ list

mercenary ➡ soldier

merchandise ➡ product

merchant ➡ seller

merciful ➡ kind

merciless ➡ mean

mercurial ➡ fickle

mercy ➡ kindness, pity, forgiveness

mere ➡ trivial

merely ➡ only

merest ➡ least

merge ➡ mix, unify

merger ➡ union

meringue ➡ icing

merit ➡ worth, deserve

meritorious ➡ praiseworthy

merriment ➡ mirth, laughter

merry ➡ happy

merrymaking ➡ party

mesa ➡ mountain, plateau

mesh ➡ net

mesmerize ➡ enchant

message ➡ announcement, letter

metamorphosis ➡ change

metaphysics ➡ philosophy

---

meteor *n* meteorite, shooting star, falling star, comet, asteroid

method *n* approach, procedure, process, technique, system, routine, manner, way ➡ **plan**

middle 1. *n* center, core, midpoint, hub, nucleus, focus, midst, interior, inside, soul, depth ➡ **essence**
2. *adj* central, inner, interior, median, mean, midmost, intermediate ➡ **inside, average**

midget *n* dwarf, pygmy, manikin

military 1. *adj* armed, militant, combative, warlike, martial, militaristic, bellicose, soldierly
2. *n* ➡ **army**

mind 1. *n* brain, intellect, intelligence, psyche, consciousness, subconscious, ego ➡ **soul, wisdom**
2. *n* ➡ **belief**

3. *vb* ➡ **protect**
4. *vb* ➡ **obey**

mine 1. *n* quarry, pit, excavation, tunnel ➡ **hole**
2. *n* ➡ **supply**

minister 1. *n* preacher, pastor, rector, chaplain, clergyman, clergywoman, clergy, cleric ➡ **priest, religious**
2. *n* ➡ **diplomat**

minus 1. *prep* less, without, diminished by
2. *n* ➡ **defect**

miracle *n* wonder, marvel, phenomenon, rarity, oddity, portent

mirror 1. *n* looking glass, glass, reflector
2. *vb* ➡ **reflect**

mirth *n* merriment, joviality, festivity, gaiety ➡ **humor, pleasure, laughter**

If the word you want is not a main entry above, look below to find it.

meteoric ➡ sudden
meteorite ➡ meteor
mete out ➡ inflict, share
meter ➡ rhythm
meticulous ➡ careful
meticulously ➡ carefully
métier ➡ specialty
metropolis ➡ town
metropolitan ➡ urban
mettle ➡ courage
microscope ➡ glass
microscopic ➡ invisible
microwave ➡ cook
midday ➡ day, afternoon
middleman ➡ agent
midmost ➡ middle
midnight ➡ night

midpoint ➡ middle, average
midriff ➡ stomach
midsection ➡ stomach
midshipman ➡ sailor
midst ➡ middle
midterm ➡ examination
mien ➡ bearing, appearance
might ➡ strength
mighty ➡ strong, huge
migrant ➡ traveler
migrate ➡ move
migration ➡ movement
mikado ➡ emperor
mild ➡ gentle, fair, insipid, warm
mildew ➡ fungus
mild-tempered ➡ patient
milestone ➡ event

milieu ➡ setting
militant ➡ belligerent, military
militaristic ➡ military
militia ➡ army
milky ➡ white
mill ➡ factory
millionaire ➡ tycoon
mimic ➡ imitate
minaret ➡ tower
mince ➡ cut
mindfully ➡ carefully
mingle ➡ mix
miniature ➡ small, model
minimal ➡ least
minimum ➡ least
minion ➡ servant
minor ➡ trivial, child, course

minority ➡ childhood
minstrel ➡ musician
minstrelsy ➡ music
minute ➡ small, trivial, moment
minutest ➡ least
miraculous ➡ awesome
mirage ➡ illusion
mire ➡ swamp, dirt, catch
misanthrope ➡ miser, skeptic
misapprehension ➡ misunderstanding
misbehave ➡ disobey
misbehavior ➡ mischief
miscalculation ➡ mistake
miscellaneous ➡ different
miscellany ➡ assortment, mixture

mischief *n* misconduct, misbehavior, devilment, tomfoolery, rascality, shenanigans (*informal*) ➡ **trouble**

mischievous *adj* naughty, disobedient, unruly, wayward, spoiled, ill-behaved, impish, elfish, elfin ➡ **rude, rebellious, bad** ⇨ *good*

miser *n* skinflint, penny-pincher, scrooge, niggard, cheapskate, tightwad, hoarder, misanthrope

misery *n* suffering, agony, anguish, distress, grief, pain, torment, torture, heartache ➡ **hardship, sorrow**

missile 1. *n* projectile, arrow, dart, lance, spear, javelin, bullet, shell, bolt, slug
2. *n* rocket, torpedo, ICBM

mistake 1. *n* error, slip, blunder, oversight, faux pas, inaccuracy, fallacy, miscalculation, blooper (*informal*), boo-boo (*informal*) ➡ **fault, defect, misunderstanding**
2. *vb* ➡ **misunderstand**

misunderstand *vb* misinterpret, misjudge, misconstrue, mistake, err

misunderstanding 1. *n* misapprehension, misconception, confusion ➡ **mistake**
2. *n* ➡ **argument**

mix 1. *vb* combine, blend, merge, mingle, compound, consolidate, stir, whip, beat, knead, roll, churn, jumble, scramble, shuffle ➡ **join**
2. *vb* associate, mingle, intermingle, socialize, fraternize, consort, hobnob (*informal*) ➡ **join**
3. *n* ➡ **assortment**

mixture *n* combination, blend, composite, compound, solution, amalgam, amalgamation, potpourri, miscellany, concoction ➡ **mess, hybrid**

mobilize *vb* muster, enlist, marshal, summon, rally ➡ **gather**

If the word you want is not a main entry above, look below to find it.

misconception ➡ **misunderstanding**
misconduct ➡ **mischief**
misconstrue ➡ **misunderstand, distort**
misdeed ➡ **crime**
misdemeanor ➡ **crime**
miserable ➡ **sad, bad**
miserly ➡ **cheap**
misfortune ➡ **hardship, disaster**
misgiving ➡ **doubt**
mishap ➡ **accident**
misinterpret ➡ **misunderstand**

misjudge ➡ **misunderstand**
mislaid ➡ **lost**
mislay ➡ **lose**
mislead ➡ **lie**
misleading ➡ **unreliable**
mispend ➡ **waste**
misplace ➡ **lose**
misplaced ➡ **lost**
misremember ➡ **forget**
misrepresent ➡ **distort**
misrepresentation ➡ **lie, pretense**
miss ➡ **lose, exclude**
misshapen ➡ **bent**

missing ➡ **absent, lost**
mission ➡ **job, committee, church**
missive ➡ **letter**
misstate ➡ **lie**
mist ➡ **fog, cloud**
mistaken ➡ **wrong**
mistreat ➡ **abuse**
mistreatment ➡ **abuse**
mistress ➡ **owner**
mistrust ➡ **doubt**
misty ➡ **wet**
misuse ➡ **abuse, waste**

mitigate ➡ **relieve**
mitt ➡ **glove**
mitten ➡ **glove**
mixer ➡ **dance**
moan ➡ **cry, complain**
moat ➡ **channel**
mob ➡ **crowd**
mobile ➡ **portable**
mobility ➡ **movement**
mock ➡ **imitate, ridicule, fake**
mockery ➡ **ridicule**
mock-up ➡ **model**
mode ➡ **fashion**

model 1. *n* paragon, ideal, archetype, exemplar, paradigm, nonpareil, standard, prototype, original ➡ **example**
2. *n* miniature, representation, reduction, mock-up ➡ **copy, duplicate**
3. *n* ➡ **make, pattern**
4. *n* subject, sitter, fashion model, poser, mannequin
5. *vb* ➡ **make**
6. *vb* pose, sit ➡ **show**
7. *adj* classic, outstanding, first-rate, excellent, authoritative, typical, archetypal, definitive ➡ **perfect**

modern 1. *adj* contemporary, current, up-to-date, stylish, recent, modernistic, newfangled, space-age, state-of-the-art, latter-day ➡ **new**
2. Modern *adj* ➡ **art**

moment 1. *n* instant, point, minute, second, twinkling, wink, jiffy, flash, trice, time ➡ **period**
2. *n* ➡ **importance**

monastery *n* abbey, convent, nunnery, cloister, priory, friary, lamasery, ashram

money *n* cash, currency, coin, revenue, capital, specie ➡ **wealth, property**

monopoly *n* trust, syndicate, cartel, corner, consortium, ownership

monster *n* beast, ogre, ghoul, brute, savage, freak, monstrosity ➡ **animal**

monument 1. *n* marker, shrine, mausoleum, memorial, tribute ➡ **reminder, statue**
2. *n* ➡ **masterpiece**

mood *n* humor, morale, temper, temperament, disposition, spirits, vein ➡ **state, setting**

mope *vb* sulk, pout, brood ➡ **worry, grieve**

more 1. *adj* additional, extra, added, further, supplementary, another, new ⇨ *less*
2. *adv* additionally, furthermore, still, yet, better, preferably, sooner, rather
3. *n* increase, supplement, extra, surplus

If the word you want is not a main entry above, look below to find it.

moderate ➡ easy, gentle, slow, conservative, negotiate

moderation ➡ abstinence

moderator ➡ host

modernistic ➡ modern

modernity ➡ novelty

modest ➡ humble, average

modesty ➡ virtue

modicum ➡ bit

modification ➡ change

modify ➡ change, adjust, soften

moist ➡ damp

moisten ➡ wet

moisture ➡ humidity

mold ➡ form, fungus

molder ➡ decay

moldy ➡ stale, bad

mole ➡ growth

molecule ➡ atom

molest ➡ abuse

mollify ➡ pacify

molt ➡ shed

molten ➡ liquid

momentarily ➡ soon

momentary ➡ temporary

momentous ➡ memorable

momentum ➡ progress, impulse

monarch ➡ king, queen

monetary ➡ financial

moneyed ➡ rich

mongrel ➡ dog, hybrid

monitor ➡ guardian

monk ➡ religious

monogram ➡ signature

monotonous ➡ dull

monotony ➡ boredom

monsoon ➡ storm

monstrosity ➡ monster

monstrous ➡ huge

monumental ➡ memorable

mooch ➡ borrow

moody ➡ temperamental, sad

moor ➡ dock, plain

mooring ➡ anchor

mop ➡ sweep

moral ➡ good

morale ➡ mood

morality ➡ virtue

moralize ➡ preach

morass ➡ maze

morbid ➡ gruesome

moreover ➡ besides

more than ➡ above

morning *n* a.m., daybreak, dawn, sunrise, sunup, morn ➡ **day** ⇨ *evening*

mortal 1. *adj* human, transient, frail, impermanent, perishable ➡ **temporary** ⇨ *eternal*
2. *adj* ➡ **deadly**
3. *n* ➡ **human being**

most 1. *adj* maximum, utmost, greatest
2. *n* majority, maximum, bulk, preponderance
3. *adv* ➡ **very, best**

motherly *adj* maternal, parental, protective ➡ **feminine, fatherly**

mountain *n* mount, peak, ridge, summit, butte, mesa ➡ **hill, cliff** ⇨ *valley*

move 1. *vb* shift, remove, budge, dislodge ➡ **carry, push**
2. *vb* transfer, relocate, migrate, emigrate, immigrate ➡ **leave, go, travel**
3. *vb* ➡ **affect**
4. *vb* ➡ **suggest**

movement 1. *n* locomotion, motion, progress, shift, mobility, play, maneuver ➡ **activity, speed**
2. *n* campaign, crusade, march, faction, demonstration ➡ **cause**
3. *n* migration, immigration, emigration, transition, displacement, removal, transfer, transmission, conveyance
4. *n* ➡ **gait**

movie *n* film, picture, show, video, flick (*informal*) ➡ **play**

movies *n* pictures, cinema, silver screen

much 1. *adv* greatly, enormously, extremely, dearly ➡ **very, far**
2. *adj* ➡ **enough, abundant**
3. *n* ➡ **abundance**

mumble *vb* murmur, mutter, whisper, breathe, sigh ➡ **complain, say, talk, stammer**

If the word you want is not a main entry above, look below to find it.

morn ➡ morning
moron ➡ fool
morose ➡ pessimistic
morrow ➡ future
morsel ➡ bite
mortgage ➡ loan, pawn
mortified ➡ ashamed
mortify ➡ embarrass
mosque ➡ church
mostly ➡ chiefly
motel ➡ hotel
motet ➡ hymn
mother ➡ parent
motherland ➡ country
motif ➡ pattern, chorus

motion ➡ movement, activity, wave
motionless ➡ stationary, passive, dead
motivate ➡ cause
motivation ➡ incentive
motive ➡ reason, incentive
motley ➡ different
motor ➡ engine
motorcade ➡ parade
motorcyclist ➡ rider
motorized ➡ automatic
mottled ➡ speckled
motto ➡ saying
mound ➡ pile, hill
mount ➡ ascend, enter, mountain, horse

mourn ➡ grieve
mournful ➡ pitiful
mouth ➡ door
mouthful ➡ bite
mouth-watering ➡ delicious
movable ➡ portable
moving ➡ emotional
mow ➡ cut
mucilage ➡ adhesive
muck ➡ dirt
mud ➡ dirt
muddle ➡ fumble, mess
muddy ➡ dirty
mudslide ➡ avalanche
muff ➡ fumble

muffle ➡ quiet
muffler ➡ wrap
mug ➡ glass, attack
mugginess ➡ humidity
muggy ➡ damp, tropical
mulish ➡ stubborn
multiple ➡ many
multiply ➡ reproduce, grow
multitude ➡ crowd
mum ➡ quiet
mummify ➡ embalm, bury
munch ➡ bite
municipal ➡ public, urban
municipality ➡ town
munificence ➡ generosity
munitions ➡ ammunition

➡ = synonym cross-reference • ⇨ = antonym cross-reference

murder 1. *n* homicide, manslaughter, assassination, bloodshed, massacre, slaughter, slaying, carnage, annihilation ➡ **crime**
2. *vb* ➡ **kill**

music *n* harmony, melody, minstrelsy ➡ **song**

musical 1. *adj* harmonious, melodious, tuneful, lyrical, symphonic, rhythmical, euphonious, assonant
2. *adj* ➡ **talented**
3. *n* ➡ **play**

musician *n* composer, player, instrumentalist, performer, entertainer, minstrel, troubadour, bard ➡ **singer, artist**

mutilate *vb* maim, disfigure, dismember, mangle, disable ➡ **hurt, destroy**

mysterious *adj* puzzling, enigmatic, perplexing, baffling, inexplicable, uncanny, mystic, mystical ➡ **magic, strange, obscure**

myth *n* legend, fable, epic, lore, folklore, tradition, mythology ➡ **story, superstition**

If the word you want is not a main entry above, look below to find it.

murderer ➡ killer
murderous ➡ deadly
murk ➡ fog
murky ➡ dark, dim
murmur ➡ mumble, hum, rustle
muscle ➡ strength
muscular ➡ strong
muse ➡ meditate
museum ➡ gallery

mushroom ➡ fungus, grow
musket ➡ gun
muss ➡ disturb
must ➡ need, necessity
muster ➡ mobilize
musty ➡ stale, trite
mutable ➡ variable
mutate ➡ change
mutation ➡ change
mute ➡ dumb, quiet

mutineer ➡ rebel
mutinous ➡ rebellious
mutiny ➡ treason, rebel
mutt ➡ dog
mutter ➡ mumble
mutual ➡ common
mutually ➡ together
muumuu ➡ dress
muzzle ➡ quiet
muzzle loader ➡ gun

myriad ➡ many
mystery ➡ secret, problem, play
mystic ➡ mysterious
mystical ➡ magic, mysterious, supernatural
mystify ➡ confuse
mythical ➡ legendary
mythological ➡ legendary
mythology ➡ myth, religion

n = noun • *vb* = verb • *adj* = adjective • *adv* = adverb • *prep* = preposition • *conj* = conjunction

nail 1. *n* spike, brad, stud, tack, bolt, rivet, screw, peg, dowel ➡ **pin**
2. *vb* pin, tack, screw, bolt, rivet ➡ **join**

naive *adj* unsophisticated, inexperienced, simple, innocent, artless, ingenuous, trusting, green, gullible, credulous ➡ **unaware, amateur, harmless**

naked *adj* undressed, nude, exposed, unclothed, unclad, bare, stripped, bald
Some people consider **nude** *to be a more polite word than* **naked** *when referring to the unclothed human body.* **Nude** *is the term regularly used in reference to works of art showing unclothed figures.*

name 1. *n* appellation, proper name, surname, designation, nickname, epithet, title, heading ➡ **label**
2. *n* ➡ **reputation**
3. *n* ➡ **celebrity**
4. *vb* christen, nickname, call, dub, designate, entitle, title, label, identify
5. *vb* ➡ **mention**
6. *vb* appoint, delegate, nominate, assign ➡ **choose**

narrow *adj* snug, thin, slender, constricted, close, slim ➡ **small** ⇨ *broad*

native 1. *adj* indigenous, aboriginal, endemic, original, domestic, local, homegrown ➡ **natural**
2. *n* ➡ **citizen**

natural 1. *adj* organic, pure, unprocessed, raw, uncooked ➡ **plain, normal**
2. *adj* inborn, inherent, instinctive, innate, hereditary, inherited, congenital, genetic, intrinsic ➡ **native**

nature 1. *n* environment, outdoors, out-of-doors, landscape ➡ **earth**
2. *n* ➡ **type**
3. *n* ➡ **personality**

nausea *n* indigestion, queasiness, vomiting, sickness, qualm ➡ **illness**

nautical *adj* maritime, marine, naval, sailing, boating, yachting, seagoing

navy 1. *n* fleet, flotilla, armada, naval forces ➡ **army**
2. *adj* ➡ **blue**

If the word you want is not a main entry above, look below to find it.

nab ➡ **arrest**

nag ➡ **bother, complain**

nah ➡ **no**

nameless ➡ **anonymous**

nap ➡ **sleep**

napping ➡ **asleep, unprepared**

narcissism ➡ **pride**

narcotic ➡ **drug**

narrate ➡ **tell**

narration ➡ **story**

narrative ➡ **story**

narrow-minded ➡ **provincial**

nascent ➡ **early**

nasty ➡ **bad**

nation ➡ **country**

national ➡ **citizen**

national park ➡ **park**

nationalistic ➡ **patriotic**

nativity ➡ **birth**

naturally ➡ **regularly**

naught ➡ **zero**

naughty ➡ **bad, mischievous**

nauseate ➡ **disgust**

nauseated ➡ **sick**

nauseating ➡ **bad**

nauseous ➡ **sick**

naval ➡ **nautical**

naval forces ➡ **navy**

navel orange ➡ **orange**

navigate ➡ **drive, pilot**

navigator ➡ **pilot**

nay ➡ **no**

near 1. *adj* close, nearby, immediate, intimate, imminent, local ➡ **adjacent, about, approximate**
2. *adj* ➡ **future**
3. *prep* ➡ **beside**
4. *vb* ➡ **approach**

neat *adj* tidy, trim, orderly, organized, shipshape, precise, spruce ➡ **clean, prim, legible** ⇨ *messy*

necessary *adj* essential, indispensable, basic, required, requisite, fundamental, mandatory, compulsory, obligatory, imperative ➡ **important**

necessity *n* requirement, essential, staple, requisite, prerequisite, qualification, must, need ➡ **reason**

need 1. *vb* require, lack ➡ **want**
2. *vb* must, should, ought, have
3. *n* ➡ **necessity, reason**
4. *n* ➡ **hardship, poverty**

neglect 1. *n* indifference, disregard, disrespect
2. *vb* ➡ **forget, exclude**

negligent *adj* neglectful, inattentive, lax, remiss, derelict, delinquent, slack, dilatory, irresponsible ➡ **thoughtless, absent-minded**

negotiate *vb* mediate, moderate, bargain, referee, confer, transact, haggle, parley, intercede, arbitrate ➡ **decide**

neighborhood *n* community, block, vicinity, quarter, precinct, ward, borough ➡ **place, zone**

nervous *adj* restless, fidgety, shaky, edgy, uptight, skittish, self-conscious, jittery, jumpy, high-strung ➡ **afraid, anxious, cowardly**

net 1. *n* screen, mesh, web, webbing, network, sieve, filter, sifter
2. *vb* ➡ **earn**

new 1. *adj* fresh, original, recent, late, latest, novel, brand-new, trendy, up-to-date, unused, unspoiled, pristine, virgin, untouched ➡ **modern** ⇨ *old*
2. *adj* ➡ **more**

If the word you want is not a main entry above, look below to find it.

nearby ➡ **near, about**
nearly ➡ **about, practically**
nearness ➡ **presence**
nebulous ➡ **obscure**
neck ➡ **cape**
necktie ➡ **tie**
needle ➡ **bother**
needless ➡ **unnecessary**
needy ➡ **poor**
ne'er-do-well ➡ **loafer**
nefarious ➡ **bad**
negative ➡ **no, pessimistic**

neglected ➡ **abandoned**
neglectful ➡ **negligent**
negligee ➡ **bathrobe**
negligible ➡ **trivial, few**
neighbor ➡ **border**
neighboring ➡ **adjacent**
neighborly ➡ **friendly**
neophyte ➡ **amateur**
nerve ➡ **audacity, courage**
nervousness ➡ **confusion**
nest ➡ **den**
nestle ➡ **snuggle**

network ➡ **net, maze**
neuter ➡ **sterilize**
neutral ➡ **fair**
neutralize ➡ **balance**
névé ➡ **snow**
nevertheless ➡ **anyway, but**
newborn ➡ **baby**
newcomer ➡ **stranger**
newfangled ➡ **modern**
newly ➡ **recently**
newness ➡ **novelty**
news ➡ **announcement**

newscaster ➡ **reporter**
newsman ➡ **reporter**
newspaper ➡ **paper**
newspaperman ➡ **reporter**
newspaperwoman ➡ **reporter**
newsprint ➡ **paper**
newswoman ➡ **reporter**
next ➡ **adjacent, following**
next door ➡ **adjacent**
next to ➡ **beside**
nib ➡ **pen**
nibble ➡ **bite**

nice 1. *adj* agreeable, delightful, fantastic
➡ **good, great, pleasant**
2. *adj* good-natured, charming, pleasant, agreeable, affable, good-humored
➡ **thoughtful, polite, friendly, kind**
3. *adj* ➡ **careful**
Nice *is a very general word to describe someone or something you like, but it is not very specific. Be careful not to overuse it. Often a stronger or more specific synonym is better.*

night *n* nighttime, p.m., bedtime, midnight, dark ➡ **evening** ⇨ **day**

no *interj* nay, negative, nope (*informal*), nah (*informal*) ⇨ **yes**

noble 1. *adj* royal, aristocratic, highborn, patrician, titled, blue-blooded, princely, kingly, regal, imperial, elite
2. *adj* worthy, generous, magnanimous, courtly, chivalrous, chivalric ➡ **grand, good**

3. *n* nobleman, noblewoman, aristocrat, peer, lord, lady

noise *n* sound, din, uproar, clamor, racket, hubbub, tumult, commotion, pandemonium, hullabaloo, peal ➡ **bang, cry, peep**

nonsense 1. *n* foolishness, stupidity, absurdity, irrationality, madness, lunacy, senselessness, silliness, folly, frivolity
2. *n* poppycock, balderdash, twaddle, gobbledygook, drivel, buncombe, bunk, claptrap, baloney, hogwash

normal *adj* typical, average, natural, standard, conventional ➡ **common, usual**

nose *n* nostril, snout, proboscis, beak, bill, trunk

notepad *n* pad, memo pad, tablet, notebook, steno pad, legal pad ➡ **paper**

If the word you want is not a main entry above, look below to find it.

niche ➡ bay
nick ➡ cut, dent
nickname ➡ name, pseudonym
niggard ➡ miser
niggardly ➡ cheap
nightclub ➡ bar
nightcrawler ➡ worm
nightfall ➡ evening
nighttime ➡ night
nil ➡ zero
nimble ➡ agile
nimbleness ➡ agility
nimbus ➡ halo
nincompoop ➡ fool
ninny ➡ fool
nip ➡ squeeze, drink, bite

nippy ➡ cool
nirvana ➡ heaven
nitwit ➡ fool
nobility ➡ aristocracy
nobleman ➡ noble
noblewoman ➡ noble
nod ➡ sleep
noiseless ➡ quiet
noisy ➡ loud
nomad ➡ traveler
nom de plume ➡ pseudonym
nominate ➡ name
nomination ➡ appointment
nominee ➡ candidate
nonattendance ➡ absence

nonbeliever ➡ skeptic, atheist
nonchalance ➡ apathy
nonchalant ➡ carefree, apathetic
none ➡ zero
nonetheless ➡ anyway
nonexistent ➡ imaginary
nonnative ➡ foreign
nonpareil ➡ model
nonpartisan ➡ fair
nonprofessional ➡ amateur
nonsensical ➡ foolish
nonstop ➡ continual
nonviolent ➡ peaceful
nook ➡ bay
nope ➡ no

nor'easter ➡ storm
norm ➡ average
normally ➡ usually
nosedive ➡ fall
nosegay ➡ bouquet
nostalgia ➡ desire
nostril ➡ nose
nosy ➡ curious
notable ➡ memorable, celebrity
notably ➡ chiefly, far
notch ➡ cut, dent
note ➡ notice, letter
notebook ➡ notepad
noted ➡ famous
notepaper ➡ paper

notice 1. *vb* observe, note, perceive
➡ **discover, look, see**
2. *n* attention, observation, regard, heed, note, publicity ➡ **warning**
3. *n* ➡ **advertisement, announcement, reminder**

novelty 1. *n* newness, originality, freshness, uniqueness, modernity ➡ **invention**
2. *n* oddity, curiosity, knickknack, curio ➡ **trinket**

now *adv* immediately, straightaway, directly, right away, instantly ➡ **quickly, soon**

nuisance *n* annoyance, inconvenience, irritation, bother, pain, pest, headache, vexation ➡ **trouble**

number 1. *n* numeral, figure, digit, cipher, integer, fraction
2. *n* amount, quantity, batch, lot, bunch, bundle ➡ **group, assortment**
3. *n* ➡ **act**
Number and **batch** *usually refer to plural nouns:* "a **number** of mistakes," "a **batch** of cookies." **Amount** *is usually used with nouns that are not plural:* "a small **amount** of sunshine," "a tiny **amount** of water."

nurse 1. *n* RN, LPN, medic, orderly
2. *vb* ➡ **heal**

If the word you want is not a main entry above, look below to find it.

noteworthy ➡ special

nothing ➡ zero

noticeable ➡ obvious

notification ➡ announcement

notify ➡ tell

notion ➡ belief, idea, fancy

notoriety ➡ fame

notorious ➡ famous

notwithstanding ➡ anyway

nought ➡ zero

nourish ➡ support

nourishing ➡ healthy

nourishment ➡ food

novel ➡ new

novelist ➡ writer

novice ➡ amateur

noxious ➡ deadly, unhealthy

nozzle ➡ faucet

nuance ➡ difference

nucleus ➡ middle

nude ➡ naked

nudge ➡ push

nugget ➡ pile

nullify ➡ abolish

numb ➡ paralyze

numeral ➡ number

numerical ➡ consecutive

numerous ➡ many

nun ➡ religious

nunnery ➡ monastery

nuptials ➡ marriage

nursery ➡ bedroom, greenhouse

nursing home ➡ hospital

nurture ➡ grow, support

nut ➡ seed, fruit

nutrition ➡ food

nutritious ➡ healthy

nuzzle ➡ snuggle

obey *vb* comply, mind, follow, heed, behave, adhere, observe, meet ⇨ **disobey**

object 1. *vb* protest, disagree, dissent, oppose, dispute, disapprove, frown ➡ **argue, complain, contradict** ⇨ **agree**
2. *n* thing, article, item, gadget, device
3. *n* objective, purpose, aim, goal, sake, target, intention, intent, ambition

obscure 1. *adj* ➡ **dim, dark**
2. *adj* ambiguous, cryptic, enigmatic, inscrutable, unclear, inexplicable, abstruse, vague, incomprehensible, foggy, cloudy, nebulous ➡ **mysterious** ⇨ **obvious, explicit**
3. *vb* ➡ **hide**

observer *n* spectator, witness, eyewitness, viewer, onlooker, bystander

obsession *n* fixation, fascination, preoccupation, compulsion, mania, fetish ➡ **desire**

obvious *adj* clear, evident, apparent, transparent, noticeable, overt, glaring, blatant, gross, conspicuous, prominent, palpable, pronounced, marked, distinct, patent ➡ **bald, easy, plain** ⇨ **obscure**

occupant *n* resident, tenant, renter, householder, inhabitant, guest

occupy *vb* fill, pervade, take up ➡ **live, own, seize**

ocean *n* sea, deep, high seas, seven seas

oddity *n* peculiarity, abnormality, irregularity, idiosyncrasy, eccentricity, aberration, anomaly ➡ **novelty, miracle**

If the word you want is not a main entry above, look below to find it.

oaf ➡ **fool, boor**
oar ➡ **paddle**
oath ➡ **promise, curse**
obdurate ➡ **stubborn**
obedient ➡ **good**
obelisk ➡ **tower**
obese ➡ **fat**
objection ➡ **complaint**
objectionable ➡ **bad**
objective ➡ **object, fair, real**
obligate ➡ **force**
obligation ➡ **duty, debt**
obligatory ➡ **necessary**
oblige ➡ **force**
obliged ➡ **grateful**

obliging ➡ **good**
oblique ➡ **zigzag**
obliquely ➡ **sideways**
obliterate ➡ **erase, abolish**
oblivious ➡ **unaware, absentminded**
obnoxious ➡ **bad**
obscene ➡ **dirty**
obsequious ➡ **servile**
observable ➡ **visible**
observation ➡ **remark, notice**
observe ➡ **look, see, notice, celebrate, obey**
obsolete ➡ **old**
obstacle ➡ **barrier**

obstinate ➡ **stubborn, wild**
obstreperous ➡ **loud**
obstruct ➡ **bar, close**
obstructed ➡ **impassable**
obstruction ➡ **barrier**
obtain ➡ **get**
obtrusive ➡ **meddlesome**
obtuse ➡ **unaware, dull**
obverse ➡ **front**
obviously ➡ **apparently**
occasion ➡ **opportunity, event, party**
occasional ➡ **periodic, rare**
occasionally ➡ **seldom**
occult ➡ **magic, supernatural**

occupation ➡ **profession**
occupied ➡ **employed**
occur ➡ **happen**
occurrence ➡ **event, presence**
odd ➡ **strange**
odious ➡ **awful**
odor ➡ **smell**
odorous ➡ **smelly**
odyssey ➡ **trip**
offend ➡ **insult, disgust, sin**
offender ➡ **criminal**
offense ➡ **crime, insult, attack**
offensive ➡ **bad, attack**

---

offer 1. *vb* propose, present, tender, bid, proffer, extend, suggest, quote ➡ **give, sell**
2. *n* ➡ **suggestion, invitation**

office 1. *n* workplace, headquarters ➡ **den**
2. *n* ➡ **function**

official 1. *adj* authentic, authorized, legitimate, approved, licensed, valid, formal ➡ **real, correct**
2. *n* leader, administrator, executive, bureaucrat, civil servant, public servant ➡ **boss, judge**

often *adv* frequently, repeatedly, oftentimes, recurrently ➡ **regularly, usually** ⇨ *seldom*

oil 1. *n* petroleum, kerosene, crude oil, fossil fuel ➡ **gasoline**
2. *n* ➡ **fat**
3. *vb* grease, lubricate, lube (*informal*)

old 1. *adj* elderly, aged, venerable, mature, senior, hoary, seasoned ⇨ *young*
2. *adj* ancient, old-fashioned, antique, archaic, antiquated, obsolete, outdated ⇨ *new*
3. *adj* worn, used, rundown, worn-out, secondhand, decrepit ➡ **shabby, ragged**

older *adj* elder, senior, prior, senior, earlier

ominous *adj* foreboding, threatening, baleful, menacing, malevolent, sinister, impending, inauspicious, unfavorable ➡ **bad**

once *adv* previously, formerly ➡ **before**

only 1. *adv* just, barely, hardly, scarcely, merely, simply, exclusively
2. *adj* single, sole, solitary, unique, one, lone

open 1. *adj* ajar, uncovered, unfastened, unlocked, accessible, unobstructed, unsealed
2. *adj* spacious, deserted, clear ➡ **empty**
3. *vb* unfasten, undo, unbolt, untie, free, clear ➡ **separate**
4. *vb* ➡ **start**

operate *vb* function, perform, run ➡ **drive, act, work, use**

opponent *n* rival, competitor, opposition, challenger, antagonist, adversary, foe, competition ➡ **contestant, enemy** ⇨ *friend*

opportunity *n* chance, occasion, excuse, opening, situation ➡ **luck**

If the word you want is not a main entry above, look below to find it.

offering ➡ **gift**

officer ➡ **police, soldier**

office-seeker ➡ **candidate**

officiate ➡ **lead**

offset ➡ **balance**

offshoot ➡ **branch, limb, product**

offspring ➡ **child**

oftentimes ➡ **often**

ogle ➡ **stare**

ogre ➡ **monster**

oink ➡ **grunt**

ointment ➡ **medicine**

OK ➡ **yes**

okay ➡ **yes**

okey-dokey ➡ **yes**

old-fashioned ➡ **old**

old wives' tale ➡ **superstition**

olive ➡ **green**

omen ➡ **warning, sign**

omit ➡ **forget, exclude**

on ➡ **above**

on account of ➡ **because**

once more ➡ **again**

one ➡ **only**

one-liner ➡ **joke**

onerous ➡ **inconvenient**

one-sided ➡ **prejudiced**

on hand ➡ **present**

ongoing ➡ **continual**

onlooker ➡ **observer, audience**

onset ➡ **beginning, attack**

onslaught ➡ **attack**

onward ➡ **forward**

onwards ➡ **forward**

ooze ➡ **dirt, drop**

opaque ➡ **dark**

open fire ➡ **shoot**

opening ➡ **hole, break, opportunity, door**

openness ➡ **freedom, truth**

operation ➡ **behavior, use, attack**

opiate ➡ **drug**

opinion ➡ **belief**

opinionated ➡ **stubborn, dogmatic**

oppose ➡ **object, face**

opposed ➡ **opposite**

opposing ➡ **opposite**

n = noun • *vb* = verb • *adj* = adjective • *adv* = adverb • *prep* = preposition • *conj* = conjunction

opposite 1. *adj* opposing, contradictory, contrary, conflicting, inverse, converse, reverse, contrasting, antithetical, counter
➡ **different**
2. *adj* facing, opposed, fronting, confronting
3. *n* reverse, contrary, converse, antithesis, inverse
4. *prep* facing, across from, against, opposed to, versus

opposition 1. *n* disapproval, dislike, aversion, antagonism, hostility, antipathy, enmity
➡ **disagreement, fight** ⇨ *support*
2. *n* ➡ **opponent**

optimistic *adj* hopeful, confident, cheerful, sanguine, expectant, bullish ➡ **idealistic, certain** ⇨ *pessimistic*

orange 1. *adj*, *n* tangerine, apricot, peach, coral, salmon

2. *n* navel orange, Seville orange, mandarin orange, tangerine, clementine, tangelo
➡ **fruit, tree**

order 1. *vb* command, direct, instruct, decree, bid, dictate, impose, prescribe, ordain, mandate
➡ **ask, tell, insist, force**
2. *vb* ➡ **arrange, straighten**
3. *n* arrangement, formation, organization, layout, disposition, alignment, placement, sequence, succession, system ➡ **plan**
4. *n* decree, command, commandment, demand, ultimatum, direction, directive, charge, mandate, edict, behest, writ
5. *n* ➡ **religion**

organization 1. *n* association, corporation, institution, foundation, society, club, fraternity, sorority ➡ **business, union, group**
2. *n* ➡ **order**

If the word you want is not a main entry above, look below to find it.

oppress ➡ abuse, sadden
oppression ➡ tyranny
oppressive ➡ bleak, sharp
opt ➡ choose
optical ➡ visible
optimist ➡ idealist
optimum ➡ best
option ➡ choice
optional ➡ voluntary, unnecessary
opulence ➡ wealth, elegance
opulent ➡ rich
opus ➡ work
oracle ➡ prophet
oral ➡ spoken

oration ➡ speech
orator ➡ speaker
oratorio ➡ hymn
orb ➡ ball
orbit ➡ circle, field
orchestra ➡ band
orchestration ➡ score
ordain ➡ order, bless
ordeal ➡ shock, trouble
orderly ➡ neat, nurse
ordinance ➡ act
ordinarily ➡ usually
ordinariness ➡ mediocrity
ordinary ➡ common, usual
ordination ➡ appointment

ordnance ➡ arms
organic ➡ natural, alive
organism ➡ animal, plant
organize ➡ arrange
organized ➡ neat
orient ➡ arrange, adjust
orientate ➡ arrange
orientation ➡ perspective
origin ➡ beginning, cause, source
original ➡ new, early, model, native
originality ➡ novelty, imagination
originate ➡ start, invent
originator ➡ creator

ornament ➡ jewel, decoration, decorate
ornamentation ➡ decoration
ornate ➡ rich, fancy
ornery ➡ stubborn
orthodox ➡ religious, conservative
orthodoxy ➡ religion
oscillate ➡ alternate, swing
oscillation ➡ vibration
ostentatious ➡ loud, fancy
ostracism ➡ exile
ostracize ➡ banish
other ➡ different
otherwise ➡ differently
ought ➡ need

---

oust *vb* eject, remove, expel, depose, dethrone, unseat ➡ **fire, banish**

outside 1. *n* exterior, surface, façade
2. *adj* exterior, external, outer, outermost, outward, outdoor, alfresco
3. *adv* outdoors, out-of-doors, out, alfresco

own 1. *vb* possess, hold, have, retain, maintain, enjoy, occupy ➡ **keep**
2. *vb* ➡ **admit**
3. *adj* ➡ **private**

owner *n* proprietor, buyer, possessor, holder, master, mistress, landowner, landlord, landlady

---

If the word you want is not a main entry above, look below to find it.

out ➡ outside
outbreak ➡ epidemic
outburst ➡ fit²
outcast ➡ exile, lonely, homeless
out cold ➡ unconscious
outcome ➡ effect, score
outcry ➡ complaint
outdated ➡ old
outdo ➡ exceed
outdoor ➡ outside
outdoors ➡ outside, nature
outer ➡ outside
outer space ➡ space
outermost ➡ outside, last
outfit ➡ dress, suit, business, supply
outfox ➡ fool
outgrowth ➡ shoot, product
outing ➡ trip
outlandish ➡ strange
outlast ➡ live¹
outlaw ➡ criminal, forbid
outlawed ➡ illegal
outlay ➡ price
outlet ➡ door
outline ➡ circumference, summary, list, plan

outlive ➡ live¹
outlook ➡ view
outlying ➡ far
outmoded ➡ unpopular
outnumber ➡ exceed
out-of-doors ➡ outside, nature
out of order ➡ broken
out-of-the-way ➡ inaccessible
out-of-towner ➡ stranger
out-of-work ➡ unemployed
outpatient ➡ patient
output ➡ productivity
outrage ➡ insult, anger
outrageous ➡ awful
outright ➡ bald, perfect, unconditional
outrun ➡ catch
outset ➡ beginning
outshine ➡ exceed
outsider ➡ stranger
outsmart ➡ fool
outspoken ➡ straightforward
outstanding ➡ good, special, model, due
outstretched ➡ long
outstrip ➡ catch
outward ➡ outside

outwit ➡ fool
oval ➡ round
over ➡ above, again, past
overabundant ➡ excessive
overbearing ➡ dogmatic
overcast ➡ dark, cloudy
overcoat ➡ coat
overcome ➡ defeat, win, weather
overconfident ➡ imprudent
overdo ➡ exaggerate
overdue ➡ late, due
overemotional ➡ emotional
overflow ➡ flood
overgrown ➡ wild
overhaul ➡ fix
overhead ➡ above
overhear ➡ listen
overjoyed ➡ ecstatic
overlap ➡ fold
overlay ➡ plate
overlook ➡ forget, exclude, tower
overlooked ➡ unnoticed
overnight bag ➡ luggage
overpass ➡ bridge
overpower ➡ defeat
overpriced ➡ expensive

overrule ➡ abolish
overrun ➡ wild, infest
overseas ➡ abroad
oversee ➡ lead
overseer ➡ guardian
oversight ➡ mistake
overspread ➡ cover
overstate ➡ exaggerate
overstatement ➡ exaggeration
overstep ➡ exceed
overt ➡ obvious
overtake ➡ catch
overthrow ➡ victory, defeat
overture ➡ introduction
overturn ➡ upset
overused ➡ trite
overweight ➡ fat
overwhelm ➡ flood, shock
overwrought ➡ frantic
ovum ➡ egg
ownership ➡ possession, monopoly
oxbow ➡ curve
oxidize ➡ corrode
oxygen ➡ air
oxymoron ➡ contradiction

n = noun • *vb* = verb • *adj* = adjective • *adv* = adverb • *prep* = preposition • *conj* = conjunction

P

pacify *vb* appease, placate, soothe, mollify ➡ **calm, satisfy**

package 1. *n* parcel, packet, bundle, pack ➡ **container, mail**
2. *vb* ➡ **wrap**

paddle 1. *n* oar, scull, sweep
2. *vb* row, scull, pole
3. *vb* ➡ **punish, hit, whip**
4. *vb* ➡ **swim**

page 1. *n* sheet, leaf, folio
2. *n* intern ➡ **servant**
3. *vb* ➡ **call**

pain 1. *n* suffering, discomfort, ache, pang, soreness, twinge, stitch, spasm, cramp, sting
2. *n* ➡ **misery**
3. *n* ➡ **nuisance**

paint 1. *n* pigment, dye, stain, tint ➡ **color, finish**
2. *vb* ➡ **draw**

pair 1. *n* couple, duo, twosome, twins, brace (*of animals*), yoke (*of oxen*), span (*of horses*) ➡ **team**
2. *vb* ➡ **join**

pale 1. *adj* pallid, pasty, wan, sallow, ashen, chalky ➡ **white, fair**
2. *vb* ➡ **bleach**

pamper *vb* coddle, spoil, indulge, dote on, humor, baby, patronize ➡ **please**

pamphlet *n* booklet, brochure, leaflet, tract ➡ **book**

paper 1. *n* stationery, notepaper, writing paper, newsprint, crepe paper, tissue, wax paper, tar paper, parchment, vellum
2. *n* ➡ **document, report**
3. *n* newspaper, magazine, journal, periodical, tabloid, gazette, daily, weekly

parade 1. *n* procession, march, demonstration, cavalcade, motorcade
2. *vb* ➡ **walk, strut**
3. *vb* ➡ **advertise**

If the word you want is not a main entry above, look below to find it.

pace ➡ speed, step, gait

pacific ➡ peaceful

pacifist ➡ peaceful

pack ➡ bag, package, load, group, herd, carry

packed ➡ full, thick

packet ➡ package

pact ➡ agreement

pad ➡ cushion, notepad, foot, protect

padding ➡ cushion

paddock ➡ pen

padlock ➡ lock

pageant ➡ play

pail ➡ container

painful ➡ sore, uncomfortable

painkiller ➡ drug

pains ➡ work

painstaking ➡ careful

painter ➡ artist, rope

painting ➡ picture

pal ➡ friend

palace ➡ castle, home

palisade ➡ cliff, wall, barrier

pall ➡ cloud

pallet ➡ cushion

palliate ➡ soften

pallid ➡ pale

palpable ➡ real, obvious

paltry ➡ poor, small, trivial

pan ➡ pot

panache ➡ class

pandemic ➡ epidemic

pandemonium ➡ noise

pander ➡ flatter

panel ➡ committee

pang ➡ pain

panhandler ➡ beggar

panic ➡ fear, hysteria

panorama ➡ view

pant ➡ breathe

pantry ➡ kitchen, closet

paparazzo, paparazzi ➡ photographer

paperback ➡ book

par ➡ average

paradigm ➡ model

---

parallel 1. *adj* equidistant, collateral, aligned, even, alongside, abreast ➡ **level**
2. *adj* ➡ **alike**
3. *n* ➡ **duplicate, similarity**
4. *vb* ➡ **compare**

paralyze *vb* disable, cripple, immobilize, numb, stun, knock out

parent *n* father, mother, foster parent, stepparent ➡ **ancestor, guardian**

park 1. *n* green, common, square, playground, recreational area
2. *n* national park, state park, reserve, preserve, reservation, refuge ➡ **zoo**
3. *vb* ➡ **put**

parody 1. *n* imitation, satire, caricature, burlesque ➡ **irony**
2. *vb* ➡ **imitate**

part 1. *n* piece, section, portion, segment, fragment, fraction, share, element, facet, aspect, component, ingredient, content ➡ **bit, block, division** ⇨ *total*

2. *vb* ➡ **divide, separate**
3. *n* ➡ **role, function**

partial 1. *adj* incomplete, unfinished, fragmentary, deficient, imperfect ⇨ *complete*
2. *adj* ➡ **prejudiced**

partly *adv* partially, partway, somewhat, incompletely, slightly

partner 1. *n* associate, co-worker, confederate, accomplice, accessory, sidekick ➡ **helper**
2. *n* ➡ **friend**
3. *n* ➡ **love, spouse**

party 1. *n* celebration, festivity, gathering, reception, soiree, fete, occasion, gala, function, revelry, jubilee, merrymaking ➡ **feast**
2. *n* faction, bloc, league, lobby, junta, cabal ➡ **organization, group**
3. *n* participant, litigant, principal ➡ **member, contestant**
4. *vb* ➡ **celebrate**

If the word you want is not a main entry above, look below to find it.

paradise ➡ heaven, utopia

paradox ➡ contradiction

paragon ➡ model

paragraph ➡ division

paramount ➡ important

paranoid ➡ suspicious, insane

paranormal ➡ supernatural

parapet ➡ wall

paraphernalia ➡ equipment

paraphrase ➡ summary, translation, quote, translate

parboil ➡ boil

parcel ➡ package

parched ➡ dry

parchment ➡ paper

pardon ➡ forgive, forgiveness

pare ➡ peel

parental ➡ motherly, fatherly

parfait ➡ ice cream

pariah ➡ exile

parish ➡ church

parishioners ➡ church

parka ➡ coat

parking garage ➡ garage

parkway ➡ highway

parley ➡ negotiate, talk

parliament ➡ government

parlor ➡ living room

parochial ➡ provincial

paroxysm ➡ fit²

parrot ➡ imitate, quote

parry ➡ repel

partiality ➡ preference, prejudice

partially ➡ partly

participant ➡ contestant, member, party

participate ➡ join

particle ➡ bit

particular ➡ special, careful, choosy, detail

particularize ➡ specify

particularly ➡ chiefly

partisan ➡ fan, prejudiced

partition ➡ wall, division, divider, divide

partnership ➡ business, union

partway ➡ partly

pasha ➡ king

pass ➡ exceed, go, throw, give, catch, elapse, ticket

passage ➡ hall, door, approval, excerpt, division, trip, travel

passageway ➡ hall

pass away ➡ die

passenger ➡ rider

passerby ➡ pedestrian

passing ➡ death

passion ➡ love, desire, enthusiasm, emotion

passionate ➡ emotional, loving, eager

pass on ➡ die

n = noun • *vb* = verb • *adj* = adjective • *adv* = adverb • *prep* = preposition • *conj* = conjunction

passive 1. *adj* idle, inactive, inert, lifeless, motionless, sedentary ➡ **listless, lazy, slow**
⇨ *active*
2. *adj* resigned, submissive, docile, deferential, compliant, yielding ➡ **patient**

past 1. *adj* former, preceding, foregoing, prior, previous, antecedent ➡ **old**
2. *adj* finished, over, ended, through, done
3. *n* history, antiquity, yesterday, yesteryear, yore
4. *prep* beyond, through, behind, over, after

pastime *n* activity, pursuit, interest, hobby, avocation, venture ➡ **game**

pastry *n* baked goods, delicacy, Danish, pie, tart, shortbread, cookie ➡ **cake, bread**

path *n* pathway, footpath, trail, track, lane, walk, walkway, runway, shortcut ➡ **road**

patience *n* tolerance, understanding, fortitude, stoicism, endurance, perserverance, persistence

patient 1. *adj* understanding, forbearing, mild-tempered, long-suffering ➡ **tolerant, calm, passive**
2. *adj* persistent, perservering, steadfast, assiduous ➡ **diligent**

3. *n* subject, victim, sufferer, convalescent, invalid, outpatient, inpatient

patriotic *adj* loyal, zealous, nationalistic, chauvinistic ➡ **faithful**

patrol 1. *n* scout, lookout, sentinel, sentry, escort, vanguard, picket, watch ➡ **guardian**
2. *vb* police, inspect, cruise, reconnoiter, scout ➡ **protect**

patron 1. *n* sponsor, benefactor, philanthropist, supporter, contributor, donor, subscriber, giver
2. *n* client, customer, buyer, shopper, regular ➡ **audience**

pattern 1. *n* design, motif, configuration ➡ **structure, plan**
2. *n* model, blueprint, template, diagram, guide, sketch
3. *vb* ➡ **form**

pawn 1. *vb* hock, pledge, mortgage ➡ **sell**
2. *n* ➡ **tool**

pay 1. *vb* compensate, recompense, spend, reward, tip, remunerate, settle, disburse, expend, atone, expiate ➡ **give, earn, refund**
2. *n* ➡ **wage**

If the word you want is not a main entry above, look below to find it.

passport ➡ **document, ticket**
paste ➡ **stick, adhesive**
pastime ➡ **game**
pastor ➡ **minister**
pastoral ➡ **rural**
pastry chef ➡ **cook**
pasture ➡ **field**
pasty ➡ **pale**
pat ➡ **pet, hit**
patch ➡ **fix, repair**

patent ➡ **license, obvious**
patently ➡ **apparently**
paternal ➡ **fatherly**
path ➡ **course**
pathetic ➡ **pitiful**
pathless ➡ **impassable**
pathway ➡ **path**
patio ➡ **porch, court**
patois ➡ **dialect**
patriarch ➡ **ancestor**

patrician ➡ **noble**
patrimony ➡ **inheritance**
patriotism ➡ **loyalty**
patrolman ➡ **police officer**
patrolwoman ➡ **police officer**
patronize ➡ **frequent, condescend, pamper**
patrons ➡ **audience**
patter ➡ **talk, knock, rustle**

paucity ➡ **want**
paunch ➡ **stomach**
pauper ➡ **beggar**
pause ➡ **stop, hesitate, break**
pave ➡ **cover**
pavilion ➡ **tent**
paw ➡ **foot, touch**
payable ➡ **due**
pay for ➡ **afford, buy**
payment ➡ **price**

---

peace *n* harmony, concord, repose, amity, reconciliation ➡ **agreement, calm, truce**

peaceful 1. *adj* ➡ **calm**
2. *adj* peaceable, pacific, amicable, nonviolent, pacifist, conciliatory ➡ **friendly**

pedestrian 1. *n* walker, hiker, passerby, rover, stroller, straggler
2. *adj* ➡ **common, poor**

peel 1. *vb* skin, pare, strip, scale, husk, shuck, flay ➡ **cut**
2. *n* skin, rind, bark ➡ **shell**

peep *n* squeak, chirp, cheep, squawk, clink, tinkle, click, ping, pop, plink, plunk ➡ **noise, bang**

pen 1. *n* corral, fold, pound, paddock, enclosure, coop, cage, sty, stall, kennel ➡ **barn, field, jail**

2. *n* ballpoint, marker, fountain pen, quill, nib
3. *vb* ➡ **write**

pension *n* benefit, support, annuity, Social Security ➡ **wage**

people 1. *n* citizenry, populace, public, population, society, civilization, community, folk, hoi polloi (*Greek*), bourgeoisie (*French*) ➡ **human being, humanity, citizen**
2. *n* ➡ **family**

perfect 1. *adj* ideal, flawless, faultless, impeccable, unblemished, immaculate, exquisite, exemplary, model ➡ **correct, infallible**
2. *adj* pure, sheer, outright ➡ **complete**
3. *vb* polish, hone, amend ➡ **fix, correct**

If the word you want is not a main entry above, look below to find it.

peaceable ➡ **peaceful**

peacefulness ➡ **calm**

peach ➡ **orange**

pea green ➡ **green**

peak ➡ **top, mountain, climax, bill**

peal ➡ **ring, noise**

pearl ➡ **ball**

peasant ➡ **farmer**

pebble ➡ **rock**

peck ➡ **abundance, stick, kiss**

peculiar ➡ **strange, special**

peculiarity ➡ **oddity, detail**

pecuniary ➡ **financial**

peddle ➡ **sell**

peddler ➡ **seller**

pedestal ➡ **post**

peek ➡ **look**

peer ➡ **stare, equal, noble**

peerless ➡ **unique**

peevish ➡ **cross**

peg ➡ **nail**

peignoir ➡ **bathrobe**

pellet ➡ **ball**

pelt ➡ **hit, hide**

penalize ➡ **punish**

penalty ➡ **punishment**

penance ➡ **punishment**

penchant ➡ **tendency**

pending ➡ **future, unresolved**

penetrate ➡ **enter, stick, know**

penetrating ➡ **profound**

peninsula ➡ **cape**

penitent ➡ **sorry**

penitentiary ➡ **jail**

penknife ➡ **knife**

penmanship ➡ **handwriting**

pen name ➡ **pseudonym**

pennant ➡ **flag**

penniless ➡ **poor**

penny-pinching ➡ **cheap**

penny-pincher ➡ **miser**

pensive ➡ **thoughtful**

penurious ➡ **cheap**

penury ➡ **poverty**

pep ➡ **energy**

peppery ➡ **spicy**

perceivable ➡ **visible**

perceive ➡ **see, notice, read**

percent ➡ **share**

percentage ➡ **share**

perceptible ➡ **audible, visible**

perception ➡ **sight, wisdom, feeling**

perceptive ➡ **smart**

perch ➡ **descend, seat**

perchance ➡ **maybe**

perennial ➡ **flower, permanent**

perfection ➡ **excellence**

perfectionist ➡ **idealist**

perfectly ➡ **certainly**

perfidious ➡ **unfaithful**

perforate ➡ **stick**

perforation ➡ **hole**

perform ➡ **act, operate, play**

performance ➡ **act, behavior, delivery, program**

performer ➡ **actor, musician**

perfume ➡ **smell**

perfumed ➡ **fragrant**

perfunctory ➡ **fast, superficial**

perhaps ➡ **maybe**

peril ➡ **danger**

perilous ➡ **dangerous**

perimeter ➡ **circumference, circle**

n = noun • *vb* = verb • *adj* = adjective • *adv* = adverb • *prep* = preposition • *conj* = conjunction

period 1. *n* interval, term, span, spell, duration, extent, stretch, streak, cycle, bout, season, phase, stage, time, shift, watch, tour, stint ➡ **round, moment**
2. *n* age, eon, era, epoch, date

periodic *adj* intermittent, cyclic, cyclical, recurrent, spasmodic, sporadic, fitful, erratic, irregular, occasional ➡ **alternate, frequent**

permanent *adj* durable, lasting, enduring, abiding, perennial, persistent, indelible ➡ **continual, eternal, stationary** ⇨ *temporary*

permission *n* consent, authorization, authority, approval, license, sanction ➡ **support**

personality 1. *n* character, disposition, temperament, temper, nature, identity

2. *n* charisma, charm, presence, allure, magnetism ➡ **bearing, attraction**
3. *n* ➡ **celebrity**

perspective *n* point of view, viewpoint, standpoint, orientation, direction, angle, position, attitude, side ➡ **view**

persuade *vb* convince, satisfy, influence, induce, dispose, coax, sway, get, wheedle, cajole, entice, prevail, snow ➡ **urge, tempt** ⇨ *discourage*

pessimistic *adj* cynical, negative, glum, sullen, morose, fatalistic ➡ **bleak, sad** ⇨ *optimistic*

pet 1. *vb* pat, caress, fondle, stroke, tickle ➡ **rub**
2. *adj, n* ➡ **favorite**

If the word you want is not a main entry above, look below to find it.

periodical ➡ paper
periphery ➡ edge, circumference, circle
perish ➡ die
perishable ➡ mortal
periwig ➡ wig
perjurer ➡ liar
perk ➡ tip
permafrost ➡ ice
permanently ➡ forever, finally
permissible ➡ legal
permissive ➡ tolerant
permit ➡ let, ticket, license
perpendicular ➡ vertical, steep
perpetrate ➡ commit
perpetrator ➡ criminal
perpetual ➡ eternal
perpetually ➡ forever

perplex ➡ confuse
perplexed ➡ doubtful
perplexing ➡ mysterious
perplexity ➡ confusion
perquisite ➡ tip
persecute ➡ abuse
perserverance ➡ diligence, patience
perservering ➡ patient
persevere ➡ continue, live[1]
persist ➡ continue, live[1]
persistence ➡ diligence, patience
persistent ➡ patient, continual, permanent
person ➡ human being
personage ➡ celebrity
personal ➡ private
personnel ➡ faculty
perspiration ➡ sweat

perspire ➡ sweat
pert ➡ rude
pertain ➡ belong, concern
pertinaceous ➡ stubborn
pertinence ➡ relevance
pertinent ➡ relevant, fit[1]
perturb ➡ disturb, scare
peruse ➡ read
pervade ➡ occupy
perverse ➡ stubborn
perversion ➡ immorality
perversity ➡ immorality
pervert ➡ debase, distort
perverted ➡ immoral
pessimist ➡ skeptic
pest ➡ nuisance, bug
pester ➡ bother
pestilence ➡ epidemic

petcock ➡ faucet
petition ➡ appeal, ask
petrified ➡ afraid
petrify ➡ scare, harden
petrol ➡ gasoline
petroleum ➡ oil
petty ➡ trivial, mean
petulant ➡ temperamental, cross
pew ➡ seat
phantom ➡ ghost
pharaoh ➡ emperor
pharmaceutical ➡ medicinal
phase ➡ state, period
Ph.D. ➡ doctor
phenomenal ➡ special
phenomenon ➡ event, miracle
philanthropist ➡ patron
philanthropy ➡ generosity

➡ = synonym cross-reference • ⇨ = antonym cross-reference

philosopher *n* thinker, sage, logician, scholar

philosophy *n* metaphysics, theory, thought, ideology, esthetics, ethics ➡ **knowledge, wisdom, belief**

photograph *n* photo, snapshot, image, slide, print, likeness ➡ **picture, X ray**

photographer *n* camerman, cinematographer, paparazzo (*Italian; plural:* paparazzi), shutterbug (*informal*) ➡ **artist**

physical *adj* bodily, corporal, corporeal, fleshly ➡ **real**

picture 1. *n* portrait, image, drawing, painting, illustration, representation, diagram, sketch, cartoon, poster, work, plate, print
➡ **description, photograph, X ray**
2. *n* ➡ **movie**
3. *vb* ➡ **imagine**
4. *vb* ➡ **draw**

pile 1. *n* heap, stack, mound, hill, lump, wad, clump, mass, nugget ➡ **bulk, assortment**
2. *vb* heap, stack ➡ **gather**
3. *n* ➡ **post**

pillage 1. *vb* plunder, ransack, sack, loot
➡ **steal, attack**
2. *n* ➡ **theft, booty**

pilot 1. *n* aviator, flier, airman, aeronaut
2. *n* helmsman, navigator, coxswain, steersman
3. *vb* sail, navigate ➡ **lead, guide, drive**

pin 1. *n* safety pin, straight pin, bobby pin, hairpin, hat pin, cotter pin, brooch, tiepin, clip ➡ **nail**
2. *vb* attach ➡ **join, nail**

pine 1. *n* fir, evergreen ➡ **tree**
2. *vb* ➡ **grieve**
3. *vb* ➡ **want**

pioneer 1. *n* settler, homesteader, backwoodsman, frontiersman, immigrant, colonist, colonizer
2. *n* ➡ **creator**
3. *adj* ➡ **early**

pipe *n* tube, drainpipe, waterpipe, duct, conduit, pipeline, tubing, hose, funnel ➡ **channel**

If the word you want is not a main entry above, look below to find it.

Philistine ➡ boor

philosophical ➡ theoretical, profound

phobia ➡ fear

phone ➡ call

phony ➡ fake

photo ➡ photograph

photocopy ➡ reproduce, print, copy

phrase ➡ saying, say

physically challenged ➡ disabled

physician ➡ doctor

physics ➡ science

physique ➡ body

piazza ➡ court, porch

pick ➡ choose, gather, choice

pickax ➡ ax, axe

picket ➡ post, patrol, protest

pickle ➡ trouble

pick up ➡ continue

picky ➡ choosy

picnic ➡ meal

pictorial ➡ scenic

pictures ➡ movies

picturesque ➡ scenic

piddling ➡ trivial

pidgin ➡ dialect

pie ➡ pastry

piebald ➡ speckled

piece ➡ part, bit, block

pièce de résistance ➡ masterpiece

pier ➡ dock, jetty, post

pierce ➡ stick

piercing ➡ loud

pig ➡ glutton

pigeonhole ➡ stereotype

pigheaded ➡ stubborn

pigment ➡ paint

pigtail ➡ braid

pilfer ➡ steal

pilgrim ➡ traveler

pilgrimage ➡ trip

pill ➡ medicine

pillar ➡ post, support

pillow ➡ cushion

pinafore ➡ dress

pinch ➡ squeeze, steal, trouble, bit

ping ➡ peep

pinion ➡ limb

pink ➡ red

pinnacle ➡ top, tower

pioneering ➡ early

pious ➡ religious

pip ➡ seed

pipeline ➡ pipe

piping ➡ high

piquant ➡ spicy

pirate 1. *n* buccaneer, privateer, freebooter, corsair, plunderer, marauder ➡ **criminal, vandal**
2. *vb* ➡ **steal**

pitiful *adj* pathetic, piteous, pitiable, mournful, woeful, distressing, heartbreaking ➡ **sad, sorry, poor, unfortunate, emotional**

pity 1. *n* sympathy, compassion, empathy, mercy, forbearance, ruth, clemency, condolence, commiseration ➡ **kindness, comfort**
2. *vb* sympathize, commiserate, comfort
3. *n* ➡ **disaster**

place 1. *n* location, position, situation, locale, site, spot, locality, region, vicinity ➡ **space, zone**
2. *vb* locate, situate, assign, store ➡ **put**
3. *vb* ➡ **arrange**
4. *n* ➡ **house**
5. *n* ➡ **profession**

plain 1. *adj* simple, uncomplicated, unadorned, unvarnished, frugal, severe, austere, stark ➡ **common, humble, natural, naked** ⇨ *complicated*
2. *adj* unattractive, homely, drab, unlovely ➡ **ugly** ⇨ *pretty*
3. *adj* ➡ **obvious, straightforward**
4. *n* prairie, range, grassland, savanna, heath, moor, tundra, downs ➡ **field, plateau**

plan 1. *n* design, project, plot, schematic, outline, map ➡ **table**
2. *n* aim, intent, goal, purpose, strategy, scheme, plot, conspiracy, program, policy, platform, plank, provision ➡ **method, recipe**
3. *vb* plot, scheme, conspire, contrive, connive, chart, map, outline ➡ **arrange, prepare, intend**

planet *n* heavenly body, celestial body, satellite ➡ **earth, space**

plant 1. *n* shrub, weed, grass, bush, shrub, vegetation, flora, foliage, organism ➡ **flower, tree, herb, vegetable, fruit**
2. *n* ➡ **factory**
3. *vb* seed, sow, pot, transplant, propagate, set, broadcast, scatter ➡ **grow**
4. *vb* ➡ **put**

plate 1. *n* dish, platter, saucer, dinnerware, china ➡ **bowl, tray**
2. *n* ➡ **picture**
3. *n* ➡ **base**
4. *vb* laminate, overlay, gild, electroplate ➡ **cover**

plateau 1. *n* tableland, table, mesa, steppe, upland, highland ➡ **plain**
2. *n* ➡ **grade**

platform 1. *n* stage, dais, pulpit, rostrum, stand, riser
2. *n* ➡ **plan**

If the word you want is not a main entry above, look below to find it.

pirouette ➡ dance
pistol ➡ gun
pit ➡ dent, hole, grave, mine, seed
pitch ➡ throw, advertise, swing, slant, advertisement
pitch-black ➡ black, dark
pitcher ➡ bottle
piteous ➡ pitiful

pitfall ➡ trap
pitiable ➡ pitiful
pitiless ➡ mean
pitter-patter ➡ knock
pivot ➡ axis, turn
pixie ➡ fairy
pizzeria ➡ restaurant
placate ➡ pacify

place-kick ➡ kick
placement ➡ order
placid ➡ calm
plagiarize ➡ steal
plague ➡ epidemic, infest, bother
plainly ➡ apparently
plait ➡ braid, weave

plane ➡ airplane, level, side
plank ➡ board, wood, plan
plantation ➡ farm
planter ➡ farmer
plastic ➡ flexible
plate ➡ base
platitude ➡ cliché
platter ➡ plate, tray

➡ = synonym cross-reference • ⇨ = antonym cross-reference

play 1. *vb* frisk, sport, disport, romp, frolic, gambol, recreate
2. *vb* ➡ **compete**
3. *vb* perform, finger, bow, strum ➡ **practice, blow²**
4. *vb* ➡ **act**
5. *vb* run, show, present, air, broadcast
6. *n* recreation, horseplay, clowning ➡ **pleasure, entertainment**
7. *n* drama, dramatization, skit, pageant, tragedy, melodrama, comedy, farce, musical, mystery ➡ **program, movie**
8. *n* ➡ **movement**

pleasant 1. *adj* pleasurable, gratifying, agreeable, pleasing, enjoyable, congenial, satisfying, appealing, desirable, delightful, sweet ➡ **happy**
2. *adj* ➡ **nice, friendly**
3. *adj* ➡ **fair**

please *vb* delight, gratify, gladden, content, hearten ➡ **satisfy, entertain, pamper**

pleasure *n* amusement, joy, happiness, fun, delight, glee, enjoyment, pride, ecstasy, bliss, rapture, content, felicity ➡ **satisfaction, entertainment, play** ⇨ *pain*

pocket 1. *n* pouch, sac ➡ **bag**
2. *vb* ➡ **steal**

poem *n* verse, poetry, lyric, rhyme ➡ **stanza, song, work**

point 1. *n* end, tip, spike, tine ➡ **top, thorn**
2. *n* ➡ **cape**
3. *n* ➡ **subject**
4. *n* ➡ **detail**
5. *n* ➡ **moment**

poison 1. *n* venom, toxin, bane, infection, virus, germ
2. *vb* ➡ **kill**

If the word you want is not a main entry above, look below to find it.

plausibility ➡ possibility
plausible ➡ possible
plausibly ➡ probably
player ➡ actor, musician, athlete, contestant
playful ➡ lively
playground ➡ park
playing field ➡ field
playmate ➡ friend
playroom ➡ den
plaything ➡ toy
playwright ➡ writer
plaza ➡ court
plea ➡ appeal
plead ➡ argue, beg
pleased ➡ grateful
pleasing ➡ pleasant
pleasurable ➡ pleasant

pleat ➡ fold
plebeian ➡ common
pledge ➡ promise, dedicate, pawn
plenteous ➡ abundant
plentiful ➡ abundant, enough
plenty ➡ abundance, enough
plethora ➡ abundance
pliable ➡ flexible
pliant ➡ flexible
plight ➡ trouble
plink ➡ peep
plod ➡ walk, lag
plot ➡ plan, property, field, story
plow ➡ dig
ploy ➡ trick

pluck ➡ pull, gather, extract
plucky ➡ brave
plug ➡ close, repair, advertise, advertisement, top
plum ➡ purple
plumb ➡ vertical
plummet ➡ fall
plump ➡ fat, fall
plunder ➡ booty, pillage
plunderer ➡ pirate
plunge ➡ fall, drop, jump, stick, swim
plunk ➡ peep
plus ➡ besides, advantage
ply ➡ act
p.m. ➡ night, afternoon
poach ➡ boil, hunt, steal
pocketbook ➡ bag, wallet

pod ➡ shell, herd
poet ➡ writer
poetry ➡ poem
poignant ➡ emotional
pointed ➡ sharp
pointer ➡ tip
pointless ➡ unnecessary
point of view ➡ perspective
pointy ➡ sharp
poise ➡ balance, tact
poised ➡ calm
poisonous ➡ deadly
poke ➡ push, stick, blow¹
poker-faced ➡ blank
polar ➡ cold
pole ➡ bar, bat, paddle
poleax ➡ ax, axe

n = noun • *vb* = verb • *adj* = adjective • *adv* = adverb • *prep* = preposition • *conj* = conjunction

police 1. *n* authorities, officer ➡ **police officer**
2. *vb* ➡ **patrol**

police officer *n* policeman, policewoman, cop (*informal*), patrolman, patrolwoman, constable, sheriff, marshal, detective

polite *adj* courteous, well-mannered, civil, chivalrous, gracious ➡ **friendly, thoughtful, nice, prim** ⇨ *rude*

pompous *adj* grandiloquent, flowery, grandiose, bombastic, pretentious, turgid, condescending ➡ **proud**

poor 1. *adj* needy, penniless, destitute, broke, impoverished, deprived, indigent, poverty-stricken ⇨ *rich*
2. *adj* pitiful, sorry, paltry, inferior, shoddy, deficient, pedestrian, tawdry, unsatisfactory, inadequate, worthless, wretched, abject, lame

porch *n* veranda, stoop, piazza, patio, breezeway, portico, gallery

portable *adj* movable, transportable, mobile ⇨ *stationary*

porter *n* redcap, skycap, bellboy, bellhop, baggage carrier ➡ **doorman**

possession 1. *n* ownership, custody, title, proprietorship, receipt ➡ **control, rule**
2. *n* ➡ **property, acquisition**
3. *n* ➡ **colony**

possibility *n* probability, likelihood, chance, plausibility, prospect, expectation, eventuality, potential, potentiality

possible *adj* plausible, conceivable, believable, credible, feasible, potential, reasonable, imaginable, practicable, viable ➡ **likely**

post 1. *n* pillar, column, pedestal, stud, upright, picket, stanchion, pier, pile
2. *n* ➡ **profession**
3. *n* ➡ **mail**
4. *n* ➡ **base**
5. *vb* ➡ **send**

If the word you want is not a main entry above, look below to find it.

policeman ➡ police officer

policewoman ➡ police officer

policy ➡ plan

polish ➡ shine, finish, perfect, class, elegance, civilization

politic ➡ careful

poll ➡ vote, study

polliwog ➡ frog

pollute ➡ dirty, debase

polluted ➡ dirty

polyp ➡ growth

pomp ➡ ceremony

pond ➡ lake

ponder ➡ meditate

ponderous ➡ heavy

pontiff ➡ priest

pony ➡ horse

pool ➡ lake, lottery

pop ➡ bang, peep, soda, jump

pope ➡ priest

poppycock ➡ nonsense

populace ➡ people

popular ➡ common, fashionable, famous, favorite

popularity ➡ fame

population ➡ people

porcelain ➡ pottery

pore ➡ hole

pore over ➡ study

pornographic ➡ dirty

port ➡ harbor

portal ➡ door

portend ➡ predict

portent ➡ miracle

portico ➡ porch

portion ➡ part, excerpt, divide

portly ➡ fat

portrait ➡ picture, description

portray ➡ act, draw

portrayal ➡ description, role

pose ➡ posture, model, act

poser ➡ model

posh ➡ rich

position ➡ place, put, deploy, grade, profession, reputation, perspective

positive ➡ certain, good

positively ➡ certainly

possess ➡ own, keep

possessive ➡ greedy, jealous

possessor ➡ owner

possibly ➡ maybe

postcard ➡ letter

poster ➡ picture, advertisement

posterior ➡ back

postlude ➡ conclusion

➡ = synonym cross-reference • ⇨ = antonym cross-reference

posture *n* pose, stance, carriage, bearing, attitude

pot 1. *n* pan, saucepan, kettle, teakettle, teapot, coffeepot, vat, cauldron ➡ **bowl, container**
2. *vb* ➡ **plant**

pottery *n* ceramics, porcelain, china, earthenware, stoneware, terra cotta

poverty *n* destitution, want, need, penury, indigence, privation, impoverishment ➡ **hardship**

practical 1. *adj* matter-of-fact, down-to-earth, realistic, reasonable, rational, sensible, unsentimental ➡ **able** ⇨ *impractical*
2. *adj* ➡ **useful, efficient**
3. *adj* ➡ **virtual**

practically *adv* virtually, effectively, essentially, fundamentally, nearly, basically, principally ➡ **about**

practice 1. *vb* rehearse, drill, train ➡ **study, learn**

2. *vb* ➡ **use**
3. *n* rehearsal, repetition, preparation ➡ **discipline**
4. *n* ➡ **habit**

praise 1. *n* applause, acclaim, compliment, approval, adulation, acclamation, kudos, congratulations, flattery ➡ **respect**
2. *vb* commend, extol, acclaim, laud, compliment, honor, decorate, congratulate, toast, rave ➡ **celebrate, clap, flatter, worship**

praiseworthy *adj* commendable, laudable, deserving, creditable, estimable, worthy, meritorious

preach *vb* exhort, sermonize, moralize, proclaim ➡ **teach**

precede *vb* preface, herald, antedate, introduce ⇨ *follow*

precisely *adv* exactly, directly, right, due ➡ **correctly, carefully**

If the word you want is not a main entry above, look below to find it.

postman ➡ **letter carrier**

postmaster ➡ **letter carrier**

postmistress ➡ **letter carrier**

postpone ➡ **delay**

postscript ➡ **conclusion**

postulate ➡ **assume**

posy ➡ **bouquet, flower**

potency ➡ **strength**

potent ➡ **strong**

potentate ➡ **ruler**

potential ➡ **possible, latent, possibility**

potentiality ➡ **possibility**

potpourri ➡ **mixture, assortment**

potter ➡ **tinker**

pouch ➡ **bag, pocket**

pounce ➡ **jump**

pound ➡ **hit, pen**

pour ➡ **flow, rain, hurry**

pour out ➡ **empty**

pout ➡ **frown, mope**

poverty-stricken ➡ **poor**

powder ➡ **grind, snow**

powder blue ➡ **blue**

power ➡ **strength, energy, ability, right**

powerful ➡ **strong, important**

powerless ➡ **weak**

powerlessness ➡ **inability**

practicable ➡ **possible**

practical joke ➡ **joke**

pragmatic ➡ **useful**

prairie ➡ **plain**

prank ➡ **joke**

prate ➡ **chatter**

prattle ➡ **chatter, talk**

pray ➡ **appeal**

prayer ➡ **worship**

preacher ➡ **minister, speaker**

preamble ➡ **introduction**

precarious ➡ **unsteady, dangerous**

precaution ➡ **protection**

preceding ➡ **before, past**

precept ➡ **rule**

precinct ➡ **neighborhood**

precious ➡ **valuable, expensive, favorite**

precious stone ➡ **jewel**

precipice ➡ **cliff**

precipitate ➡ **sudden, rain**

precipitation ➡ **rain**

precipitous ➡ **steep**

précis ➡ **summary**

precise ➡ **correct, careful, neat, punctual, explicit**

precision ➡ **accuracy**

precocious ➡ **gifted, early**

---

n = noun • *vb* = verb • *adj* = adjective • *adv* = adverb • *prep* = preposition • *conj* = conjunction

predatory *adj* voracious, rapacious, ravenous, bloodthirsty, carnivorous ➡ **greedy**

predict *vb* forecast, foretell, prophesy, prognosticate, project, divine, tell, foresee, augur, portend, presage ➡ **anticipate**

prediction 1. *n* forecast, prognostication 2. *n* prophecy, divination, fortune telling, augury

predominant *adj* dominant, preeminent, prevalent, prevailing ➡ **important**

prefer *vb* favor, endorse, advocate ➡ **choose, like, want**

preference *n* favorite, partiality, predilection, inclination, proclivity ➡ **choice, tendency**

pregnant 1. *adj* expecting, expectant, with child, gravid 2. *adj* ➡ **meaningful**

prejudice *n* intolerance, bigotry, bias, partiality, predisposition, predilection, favoritism, discrimination, racism, sexism, chauvinism, ageism ➡ **hatred**

prejudiced *adj* biased, unfair, unjust, partial, one-sided, partisan, predisposed, bigoted, intolerant, discriminatory

prepare *vb* develop, provide, ready, plan, adapt, prime, process, refine ➡ **arrange, cook, make, invent**

presence 1. *n* proximity, nearness, closeness ⇨ *absence* 2. *n* attendance, occurrence ➡ **existence** ⇨ *absence* 3. *n* ➡ **bearing, personality**

present 1. *adj* here, on hand ➡ **near** ⇨ *absent* 2. *vb* ➡ **give, offer** 3. *vb* ➡ **introduce** 4. *vb* ➡ **play, show** 5. *n* ➡ **gift**

If the word you want is not a main entry above, look below to find it.

predecessor ➡ **ancestor**

predicament ➡ **trouble**

predicate ➡ **base**

predilection ➡ **prejudice, preference**

predisposed ➡ **prejudiced, ready**

predisposition ➡ **prejudice**

predominantly ➡ **chiefly**

preeminent ➡ **best, predominant**

preface ➡ **introduction, introduce, precede**

preferable ➡ **better**

preferably ➡ **more, instead**

preferment ➡ **promotion**

preferred ➡ **favorite**

prehistoric ➡ **early**

preliminary ➡ **early**

prelude ➡ **introduction**

premature ➡ **early**

premier ➡ **ruler**

premise ➡ **theory**

premises ➡ **property**

premium ➡ **best, prize**

premonition ➡ **warning**

preoccupation ➡ **obsession**

preoccupied ➡ **absorbed, absentminded**

preoccupy ➡ **interest**

preparation ➡ **practice**

preparatory school ➡ **school**

prepared ➡ **ready**

preponderance ➡ **most**

preposterous ➡ **foolish**

prerequisite ➡ **necessity**

prerogative ➡ **right**

presage ➡ **predict**

prescience ➡ **foresight**

prescribe ➡ **order, suggest**

prescribed ➡ **legal**

prescription ➡ **medicine, recipe**

presentation ➡ **display, introduction, program, delivery**

presenter ➡ **host**

presently ➡ **soon**

preservation ➡ **salvation**

preserve ➡ **save, keep, embalm, park, jelly**

preside ➡ **lead**

president ➡ **ruler**

press ➡ **push, squeeze, iron, urge**

pressing ➡ **urgent**

pressure ➡ **weight, energy, stress, force**

prestidigitator ➡ **magician**

prestige ➡ **fame, respect**

presumably ➡ **apparently, probably**

presume ➡ **assume, dare**

presumption ➡ **theory**

presumptuous ➡ **rude**

presuppose ➡ **assume**

➡ = synonym cross-reference • ⇨ = antonym cross-reference

pretend *vb* feign, affect, simulate, profess ➡ **act, assume, imagine, lie, fake**

pretense 1. *n* affectation, deceit, deception, fabrication, trickery, misrepresentation, fraud ➡ **act, lie, disguise, dishonesty**
2. *n* excuse, pretext, subterfuge ➡ **trick**

pretty *adj* lovely, handsome, attractive, good-looking, fair, becoming, comely, striking ➡ **beautiful, cute** ⇨ *ugly*

prevent *vb* avert, hinder, forestall, check, restrain, thwart, foil, frustrate, deter, inhibit, stunt, hobble, leash ➡ **stop, block, discourage, contain** ⇨ *let*

prey 1. *n* quarry, victim, target
2. *vb* ➡ **eat**
3. *vb* ➡ **cheat**

price *n* charge, expense, cost, fare, payment, amount, fee, consideration, outlay ➡ **worth, bill**

pride 1. *n* self-respect, self-esteem, dignity, self-confidence ➡ **respect**
2. *n* vanity, conceit, arrogance, vainglory, egotism, hubris, narcissism, haughtiness
3. *n* ➡ **pleasure**

priest *n* vicar, bishop, cardinal, pope, pontiff, rabbi ➡ **minister, religious**

prim *adj* proper, formal, stiff, wooden, stilted, decorous ➡ **correct, neat, polite**

primitive 1. *adj* ➡ **basic**
2. *adj* ➡ **early**
3. *adj* uncivilized, simple, crude, rough, rustic, unsophisticated, untamed, aboriginal, pristine

principal 1. *adj* ➡ **important**
2. *n* headmaster, master, administrator, superintendent, dean ➡ **boss**
3. *n* ➡ **party**

print 1. *vb* publish, issue, reprint ➡ **write**
2. *vb* imprint, impress, engrave, stamp, emboss, inscribe
3. *n* etching, engraving, woodcut, lithograph, photocopy ➡ **photograph, picture**
4. *n* impression, imprint, indentation, fingerprint, footprint ➡ **track**
5. *n* text, printing, type, typescript, writing

prisoner *n* captive, inmate, detainee, internee, slave, hostage, jailbird (*informal*)

privacy *n* solitude, seclusion, isolation, retirement, withdrawal, confinement, quarantine, segregation ➡ **secrecy**

If the word you want is not a main entry above, look below to find it.

pretentious ➡ **pompous, proud**

preternatural ➡ **supernatural**

pretext ➡ **pretense**

prettiness ➡ **beauty**

prevail ➡ **win, excel, persuade**

prevailing ➡ **predominant**

prevalent ➡ **predominant, common**

prevaricate ➡ **lie**

prevaricator ➡ **liar**

previous ➡ **past**

previously ➡ **once, before**

priceless ➡ **valuable**

prick ➡ **stick**

prickle ➡ **tingle**

primal ➡ **early**

primarily ➡ **chiefly**

primary ➡ **basic, important, early**

prime ➡ **best, important, top, prepare**

prime minister ➡ **ruler**

primeval ➡ **early**

primordial ➡ **early**

prince ➡ **ruler**

princely ➡ **noble**

principally ➡ **chiefly, practically**

principle ➡ **rule, belief, cause, virtue**

printing ➡ **print, handwriting**

prior ➡ **past, older, religious**

prior to ➡ **before**

prioress ➡ **religious**

priory ➡ **monastery**

prison ➡ **jail**

pristine ➡ **clean, new, primitive**

private 1. *adj* secluded, isolated, remote, withdrawn, insular, quarantined
2. *adj* personal, individual, intimate, own ⇨ *public*
3. *adj* exclusive, restricted, reserved, special ⇨ *public*
4. *adj* ➡ **secret**

prize 1. *n* reward, premium, bonus, trophy, garland, laurel, winnings, purse ➡ **award, gift, booty**
2. *vb* ➡ **appreciate, respect**

probably *adv* presumably, apparently, plausibly, seemingly ➡ **maybe**
Note that **probably** *and its synonyms also express a degree of uncertainty about something, but not as much as* **maybe** *and its synonyms.*

problem 1. *n* mystery, puzzle, riddle, dilemma, enigma, ambiguity, conundrum ➡ **contradiction, question**
2. *n* ➡ **trouble**

product 1. *n* merchandise, commodity, goods, wares
2. *n* by product, outgrowth, derivative, derivation, offshoot, spin off ➡ **answer, effect**

productivity *n* turnout, output, production, volume ➡ **growth, efficiency**

profession *n* occupation, employment, appointment, vocation, avocation, calling, career, livelihood, post, position, situation, place, craft, trade ➡ **job, field, business, specialty**

profound *adj* deep, sage, sagacious, intellectual, philosophical, penetrating, discerning, erudite, cerebral ➡ **smart, thoughtful, serious**

program 1. *n* performance, concert, recital, show, production, broadcast, telecast, presentation, series ➡ **play, movie, entertainment**
2. *n* ➡ **list**
3. *n* ➡ **plan, course**

If the word you want is not a main entry above, look below to find it.

privateer ➡ pirate

privation ➡ poverty

privilege ➡ right

prized ➡ valuable

prizewinner ➡ winner

probability ➡ possibility

probable ➡ likely

probe ➡ stick, hunt, study, examine

proboscis ➡ nose

procedure ➡ method

proceed ➡ go, continue

process ➡ method, prepare

procession ➡ parade

proclaim ➡ advertise, preach

proclamation ➡ announcement

proclivity ➡ tendency, preference

procrastinate ➡ delay

procreate ➡ reproduce

procure ➡ get

procurement ➡ acquisition

prod ➡ push, urge

prodigal ➡ wasteful, abundant

prodigious ➡ huge

prodigy ➡ genius

produce ➡ make, cause, give, show, vegetable

production ➡ program, assembly, productivity

productive ➡ successful, efficient, fertile

profanity ➡ curse

profess ➡ pretend, tell

professor ➡ teacher, doctor

proffer ➡ offer

proficiency ➡ ability, efficiency

proficient ➡ able, expert, efficient

profile ➡ face, description

profit ➡ advantage, wage, earn

profitable ➡ useful

profligate ➡ wasteful

profoundness ➡ depth

profundity ➡ depth

profuse ➡ abundant, thick, rich

profusion ➡ abundance

progenitor ➡ ancestor

progeny ➡ child

prognosticate ➡ predict

prognostication ➡ prediction

progression ➡ progress

progressive ➡ forward, gifted, consecutive, liberal

prohibit ➡ forbid

prohibited ➡ illegal

prohibition ➡ ban

---

progress 1. *n* improvement, progression, headway, advance, advancement, momentum ➡ **movement, growth, success**
2. *vb* ➡ **go**

promise 1. *n* oath, vow, word, pledge, assurance, commitment, covenant, guarantee
2. *vb* swear, pledge, vow, assure, warrant ➡ **guarantee**

promote 1. *vb* raise, advance, elevate, graduate, upgrade
2. *vb* ➡ **back, support**
3. *vb* ➡ **advertise**

promotion 1. *n* advancement, preferment, elevation, raise
2. *n* ➡ **advertisement, advertising**

prone 1. *adj* ➡ **likely**
2. *adj* prostrate, flat, supine, recumbent, lying (down), reclining, horizontal
3. *adj* ➡ **vulnerable**

pronounce *vb* enunciate, articulate, utter, vocalize ➡ **say, tell**

proof *n* evidence, testimony, verification, certification, documentation, data, corroboration, confirmation, substantiation, authentication

property 1. *n* possessions, belongings, effects, goods, assets, holdings, capital, things, stuff ➡ **wealth, acquisition**
2. *n* land, lot, estate, yard, grounds, premises, plot, tract
3. *n* ➡ **quality**

prophet *n* seer, soothsayer, oracle, clairvoyant, medium, fortune teller, astrologer, diviner ➡ **magician**

prosper *vb* flourish, thrive, succeed, benefit, flower ➡ **blossom, grow, excel**

protect 1. *vb* defend, guard, shield, safeguard, fortify, watch, mind, tend ➡ **save, patrol** ⇨ *attack*
2. *vb* shelter, cover, cushion, pad

If the word you want is not a main entry above, look below to find it.

project ➡ **plan, job, development, shoot, throw, swell, predict**
projected ➡ **future**
projectile ➡ **missile**
projection ➡ **branch**
proliferate ➡ **reproduce**
proliferation ➡ **growth**
prolific ➡ **fertile**
prologue ➡ **introduction**
prolong ➡ **lengthen**
prom ➡ **dance**
prominence ➡ **accent**
prominent ➡ **famous, obvious, important**
promiscuous ➡ **indiscriminate**

promised land ➡ **utopia**
promontory ➡ **cape, cliff**
prompt ➡ **early, fast, punctual, reminder, cause, urge**
promptly ➡ **quickly**
pronounced ➡ **obvious**
pronouncement ➡ **announcement**
pronunciation ➡ **accent, delivery**
prop ➡ **support**
propaganda ➡ **advertising**
propagate ➡ **reproduce, plant**
propel ➡ **shoot, throw, drive**

propensity ➡ **tendency**
proper ➡ **fit[1], correct, prim, good, special**
properly ➡ **well, correctly**
proper name ➡ **name**
prophecy ➡ **prediction**
prophesy ➡ **predict**
proportion ➡ **balance, size, share**
proposal ➡ **suggestion**
propose ➡ **offer, suggest, intend**
proposition ➡ **suggestion**
proprietor ➡ **owner**
proprietorship ➡ **possession**

propulsion ➡ **energy**
prosaic ➡ **dull**
proscribe ➡ **forbid**
proscription ➡ **ban**
prosecute ➡ **try**
prospect ➡ **view, possibility, hunt**
prospective ➡ **future**
prosperity ➡ **wealth, welfare, success**
prosperous ➡ **rich**
prostrate ➡ **prone**
prostration ➡ **exhaustion**
protected ➡ **safe**
protective ➡ **motherly, fatherly**

protection 1. *n* security, safety, defense, caution, precaution, care, safeguard
➡ **support**
2. *n* shelter, refuge, cover, retreat, harbor, haven, sanctuary, asylum, shield, buffer

protest 1. *n* demonstration, strike, sit-in, teach-in, rally ➡ **complaint**
2. *vb* demonstrate, picket, strike, walk out ➡ **complain, object**
3. *vb* ➡ **complain, object, argue**

proud 1. *adj* egotistic, conceited, vain, arrogant, egocentric, haughty, smug, superior, pretentious ➡ **pompous** ⇨ *humble*
2. *adj* ➡ **grand**
3. *adj* ➡ **happy**

provincial 1. *adj* ➡ **rural**
2. *adj* narrow-minded, unsophisticated, parochial, unpolished, intolerant, insular, hidebound ➡ **naive, primitive, mean**

pseudonym *n* pen name, alias, stage name, nom de plume, nickname, sobriquet

public 1. *adj* civic, civil, governmental, communal, municipal, federal, social
➡ **common** ⇨ *private*
2. *n* ➡ **people**
3. *n* ➡ **following**

pull 1. *vb* tow, drag, haul, draw, tug, yank, jerk, pluck, attract, bring, tighten, strain
➡ **extract** ⇨ *push*
2. *vb* sprain, strain ➡ **hurt**
3. *n* tug, yank, drag, jerk, wrench
➡ **attraction**

punch 1. *vb* slap, belt, pummel, box ➡ **hit**
2. *n* ➡ **blow**[1]

punctual *adj* timely, prompt, precise, expeditious, punctilious ⇨ *late*

punish *vb* discipline, penalize, sentence, correct, fine ➡ **abuse, hurt, hit, scold, whip**

If the word you want is not a main entry above, look below to find it.

protector ➡ **savior**
protocol ➡ **ceremony**
prototype ➡ **model**
protract ➡ **lengthen**
protracted ➡ **long**
protrude ➡ **swell**
protrusion ➡ **bulge**
protuberance ➡ **bulge**
prove ➡ **verify**
proverb ➡ **saying**
proverbial ➡ **legendary**
provide ➡ **supply, prepare**
providential ➡ **lucky**
province ➡ **state, field**
provision ➡ **plan, supply, excerpt**
provisional ➡ **temporary, experimental**

provisions ➡ **food**
provocative ➡ **interesting**
provoke ➡ **anger, dare, urge**
prow ➡ **front**
prowess ➡ **talent**
prowl ➡ **sneak**
proximity ➡ **presence**
prudence ➡ **foresight, economy**
prudent ➡ **careful, cheap**
prudently ➡ **carefully**
prune ➡ **cut, condense**
pry ➡ **lift, meddle, spy**
prying ➡ **curious, interference**
psalm ➡ **hymn**
pseudonymous ➡ **anonymous**

psyche ➡ **mind, soul**
psychic ➡ **supernatural**
psychology ➡ **science**
psychotic ➡ **insane**
pub ➡ **bar**
puberty ➡ **childhood**
public assistance ➡ **welfare**
publication ➡ **book**
publicity ➡ **advertising, notice**
publicize ➡ **advertise**
public servant ➡ **official**
publish ➡ **print, write**
pucker ➡ **wrinkle**
pudgy ➡ **fat**
puerile ➡ **childish**
puff ➡ **wind, smoke, breathe**

puff up ➡ **swell**
pugnacious ➡ **belligerent**
puke ➡ **vomit**
pulchritude ➡ **beauty**
pull out ➡ **retreat**
pulpit ➡ **platform**
pulsar ➡ **star**
pulsate ➡ **shake**
pulsation ➡ **impulse**
pulse ➡ **rhythm, impulse**
pulverize ➡ **grind**
pummel ➡ **punch**
pun ➡ **joke**
punctilious ➡ **punctual**
puncture ➡ **hole, stick**
pungent ➡ **fragrant, spicy**

---

punishment *n* penalty, sentence, penance, deserts, retribution, consequence, discipline ➡ **abuse**

puppet 1. *n* marionette, dummy, mannequin ➡ **doll**
2. *n* ➡ **tool**

purple *adj, n* violet, magenta, lilac, mauve, plum, lavender

purposely *adv* deliberately, purposefully, intentionally, consciously, knowingly, willfully ⇨ *accidentally*

push 1. *vb* press, shove, impel, thrust, jostle, nudge, elbow, shoulder, shove, slide, thrust, prod, poke, ram, jam, wedge ➡ **move, force** ⇨ *pull*
2. *vb* ➡ **urge**
3. *n* ➡ **blow, impulse**

put *vb* set, lay, park, deposit, plant, position, implant, install, insert ➡ **place**

If the word you want is not a main entry above, look below to find it.

punk ➡ vandal

punt ➡ kick

puny ➡ weak

pupil ➡ student

puppy ➡ dog

purchase ➡ acquisition, sale, buy

pure ➡ innocent, perfect, natural, real

purify ➡ clean

purity ➡ virtue

purloin ➡ steal

purpose ➡ reason, object, plan, use, intend

purposefully ➡ purposely

purr ➡ hum

purse ➡ bag, wallet, prize

pursue ➡ follow

pursuit ➡ pastime, hunt

pushy ➡ meddlesome

put-down ➡ insult

put off ➡ delay

put out ➡ extinguish

putrefy ➡ decay

putrid ➡ smelly, bad

putter ➡ tinker

put up ➡ house

puzzle ➡ problem, confuse

puzzlement ➡ confusion

puzzle out ➡ solve

puzzling ➡ mysterious

pygmy ➡ midget

pyre ➡ fire

pyrotechnics ➡ fireworks

---

n = noun • *vb* = verb • *adj* = adjective • *adv* = adverb • *prep* = preposition • *conj* = conjunction

Q

quality *n* property, characteristic, character, trait, attribute, air, atmosphere, texture, tone ➡ **class, feeling**

queen *n* monarch, sovereign, maharani *(India)*, rani *(India)*, sultana *(Muslim)* ➡ **ruler, empress**

question 1. *n* query, inquiry, interrogation, interrogative ➡ **problem** ⇨ *answer*
2. *n* ➡ **doubt**
3. *n* ➡ **subject**
4. *vb* ➡ **ask**

quickly *adv* speedily, hastily, hurriedly, fast, rapidly, expeditiously, instantaneously, promptly, headlong ➡ **now, soon**

quiet 1. *adj* silent, still, hushed, noiseless, soundless, inaudible, mute, mum, speechless ➡ **low** ⇨ *loud*
2. *n* ➡ **calm**
3. *vb* hush, silence, soften, mute, muffle, stifle, muzzle, gag

quote 1. *vb* cite, repeat, parrot, paraphrase, recite, declaim, render ➡ **mention, say, tell**
2. *n* ➡ **estimate**

If the word you want is not a main entry above, look below to find it.

quack ➡ cheat, hypocrite

quad ➡ court

quadrangle ➡ square, court

quadrilateral ➡ square

quaff ➡ drink

quagmire ➡ swamp

quail ➡ fear, retreat

quaint ➡ strange, cute

quake ➡ shake, fear, vibration, earthquake

qualification ➡ necessity, term

qualified ➡ able, ready

qualify ➡ let, soften

qualm ➡ doubt, nausea

quandary ➡ trouble

quantity ➡ number, size

quarantine ➡ privacy, separate

quarantined ➡ private

quarrel ➡ argue, argument

quarrelsome ➡ unfriendly

quarry ➡ prey, mine

quarter ➡ term, zone, neighborhood, divide, house

quash ➡ subdue, contain

quaver ➡ vibration, shake

quay ➡ dock

queasiness ➡ nausea

queasy ➡ sick

queer ➡ strange, suspicious

quell ➡ contain

quench ➡ extinguish, contain, satisfy

query ➡ question, ask

quest ➡ hunt

questionable ➡ doubtful

queue ➡ braid, row

quibble ➡ argue

quick ➡ fast, agile, smart, alive

quicken ➡ hurry

quill ➡ pen

quilt ➡ blanket

quintessence ➡ essence

quip ➡ joke

quirk ➡ habit

quit ➡ abandon, leave, surrender

quite ➡ completely, very

quiver ➡ shake, vibration

quixotic ➡ impractical

quiz ➡ examination, examine, ask

quota ➡ share

quotation ➡ excerpt, estimate

R

race 1. *n* run, dash, sprint, relay, marathon, footrace, horse race, steeplechase, derby ➡ **game**
2. *vb* ➡ **run, hurry**
3. *n* ➡ **type**
4. *n* ➡ **humanity**

ragged *adj* tattered, frayed, threadbare, torn, rent ➡ **old, shabby**

rain 1. *n* precipitation, shower, downpour, drizzle, cloudburst, torrent ➡ **storm**
2. *vb* pour, drizzle, sprinkle, shower, teem, precipitate

range 1. *n* extent, scope, spread, reach, compass, sweep, spectrum ➡ **assortment, space, horizon**
2. *n* ➡ **plain**
3. *vb* ➡ **wander**
4. *vb* ➡ **spread**

rare *adj* uncommon, scarce, infrequent, occasional ➡ **special, valuable**

rascal *n* scoundrel, villain, knave, wretch, scamp, imp, sneak, charlatan, fraud, swindler, rogue, rake, libertine, lecher ➡ **bully, criminal**

If the word you want is not a main entry above, look below to find it.

rabbi ➡ priest
racetrack ➡ course
rack ➡ shelf
racket ➡ noise
racy ➡ dirty
radiance ➡ light[1]
radiant ➡ bright
radiate ➡ shine, throw
radiation ➡ X ray
radical ➡ excessive, liberal, extremist
radiograph ➡ X ray
raffle ➡ lottery
rafter ➡ beam, board
rag ➡ cloth
ragamuffin ➡ urchin
rage ➡ anger, hysteria, fashion
raging ➡ rough, wild
raid ➡ attack
rail ➡ bar
raincoat ➡ coat
raindrop ➡ drop

rainforest ➡ forest
rainspout ➡ gargoyle
rainstorm ➡ storm
rainy ➡ wet, stormy
raise ➡ lift, grow, adopt, build, broach, promote, promotion
raison d'être ➡ basis
rajah ➡ king
rake ➡ dig, rascal
rally ➡ mobilize, protest
ram ➡ push
ramble ➡ wander, chatter
rambling ➡ indirect
rambunctious ➡ loud
ramp ➡ channel
rampage ➡ disturbance
rampant ➡ wild
rampart ➡ wall
ranch ➡ farm
rancher ➡ farmer
ranching ➡ farming
rancid ➡ sour, smelly, bad

random ➡ arbitrary
R & R ➡ vacation
range ➡ plain
rani ➡ queen
rank ➡ grade, row, arrange, smelly
rankle ➡ bother
ransack ➡ pillage, hunt
ransom ➡ recover
rant ➡ yell
rap ➡ knock, talk
rapacious ➡ greedy, predatory
rapid ➡ fast, sharp
rapidity ➡ speed
rapidly ➡ quickly
rapier ➡ sword
rapport ➡ relationship
rapture ➡ pleasure
rarely ➡ seldom
rarity ➡ miracle
rascality ➡ mischief
rash ➡ thoughtless, imprudent, epidemic

rasp ➡ squeak
raspy ➡ hoarse
rate ➡ speed, deserve
rather ➡ very, more, instead
ratification ➡ approval
ratify ➡ approve
ratio ➡ share
ration ➡ share, budget
rational ➡ practical, sane
rationale ➡ reason
rations ➡ food
rattle ➡ embarrass, bang
raucous ➡ loud
ravage ➡ destroy, attack
rave ➡ yell, praise, good
raven ➡ black
ravenous ➡ hungry, predatory
ravine ➡ canyon
ravishing ➡ beautiful
raw ➡ natural, cold, sore
rawhide ➡ hide
ray ➡ light[1]

n = noun • *vb* = verb • *adj* = adjective • *adv* = adverb • *prep* = preposition • *conj* = conjunction

read 1. *vb* peruse, skim, scan, browse ➡ **study**
2. *vb* comprehend, decipher, decode, perceive
3. *vb* indicate, register, record ➡ **show**

ready 1. *adj* prepared, set, qualified, ripe, equipped ➡ **available**
2. *adj* willing, disposed, predisposed ➡ **eager, likely**
3. *vb* ➡ **prepare**

real 1. *adj* actual, material, tangible, substantive, concrete, objective, solid, true, palpable ➡ **physical** ⇨ *imaginary*
2. *adj* actual, genuine, authentic, bona fide, veritable, literal, legitimate, pure ➡ **natural** ⇨ *fake*

really 1. *adv* actually, genuinely, literally, indeed, veritably ➡ **certainly**
2. *adv* ➡ **very**

reason 1. *n* purpose, cause, motive, explanation, call, grounds, need, rationale ➡ **necessity, incentive, justification**
2. *n* logic, reasoning, thinking, induction, deduction, analysis ➡ **wisdom**
3. *vb* ➡ **think, infer**
4. *n* sanity, mental health, lucidity, saneness

rebel 1. *vb* revolt, mutiny, resist, defy ➡ **face, dare**
2. *n* revolutionary, insurgent, mutineer, subversive, dissident, freedom fighter, traitor, turncoat ➡ **extremist**

rebellious *adj* disobedient, mutinous, defiant, insubordinate, seditious

receive 1. *vb* accept, admit, take, inherit, greet ➡ **get** ⇨ *give, refuse*
2. *vb* ➡ **welcome, entertain**

recently *adv* lately, newly, just, latterly

recipe *n* formula, directions, instructions, prescription ➡ **plan**

If the word you want is not a main entry above, look below to find it.

raze ➡ **destroy**

razor ➡ **knife**

reach ➡ **come, touch, range**

react ➡ **answer**

reaction ➡ **answer**

reactionary ➡ **conservative**

readable ➡ **legible**

readers ➡ **audience**

reading ➡ **tryout**

realign ➡ **straighten**

realistic ➡ **practical, explicit**

reality ➡ **existence, certainty**

realize ➡ **learn, know, earn**

realm ➡ **country, field**

reap ➡ **cut, gather**

reappear ➡ **return**

reappearance ➡ **return**

rear ➡ **back, adopt, grow, lift, tower**

rearend ➡ **back**

rearend ➡ **collide**

rearward ➡ **backward**

reasonable ➡ **practical, sane, possible, cheap**

reasoning ➡ **reason**

reassure ➡ **comfort**

reawaken ➡ **renew**

reawakening ➡ **revival**

rebate ➡ **refund**

rebellion ➡ **revolution, disobedience**

rebirth ➡ **revival**

rebound ➡ **reflect, return**

rebuff ➡ **rejection, refuse**

rebuild ➡ **fix**

rebuke ➡ **scold**

rebut ➡ **disprove**

recall ➡ **remember, memory**

recapitulate ➡ **repeat**

recede ➡ **retreat**

receipt ➡ **ticket, possession**

receivable ➡ **due**

recent ➡ **new, modern**

receptacle ➡ **container**

reception ➡ **welcome, party, treatment**

recess ➡ **break, vacation, bay**

recession ➡ **depression**

reciprocate ➡ **alternate, answer**

reciprocation ➡ **answer**

recital ➡ **program**

recite ➡ **quote, tell**

reckless ➡ **thoughtless, wasteful**

reckon ➡ **guess, estimate**

reckoning ➡ **score, addition**

reclaim ➡ **recover**

recline ➡ **lie**

reclining ➡ **prone**

recluse ➡ **hermit**

recognition ➡ **gratitude**

recognize ➡ **remember, distinguish, know**

recoil ➡ **retreat, jump**

recollect ➡ **remember**

recollection ➡ **memory**

recommence ➡ **continue**

recommend ➡ **suggest, approve**

recommendation ➡ **advice, suggestion**

➡ = synonym cross-reference • ⇨ = antonym cross-reference

recover *vb* regain, retrieve, recoup, reclaim, redeem, ransom ➡ **find, save**

red 1. *adj, n* pink, scarlet, crimson, maroon, vermilion, carmine, ruby, rose
2. *adj* ruddy, rosy, flushed, florid, blushing

reflect 1. *vb* echo, mirror, ricochet, rebound, bounce
2. *vb* ➡ **consider, meditate**

refrigerator *n* icebox, fridge, freezer, cooler

refund 1. *vb* reimburse, repay, remit, compensate ➡ **pay**

2. *n* reimbursement, repayment, compensation, rebate

refuse 1. *vb* deny, reject, decline, dismiss, disapprove, spurn, repudiate, rebuff, snub, scorn, flout ➡ **deprive, repel**
2. *n* ➡ **trash**

regret 1. *vb* repent, apologize, bewail, bemoan, lament, deplore, rue ➡ **grieve**
2. *n* compunction, repentance
➡ **disappointment, sorrow, shame**

If the word you want is not a main entry above, look below to find it.

recompense ➡ pay

reconcile ➡ correct, decide

reconciliation ➡ peace

recondition ➡ fix

reconnoiter ➡ patrol

record ➡ document, list, write, read

recount ➡ describe, repeat

recoup ➡ recover

recourse ➡ choice

recovery ➡ return, cure

recreate ➡ play

recreation ➡ game, leisure, entertainment, play

recreational area ➡ park

recreation center ➡ gymnasium

recreation room ➡ den

rec room ➡ den

recruit ➡ soldier, hire

rectangle ➡ square

rectangular ➡ square

rectification ➡ correction

rectify ➡ correct

rectilinear ➡ square

rector ➡ minister

recumbent ➡ prone

recuperate ➡ rest

recuperation ➡ cure

recur ➡ repeat, return, happen

recurrence ➡ return, relapse

recurrent ➡ frequent, periodic

recurrently ➡ often

recycling center ➡ dump

redcap ➡ porter

redden ➡ blush

redecorate ➡ decorate

redecoration ➡ decoration

redeem ➡ balance, recover

redeemer ➡ savior

redemption ➡ salvation

redirect ➡ detour

redo ➡ repeat

redolent ➡ fragrant

redress ➡ correct

reduce ➡ decrease

reduced ➡ less

reduction ➡ subtraction, drop, bargain, model

redundant ➡ unnecessary, talkative

reduplicate ➡ repeat

reek ➡ smell

reel ➡ swing

reestablish ➡ renew

referee ➡ judge, negotiate

referendum ➡ vote

refer to ➡ mention, concern, use

refill ➡ renew

refine ➡ prepare

refinement ➡ class, civilization

reflective ➡ thoughtful

reflector ➡ mirror

reflex ➡ automatic, habit

reform ➡ correct

reformatory ➡ jail

reformist ➡ liberal

refrain ➡ abstain, chorus, stanza

refresh ➡ renew

refreshment ➡ meal, food, drink

refrigerate ➡ cool

refuge ➡ protection, park

refugee ➡ exile

refurbish ➡ decorate

refusal ➡ rejection

refute ➡ contradict, disprove

regain ➡ recover

regal ➡ noble, grand

regale ➡ entertain

regard ➡ look, notice, respect, concern

regarding ➡ about

regardless ➡ anyway

regime ➡ government

regimen ➡ discipline

regimentation ➡ discipline

region ➡ zone, place

register ➡ read, join, list, table, cash register

registration ➡ license

regress ➡ relapse

regression ➡ relapse

regressive ➡ backward

regressively ➡ backward

regrets ➡ apology

regrettable ➡ unfortunate

regular ➡ usual, frequent, straight, patron

regularly *adv* constantly, invariably, always, ever, continually, habitually, routinely, religiously, naturally, typically ➡ **often, usually, forever**

rejection *n* refusal, rebuff, denial, dismissal, renunciation, repudiation, veto

relapse 1. *vb* regress, backslide, revert, deteriorate, lapse, retrogress, worsen
2. *n* regression, reversion, recurrence, reverse, setback

relationship *n* relation, kinship, affinity, rapport, compatibility ➡ **link, friendship**

relevance *n* connection, bearing, significance, pertinence ➡ **importance**

relevant *adj* pertinent, germane, apposite, applicable, apropos, related, relative ➡ **fit**

reliable *adj* dependable, trustworthy, responsible, reputable, unimpeachable, solid, conscientious, sure, sure-fire ➡ **faithful, able, indisputable**

relieve 1. *vb* alleviate, ease, soothe, lessen, lighten, mitigate, allay ➡ **help, please**

2. *vb* dismiss, replace, discharge, substitute, excuse ➡ **free**

religion 1. *n* faith, mythology, theology, religiosity, spirituality, orthodoxy ➡ **belief, philosophy**
2. *n* denomination, sect, order, cult

religious 1. *adj* devout, pious, spiritual, orthodox, godly, reverent, God-fearing, reverential, churchgoing ➡ **faithful**
2. *adj* sacred, divine, ecclesiastical, clerical, liturgical, theological ➡ **holy**
3. *n* monk, friar, brother, abbot, prior, nun, sister, abbess, prioress ➡ **priest, minister**

reluctant *adj* hesitant, unwilling, grudging, disinclined, loath, averse, diffident, squeamish

remainder *n* remains, rest, remnant, residue, balance, surplus

remark 1. *n* comment, statement, mention, observation, commentary, utterance ➡ **saying**
2. *vb* ➡ **say**
3. *vb* ➡ **see**

If the word you want is not a main entry above, look below to find it.

regulate ➡ adjust, control

regulation ➡ rule

regurgitate ➡ vomit

rehabilitation ➡ cure

rehabilitation center ➡ hospital

rehash ➡ repeat

rehearsal ➡ practice

rehearse ➡ practice, repeat

reign ➡ govern

reimburse ➡ refund

reimbursement ➡ refund, return

rein ➡ rope

reinforce ➡ strengthen

reinforcement ➡ support

reins ➡ wheel

reiterate ➡ repeat

reject ➡ refuse, exclude, discard

rejected ➡ abandoned

rejoice ➡ celebrate

rejoinder ➡ answer

rejuvenate ➡ renew

rejuvenation ➡ revival

rekindle ➡ renew

relate ➡ tell, belong

related ➡ relevant

relating to ➡ about

relation ➡ family, relationship

relative ➡ family, relevant

relax ➡ calm, rest

relaxation ➡ comfort, leisure, rest

relaxed ➡ calm

relay ➡ race, broadcast

release ➡ free

relegate ➡ entrust

relent ➡ surrender

relentless ➡ continual, mean

relic ➡ antique

relief ➡ help

religiosity ➡ religion

religiously ➡ regularly

relinquish ➡ surrender

relish ➡ like, appreciate, spice

relocate ➡ move

rely ➡ depend

remain ➡ wait, continue

remains ➡ remainder, body

remand ➡ jail

remarkable ➡ great, special

remedial ➡ medicinal

remedy ➡ cure, correction, heal, correct

---

remember *vb* recall, recollect, reminisce, remind, recognize, commemorate, memorialize ➡ **know, learn** ⇨ *forget*

reminder 1. *n* hint, cue, notice, prompt ➡ **warning, letter**
2. *n* souvenir, memento, token, remembrance, keepsake, memorial

renew 1. *vb* restore, revive, rejuvenate, refresh, reawaken, invigorate, reestablish, rekindle, update ➡ **continue**
2. *vb* refill, replenish, replace, restock
3. *vb* ➡ **fix**

repair 1. *n* adjustment, improvement, renovation, restoration, patch, plug, mend, service, servicing ➡ **correction**
2. *vb* ➡ **fix**

repeat 1. *vb* redo, replicate, duplicate, reduplicate ➡ **reproduce**
2. *vb* recur, reoccur
3. *vb* reiterate, restate, recapitulate, echo, rehearse, rehash, recount ➡ **quote**

repel 1. *vb* repulse, foil, ward off, stave off, fend off, withstand, parry ➡ **refuse**
2. *vb* ➡ **disgust**

report 1. *n* essay, paper, composition, theme, treatise, thesis, dissertation, article ➡ **announcement, speech, story, study**
2. *n* ➡ **bang**
3. *vb* ➡ **tell**

reporter *n* journalist, correspondent, newspaperman, newspaperwoman, newsman, newswoman, newscaster, anchor ➡ **writer**
Note that **reporters** and other newspeople are referred to as a group as the press, the media, *and* the fourth estate.

If the word you want is not a main entry above, look below to find it.

remembrance ➡ reminder, memory

remind ➡ remember

reminisce ➡ remember

reminiscence ➡ memory

remiss ➡ negligent

remission ➡ forgiveness

remit ➡ refund

remnant ➡ remainder, cloth

remorse ➡ shame

remorseful ➡ sorry

remote ➡ far, foreign, private, cool

removal ➡ suspension, movement

remove ➡ move, subtract, exclude, oust, empty, extract, shed

removed ➡ far

remunerate ➡ pay

renaissance ➡ revival

rend ➡ rip

render ➡ quote, translate, give, act, do

rendezvous ➡ meeting, gather

rendition ➡ translation

renegade ➡ runaway

renewal ➡ revival

renounce ➡ abstain, abandon

renovate ➡ fix

renovation ➡ repair

renown ➡ fame

renowned ➡ famous

rent ➡ hire, borrow, ragged, rip

rental ➡ loan

renter ➡ occupant

renunciation ➡ rejection, surrender

reoccur ➡ repeat, return

reoccurrence ➡ return

repairman ➡ mechanic

repair shop ➡ garage

reparation ➡ correction

repast ➡ meal, feast

repay ➡ refund, revenge

repayment ➡ refund, return, revenge

repeal ➡ abolish

repeatedly ➡ often

repellent ➡ ugly

repent ➡ regret

repentance ➡ regret

repentant ➡ sorry

repetition ➡ practice

repetitious ➡ talkative

replace ➡ renew, change, relieve, follow

replacement ➡ alternate

replenish ➡ renew

replete ➡ full

replica ➡ duplicate

replicate ➡ repeat

reply ➡ answer

repose ➡ peace, sleep, leisure, rest, comfort, lie

repository ➡ bank

represent ➡ describe, embody

representation ➡ picture, model, example

representative ➡ example, agent

repress ➡ abuse, contain

repression ➡ tyranny

reprieve ➡ forgiveness

reprimand ➡ scold

reprint ➡ print

reproach ➡ scold, complaint

n = noun • *vb* = verb • *adj* = adjective • *adv* = adverb • *prep* = preposition • *conj* = conjunction

reproduce 1. *vb* copy, duplicate, photocopy, clone ➡ **imitate**
2. *vb* procreate, breed, propagate, multiply, proliferate, generate, beget, spawn, hatch

reptile *n* reptilian, amphibian, lizard ➡ **snake, animal**

reputation *n* status, position, repute, estimation, character, name

resemble *vb* look like, take after, match, approximate, favor, correspond

resolute *adj* strong-minded, determined, resolved, steadfast, unwavering, staunch, unyielding, adamant, uncompromising, assured, decisive ➡ **brave, faithful, stubborn**

respect 1. *n* admiration, honor, reverence, dignity, homage, esteem, regard, estimation, deference, courtesy, awe, wonder, prestige ➡ **pride**
2. *vb* esteem, admire, revere, value, prize, cherish ➡ **appreciate**
3. *vb* ➡ **keep**

rest 1. *vb* relax, repose, unwind, recuperate, lounge, loaf, laze, idle, vegetate (*informal*) ➡ **sleep, lie**
2. *vb* ➡ **depend**
3. *n* relaxation, repose, ease ➡ **sleep, break, vacation**
4. *n* ➡ **remainder**

restaurant *n* café, inn, deli, diner, cafeteria, tavern, luncheonette, bistro, pizzeria, canteen, tearoom, coffeehouse

---

If the word you want is not a main entry above, look below to find it.

reproduction ➡ copy
reprove ➡ scold
reptilian ➡ reptile
republic ➡ country
repudiate ➡ refuse
repudiation ➡ rejection
repugnance ➡ disgust
repugnant ➡ ugly
repulse ➡ repel
repulsive ➡ ugly, bad
reputable ➡ good, reliable
repute ➡ reputation
reputedly ➡ apparently
request ➡ ask, appeal, invitation
requiem ➡ dirge
require ➡ force, need, insist
required ➡ necessary

requirement ➡ necessity
requisite ➡ necessary, necessity
requite ➡ revenge
rescind ➡ abolish
rescue ➡ save, escape
rescuer ➡ savior
research ➡ study
resemblance ➡ similarity
resent ➡ envy
resentful ➡ jealous
resentment ➡ envy
reservation ➡ park, doubt, term
reserve ➡ park, supply
reserved ➡ shy, private, cool
reservoir ➡ well, lake, supply
reside ➡ live[1]

residence ➡ home
resident ➡ citizen, occupant
residential ➡ family
residue ➡ remainder
resign ➡ surrender, abandon
resignation ➡ surrender
resigned ➡ passive
resilient ➡ tough, flexible
resist ➡ rebel, fight
resistance ➡ fight, friction
resistant ➡ unbreakable
resolution ➡ will, answer, decision, clarity
resolve ➡ decide, solve, will
resolved ➡ resolute
resonant ➡ loud
resort ➡ hotel
resort to ➡ use

resound ➡ ring
resounding ➡ loud
resource ➡ support
resourceful ➡ ambitious
resources ➡ budget
respectable ➡ correct, good
respectful ➡ good
respective ➡ special
respiration ➡ breath
respire ➡ breathe
respite ➡ break, vacation
resplendent ➡ rich
respond ➡ answer
response ➡ answer
responsibility ➡ duty, guilt
responsible ➡ reliable, guilty
restate ➡ repeat

➡ = synonym cross-reference • ⇨ = antonym cross-reference

retreat 1. *vb* withdraw, retire, recede, ebb, back out, back down, recoil, shrink, quail, pull out ➡ **abandon, leave**
2. *n* ➡ **protection**
3. *n* ➡ **hotel**

return 1. *vb* come back, go back, revisit, recur, reoccur, resurface, reappear, rebound ➡ **renew**
2. *n* arrival, homecoming, reappearance, recurrence, reoccurrence, resurgence
3. *n* recovery, restoration, restitution, reimbursement, repayment
4. *n* ➡ **wage**

reveal 1. *vb* disclose, divulge, confess, bare, betray ➡ **discover** ⇨ *hide*
2. *vb* expose, uncover, unveil, unearth ➡ **show**

revenge 1. *n* vengeance, retaliation, repayment, compensation, satisfaction, vindication
2. *vb* avenge, retaliate, repay, requite, vindicate

revengeful *adj* vindictive, vengeful, avenging, retaliatory, spiteful ➡ **mean**

revival *n* rebirth, renaissance, resurrection, renewal, reawakening, rejuvenation, revitalization

revolution 1. *n* rebellion, revolt, insurrection, uprising, coup, coup d'état, insurgence ➡ **treason, disturbance**
2. *n* ➡ **change**
3. *n* ➡ **circle**

rhythm *n* beat, cadence, meter, tempo, time, measure, swing, pulse

---

If the word you want is not a main entry above, look below to find it.

restful ➡ comfortable

resting ➡ asleep

restitution ➡ return

restless ➡ nervous

restock ➡ renew

restoration ➡ repair, return

restore ➡ fix, renew

restrain ➡ prevent, contain

restraint ➡ bond

restrict ➡ bar

restricted ➡ finite, private

restriction ➡ ban, term

restroom ➡ bathroom

result ➡ effect, answer

resume ➡ continue

resurface ➡ return

resurgence ➡ return

resurrection ➡ revival

retail ➡ sell

retain ➡ keep, own

retainer ➡ servant

retaliate ➡ revenge

retaliation ➡ revenge

retaliatory ➡ revengeful

retard ➡ delay

retch ➡ vomit

retinue ➡ court, following

retire ➡ retreat

retirement ➡ privacy

retiring ➡ shy

retort ➡ answer

retract ➡ extract

retribution ➡ punishment

retrieve ➡ recover, find

retrograde ➡ backward

retrogress ➡ relapse

reunion ➡ meeting

revel ➡ celebrate

revelation ➡ announcement

revelry ➡ party

revenue ➡ money, wage

revere ➡ respect, love, worship

reverence ➡ respect, worship

reverent ➡ religious

reverential ➡ religious

reverie ➡ dream

reverse ➡ back, opposite, relapse, change

reversed ➡ backward, upside down

reversion ➡ relapse

revert ➡ relapse

review ➡ study

reviewer ➡ judge

revile ➡ curse

revise ➡ correct

revision ➡ correction

revisit ➡ return

revitalization ➡ revival

revive ➡ renew

revoke ➡ abolish

revolt ➡ revolution, rebel, disgust

revolting ➡ ugly

revolutionary ➡ rebel

revolve ➡ turn

revolver ➡ gun

revulsion ➡ hatred, disgust

reward ➡ prize, pay, tip

rhetorical ➡ theoretical

rhetorician ➡ speaker

rhyme ➡ poem

rhythmical ➡ musical

rib ➡ bar

ribald ➡ dirty

ribbon ➡ band, award

ribcage ➡ chest

ribs ➡ chest

---

n = noun • *vb* = verb • *adj* = adjective • *adv* = adverb • *prep* = preposition • *conj* = conjunction

rich 1. *adj* wealthy, affluent, prosperous, well-to-do, moneyed, well-off, comfortable, posh ➡ **successful** ⇨ *poor*
2. *adj* opulent, resplendent, ornate, lavish, lush, luxurious, profuse ➡ **grand, fashionable, expensive, fancy**
3. *adj* sweet, sugary, creamy, buttery, fattening, luscious, succulent, cloying, saccharine, honeyed ➡ **delicious**
4. *n* ➡ **aristocracy**

rider 1. *n* passenger, hitchhiker, cyclist, bicyclist, motorcyclist
2. *n* jockey, equestrian, horseman, horsewoman
3. *n* ➡ **addition**

ridicule 1. *n* derision, mockery, scorn, disdain ➡ **laughter**
2. *vb* jeer, belittle, deprecate, disparage, mock, deride, scoff, gibe ➡ **insult**

right 1. *n* power, privilege, prerogative, authority, license ➡ **freedom**
2. *adj* ➡ **correct, fit, fair** ⇨ *wrong*
3. *adv* ➡ **correctly**

4. *adv* ➡ **soon**
5. *adv* ➡ **precisely**

ring 1. *n* hoop, circlet ➡ **band, circle**
2. *n* chime, knell, toll, peal, clang, jingle, jangle, tinkle, clang, tintinnabulation ➡ **noise**
3. *n* ➡ **group**
4. *vb* circle, encircle, encompass, surround, enclose, loop, gird
5. *vb* resound, peal, knell, chime, toll, jingle, jangle, clang, bong, ding, sound, tinkle
6. *vb* ➡ **call**

rip 1. *vb* tear, rend, shred ➡ **cut, separate**
2. *n* tear, rent ➡ **hole, cut**

river 1. *n* stream, creek, brook, rivulet, tributary, estuary
2. *n* ➡ **flood**
Both **creek** *and* **brook** *are widely used terms for a small stream. Both words often refer to streams of the same size, but some people use* **brook** *to refer to a stream smaller than one they would call a* **creek**.

If the word you want is not a main entry above, look below to find it.

riches ➡ **wealth**
rickety ➡ **weak**
ricochet ➡ **reflect**
rid ➡ **exclude**
riddle ➡ **problem, stick**
ride ➡ **drive**
ridge ➡ **mountain, hill**
ridiculous ➡ **foolish, funny**
rifle ➡ **steal, gun**
rift ➡ **break**

rig ➡ **supply, tinker**
right away ➡ **now**
righteous ➡ **good**
right-wing ➡ **conservative**
rigid ➡ **firm**
rigorous ➡ **hard, strict**
rile ➡ **anger**
rim ➡ **edge**
rind ➡ **peel**
ringlet ➡ **lock**

rinse ➡ **clean, wet, cleaning**
riot ➡ **disturbance**
ripe ➡ **ready, adult**
ripen ➡ **grow**
riposte ➡ **answer**
ripple ➡ **wave, rustle**
rise ➡ **ascend, climb, appear, tower, slant, growth**
riser ➡ **platform**
risk ➡ **danger, bet, dare, jeopardize**

risky ➡ **dangerous**
risqué ➡ **dirty**
rite ➡ **ceremony**
ritual ➡ **ceremony**
rival ➡ **enemy, opponent, competitive, compete**
rivalry ➡ **competition**
rivet ➡ **nail**
riveting ➡ **exciting**

---

road *n* street, avenue, boulevard, thoroughfare, artery, roadway, lane, alley ➡ **highway, path**

rock 1. *n* stone, pebble, boulder, gravel, cobblestone ➡ **jewel**
2. *vb* ➡ **swing**

role *n* character, part, portrayal, bit ➡ **function**

room 1. *n* chamber, apartment, salon, suite, lodging, flat, gallery ➡ **living room, kitchen, bedroom, dining room, bathroom, den, basement, hall, attic**
2. *n* ➡ **space**
3. *vb* ➡ **live**[1]

rope *n* line, lasso, lariat, cable, wire, guy, painter, tether, leash, rein, strap ➡ **string**

rough 1. *adj* coarse, uneven, rugged, irregular, bumpy, jagged, crumpled, rumpled, harsh, scratchy ➡ **hoarse**
2. *adj* choppy, raging, ruffled, wild ➡ **stormy**
3. *adj* ➡ **rude, primitive**
4. *adj* ➡ **hard**
5. *adj* ➡ **approximate**

round 1. *adj* circular, spherical, cylindrical, oval, globular, rotund
2. *adv* ➡ **about**
3. *n* circuit, cycle, loop, beat, turn ➡ **period**

row 1. *n* line, string, file, rank, column, chain, queue, series, sequence
2. *n* ➡ **argument**
3. *vb* ➡ **paddle**

rub 1. *vb* scrape, chafe, graze, skim, brush, abrade, scuff, scratch ➡ **grind**
2. *vb* knead, massage, smooth, stroke ➡ **touch, pet**
3. *vb* daub, smear, spread, slather, anoint, dab, swab

rubber band *n* elastic, elastic band, gum band

rude *adj* impolite, insolent, discourteous, ungracious, impertinent, impudent, fresh, uncouth, crude, coarse, crass, bold, brash, presumptuous, audacious, sassy, forward, surly, pert, flip, disrespectful, irreverent, cheeky ➡ **abrupt, cross, thoughtless** ⇨ *polite*

If the word you want is not a main entry above, look below to find it.

rivulet ➡ river
RN ➡ nurse
roadblock ➡ barrier
roadway ➡ road
roam ➡ wander, travel
roar ➡ laugh, cry
roast ➡ cook
roasting ➡ hot
rob ➡ steal, deprive
robber ➡ criminal
robbery ➡ theft
robe ➡ bathrobe, dress
robust ➡ strong
rocket ➡ missile
rocket scientist ➡ genius

rockslide ➡ avalanche
rocky ➡ hard
rod ➡ bar
roe ➡ egg
Roentgen ray ➡ X ray
rogue ➡ rascal
roll ➡ bread, swing, mix
roller ➡ wheel, wave
romance ➡ court
romantic ➡ loving, idealistic, idealist
romp ➡ play, dance
roomy ➡ comfortable
roost ➡ seat
root ➡ base, essence, clap

rose ➡ red
roster ➡ list
rostrum ➡ platform
rosy ➡ red
rot ➡ decay, corrode, fungus
rotate ➡ turn
rotten ➡ bad
rotund ➡ round
roughly ➡ about
roundabout ➡ indirect
rouse ➡ wake
rousing ➡ exciting
rout ➡ defeat
route ➡ course

routine ➡ habit, method, act, average
routinely ➡ regularly
rove ➡ wander
rover ➡ pedestrian
rowdy ➡ loud, bully
royal ➡ noble
royal blue ➡ blue
royal household ➡ court
rubbing ➡ friction
rubbish ➡ trash
rubble ➡ trash
ruby ➡ red
ruddy ➡ red

n = noun • *vb* = verb • *adj* = adjective • *adv* = adverb • *prep* = preposition • *conj* = conjunction

rudeness *n* discourtesy, insolence, vulgarity, impudence, disrespect, crudity, crudeness, coarseness, boorishness

rug 1. *n* carpet, mat, carpeting, runner
2. *n* ➡ **wig**

ruin 1. *vb* ➡ **destroy**
2. *vb* impoverish, bankrupt, beggar
3. *n* ➡ **damage**
4. *n* ➡ **fate**

rule 1. *n* law, regulation, custom, principle, axiom, guideline, code, precept, canon, ultimatum ➡ **act, habit**
2. *n* command, control, authority, mastery, sway, sovereignty, charge, government, jurisdiction, dominion ➡ **leadership**
3. *n* ➡ **measure**
4. *vb* ➡ **govern**
5. *vb* ➡ **decide**

ruler *n* potentate, prince, lord, governor, leader, president, premier, prime minister ➡ **king, queen, emperor, empress, dictator**

rumor *n* gossip, hearsay, scandal, talk

run 1. *vb* jog, trot, dash, sprint, bolt, dart, streak, gallop, lope, canter ➡ **hurry, race**
2. *vb* ➡ **escape, leave**
3. *vb* ➡ **lead**
4. *vb* ➡ **operate**
5. *vb* ➡ **play**
6. *vb* ➡ **flow**
7. *n* ➡ **race**

runaway *n* fugitive, deserter, escapee, renegade, defector, truant, absentee

rural *adj* rustic, pastoral, provincial, backwoods ➡ **farming** ⇨ *urban*

rustle 1. *n* whisper, swish, ripple, crackle, patter, stir
2. *vb* whisper, swish, crackle, sigh, murmur, shuffle, flutter

rusty *adj* corroded, decayed ➡ **old**

If the word you want is not a main entry above, look below to find it.

rudiment ➡ basis
rudimentary ➡ basic
rue ➡ grieve, regret
ruffian ➡ bully
ruffle ➡ disturb
ruffled ➡ rough
rugged ➡ rough, tough, unbreakable

ruinous ➡ destructive
ruling ➡ decision
rumble ➡ bang, fight
rummage ➡ hunt
rump ➡ back
rumple ➡ wrinkle, disturb
rumpled ➡ rough

rundown ➡ old, summary
rung ➡ step
run-in ➡ meeting
runner ➡ messenger, shoot, rug
runway ➡ path
rupture ➡ break, hole

ruse ➡ trick
rush ➡ hurry, flood
rust ➡ corrode, fungus
rustic ➡ rural, primitive
rut ➡ channel
ruth ➡ pity
ruthless ➡ mean

➡ = synonym cross-reference • ⇨ = antonym cross-reference

S

sad *adj* unhappy, miserable, depressed, gloomy, dismal, melancholy, blue, downhearted, downcast, dejected, despondent, doleful, forlorn, moody, down, low, bad, glum ➡ **lonely, pitiful, sorry, thoughtful, pessimistic** ⇨ *happy*

sadden *vb* dishearten, disappoint, grieve, sorrow, oppress, depress, desolate

safe 1. *adj* secure, protected, harmless, snug, guarded, impregnable, invulnerable, immune ➡ **invincible** ⇨ *dangerous*
2. *n* vault, strongbox, chest, coffer, treasury, safe-deposit box ➡ **cash register**

sailor *n* seaman, mariner, seafarer, boatman, yachtsman, midshipman ➡ **soldier**

sale 1. *n* deal, transaction, purchase, marketing, auction ➡ **trade**
2. *n* bargain, deal, clearance, closeout, discount

salty 1. *adj* briny, brackish, saline
2. *adj* ➡ **dirty**

salvation *n* redemption, deliverance, preservation, liberation, emancipation, delivery ➡ **forgiveness, escape**

same *adj* identical, equal, equivalent, corresponding, matching, uniform, consistent, like ➡ **alike** ⇨ *different*

sane *adj* rational, sensible, reasonable, lucid, balanced, sound ⇨ *insane*

If the word you want is not a main entry above, look below to find it.

sabbatical ➡ vacation

saber ➡ sword

sable ➡ black, dark

sabotage ➡ damage, weaken

sac ➡ pocket

saccharine ➡ rich

sachem ➡ king

sack ➡ bag, base, pillage, attack, fire

sacramental ➡ holy

sacred ➡ holy, religious

sacrifice ➡ surrender, kill, gift

sadistic ➡ gruesome

sadness ➡ sorrow

safe-deposit box ➡ safe

safeguard ➡ protect, protection

safety ➡ protection

safety pin ➡ pin

saffron ➡ yellow

sag ➡ slant, weaken

saga ➡ story

sagacious ➡ profound

sagacity ➡ wisdom

sage ➡ philosopher, herb, profound

sail ➡ blow², fly, travel, pilot

sailing ➡ nautical

sake ➡ object

salaam ➡ good-bye

salary ➡ wage

salesman ➡ seller

salesperson ➡ seller

sales slip ➡ ticket

saleswoman ➡ seller

saline ➡ salty

sallow ➡ pale

sally ➡ attack, hurry

salmon ➡ orange

salon ➡ gallery, living room, room

saloon ➡ bar

salutation ➡ welcome

salute ➡ wave, welcome

salvage ➡ save

salver ➡ tray

sameness ➡ unity

sample ➡ example, try

sampling ➡ study

sanatorium ➡ hospital

sanctify ➡ bless, worship

sanctimonious ➡ self-righteous

sanction ➡ approve, forbid, permission, ban

sanctioned ➡ legal

sanctuary ➡ protection

sand ➡ dirt

sandy ➡ yellow

saneness ➡ reason

sanguine ➡ optimistic

sanitarium ➡ hospital

sanitary ➡ sterile

sanity ➡ reason

sap ➡ liquid, tire

sapling ➡ tree

sarcasm ➡ irony

n = noun • *vb* = verb • *adj* = adjective • *adv* = adverb • *prep* = preposition • *conj* = conjunction

sarcastic *adj* scornful, snide, ironic, ironical, satiric, satirical, sardonic, caustic, derisive

satisfaction 1. *n* gratification, fulfillment, contentment ➡ **pleasure**
2. *n* ➡ **revenge**

satisfied *adj* content, contented, self-satisfied, complacent ➡ **happy**

satisfy 1. *vb* appease, slake, quench, sate, satiate ➡ **please, relieve, pacify**
2. *vb* ➡ **persuade**
3. *vb* suffice, serve, do, fulfill, answer

save 1. *vb* keep, preserve, conserve, maintain, hoard, stockpile, stash ➡ **gather** ⇨ *discard, abolish, waste*
2. *vb* rescue, deliver, salvage, spare ➡ **free, protect**
3. *vb* ➡ **bank**
4. *prep* ➡ **but**

savior *n* rescuer, deliverer, protector, hero, champion, redeemer, lifesaver ➡ **guardian**

say *vb* state, speak, remark, exclaim, phrase, verbalize, express, signify, air, vent, dictate
➡ **talk, tell, pronounce, reveal**

saying *n* expression, motto, proverb, maxim, adage, aphorism, axiom, slogan, byword, saw, phrase ➡ **remark, cliché**

scar 1. *n* blemish, cicatrix, injury, disfigurement, mark, discoloration
2. *vb* ➡ **damage**

scare 1. *vb* frighten, alarm, startle, terrify, petrify, shock, horrify, perturb, unnerve, cow
➡ **threaten**
2. *n* ➡ **fear**

scarf *n* sash, bandanna, veil, ascot, handkerchief, do-rag ➡ **wrap**

scary *adj* frightening, frightful, dreadful, terrifying, terrible, horrifying, unnerving, appalling, fearful, awesome

scenic *adj* picturesque, pictorial, spectacular, striking ➡ **pretty**

If the word you want is not a main entry above, look below to find it.

sarcoma ➡ growth
sardonic ➡ sarcastic, dry
sari ➡ dress
sarong ➡ dress
sash ➡ band, scarf
sashay ➡ strut
sassy ➡ rude
satchel ➡ bag
sate ➡ satisfy
sated ➡ full
satellite ➡ colony, planet
satiate ➡ satisfy
satiny ➡ shiny
satire ➡ irony, parody
satiric ➡ sarcastic
satirical ➡ sarcastic
satirize ➡ imitate

satisfactorily ➡ well, correctly
satisfactory ➡ fair
satisfying ➡ pleasant
saturate ➡ wet
saturated ➡ wet
saucepan ➡ pot
saucer ➡ plate
saunter ➡ wander, lag
sauté ➡ cook
savage ➡ wild, mean, violent, monster, vandal
savagery ➡ violence
savanna ➡ plain
savings and loan ➡ bank
savings bank ➡ bank
savoir faire ➡ tact

savor ➡ spice, flavor, appreciate
savory ➡ delicious, fragrant
saw ➡ saying
scaffold ➡ gallows
scalding ➡ hot
scale ➡ climb, measure, peel, coat
scalpel ➡ knife
scamp ➡ rascal
scamper ➡ dance, hurry
scan ➡ read, examine
scandal ➡ rumor
scandalous ➡ sensational, shameful
scant ➡ few, light[2]
scanty ➡ small, few
scarce ➡ rare

scarcely ➡ only, seldom
scarcity ➡ want
scared ➡ afraid
scarlet ➡ red
scatter ➡ spread, plant
scatterbrained ➡ absentminded
scenario ➡ story
scene ➡ view, division
scenery ➡ view, setting
scent ➡ smell
scented ➡ fragrant
schedule ➡ list, table, arrange
scheduled ➡ due
schematic ➡ plan
scheme ➡ plan

---

school 1. *n* academy, institute ➡ **college**
2. *vb* ➡ **teach**
3. *n* ➡ **herd**

science *n* discipline, technique ➡ **education, knowledge**

scold *vb* rebuke, admonish, reprimand, chastise, chide, castigate, berate, reproach, upbraid, reprove ➡ **punish, blame** ⇨ *praise*

score 1. *n* count, tally, reckoning, outcome ➡ **grade**
2. *n* transcription, arrangement, composition, orchestration *vb* ➡ **get, add, win**

seat *n* chair, bench, sofa, couch, settee, stool, pew, bleachers, grandstand, stands, perch, roost

secrecy *n* stealth, hiding, confidence, subterfuge, furtiveness ➡ **privacy**

secret 1. *adj* hidden, arcane, cryptic, esoteric ➡ **mysterious, anonymous**
2. *adj* clandestine, confidential, classified, top secret, private, covert, undercover, surreptitious, underground ➡ **sly**
3. *n* mystery, confidence, intrigue ➡ **problem**

If the word you want is not a main entry above, look below to find it.

scheming ➡ sly
schism ➡ break
scholar ➡ student, teacher, philosopher
scholarly ➡ intellectual, educated
scholarship ➡ education, award
scholastic ➡ intellectual
schoolboy ➡ student
schoolchild ➡ student
schooled ➡ educated
schoolgirl ➡ student
schooling ➡ education
schoolmaster ➡ teacher
schoolmistress ➡ teacher
scimitar ➡ sword
scoff ➡ ridicule
scoop ➡ spoon, dig, catch
scope ➡ space, range
scorch ➡ burn
scorn ➡ hatred, hate, ridicule, refuse, insult
scornful ➡ sarcastic
Scotch® tape ➡ adhesive
scoundrel ➡ rascal
scour ➡ clean, shine, hunt

scourge ➡ whip
scout ➡ patrol
scowl ➡ frown
scramble ➡ mix, hurry, climb
scrap ➡ fight, bite, bit, discard
scrape ➡ clean, rub, cut, damage
scraping ➡ friction
scratch ➡ cut, rub, damage, erase
scratchy ➡ rough
scrawl ➡ write
scrawny ➡ thin
scream ➡ yell, cry
screamer ➡ headline
screech ➡ yell, cry, squeak
screen ➡ divider, net, hide, sift
screening ➡ tryout
screenwriter ➡ writer
screw ➡ nail, turn
scribble ➡ write
script ➡ handwriting, book
scriptwriter ➡ writer
scrooge ➡ miser
scrounge ➡ borrow

scrub ➡ clean, brush, cleaning
scruffy ➡ shabby
scrumptious ➡ delicious
scrupulous ➡ careful, good
scrutinize ➡ examine
scrutiny ➡ look
scuff ➡ rub
scuffle ➡ fight
scull ➡ paddle
scullery ➡ kitchen
sculpt ➡ carve
sculptor ➡ artist
sculpture ➡ statue, carve
scum ➡ foam
scurry ➡ hurry
scuttle ➡ hurry, abandon
sea ➡ ocean
seafarer ➡ sailor
seagoing ➡ nautical
seagull ➡ bird
seal ➡ close, signature
sealed ➡ tight
seam ➡ band
seaman ➡ sailor

sear ➡ burn
search ➡ hunt
seashore ➡ shore
seaside ➡ shore
season ➡ period, weather
seasoned ➡ old
seasoning ➡ spice, herb
sea wall ➡ jetty
seclude ➡ separate
secluded ➡ private
seclusion ➡ privacy
second ➡ moment, latter
secondary ➡ subordinate
secondhand ➡ old
second-rate ➡ cheap
secret agent ➡ spy
secrete ➡ hide, sweat
secretive ➡ sly
sect ➡ religion
section ➡ part, excerpt, division, department
secure ➡ safe, guarantee, lock, tie
security ➡ protection
sedate ➡ serious
sedative ➡ drug

n = noun • *vb* = verb • *adj* = adjective • *adv* = adverb • *prep* = preposition • *conj* = conjunction

see 1. *vb* behold, discern, observe, perceive, notice, glimpse, spot, remark ➡ **look**
2. *vb* ➡ **know, learn**
3. *vb* ➡ **imagine**

seed 1. *n* kernel, grain, pit, pip, nut, bulb ➡ **egg, fruit**
2. *vb* ➡ **plant**

seize *vb* take, grab, snatch, clutch, wrest, abduct, kidnap, hijack, skyjack, carjack, occupy, intercept, tackle ➡ **catch, get**

seldom *adv* rarely, occasionally, infrequently, sometimes, scarcely, hardly, barely ⇨ *often*

self-righteous *adj* sanctimonious, holier-than-thou, unctuous ➡ **hypocritical**

sell *vb* carry, stock, retail, handle, trade (in), market, peddle, vend, barter, hawk ➡ **offer**

seller *n* salesperson, salesman, saleswoman, dealer, merchant, vendor, tradesman, shopkeeper, peddler, trader, supplier, wholesaler ➡ **agent**

send 1. *vb* dispatch, transmit, mail, post, e-mail, forward, convey, ship, transfer, export ➡ **spread, broadcast**
2. *vb* ➡ **lead**
3. *vb* ➡ **throw**

sensational 1. *adj* scandalous, shocking, lurid, dramatic, melodramatic, vulgar, exaggerated
2. *adj* ➡ **exciting, awesome**

sense 1. *n* sensation, function, capability ➡ **feeling, ability**
2. *n* ➡ **wisdom**
3. *n* ➡ **meaning**

separate 1. *vb* part, sever, undo, detach, cleave, sunder ➡ **divide, rip, share, open**
2. *vb* isolate, insulate, segregate, discriminate, sequester, quarantine, seclude ➡ **distinguish**
3. *vb* divorce, split up, break up
4. *adj* ➡ **different**

If the word you want is not a main entry above, look below to find it.

sedentary ➡ **passive**
sedition ➡ **treason**
seditious ➡ **rebellious**
seduce ➡ **tempt**
seduction ➡ **attraction**
seedling ➡ **tree**
seedy ➡ **shabby**
seek ➡ **hunt**
seem ➡ **act, look**
seemingly ➡ **apparently, probably**
seemly ➡ **correct**
seep ➡ **drop**
seer ➡ **prophet**
seethe ➡ **boil**
see-through ➡ **transparent**
segment ➡ **part, divide**
segregate ➡ **separate**

segregation ➡ **privacy**
seizure ➡ **arrest, fit²**
select ➡ **choose, special**
selection ➡ **choice, assortment, excerpt, appointment**
self-acting ➡ **automatic**
self-confidence ➡ **pride, certainty**
self-confident ➡ **certain**
self-conscious ➡ **nervous**
self-control ➡ **discipline**
self-denial ➡ **abstinence**
self-deprecating ➡ **humble**
self-effacing ➡ **humble**
self-esteem ➡ **pride**
self-governing ➡ **free**
selfish ➡ **greedy, mean**
selfishness ➡ **greed**

self-possessed ➡ **calm**
self-respect ➡ **pride**
self-restraint ➡ **abstinence, discipline**
self-satisfied ➡ **satisfied**
self-starting ➡ **automatic**
semester ➡ **term**
seminar ➡ **course**
senate ➡ **government**
senior ➡ **old, older, student**
sensation ➡ **feeling, sense**
senseless ➡ **unconscious**
senselessness ➡ **nonsense**
sensible ➡ **practical, sane**
sensitive ➡ **sore, thoughtful, delicate, emotional, temperamental**
sensitivity ➡ **feeling**

sentence ➡ **punish, punishment, decision**
sentience ➡ **life**
sentiment ➡ **emotion, belief**
sentimental ➡ **emotional**
sentimentality ➡ **feeling**
sentinel ➡ **patrol**
sentry ➡ **patrol**
separately ➡ **apart, differently**
separation ➡ **division**
sepulcher ➡ **grave, cemetery**
sequence ➡ **order, row**
sequential ➡ **consecutive**
sequester ➡ **separate**
seraph ➡ **angel**
serendipitous ➡ **lucky**
serendipity ➡ **chance**

---

serious 1. *adj* solemn, grave, somber, earnest, sedate, sober, heavy ➡ **important, profound, dignified**
2. *adj* ➡ **sincere**

servant *n* retainer, domestic, employee, minion, attendant, subordinate ➡ **helper**

servile *adj* obsequious, submissive, subservient, slavish, fawning, sycophantic, spineless, mealy-mouthed, abject ➡ **passive, humble**

setting *n* environment, surroundings, framework, background, context, backdrop, scenery, climate, ambiance, mood, medium, milieu

sew *vb* stitch, mend, embroider, baste, tailor ➡ **weave**

shabby *adj* dilapidated, deteriorated, broken-down, decayed, scruffy, seedy, mangy ➡ **old, ragged, sorry**

shack *n* cabin, hut, shanty, hovel, shed ➡ **house**

shake 1. *vb* vibrate, tremble, shudder, shiver, quiver, quake, quaver, flutter, wobble, wag, waggle, pulsate, throb, jar ➡ **tingle**
2. *vb* ➡ **spread**
3. *n* ➡ **vibration**

shame 1. *n* disgrace, dishonor, discredit, humiliation, remorse, regret, contrition, embarrassment, chagrin ➡ **guilt**
2. *vb* humiliate, dishonor, disgrace, debase, abase, demean, discredit ➡ **embarrass**

shameful *adj* disgraceful, contemptible, scandalous, shocking, disreputable, dishonorable, ignoble, deplorable ➡ **improper, bad**

share 1. *n* division, percentage, allowance, allotment, stake, quota, ration, proportion, fraction, percent, ratio ➡ **part, interest**
2. *vb* distribute, apportion, split (up), deal out, ration, mete out ➡ **divide, budget**

If the word you want is not a main entry above, look below to find it.

serene ➡ **calm**
serenity ➡ **calm**
serf ➡ **farmer**
serfdom ➡ **slavery**
serial ➡ **consecutive**
series ➡ **row, assortment, program, game**
sermon ➡ **speech**
sermonize ➡ **preach**
serpent ➡ **snake**
serve ➡ **help, satisfy, act, give**
service ➡ **ceremony, army, tray, help, repair, fix**
serviceman ➡ **soldier**
service mark ➡ **label**
service station ➡ **garage**

servicewoman ➡ **soldier**
servicing ➡ **repair**
servitude ➡ **slavery**
session ➡ **meeting**
set ➡ **put, group, harden, plant, fall, ready, usual**
set apart ➡ **dedicate**
setback ➡ **relapse, accident**
set off ➡ **leave**
set out ➡ **leave**
settee ➡ **seat**
settle ➡ **decide, pay, descend**
settlement ➡ **town, colony**
settler ➡ **pioneer**
set up ➡ **arrange**

seven seas ➡ **ocean**
sever ➡ **separate**
several ➡ **few**
severance ➡ **division**
severe ➡ **sharp, hard, plain, strict**
severity ➡ **strength**
Seville orange ➡ **orange**
shackle ➡ **bond**
shade ➡ **dark, color, bit, ghost, hide**
shades ➡ **glasses**
shadow ➡ **dark, cloud, follow**
shadowy ➡ **dim**
shady ➡ **dark, suspicious**
shaft ➡ **bar, well, channel**

shaggy ➡ **fuzzy**
shah ➡ **king**
shaky ➡ **unsteady, nervous**
shallow ➡ **superficial, dull**
shalom ➡ **good-bye, hello**
sham ➡ **fake**
shaman ➡ **magician**
shamed ➡ **ashamed**
shameless ➡ **immoral**
Shangri-la ➡ **utopia**
shanty ➡ **shack**
shape ➡ **form, structure, health**
sharecropper ➡ **farmer**
sharecropping ➡ **farming**
shared ➡ **common**

sharp 1. *adj* keen, acute, honed, pointed, pointy, sharp-edged, knife-edged
2. *adj* ➡ **smart**
3. *adj* acute, abrupt, rapid ➡ **sudden**
4. *adj* ➡ **steep**
5. *adj* severe, biting, caustic, bitter, harsh, cutting, fierce, brutal, oppressive
6. *adj* ➡ **spicy, sour**
7. *adj* ➡ **smelly**
8. *adj* ➡ **fashionable**

sharpen *vb* whet, hone, file, grind, strop

shed 1. *n* ➡ **shack, barn, building**
2. *vb* remove, take off, cast off, drop, molt, slough ➡ **discard**

shelf *n* rack, counter, stand, ledge, mantel, mantelpiece

shell 1. *n* husk, pod, casing, sheath, carapace, eggshell ➡ **peel**
2. *n* ➡ **framework**
3. *n* ➡ **missile**
4. *vb* ➡ **shoot**

shine 1. *vb* radiate, beam, sparkle, gleam, glow, shimmer, glisten, twinkle
2. *vb* polish, burnish, buff, wax, scour ➡ **clean, finish**
3. *n* ➡ **light**[1]

shiny *adj* lustrous, gleaming, glossy, sleek, glistening, sparkling, silky, satiny ➡ **bright**

shock 1. *vb* astound, appall, dismay, devastate, overwhelm, stun, electrify, stagger, awe, horrify ➡ **surprise, scare**
2. *n* ➡ **blow**[1]**, vibration**
3. *n* ➡ **earthquake**
4. *n* blow, upset, jolt, ordeal, trauma ➡ **surprise**
5. *n* ➡ **lock**

shoe *n* boot, footwear

shoot 1. *vb* fire, discharge, open fire, blast, gun down, shell, propel, launch, project
2. *vb* ➡ **hunt, kill**
3. *n* sprout, bud, runner, twig, outgrowth ➡ **stick**

If the word you want is not a main entry above, look below to find it.

sharp-edged ➡ sharp

sharpness ➡ clarity

shatter ➡ break

shattered ➡ broken

shave ➡ cut

shawl ➡ wrap

shear ➡ cut

sheath ➡ dress, shell

sheathe ➡ wrap

sheen ➡ light[1]

sheer ➡ steep, perfect, thin, transparent

sheet ➡ layer, page, blanket

shellac ➡ finish

shelling ➡ fire

shells ➡ ammunition

shelter ➡ protect, protection, house, building

shenanigans ➡ mischief

shepherd ➡ guide

sherbet ➡ ice cream

sheriff ➡ police officer

shield ➡ protect, protection, badge

shift ➡ move, change, swerve, movement, period, dress

shiftless ➡ lazy

shifty ➡ sly

shimmer ➡ shine

ship ➡ boat, send

shipment ➡ load, delivery

shipshape ➡ neat

shirk ➡ avoid

shirtwaist ➡ dress

shiver ➡ shake

shock absorber ➡ cushion

shocking ➡ sensational, shameful

shoddy ➡ cheap, poor

shooting ➡ fire

shooting star ➡ meteor

shop ➡ market, factory, buy

shopkeeper ➡ seller

shoplift ➡ steal

shoplifting ➡ theft

shopper ➡ patron

shopping mall ➡ market

---

shore *n* beach, coast, seashore, seaside, strand, bank ➡ **edge**

short 1. *adj* slight, low, undersized, skimpy, brief ➡ **small** ⇨ *long*
2. *adj* brief, concise, compact, succinct, abbreviated, terse, laconic, abridged, fleeting, transient, short-lived ➡ **fast, temporary**
3. *adj* ➡ **abrupt**
4. *adj* ➡ **inadequate**

show 1. *vb* display, exhibit, present, manifest, produce ➡ **reveal, advertise, model**
2. *vb* ➡ **lead**
3. *vb* ➡ **explain, verify**
4. *n* spectacle, display ➡ **play, movie, program**

shrink 1. *vb* contract, shrivel, deflate, constrict ➡ **condense, decrease** ⇨ *grow, lengthen*
2. *vb* ➡ **retreat**

shy *adj* bashful, timid, meek, retiring, diffident, reserved, demure, deferential, timorous, tentative ➡ **humble**

sick 1. *adj* ill, ailing, sickly, unwell, unhealthy, nauseous, nauseated, queasy, infirm, indisposed, funny ➡ **weak** ⇨ *healthy*
2. *adj* ➡ **gruesome**

side 1. *n* surface, face, end, facet, plane ➡ **edge**
2. *n* ➡ **perspective**
3. *n* ➡ **team**

sideways *adv* broadside, obliquely, askance, indirectly

sift 1. *vb* strain, filter, screen, winnow, sort
2. *vb* ➡ **hunt**

sight 1. *n* vision, eyesight, perception ➡ **sense**
2. *n* ➡ **view**
3. *vb* ➡ **look**

sign 1. *n* symbol, signal, token, omen, clue, index, indication, manifestation, symptom, gesture, expression ➡ **track, warning**
2. *vb* autograph, inscribe, endorse, countersign, initial ➡ **write**

If the word you want is not a main entry above, look below to find it.

shortage ➡ want
shortbread ➡ pastry
shortcoming ➡ defect
shortcut ➡ path
shorten ➡ condense
shortening ➡ abbreviation, fat
short-lived ➡ short
shortly ➡ soon
shot ➡ medicine, try
shotgun ➡ gun
should ➡ need
shoulder ➡ push, bear
shout ➡ yell, cry
shove ➡ push, impulse

shovel ➡ dig
showdown ➡ fight
shower ➡ rain, cleaning
showery ➡ wet
show off ➡ boast
showpiece ➡ masterpiece
showroom ➡ gallery
show up ➡ appear
showy ➡ loud
shred ➡ cut, rip, bit
shrewd ➡ sly, smart
shriek ➡ yell, cry, laugh
shrill ➡ loud, high
shrine ➡ monument
shrivel ➡ shrink, decrease, dry

shroud ➡ blanket, wrap, hide
shrub ➡ plant
shrubbery ➡ hedge, brush
shuck ➡ peel
shudder ➡ shake
shuffle ➡ limp, rustle, mix
shun ➡ avoid, abstain
shut ➡ close
shut-eye ➡ sleep
shut-in ➡ hermit
shutterbug ➡ photographer
shyster ➡ cheat
sicken ➡ disgust
sickening ➡ bad
sickly ➡ sick

sickness ➡ illness, nausea
sidearm ➡ gun
sideboard ➡ cupboard
sideburns ➡ beard
sidekick ➡ partner
sidestep ➡ avoid
sideswipe ➡ collide
sidetrack ➡ distract
siesta ➡ sleep
sieve ➡ net
sifter ➡ net
sigh ➡ mumble, rustle
sighting ➡ discovery
sightless ➡ blind
signal ➡ sign, warning, wave, bell, light[1]

n = noun • *vb* = verb • *adj* = adjective • *adv* = adverb • *prep* = preposition • *conj* = conjunction

signature *n* autograph, John Hancock, seal, monogram, mark, stamp, imprint

similarity *n* likeness, resemblance, correspondence, parallel, similitude, affinity, congruity, analogy, comparison

simultaneous *adj* concurrent, coincident, coinciding, synchronized, synchronous, contemporary, contemporaneous

sin 1. *vb* err, offend, transgress, trespass ➡ **disobey**
2. *n* ➡ **crime, immorality**

sincere *adj* genuine, honest, heartfelt, wholehearted, true, trustworthy, serious, straight ➡ **straightforward**

sincerely *adv* truly, honestly, earnestly, genuinely, heartily, frankly

sing *vb* chant, harmonize, vocalize, croon, warble, chirp ➡ **hum**

singer *n* vocalist, chorister, soloist, songster, cantor ➡ **choir, musician**

single 1. *adj* ➡ **only**
2. *adj* alone, unmarried, unwed, unattached, eligible, divorced ⇨ *married*

sink 1. *vb* submerge, submerse, swamp, engulf, immerse, duck, dunk, dip ➡ **descend, fall, flood**
2. *n* washbasin, basin, lavatory, washstand ➡ **bowl**

size *n* magnitude, mass, volume, bulk, quantity, proportion, capacity

skeptic *n* cynic, pessimist, doubter, doubting Thomas

If the word you want is not a main entry above, look below to find it.

significance ➡ **importance, meaning, relevance**

significant ➡ **important, meaningful**

signify ➡ **mean, matter, say**

silence ➡ **quiet, calm**

silent ➡ **dumb, quiet**

silhouette ➡ **circumference**

silky ➡ **shiny**

sill ➡ **threshold**

silliness ➡ **nonsense**

silly ➡ **foolish**

silo ➡ **warehouse**

silver screen ➡ **movies**

silvery ➡ **white**

similar ➡ **alike, compatible**

similarly ➡ **alike**

similitude ➡ **similarity**

simmer ➡ **boil**

simple ➡ **plain, easy, naive, primitive**

simple-minded ➡ **stupid**

simpleton ➡ **fool**

simplicity ➡ **clarity, ignorance**

simplify ➡ **facilitate**

simply ➡ **only**

simulate ➡ **imitate, pretend**

simultaneously ➡ **together**

since ➡ **because**

sincerity ➡ **truth**

sinful ➡ **bad**

singe ➡ **burn**

single-handed ➡ **alone**

singular ➡ **unique**

sinister ➡ **ominous**

sinless ➡ **innocent**

sip ➡ **drink**

sister ➡ **religious**

sisterhood ➡ **friendship**

sit ➡ **model**

site ➡ **place**

sit-in ➡ **protest**

sitter ➡ **model**

sitting room ➡ **living room**

situate ➡ **place, base**

situation ➡ **place, state, opportunity, profession**

sizzling ➡ **hot**

skate ➡ **slide**

skeleton ➡ **framework, body**

skeptical ➡ **doubtful**

skepticism ➡ **doubt**

sketch ➡ **picture, pattern, act, draw**

skid ➡ **slide**

skill ➡ **talent, art, experience**

skilled ➡ **expert**

skillful ➡ **able**

skim ➡ **read, slide, rub**

skimpy ➡ **small, short**

skin ➡ **peel, hide**

skin-deep ➡ **superficial**

skinflint ➡ **miser**

skinny ➡ **thin**

skintight ➡ **tight**

skip ➡ **exclude, jump**

skipper ➡ **boss**

skirmish ➡ **fight**

skirt ➡ **dress, border, detour**

skit ➡ **act, play**

skittish ➡ **nervous**

skulk ➡ **sneak**

sky ➡ **air**

sky blue ➡ **blue**

skycap ➡ **porter**

skyjack ➡ **seize**

skyline ➡ **horizon**

skyscraper ➡ **tower**

slab ➡ **block**

slack ➡ **limp, negligent**

slacker ➡ **loafer**

slake ➡ **satisfy**

slant 1. *vb* tilt, lean, list, incline, slope, bank, sag, pitch, cant ➡ **bend**
2. *n* slope, incline, climb, ascent, rise, descent, declivity, grade, hill

slavery *n* bondage, servitude, enslavement, serfdom, subjugation, vassalage ⇨ *freedom*

sleep 1. *vb* slumber, doze, snooze, nod, nap, hibernate ➡ **rest**
2. *n* slumber, doze, rest, repose, siesta, nap, catnap, shut-eye (*informal*)

slide 1. *vb* glide, skim, coast, skid, slip, skate ➡ **push**
2. *n* ➡ **channel**
3. *n* ➡ **photograph**
4. *n* ➡ **avalanche**

slippery *adj* smooth, slick, glassy, icy, waxy, soapy

slow 1. *adj* leisurely, gradual, sluggish, deliberate, moderate, torpid ⇨ *fast*
2. *adj* dilatory, lackadaisical ➡ **passive, lazy, listless**
3. *adj* ➡ **dull, stupid**

sly 1. *adj* devious, crafty, cunning, shrewd, subtle, tricky, sneaky, wily, slick, shifty, artful, scheming, underhanded ➡ **dishonest**
2. *adj* secretive, furtive, sneaky, surreptitious, stealthy, elusive ➡ **private**

small 1. *adj* little, tiny, miniature, minute, diminutive, Lilliputian, compact ➡ **trivial** ⇨ *big*
2. *adj* scanty, meager, slight, spare, skimpy, stingy, paltry ➡ **inadequate**

smart 1. *adj* intelligent, clever, bright, wise, learned, brilliant, keen, acute, quick, alert, apt, astute, perceptive, insightful, discerning, incisive, canny, shrewd ➡ **precocious, educated, profound** ⇨ *foolish, stupid*
2. *adj* ➡ **fashionable**
3. *vb* ➡ **hurt**
In general, **smart, clever,** *and* **bright,** *which all suggest quickness in learning, are more often applied to young people than are* **intelligent, wise,** *and* **learned,** *which suggest the wisdom that comes from experience, education, and age.*

If the word you want is not a main entry above, look below to find it.

slam ➡ close
slammer ➡ jail
slander ➡ insult
slang ➡ dialect
slap ➡ punch, blow[1]
slash ➡ cut, decrease
slat ➡ board
slate ➡ gray, ballot
slather ➡ rub
slaughter ➡ kill, murder
slave ➡ servant, prisoner, work
slavish ➡ servile
slay ➡ kill
slayer ➡ killer
slaying ➡ murder
sled ➡ vehicle

sledge ➡ hammer
sledgehammer ➡ hammer
sleek ➡ shiny
sleeping ➡ asleep
sleepless ➡ awake
sleepy ➡ tired
sleet ➡ ice
slender ➡ thin, narrow, light[2]
slew ➡ abundance
slice ➡ cut, block
slick ➡ slippery, sly
slight ➡ small, thin, short, light[2], insult
slightest ➡ least
slightly ➡ partly
slim ➡ thin, narrow
slime ➡ dirt

sling ➡ throw
slink ➡ sneak
slip ➡ mistake, trip, dock, ticket, slide, fall
slip by ➡ elapse
slit ➡ cut
slither ➡ crawl
slogan ➡ saying
slop ➡ dirt
slope ➡ slant
sloppy ➡ messy
slosh ➡ splash
sloth ➡ laziness
slothful ➡ lazy
slouch ➡ bend
slough ➡ shed
slovenly ➡ messy

sludge ➡ dirt
slug ➡ hit, missile
sluggard ➡ loafer
sluggish ➡ slow, listless
sluice ➡ channel
slumber ➡ sleep
slumbering ➡ asleep
slump ➡ depression, fall, drop, bend
slush ➡ snow
slushy ➡ wet
smack ➡ hit, kiss, blow[1]
smaller ➡ less
smallest ➡ least
small-minded ➡ mean
smash ➡ break, hit, collide
smear ➡ rub, insult

smell 1. *n* scent, odor, aroma, fragrance, perfume, incense, bouquet, stench
2. *vb, n* sniff, whiff, scent ➡ **sense**
3. *vb, n* stink, reek

smelly *adj* odorous, rancid, rank, foul, putrid, acrid, sharp, strong ➡ **fragrant**

smile *vb, n* beam, grin, smirk, sneer ➡ **laugh**
⇨ *frown*

smoke 1. *n* vapor, fumes, gas, steam ➡ **fog**
2. *vb* smolder, fume ➡ **burn**
3. *vb* inhale, puff

snake *n* serpent, viper ➡ **reptile**

sneak 1. *vb* creep, slink, prowl, skulk, steal, tiptoe, lurk
2. *n* ➡ **rascal**

snow 1. *n* snowfall, snowstorm, blizzard, flurry ➡ **storm**
2. *n* snowflake, powder, slush, hail, graupel, névé, firn
3. *vb* ➡ **enchant, persuade**

snuggle *vb* cuddle, nuzzle, nestle, huddle

soda *n* pop, soda pop, soft drink, cola, Coke (*trademark*), tonic ➡ **drink**

soften 1. *vb* ➡ **melt**
2. *vb* modify, assuage, temper, qualify, appease, palliate ➡ **change, quiet**

soldier *n* fighter, warrior, volunteer, conscript, draftee, recruit, cadet, veteran, officer, serviceman, servicewoman, combatant, mercenary, soldier of fortune, gladiator ➡ **army, troop**

If the word you want is not a main entry above, look below to find it.

smirk ➡ smile
smock ➡ dress
smog ➡ fog
smoky ➡ gray
smolder ➡ smoke
smoldering ➡ burning
smooch ➡ kiss
smooth ➡ level, slippery, suave, rub
smother ➡ extinguish, choke
smudge ➡ spot, dirty
smug ➡ proud
snack ➡ meal
snag ➡ knot, catch
snap ➡ break, bite, clasp, fast
snapshot ➡ photograph
snare ➡ trap, catch
snarl ➡ bark, knot
snatch ➡ seize, steal, bit
sneaky ➡ sly
sneer ➡ smile
snicker ➡ laugh

snide ➡ sarcastic
sniff ➡ smell
snigger ➡ laugh
snip ➡ cut
snippet ➡ bit
snit ➡ fit[2]
snoop ➡ meddle, spy
snooze ➡ sleep
snort ➡ grunt
snout ➡ nose
snowfall ➡ snow
snowflake ➡ snow
snowstorm ➡ snow, storm
snow-white ➡ white
snowy ➡ white, wet
snub ➡ refuse, insult
snug ➡ safe, comfortable, warm, narrow, tight
so ➡ therefore
soak ➡ wet, cleaning, absorb
soaked ➡ wet
soapy ➡ slippery

soar ➡ fly
soaring ➡ high, flight
sob ➡ cry
sober ➡ serious
sobriquet ➡ pseudonym
sociable ➡ friendly
social ➡ friendly, public, dance
socialize ➡ mix
Social Security ➡ pension
society ➡ humanity, people, friendship, organization, aristocracy
sociology ➡ science
soda pop ➡ soda
sodden ➡ wet
sofa ➡ seat
soft ➡ gentle, flexible, fuzzy
soft drink ➡ soda
soggy ➡ wet
soil ➡ dirt, dirty
soiled ➡ dirty

soiree ➡ party
sojourn ➡ live[1], visit
solace ➡ comfort
solder ➡ join
soldier of fortune ➡ soldier
soldierly ➡ military
sole ➡ only
solemn ➡ serious, dignified
solemnity ➡ ceremony
solemnize ➡ celebrate
solicit ➡ beg
solicitous ➡ thoughtful
solid ➡ firm, strong, reliable, real
solidify ➡ harden
solitary ➡ alone, only, lonely
solitude ➡ privacy
solo ➡ alone
soloist ➡ singer
so long ➡ good-bye
solution ➡ answer, mixture

➡ = synonym cross-reference • ⇨ = antonym cross-reference

solve *vb* figure out, puzzle out, resolve, decode, decipher, answer, do, work (out), unravel, unscramble ➡ **explain**

song *n* tune, melody, lyric, theme, ballad, lullaby, ditty, madrigal ➡ **hymn, poem, music**

soon *adv* presently, shortly, forthwith, momentarily, anon ➡ **quickly, now**

sore 1. *adj* painful, sensitive, tender, raw, hurtful, irritated, inflamed, bruised, livid
2. *adj* ➡ **angry**
3. *n* boil, abscess, ulcer, inflammation, welt, swelling ➡ **cut, pain**

sorrow 1. *n* grief, sadness, regret, anguish, melancholy, distress, gloom, woe, heartache ➡ **misery, depression**
2. *vb* ➡ **sadden**

sorry 1. *adj* sorrowful, repentant, apologetic, contrite, penitent, remorseful ➡ **sad**
2. *adj* forlorn, wretched, depressing ➡ **sad, pitiful**
3. *adj* ➡ **poor**

soul 1. *n* spirit, psyche, essence, genius, ego ➡ **mind, ghost**
2. *n* ➡ **human being**
3. *n* ➡ **feeling**
4. *n* ➡ **middle**

sour *adj* tart, bitter, rancid, acidic, sharp, acid, tangy, dry ⇨ *sweet*

source 1. *n* origin, derivation, birthplace, cradle, fountain, fountainhead, font, fount, well, wellspring
2. *n* ➡ **beginning, cause**

space 1. *n* universe, cosmos, heavens, outer space, infinity, void ➡ **air**
2. *n* room, area, scope, range, expanse, territory, elbowroom

speaker *n* lecturer, orator, speechmaker, rhetorician, preacher, talker

special 1. *adj* distinct, particular, specific, especial, distinctive, respective, proper, certain ➡ **unique**
2. *adj* select, choice, extraordinary, exceptional, unusual, peculiar, remarkable, noteworthy, phenomenal, outstanding ➡ **rare, striking, strange**

If the word you want is not a main entry above, look below to find it.

somber ➡ **serious, bleak, dark**
some ➡ **any**
sometimes ➡ **seldom**
somewhat ➡ **partly**
somnolent ➡ **asleep**
son ➡ **child**
songbird ➡ **bird**
songster ➡ **singer**
sooner ➡ **more**
soothe ➡ **relieve, pacify, calm**
soothsayer ➡ **prophet**
sophisticated ➡ **cosmopolitan, complicated**
sophistication ➡ **elegance**
sophomore ➡ **student**

sophomoric ➡ **childish**
sop up ➡ **absorb**
sorbet ➡ **ice cream**
sorcerer ➡ **magician**
sorcery ➡ **magic**
soreness ➡ **pain**
sorority ➡ **organization**
sorrowful ➡ **sorry**
sort ➡ **type, arrange, sift**
sortie ➡ **attack**
sot ➡ **drunkard**
sound ➡ **noise, valid, healthy, sane, strong, blow^2, ring**
soundless ➡ **quiet**
sous-chef ➡ **cook**

souse ➡ **drunkard**
souvenir ➡ **reminder**
sovereign ➡ **king, queen, free**
sovereignty ➡ **freedom, rule**
sow ➡ **plant**
spa ➡ **hotel**
space-age ➡ **modern**
space flight ➡ **flight**
spacey ➡ **absentminded**
spacious ➡ **open, comfortable**
span ➡ **period, life, bridge, width, pair, team**
spank ➡ **whip**
spar ➡ **joke**
spare ➡ **save, small, thin**

spark ➡ **light^1, incentive, start**
sparkle ➡ **shine, light^1**
sparkling ➡ **shiny**
sparse ➡ **light^2, inadequate**
spasm ➡ **pain, fit^2**
spasmodic ➡ **periodic**
spat ➡ **argument**
spate ➡ **flood**
spatter ➡ **splash**
spawn ➡ **reproduce, egg**
spay ➡ **sterilize**
speak ➡ **say, talk**
speak to ➡ **approach**
spear ➡ **stick, missile**

n = noun • *vb* = verb • *adj* = adjective • *adv* = adverb • *prep* = preposition • *conj* = conjunction

specialty *n* speciality, forte, métier, specialization ➡ **talent, field, profession**

specify *vb* stipulate, define, particularize, detail ➡ **name, mention, list**

speckled *adj* spotted, mottled, variegated, dappled, piebald

speech 1. *n* voice, communication, discourse, intercourse, utterance, articulation, diction, locution, enunciation, expression ➡ **talk, language, remark, accent, dialect**
2. *n* lecture, talk, sermon, address, report, oration

speed 1. *n* velocity, acceleration, swiftness, pace, rate, tempo, rapidity, celerity, dispatch ➡ **hurry**
2. *vb* ➡ **hurry**

spice 1. *n* seasoning, zest, savor, relish ➡ **herb**
2. *n* ➡ **excitement**

spicy *adj* zesty, piquant, tangy, tart, sharp, hot, pungent, peppery

splash *vb*, *n* splatter, sprinkle, squirt, spray, spatter, slosh ➡ **drop, wet**

spoken *adj* verbal, oral, voiced, stated, unwritten, vocal

spontaneous *adj* impromptu, impulsive, unplanned, extemporaneous, casual ➡ **automatic, voluntary**

spoon *n* ladle, scoop, dipper, tablespoon, teaspoon

spot 1. *n* speck, dot, mark, taint, stain, blot, blemish, blotch, smudge
2. *n* ➡ **place**
3. *n* ➡ **trouble**
4. *vb* ➡ **find, see**

If the word you want is not a main entry above, look below to find it.

specialist ➡ expert
speciality ➡ specialty
specialization ➡ specialty
specie ➡ money
species ➡ type
specific ➡ special, detail
specimen ➡ example
speck ➡ spot
spectacle ➡ show, view
spectacles ➡ glasses
spectacular ➡ great, scenic
spectator ➡ observer
spectators ➡ audience
specter ➡ ghost
spectrum ➡ range
speculate ➡ guess, meditate
speculation ➡ theory
speculative ➡ theoretical
speechless ➡ dumb, quiet

speechmaker ➡ speaker
speedily ➡ quickly
speedy ➡ fast
spell ➡ period, curse, enchantment, dream, fit², mean
spellbind ➡ enchant
spellbinding ➡ magic
spend ➡ pay
spendthrift ➡ wasteful
sphere ➡ ball, field
spherical ➡ round
spider ➡ bug
spigot ➡ faucet
spike ➡ nail, point
spill ➡ flow, fall
spin ➡ turn, trip
spine ➡ thorn
spineless ➡ servile

spinoff ➡ product
spire ➡ tower
spirit ➡ courage, soul, angel, ghost, fairy
spirited ➡ active, lively
spirits ➡ mood, drink
spiritual ➡ religious, heavenly
spirituality ➡ religion
spit ➡ cape
spite ➡ envy
spiteful ➡ revengeful
splatter ➡ splash
splendid ➡ grand, good
splendidly ➡ well
splendor ➡ elegance
splice ➡ knot
splinter ➡ break
split ➡ hole, divide, break

split up ➡ separate, share
spoil ➡ decay, destroy, pamper
spoilage ➡ decay
spoiled ➡ stale, mischievous, bad
spoils ➡ booty
spokesperson ➡ agent
sponsor ➡ patron, back
spontaneity ➡ freedom
spook ➡ ghost, spy
spoor ➡ track
sporadic ➡ few, periodic
sport ➡ game, play
sport coat ➡ coat
sport jacket ➡ coat
sports center ➡ gymnasium
sportsman ➡ athlete
sportswoman ➡ athlete

---

spouse *n* mate, partner, husband, wife, bride, groom, consort, helpmate

spread 1. *vb* distribute, disseminate, disperse, circulate, strew, shake, sprinkle, scatter
➡ **send, broadcast**
2. *vb* extend, stretch, range, unfold, expand, widen, gape, yawn
3. *vb* ➡ **cover**
4. *vb* ➡ **rub**
5. *n* ➡ **growth**
6. *n* ➡ **range**
7. *n* ➡ **farm**
8. *n* ➡ **feast**
9. *n* ➡ **flow**

spy 1. *n* agent, counterspy, secret agent, double agent, spook (*informal*)
2. *vb* eavesdrop, pry, snoop
3. *vb* ➡ **look**

spying *n* espionage, surveillance, intelligence, counterespionage, counterintelligence

square 1. *adj* foursquare, four-sided, quadrilateral
2. *adj* ➡ **dull**
3. *n* box, rectangle, quadrilateral, quadrangle
4. *n* ➡ **court, park**

squeak 1. *vb* creak, screech, squeal, rasp, grate
2. *n* ➡ **peep**

squeeze 1. *vb* pinch, clasp ➡ **embrace**
2. *vb* compress, wring, press ➡ **tighten**
3. *n* pinch, nip, tweak ➡ **embrace**

stage 1. *n* ➡ **platform, floor**
2. *n* theater, boards
3. *n* ➡ **state, period**
4. *vb* ➡ **act, give**

stale 1. *adj* moldy, spoiled, wilted, flat, musty
➡ **dry, bad**
2. *adj* ➡ **trite**

stammer 1. *n* stutter, stammering
2. *vb* stutter, hem and haw, sputter
➡ **mumble**

If the word you want is not a main entry above, look below to find it.

spotless ➡ clean

spotted ➡ speckled

spout ➡ fountain, faucet

sprain ➡ pull

sprawl ➡ lie, trip

spray ➡ foam, bouquet, fountain, splash

spreadable ➡ contagious

spreadsheet ➡ table

spree ➡ binge, adventure

sprightly ➡ lively, agile

spring ➡ jump, descend, well

spring peeper ➡ frog

sprinkle ➡ wet, rain, splash, spread

sprint ➡ run, race

sprite ➡ angel, fairy

sprout ➡ grow, shoot

spruce ➡ neat

spry ➡ lively, agile

spryness ➡ agility

spume ➡ foam

spumoni ➡ ice cream

spur ➡ urge, incentive

spurious ➡ fake

spurn ➡ refuse

spurt ➡ flow

sputter ➡ stammer

spyglass ➡ glass

squabble ➡ argue, argument

squad ➡ troop, team

squalid ➡ dirty

squall ➡ storm, yell

squander ➡ waste

squash ➡ trample, break

squat ➡ low, fat, bend

squawk ➡ peep, cry, complain

squeal ➡ cry, squeak

squeamish ➡ reluctant

squirm ➡ crawl, fidget

squirrel (away) ➡ hide

squirt ➡ flow, splash, fountain

squish ➡ trample

stab ➡ stick, blow[1], try

stability ➡ balance

stabilize ➡ balance

stable ➡ stationary, barn

stack ➡ pile

stadium ➡ field

staff ➡ stick, faculty

stage name ➡ pseudonym

stagecoach ➡ wagon

stagger ➡ limp, shock

stagnant ➡ stationary, stuffy, dead

stain ➡ spot, dirty, finish, paint

stair ➡ step

stake ➡ bar, share, bet, interest

stalement ➡ tie

stalk ➡ stick, follow

stall ➡ booth, pen, barn, delay

stallion ➡ horse

stalwart ➡ brave, strong

stamina ➡ energy

stammering ➡ stammer

stamp ➡ print, signature, trample

stanza *n* verse, canto, strophe, stave, refrain, strain ➡ **poem**

star 1. *n* sun
2. *n* ➡ **celebrity, actor**

stare *vb* gaze, peer, gape, ogle, gawk ➡ **look**

start 1. *vb* begin, commence, initiate, cause, activate, launch, originate, stem, inaugurate, introduce, innovate, open, trigger, touch off, spark ➡ **continue** ⇨ *finish, stop*
2. *n* ➡ **beginning**
3. *vb* ➡ **jump**

state 1. *n* condition, circumstance, situation, status, stage, phase ➡ **grade**
2. *n* territory, province, dominion, commonwealth ➡ **country, colony, zone**
3. *vb* ➡ **mention, say, tell**

stationary *adj* fixed, immobile, permanent, motionless, steady, stable, still, stock-still, inert, stagnant ⇨ *portable*

statue *n* sculpture, statuette, figure, figurine, bust, bronze, likeness, image, effigy, idol, statuary ➡ **monument**

steal 1. *vb* rob, swipe, snatch, shoplift, purloin, embezzle, burglarize, rifle, poach, pinch, pilfer, pocket, plagiarize, pirate, filch ➡ **take, seize, pillage**
2. *vb* ➡ **sneak**
3. *n* ➡ **bargain**

steep 1. *adj* sheer, abrupt, precipitous, sharp, perpendicular, vertical, uphill
2. *vb* ➡ **wet**

step 1. *n* footstep, stride, pace, tread, footfall
2. *n* ➡ **gait**
3. *n* ➡ **act**
4. *n* rung, tread, stair ➡ **grade**
5. *vb* ➡ **walk, dance**

stereotype 1. *n* convention, generalization, categorization, characterization ➡ **cliché**
2. *vb* categorize, pigeonhole, characterize, label, generalize

---

If the word you want is not a main entry above, look below to find it.

stampede ➡ **hurry**

stance ➡ **posture**

stanchion ➡ **post**

stand ➡ **bear, booth, platform, shelf, table**

standdown ➡ **truce**

standard ➡ **normal, average, model, measure, flag**

standing ➡ **fame, grade**

standoff ➡ **tie**

standpoint ➡ **perspective**

stands ➡ **seat**

staple ➡ **necessity, basic**

stark ➡ **plain, hard, completely**

startle ➡ **surprise, scare**

starvation ➡ **hunger**

starve ➡ **die**

starved ➡ **hungry**

starving ➡ **hungry**

stash ➡ **save**

stated ➡ **spoken**

state-of-the-art ➡ **modern**

stately ➡ **grand, dignified**

statement ➡ **remark, announcement, bill**

state park ➡ **park**

statesman ➡ **diplomat**

station ➡ **base, destination**

stationery ➡ **paper**

statuary ➡ **statue**

statuette ➡ **statue**

stature ➡ **height, importance**

status ➡ **reputation, state**

statute ➡ **act**

statutory ➡ **legal**

staunch ➡ **resolute, faithful**

stave ➡ **stick, stanza**

stave off ➡ **repel**

stay ➡ **live[1], wait, anchor, visit, support**

stay with ➡ **visit**

steadfast ➡ **faithful, resolute, patient**

steady ➡ **balance, firm, stationary, continual**

stealing ➡ **theft**

stealth ➡ **secrecy**

stealthy ➡ **sly**

steam ➡ **cook, iron, smoke, energy**

steed ➡ **horse**

steeple ➡ **tower**

steeplechase ➡ **race**

steer ➡ **lead, drive**

steering wheel ➡ **wheel**

steersman ➡ **pilot**

stem ➡ **stick, start, stop**

stench ➡ **smell**

steno pad ➡ **notepad**

stentorian ➡ **loud**

stepparent ➡ **parent**

steppe ➡ **plateau**

➡ = synonym cross-reference • ⇨ = antonym cross-reference

sterile 1. *adj* antiseptic, sterilized, disinfected, sanitary, hygienic, germ-free ➡ **clean**
2. *adj* infertile, childless, barren, impotent ⇨ *fertile*
3. *adj* waste, desert, arid, barren ➡ **abandoned, empty**

sterilize 1. *vb* ➡ **clean**
2. *vb* spay, neuter, fix, geld, castrate

stick 1. *vb* poke, jab, probe, stab, plunge, pierce, prick, spear, puncture, lance, gore, peck, penetrate, perforate, riddle ➡ **hit**
2. *vb* adhere, cohere, glue, paste, tape, cling, cleave ➡ **join**
3. *n* branch, limb, twig, stem, stalk, staff, stave, wand, cane, club, baton ➡ **bar, bat**

sticky 1. *adj* adhesive, gummy, tacky, viscid, viscous
2. *adj* ➡ **damp**
3. *adj* ➡ **delicate**

stomach 1. *n* abdomen, midsection, paunch, belly, tummy, gut, midriff
2. *vb* ➡ **bear**
3. *n* ➡ **courage**

stop 1. *vb* halt, pause, cease, terminate, brake, arrest, check, stem, discontinue, lift ➡ **finish**
⇨ *start*
2. *vb* ➡ **prevent, bar**
3. *vb* ➡ **close**

storm 1. *n* tempest, gale, rainstorm, snowstorm, blizzard, hailstorm, ice storm, hurricane, typhoon, cyclone, monsoon, tornado, nor'easter, squall ➡ **rain, wind, snow**
2. *n* ➡ **flood**
3. *vb* ➡ **attack**
4. *vb* ➡ **hurry**

stormy *adj* rainy, blustery, inclement, tempestuous, turbulent, tumultuous, wild, fierce, violent ➡ **wet, windy**

story 1. *n* narrative, account, history, saga, chronicle, tale, narration, anecdote, yarn, plot, scenario, version ➡ **report, myth, joke, description**
2. *n* ➡ **lie**
3. *n* ➡ **floor**

If the word you want is not a main entry above, look below to find it.

sterilized ➡ sterile
stern ➡ strict, hard, back
stew ➡ cook, boil, worry
sticker ➡ label
sticks ➡ country
stiff ➡ firm, thick, prim
stiffen ➡ tighten
stifle ➡ choke, extinguish, quiet
stifling ➡ stuffy
stiletto ➡ knife
still ➡ quiet, more, dead, stationary, anyway
stillness ➡ calm
stilted ➡ prim
stimulate ➡ excite

stimulated ➡ excited
stimulating ➡ interesting
stimulation ➡ excitement
stimulus ➡ cause, incentive
sting ➡ hurt, pain
stingy ➡ cheap, greedy, small
stink ➡ smell
stint ➡ period
stipend ➡ wage
stipulate ➡ specify
stipulation ➡ term
stir ➡ mix, fidget, rustle, jail
stir up ➡ fan
stirring ➡ interesting

stitch ➡ sew, pain
stock ➡ sell, supply, load, family, trite
stockade ➡ wall, jail
stockpile ➡ supply, save
stockroom ➡ warehouse
stock-still ➡ stationary
stocky ➡ big, fat
stodgy ➡ stuffy
stoicism ➡ patience
stole ➡ wrap
stolid ➡ dull
stomp ➡ trample
stone ➡ rock, jewel
stoneware ➡ pottery

stony ➡ hard
stooge ➡ tool
stool ➡ seat
stoop ➡ descend, bend, condescend, porch
stopgap ➡ temporary
stopper ➡ top
stopwatch ➡ clock
store ➡ market, place, supply
storehouse ➡ warehouse
storeroom ➡ closet
storm cellar ➡ basement
storyteller ➡ liar
stout ➡ big, tough, fat
stove ➡ furnace

straight 1. *adj* direct, undeviating, even, unbent, regular, linear, true ➡ **level, vertical** ⇨ *bent, zigzag*
2. *adj* ➡ **sincere**

straighten 1. *vb* unbend, untwist, order, arrange, align, realign ➡ **level** ⇨ *bend*
2. *vb* ➡ **comb**

straightforward 1. *adj* frank, outspoken, plain, candid, forthright, ingenuous, blunt, vocal ➡ **sincere, explicit**
2. *adj* ➡ **easy**

strange 1. *adj* unfamiliar, unusual, unknown, unaccustomed, outlandish ➡ **foreign, new** ⇨ *common*
2. *adj* odd, peculiar, curious, abnormal, eccentric, quaint, queer, weird, eerie, bizarre, unnatural, ludicrous, different, irregular ➡ **mysterious, funny**

stranger *n* newcomer, outsider, out-of-towner ➡ **foreigner**

strength *n* power, force, might, potency, muscle, fortitude, intensity, vehemence, violence, severity ➡ **ability, energy**

strengthen 1. *vb* intensify, magnify, amplify, increase, expand, enhance, enlarge, boost, augment, swell ➡ **grow**
2. *vb* fortify, brace, buttress, reinforce ➡ **harden, support**

stress 1. *n* pressure, tension, strain, duress ➡ **worry**
2. *n* ➡ **accent**
3. *vb* ➡ **emphasize**

strict *adj* stern, stringent, austere, severe, rigorous, exacting, unyielding, uncompromising

striking *adj* conspicuous, impressive, dazzling, stunning, unusual ➡ **obvious, special, attractive, pretty, scenic**

string 1. *n* cord, line, twine, thread, lace, strap, yarn, fiber, filament, strand, tendril ➡ **rope**
2. *n* ➡ **row**
3. *n* ➡ **team**

strong 1. *adj* powerful, mighty, almighty, hardy, stalwart, robust, muscular, vigorous, athletic, virile, burly ➡ **tough, invincible, healthy** ⇨ *weak*
2. *adj* solid, sturdy, durable, sound, substantial ➡ **tough**
3. *adj* potent, powerful, formidable, violent, forceful, intense
4. *adj* ➡ **smelly**

If the word you want is not a main entry above, look below to find it.

stow ➡ load

straggle ➡ lag

straggler ➡ pedestrian

straightaway ➡ now

straight pin ➡ pin

strain ➡ hurt, pull, work, sift, stress, chorus, stanza, type, family

strait ➡ trouble

strand ➡ leave, string, shore

strangle ➡ choke

strap ➡ string, rope, tie

strategem ➡ trick, tactic

strategy ➡ plan

stratosphere ➡ air

stratum ➡ layer

stray ➡ wander, homeless, arbitrary

streak ➡ band, period, tendency, run

stream ➡ river, fountain, flow, flood

street ➡ road

streetlight ➡ light[1]

strenuous ➡ active, hard

stretch ➡ distance, period, spread, lengthen, distort

stretched ➡ tense

stretcher ➡ bed

strew ➡ spread

stride ➡ step, gait, walk

strident ➡ loud

strife ➡ fight, disagreement

strike ➡ hit, blow[1], attack, protest, discover, light[1], make

stringent ➡ strict

strip ➡ bar, band, peel, undress

stripe ➡ bar, band

stripped ➡ naked

strive ➡ fight, try, work

stroke ➡ blow[1], pet, rub

stroll ➡ walk

stroller ➡ pedestrian

strongbox ➡ safe

stronghold ➡ castle

strong-minded ➡ resolute

➡ = synonym cross-reference • ⇨ = antonym cross-reference

structure 1. *n* composition, arrangement, shape, form ➡ **pattern**
2. *n* ➡ **building**
3. *vb* ➡ **arrange**

strut 1. *vb* parade, swagger, sashay, flounce ➡ **walk**
2. *n* ➡ **gait**

stubborn *adj* obstinate, headstrong, pertinaceous, dogged, opinionated, obdurate, tenacious, pigheaded, unrelenting, unruly, intractable, difficult, perverse, unmanageable, mulish, ornery ➡ **resolute, dogmatic, wild**

student *n* pupil, learner, scholar, disciple, schoolchild, schoolgirl, schoolboy, freshman, sophomore, junior, senior, undergraduate, trainee, apprentice

study 1. *vb* analyze, evaluate, think through, pore over, review, research, criticize, survey, poll, canvass ➡ **examine, consider, learn, read**
2. *n* examination, analysis, investigation, inquiry, exploration, survey, poll, census, sampling, probe
3. *n* ➡ **report**
4. *n* ➡ **den**
5. *n* ➡ **dream**

stuffy 1. *adj* close, stifling, airless, suffocating, claustrophic, stagnant
2. *adj* congested, clogged
3. *adj* stodgy, conservative, conventional ➡ **dull**

stupid *adj* ignorant, unintelligent, dumb (*informal*), vacuous ➡ **foolish, dull, thoughtless** ⇨ *smart*
   Some people consider it rude to use **dumb** *in reference to people. When you are writing, it might be better to use one of the other more specific synonyms.*

suave *adj* urbane, debonair, diplomatic, cultured, charming, smooth, glib, facile ➡ **fashionable**

subdue *vb* subjugate, suppress, quash ➡ **defeat, contain**

subject 1. *n* theme, topic, question, substance, matter, thesis, gist, point, text, issue ➡ **field**
2. *n* ➡ **course**
3. *n* ➡ **model, patient**
4. *n* ➡ **citizen**
5. *vb* ➡ **control**

subordinate 1. *adj* inferior, secondary, auxiliary, junior, lower ➡ **under**
2. *n* ➡ **helper, servant**

If the word you want is not a main entry above, look below to find it.

strop ➡ **sharpen**

strophe ➡ **stanza**

struggle ➡ **fight, try, work**

strum ➡ **play**

stubble ➡ **beard**

stud ➡ **nail, beam, post**

studio ➡ **gallery**

studious ➡ **careful, educated**

stuff ➡ **matter, property, load**

stuffed ➡ **full**

stumble ➡ **trip, fumble**

stumble across ➡ **find**

stump ➡ **confuse**

stun ➡ **shock, paralyze**

stunned ➡ **unconscious**

stunning ➡ **beautiful, striking**

stunt ➡ **trick, prevent**

stupidity ➡ **ignorance, nonsense**

stupor ➡ **dream**

sturdy ➡ **tough, strong**

stutter ➡ **stammer**

sty ➡ **pen**

style ➡ **type, class, fashion, elegance**

stylish ➡ **fashionable, modern**

stymie ➡ **confuse**

stymied ➡ **disabled**

subcommittee ➡ **committee**

subconscious ➡ **mind**

subdivide ➡ **divide**

subdivision ➡ **division, development**

subject to ➡ **under**

subjective ➡ **arbitrary**

subjugate ➡ **subdue**

subjugation ➡ **slavery, victory**

sublet ➡ **hire**

sublime ➡ **heavenly**

submerge ➡ **flood, sink**

submerse ➡ **sink**

submission ➡ **surrender**

submissive ➡ **passive, servile**

submit ➡ **surrender, give, suggest**

subordinate to ➡ **under**

subtract *vb* deduct, remove, withhold, diminish ➡ **decrease** ⇨ *add*

subtraction *n* deduction, reduction, diminution, discount ⇨ *addition*

success *n* accomplishment, achievement, attainment, progress, prosperity ➡ **victory, luck**

successful 1. *adj* fortunate, accomplished ➡ **rich, famous**
2. *adj* effective, fortuitous, favorable, productive, victorious, triumphant, auspicious

sudden *adj* immediate, abrupt, swift, meteoric, precipitate, instantaneous, unexpected, unforeseen ➡ **sudden, sharp, early**

suggest 1. *vb* recommend, urge, propose, advise, counsel, move, submit, prescribe ➡ **offer**

2. *vb* imply, hint, intimate, insinuate

suggestion 1. *n* proposal, proposition, offer, recommendation ➡ **advice, idea, tip**
2. *n* ➡ **bit**

suit 1. *vb* fit, become, befit, enhance, flatter, agree with, complement
2. *n* outfit, ensemble, uniform, costume ➡ **clothes**
3. *n* lawsuit, litigation, action, hearing, case

summary *n* outline, synopsis, abstract, paraphrase, condensation, abridgment, digest, précis, rundown ➡ **essence**

superficial *adj* cursory, perfunctory, shallow, surface, skin-deep, cosmetic, uncritical, glib ➡ **trivial, trite**

If the word you want is not a main entry above, look below to find it.

subscriber ➡ patron

subsequent ➡ following

subservient ➡ servile

subside ➡ decrease, fall

subsidiary ➡ department

subsist ➡ live[1]

substance ➡ matter, essence, existence, density, weight, subject, support

substantial ➡ big, strong

substantially ➡ chiefly

substantiate ➡ verify

substantiation ➡ proof

substantive ➡ real

substitute ➡ change, trade, relieve, alternate

substitution ➡ trade

subterfuge ➡ pretense, trick, secrecy

subterranean ➡ underground

subtle ➡ sly, complicated, smart

suburb ➡ town

subversive ➡ rebel

subvert ➡ weaken

succeed ➡ prosper, win, follow

succeeding ➡ following

succession ➡ order

successive ➡ consecutive

succinct ➡ short

succinctness ➡ brevity

succor ➡ support, comfort, help

succulent ➡ rich

succumb ➡ surrender, lose, die

suck up ➡ absorb

suds ➡ foam

sue ➡ appeal, try

suet ➡ fat

suffer ➡ bear

sufferer ➡ patient

suffering ➡ pain, misery

suffice ➡ satisfy

sufficient ➡ enough

suffocate ➡ choke

suffocating ➡ stuffy

suffuse ➡ instill

sugary ➡ rich

suitable ➡ fit[1], able, good

suitcase ➡ luggage

suite ➡ room

sulk ➡ mope

sulky ➡ temperamental

sullen ➡ pessimistic, cross

sully ➡ dirty

sultan ➡ king

sultana ➡ queen

sultry ➡ damp, tropical

sum ➡ total, add, all

summation ➡ addition

summit ➡ top, mountain

summon ➡ call, mobilize

summons ➡ invitation

sumptuous ➡ grand

sun ➡ star

sundae ➡ ice cream

sunder ➡ separate

sundial ➡ clock

sundown ➡ evening

sundry ➡ many

sunglasses ➡ glasses

sunken ➡ underground

sunny ➡ bright, fair

sunrise ➡ morning

sunset ➡ evening

sunup ➡ morning

super ➡ great

superb ➡ grand, great

superfluous ➡ unnecessary

---

supernatural *adj* preternatural, superhuman, paranormal, unearthly, occult, mystical, psychic ➡ **invisible, heavenly**

superstition *n* old wives' tale, fable, lore ➡ **myth, belief**

superstitious 1. *adj* credulous, fearful
2. *adj* unfounded, groundless

supply 1. *n* stock, store, stockpile, inventory, reserve, hoard, cache, mine, holding, account, fund, reservoir
2. *vb* provide, equip, outfit, furnish, provision, rig ➡ **give, sell**

support 1. *vb* bear, hold (up), bolster (up), brace, sustain, prop (up), buttress, carry, nourish, nurture, feed, promote, foster ➡ **strengthen**
2. *vb* uphold, sustain, maintain, champion, enforce ➡ **back, help, approve**
3. *vb* ➡ **afford**
4. *n* backing, encouragement, assistance, succor, maintenance, livelihood, subsistence, upkeep, resource ➡ **help, protection, approval, permission, incentive, pension** ⇨ *opposition*

5. *n* mainstay, pillar, backer, champion ➡ **patron, fan**
6. *n* brace, prop, buttress, stay, bolster, truss, reinforcement ➡ **base, basis**

surprise 1. *vb* startle, amaze, astonish, daze, dazzle, bedazzle, flabbergast, throw, floor ➡ **shock**
2. *n* amazement, astonishment, wonder, incredulity ➡ **shock**
3. *n* ➡ **gift**

surrender 1. *vb* yield, concede, submit, resign, relinquish, sacrifice, acquiesce, capitulate, quit, give (in), bow, accede, defer, succumb, relent ➡ **lose, abandon**
2. *n* submission, capitulation, resignation, acquiescence, concession, abdication, renunciation, forfeit, sacrifice

suspense *n* uncertainty, apprehension, anticipation ➡ **doubt, fear**

suspension 1. *n* ➡ **break**
2. *n* expulsion, banishment, discharge, removal ➡ **exile**

If the word you want is not a main entry above, look below to find it.

superhuman ➡ **supernatural**

superintendent ➡ **principal**

supersede ➡ **follow**

superior ➡ **better, proud, boss**

superiority ➡ **excellence, advantage**

superlative ➡ **best**

supermarket ➡ **market**

superstar ➡ **celebrity**

supervise ➡ **lead**

supervision ➡ **leadership**

supervisor ➡ **boss**

supine ➡ **prone**

supplant ➡ **follow**

supple ➡ **flexible, agile**

supplement ➡ **add, more, addition**

supplementary ➡ **more**

supplicate ➡ **appeal**

supplier ➡ **seller**

suppose ➡ **guess**

supposedly ➡ **apparently**

supposition ➡ **theory**

suppress ➡ **subdue, contain, abuse**

supreme ➡ **best**

sure ➡ **certain, reliable**

sure-fire ➡ **reliable**

surely ➡ **certainly**

sure thing ➡ **certainty**

surf ➡ **wave**

surface ➡ **outside, top, side, appear, cover, superficial**

surge ➡ **wave, flood, impulse, hurry**

surly ➡ **rude, cross**

surmise ➡ **assume, guess, theory**

surmount ➡ **defeat, tower**

surname ➡ **name**

surpass ➡ **exceed**

surplus ➡ **remainder, abundance, more, unnecessary**

surprised ➡ **dumbfounded**

surreptitious ➡ **sly, secret**

surrogate ➡ **alternate**

surround ➡ **ring**

surroundings ➡ **setting**

surveillance ➡ **watch, spying**

survey ➡ **look, study, tower**

survive ➡ **live[1]**

susceptible ➡ **vulnerable**

suspect ➡ **guess, doubt, suspicious, defendant**

suspend ➡ **hang, exclude**

suspicious 1. *adj* distrustful, wary, leery, paranoid, apprehensive ➡ **jealous**
2. *adj* suspect, queer, shady, dubious ➡ **doubtful, strange**

swamp 1. *n* marsh, bog, marshland, bottomland, bayou, fen, quagmire, mire
2. *vb* ➡ **flood, sink**

sweat 1. *vb* perspire, swelter, secrete, exude
2. *n* perspiration, body odor, B.O.

sweep 1. *vb* wipe, whisk, brush, swish, dust, mop, vacuum ➡ **clean**
2. *n* ➡ **range**
3. *n* ➡ **paddle**

swell 1. *vb* bulge, distend, protrude, project, jut, balloon, dilate, expand, inflate, puff up

2. *vb* ➡ **strengthen**
3. *n* ➡ **wave**

swerve *vb* veer, shift, diverge, deviate, dodge ➡ **turn**

swim 1. *vb* float, paddle, bathe
2. *n* dip, plunge, swimming, bathing

swing 1. *vb* sway, rock, oscillate, vibrate, fluctuate, undulate, wave, roll, wobble, pitch, lurch, reel, waddle ➡ **turn**
2. *vb* wave, brandish, flourish, wield, whirl, twirl
3. *vb* ➡ **hang**
4. *n* ➡ **rhythm, music**

sword *n* rapier, cutlass, foil, épée, saber, broadsword, scimitar ➡ **knife**

If the word you want is not a main entry above, look below to find it.

suspicion ➡ doubt, belief

sustain ➡ support, keep

sustained ➡ long

sustenance ➡ food

swab ➡ rub

swaddle ➡ wrap

swagger ➡ boast, gait, strut

swallow ➡ drink, take, contain

swap ➡ trade, change

swarm ➡ herd, crowd, hurry, infest

swarthy ➡ dark

swat ➡ hit, blow[1]

swathe ➡ wrap, bandage

sway ➡ swing, wave, affect, persuade, rule

swear ➡ promise, testify, curse

sweepstakes ➡ lottery

sweet ➡ rich, pleasant, friendly

sweetheart ➡ love

swelling ➡ bulge, growth, sore

swelter ➡ sweat

sweltering ➡ hot

swift ➡ fast, sudden

swiftness ➡ speed

swig ➡ drink

swimming ➡ swim

swindle ➡ cheat

swindler ➡ cheat, rascal

swipe ➡ steal

swirl ➡ turn

swish ➡ rustle, sweep

switch ➡ trade, change, alternate, whip

swivel ➡ turn, axis

swoon ➡ dream

swoop ➡ descend

sycophantic ➡ servile

syllable ➡ word

symbol ➡ sign

symbolize ➡ mean

symmetry ➡ balance

sympathetic ➡ thoughtful

sympathize ➡ pity

sympathy ➡ pity, agreement

symphonic ➡ musical

symptom ➡ sign

synagogue ➡ church

synchronized ➡ simultaneous

synchronous ➡ simultaneous

syndicate ➡ group, monopoly

syndrome ➡ disease

synopsis ➡ summary

synthetic ➡ manufactured

syrupy ➡ thick

system ➡ method, order

systematize ➡ arrange

T

table 1. *n* desk, stand, counter, bar, dresser
2. *n* chart, graph, spreadsheet, timetable, schedule, table of contents, catalog, register, appendix ➡ **plan**
3. *n* ➡ **plateau**

tact *n* judgment, poise, diplomacy, savoir faire, discretion, delicacy, circumspection, finesse

tactic *n* strategem, maneuver, gambit, feint ➡ **plan, trick**

take 1. *vb* convey, deliver, transport ➡ **carry, bring, lead**
2. *vb* ➡ **get, receive**
3. *vb* confiscate, appropriate, expropriate, commandeer, usurp, gain ➡ **seize, catch**
4. *vb* ingest, swallow ➡ **eat, drink**
5. *vb* ➡ **bear**
6. *vb* ➡ **choose**
7. *vb* take in ➡ **earn**

talent *n* gift, aptitude, genius, skill, expertise, flair, knack, prowess, adroitness, facility ➡ **ability, agility, specialty, art**

talented *adj* gifted, artistic, musical, creative, inventive, versatile, imaginative, ingenious, fertile ➡ **able**

talk 1. *vb* speak, converse, discuss, chat, communicate, confer, consult, parley, rap ➡ **argue, chatter, say, tell**
2. *n* conversation, discussion, dialogue, consultation, word, chat, chitchat, patter, prattle, gibberish ➡ **speech, rumor, meeting**

talkative *adj* voluble, loquacious, verbose, garrulous, long-winded, effusive, chatty

tame 1. *adj* housebroken, house-trained, trained, manageable, domestic, domesticated, docile, broken ➡ **gentle**
2. *vb* ➡ **control**

If the word you want is not a main entry above, look below to find it.

tab ➡ bill, label
tableland ➡ plateau
tablespoon ➡ spoon
tablet ➡ medicine, notepad
tabloid ➡ paper
taboo ➡ illegal
tabulate ➡ list
tabulating ➡ addition
tack ➡ nail
tackle ➡ equipment, try, seize
tacky ➡ sticky, loud
tactful ➡ thoughtful
tactless ➡ insensitive
tadpole ➡ frog

tag ➡ label
tail ➡ follow, back
tailor ➡ adjust, sew
taint ➡ dirty, spot
take after ➡ resemble
take-home ➡ examination
take in ➡ adopt, take
take off ➡ shed
take on ➡ try
takeover ➡ acquisition
take prisoner ➡ arrest
take up ➡ occupy
tale ➡ story, lie
talker ➡ speaker
tall ➡ high, long

tallness ➡ height
tallow ➡ fat
tally ➡ add, bill, score, vote
talon ➡ foot
tamper ➡ tinker, meddle
tan ➡ brown, dark
tandem ➡ team
tang ➡ flavor, bit
tangelo ➡ orange
tangent ➡ adjacent
tangerine ➡ orange
tangible ➡ real
tangle ➡ knot, mess, maze, bend
tangy ➡ spicy, sour

tank ➡ container
tantalize ➡ tempt
tantrum ➡ fit²
tap ➡ knock, faucet
tape ➡ adhesive, band, stick
taper ➡ decrease
tardily ➡ late
tardy ➡ late
target ➡ object, prey, destination
tariff ➡ tax
tarnish ➡ corrode, dirty
tarp ➡ tent
tar paper ➡ paper
tarpaulin ➡ tent

n = noun • *vb* = verb • *adj* = adjective • *adv* = adverb • *prep* = preposition • *conj* = conjunction

tax 1. *n* duty, tariff, toll, levy, fee, assessment, tribute
2. *vb* ➡ **tire**

taxi *n* cab, taxicab, limousine, limo, hack ➡ **vehicle**

teach *vb* instruct, educate, train, school, tutor, coach, lecture, inform, drill, enlighten ➡ **explain, preach**

teacher *n* instructor, educator, schoolmaster, schoolmistress, scholar, tutor, mentor, guru, professor, lecturer, academic, don, coach ➡ **adviser, faculty**

team 1. *n* squad, company, unit, crew, side ➡ **group**
2. *n* (*in reference to horses, mules, or oxen*) pair, span, yoke, string, tandem

teenager *n* adolescent, teen, youth, juvenile ➡ **child**

tell *vb* report, narrate, relate, recite, declare, inform, announce, disclose, communicate, convey, notify, state, profess, pronounce, tattle ➡ **say, talk, order, warn, testify, predict**

temperamental *adj* moody, touchy, volatile, sensitive, testy, petulant, sulky ➡ **fickle, emotional**

temporary *adj* transitory, fleeting, momentary, ephemeral, provisional, stopgap, makeshift, interim, acting ➡ **short** ⇨ *permanent*

tempt *vb* entice, tantalize, lure, seduce, decoy, bait ➡ **persuade**

tendency *n* disposition, propensity, trend, proclivity, penchant, streak, inclination, leaning, bias ➡ **habit, preference**

tense 1. *adj* taut, stretched, drawn ➡ **firm, tight**
2. *adj* high-strung, agitated ➡ **anxious, nervous**
3. *vb* ➡ **tighten**

If the word you want is not a main entry above, look below to find it.

tarry ➡ wait

tart ➡ sour, spicy, pastry

task ➡ job

taste ➡ bite, drink, flavor, elegance, try

tasteless ➡ insipid

tasty ➡ delicious

tattered ➡ ragged

tattle ➡ tell, chatter

taunt ➡ insult

taupe ➡ brown

taut ➡ tense

tavern ➡ bar, restaurant

tawdry ➡ poor

tawny ➡ brown

taxicab ➡ taxi

teach-in ➡ protest

teaching ➡ education, lesson

teakettle ➡ pot

team up ➡ help

teapot ➡ pot

tear ➡ drop, hurt, rip

teardrop ➡ drop

tearful ➡ emotional

tearoom ➡ restaurant

tease ➡ bother, insult, joke, comb

teaspoon ➡ spoon

teaspoonful ➡ dose

teatime ➡ afternoon

technician ➡ mechanic

technique ➡ art, method

tedious ➡ dull

tedium ➡ boredom

teem ➡ rain

teeming ➡ fertile

teen ➡ teenager

telecast ➡ broadcast, program

telephone ➡ call

telescope ➡ glass, condense

televise ➡ broadcast

tell on ➡ betray

telling ➡ meaningful, valid

temerity ➡ audacity

temper ➡ personality, anger, mood, harden, soften

temperament ➡ personality, mood

temperance ➡ abstinence

temperate ➡ gentle

tempest ➡ wind, storm

tempestuous ➡ stormy

template ➡ pattern

temple ➡ church

tempo ➡ speed, rhythm

temptation ➡ attraction

tenacious ➡ stubborn, faithful

tenant ➡ occupant

tend ➡ protect

tender ➡ gentle, offer, loving, sore

tenderhearted ➡ kind

tenderness ➡ love, kindness

tendril ➡ string

tent *n* pavilion, canopy, tarp, tarpaulin, fly
➡ **protection**

term 1. *n* ➡ **word**
2. *n* semester, trimester, quarter, tenure
➡ **period**
3. *n* qualification, limitation, condition, restriction, stipulation, reservation, clause

terrain *n* ground, land, territory, landscape, environment, topography

testify *vb* affirm, swear, certify, vouch, attest
➡ **tell**

thankless 1. *adj* ➡ **thoughtless**
2. *adj* unappreciated, unrewarded, unrewarding, disagreeable, distasteful ➡ **useless**

theft *n* robbery, burglary, stealing, larceny, thievery, fraud, extortion, shoplifting, looting, pillage, embezzlement ➡ **crime**

theoretical *adj* hypothetical, academic, abstract, philosophical, rhetorical, speculative, conjectural

theory *n* hypothesis, conjecture, speculation, supposition, premise, presumption, assumption, surmise ➡ **idea, reason, philosophy**

therefore *adv* consequently, hence, accordingly, thus, ergo, wherefore, for, so

thick 1. *adj* dense, compact, close, condensed, packed, impenetrable, profuse ⇨ **thin**
2. *adj* stiff, firm, viscous, syrupy, gelatinous, glutinous, viscid
3. *adj* ➡ **broad**

thin 1. *adj* flimsy, slim, slender, sheer, delicate, diaphanous, insubstantial, gossamer ➡ **weak** ⇨ **thick, heavy**
2. *adj* ➡ **narrow**
3. *adj* slender, slim, lean, slight, skinny, scrawny, lanky, lank, wiry, spare, gaunt, haggard, emaciated ⇨ **big, tough**
4. *vb* ➡ **weaken, disappear**

think 1. *vb* reason, deliberate, cogitate
➡ **consider, meditate, believe**
2. *vb* ➡ **guess**

If the word you want is not a main entry above, look below to find it.

tension ➡ **stress**

tentative ➡ **doubtful, shy**

tenure ➡ **term**

tepee ➡ **tent**

tepid ➡ **warm**

terminal ➡ **base, destination, deadly, last**

terminally ➡ **deadly**

terminate ➡ **finish, stop, fire**

termination ➡ **finish**

terminus ➡ **destination**

terra cotta ➡ **pottery**

terrarium ➡ **zoo**

terrible ➡ **awful, scary**

terribly ➡ **very**

terrific ➡ **great, awesome**

terrified ➡ **afraid**

terrify ➡ **scare**

terrifying ➡ **scary**

territory ➡ **space, terrain, state**

terror ➡ **fear**

terrorize ➡ **threaten**

terse ➡ **short**

terseness ➡ **brevity**

test ➡ **examination, experiment, try, examine, experimental**

testament ➡ **will**

testimony ➡ **proof**

testy ➡ **temperamental, cross**

tether ➡ **tie, rope**

text ➡ **book, print, subject**

textile ➡ **cloth**

texture ➡ **quality**

thank ➡ **appreciate**

thankful ➡ **grateful**

thankfulness ➡ **gratitude**

thanks ➡ **gratitude**

thaw ➡ **melt**

theater ➡ **stage, hall**

theme ➡ **subject, report, song, chorus**

theme park ➡ **carnival**

theological ➡ **religious**

theology ➡ **religion**

therapeutic ➡ **medicinal**

therapy ➡ **cure**

thesaurus ➡ **dictionary**

thesis ➡ **report, subject**

thespian ➡ **actor**

thicken ➡ **concentrate, harden**

thicket ➡ **brush, forest**

thief ➡ **criminal**

thievery ➡ **theft**

thing ➡ **object, fashion**

things ➡ **property**

think through ➡ **study**

thinker ➡ **philosopher**

thinking ➡ **reason**

thirst ➡ **appetite**

thorn n briar, brier, bramble, barb, spine
➡ **point**

thoughtful 1. adj considerate, sympathetic, tactful, solicitous, sensitive ➡ **friendly, polite, kind, nice** ⇨ *thoughtless*
2. adj meditative, contemplative, pensive, reflective, wistful ➡ **sad, absorbed, intellectual**

thoughtless adj inconsiderate, careless, reckless, wanton, heedless, rash, foolhardy, ungrateful, thankless, unappreciative ➡ **rude, abrupt, indiscriminate, negligent** ⇨ *thoughtful*

threaten 1. vb intimidate, menace, torment, bully, terrorize ➡ **scare**
2. vb ➡ **jeopardize**

threshold 1. n sill, doorsill, doorstep, entryway, entranceway ➡ **door, porch**
2. n ➡ **beginning**

through 1. prep among, around, between ➡ **past**
2. prep ➡ **during**
3. adj ➡ **past**

throw 1. vb pitch, toss, hurl, fling, cast, pass, heave, chuck, sling
2. vb project, propel, launch, catapult, emit, radiate, send, give off ➡ **shoot**
3. vb ➡ **confuse, surprise**
4. vb ➡ **defeat**
5. n toss, pitch, pass, cast

tick 1. n ticktock, beat, click, clack
2. n check, check mark, mark, x, cross

ticket 1. n pass, admission, voucher, permit, visa, passport, receipt, sales slip, slip
2. n ➡ **ballot**
3. n, vb ➡ **label**

tie 1. vb fasten, secure, knot, bind, lash, tether, hitch, lace, strap ➡ **join, link**
2. n necktie, bow tie, cravat, ascot
3. n draw, deadlock, stalemate, standoff

tight 1. adj fast, unyielding, immovable, fixed ➡ **tense, firm, stationary**
2. adj sealed, airtight, watertight, impermeable
3. adj snug, close-fitting, skintight, formfitting, constricting
4. adj ➡ **cheap**

If the word you want is not a main entry above, look below to find it.

thirsty ➡ **dry**

thorax ➡ **chest**

thorough ➡ **complete, comprehensive, careful**

thoroughfare ➡ **road**

thoroughly ➡ **completely, well, carefully**

thoroughness ➡ **diligence**

though ➡ **but**

thought ➡ **idea, philosophy, attention**

thoughtfulness ➡ **kindness**

thrash ➡ **whip**

thrashing ➡ **defeat**

thread ➡ **string, bend**

threadbare ➡ **ragged**

threat ➡ **danger, warning**

threatening ➡ **ominous**

threnody ➡ **dirge**

thrift ➡ **economy**

thriftiness ➡ **economy**

thrifty ➡ **cheap**

thrill ➡ **excitement, excite**

thrilled ➡ **ecstatic, excited**

thrilling ➡ **exciting**

thrive ➡ **prosper, live[1]**

throaty ➡ **hoarse**

throb ➡ **shake, hurt**

throng ➡ **crowd**

throughout ➡ **during**

throw away ➡ **discard**

throw up ➡ **vomit**

thrust ➡ **impulse, energy, push**

thruway ➡ **highway**

thud ➡ **bang**

thug ➡ **vandal**

thump ➡ **knock**

thunder ➡ **bang, yell**

thunderous ➡ **loud**

thunderstruck ➡ **dumbfounded**

thus ➡ **therefore**

thwack ➡ **blow[1]**

thwart ➡ **prevent, bar**

thwarted ➡ **disabled**

tiara ➡ **crown**

tickle ➡ **pet**

ticklish ➡ **delicate**

ticktock ➡ **tick**

tidal wave ➡ **wave**

tide ➡ **flood**

tidings ➡ **announcement**

tidy ➡ **neat, clean**

tiepin ➡ **pin**

tier ➡ **layer, floor**

tiff ➡ **argument**

---

tighten *vb* stiffen, tense, clench, contract, squeeze ➡ **pull**

tingle *vb* prickle, itch, creep ➡ **hurt, shake**

tinker 1. *vb* putter, fiddle, dabble, mess, potter, twiddle, fidget, toy ➡ **fix**
2. *vb* tamper, juggle, rig, manipulate, fiddle ➡ **change**

tip 1. *n* ➡ **top, point**
2. *n* pointer, suggestion, hint ➡ **advice**
3. *n* gratuity, bonus, perk, perquisite, reward ➡ **wage**
4. *vb* ➡ **pay**
5. *vb* ➡ **upset**
6. *vb* ➡ **warn**

tire 1. *vb* exhaust, fatigue, tax, sap, fade, weary, bore ➡ **weaken**
2. *n* ➡ **wheel**

tired 1. *adj* exhausted, weary, worn out, sleepy, fatigued, listless, drained, dead
2. *adj* ➡ **trite**

together 1. *adv* jointly, mutually, collectively, en masse, cooperatively ⇨ *apart*
2. *adv* simultaneously, concurrently, contemporaneously

tolerant *adj* permissive, lenient, indulgent, easygoing ➡ **liberal, kind, patient**

tool 1. *n* instrument, utensil, machine, appliance, gadget, implement, device, mechanism, apparatus, means, vehicle, medium ➡ **equipment, hammer**
2. *n* instrument, pawn, puppet, stooge, dupe, victim

top 1. *n* peak, summit, pinnacle, apex, apogee, zenith, crest, tip, surface, climax, acme, prime, ultimate ⇨ *base*
2. *n* cover, lid, cap, hood, stopper, cork, plug, bung
3. *adj* ➡ **best**
4. *vb* ➡ **defeat, exceed**

If the word you want is not a main entry above, look below to find it.

tight-fisted ➡ cheap

tightwad ➡ miser

till ➡ until, farm, cash register

tiller ➡ wheel

tilt ➡ slant

timber ➡ wood, board, beam

timberland ➡ forest

time ➡ moment, period, rhythm, measure

timely ➡ punctual

timepiece ➡ clock

timer ➡ clock

timetable ➡ table

timid ➡ shy, cowardly

timorous ➡ shy, cowardly, afraid

timothy ➡ hay

tine ➡ point

tinge ➡ color

tiniest ➡ least

tinkle ➡ ring, peep

tint ➡ color, paint

tintinnabulation ➡ ring

tiny ➡ small

tippler ➡ drunkard

tipsy ➡ drunk, dizzy

tiptoe ➡ sneak

tiptop ➡ good

tiredness ➡ exhaustion

tireless ➡ diligent

tiresome ➡ dull

tissue ➡ paper

titan ➡ giant

titanic ➡ huge

title ➡ name, possession, headline

titled ➡ noble

titter ➡ laugh

to ➡ until

toadstool ➡ fungus

toast ➡ praise

toddler ➡ baby

toil ➡ work

toilet ➡ bathroom

token ➡ sign, reminder

tolerance ➡ patience

tolerate ➡ bear, let

toll ➡ tax, ring

tomahawk ➡ ax, axe

tomb ➡ grave

tome ➡ book

tomfoolery ➡ mischief

tomorrow ➡ future

ton ➡ abundance

tone ➡ color, quality

tongue ➡ language, lick

tongue-tied ➡ dumb

tonic ➡ soda

too ➡ besides, very

toodle-oo ➡ good-bye

toot ➡ blow^2

topic ➡ subject

topography ➡ terrain

topping ➡ icing

topple ➡ fall, upset

n = noun • *vb* = verb • *adj* = adjective • *adv* = adverb • *prep* = preposition • *conj* = conjunction

total 1. *n* sum, whole, aggregate, amount, totality, entirety ➡ **all** ⇨ *part*
2. *adj* ➡ **all, complete**
3. *vb* ➡ **add**

touch 1. *vb* feel, handle, caress, manipulate, paw, clutch, grope ➡ **rub**
2. *vb* contact, meet, reach ➡ **border**
3. *vb* ➡ **concern**
4. *n* ➡ **feeling, sense**
5. *n* ➡ **bit**

tough 1. *adj* sturdy, durable, stout, unbreakable, rugged, resilient, firm ➡ **strong**
2. *adj* ➡ **hard**
3. *n* ➡ **bully, vandal**

tower 1. *n* spire, steeple, turret, belfry, campanile, keep, minaret, pinnacle, obelisk, skyscraper
2. *vb* overlook, survey, loom, rise, rear, surmount

town *n* city, village, municipality, township, hamlet, community, borough, suburb, metropolis, megalopolis, settlement ➡ **neighborhood**

toy 1. *n* plaything, amusement ➡ **trinket, pastime, game**
2. *vb* ➡ **tinker**

track 1. *n* ➡ **path, course, field**
2. *n* trail, footprint, print, impression, imprint, spoor, sign, trace
3. *vb* ➡ **follow, hunt**

trade 1. *vb* exchange, swap, barter, switch, substitute, interchange, traffic, trade in ➡ **sell, change**
2. *n* exchange, swap, switch, substitution ➡ **sale**
3. *n* ➡ **business, profession**

If the word you want is not a main entry above, look below to find it.

top secret ➡ **secret**

topsoil ➡ **dirt**

topsy-turvy ➡ **upside down**

torch ➡ **light[1]**

torment ➡ **abuse, threaten, misery**

tormentor ➡ **bully**

torn ➡ **ragged**

tornado ➡ **storm**

torpedo ➡ **missile**

torpid ➡ **slow**

torpor ➡ **laziness**

torrent ➡ **rain, flood**

torrid ➡ **hot, tropical**

torso ➡ **body**

torte ➡ **cake**

tortilla ➡ **bread**

tortuous ➡ **indirect**

torture ➡ **misery, abuse**

toss ➡ **throw**

tot ➡ **baby**

totalitarian ➡ **dictator, dictatorial**

totalitarianism ➡ **tyranny**

totality ➡ **all, total**

totally ➡ **completely**

tote ➡ **bag, carry**

tote bag ➡ **bag**

totter ➡ **limp**

touching ➡ **about, emotional**

touch off ➡ **start**

touch on ➡ **mention**

touchstone ➡ **measure**

touchy ➡ **temperamental, delicate**

toughen ➡ **harden**

toupee ➡ **wig**

tour ➡ **trip, travel, period**

touring ➡ **abroad**

tourist ➡ **traveler, visitor**

tournament ➡ **game**

tow ➡ **pull**

towering ➡ **high**

township ➡ **town**

toxic ➡ **deadly, unhealthy**

toxin ➡ **poison**

trace ➡ **bit, draw, track**

trackless ➡ **impassable**

tract ➡ **property, pamphlet**

tractable ➡ **gentle**

traction ➡ **friction**

trademark ➡ **label**

trader ➡ **seller**

tradesman ➡ **seller**

tradition ➡ **myth, ceremony**

traditional ➡ **legendary, conservative**

traffic ➡ **business, trade, travel**

tragedy ➡ **disaster, play**

tragic ➡ **unfortunate**

trail ➡ **path, track, course, follow, lag**

train ➡ **teach, practice, exercise**

trained ➡ **tame**

trainee ➡ **student**

training ➡ **education, experience, discipline, exercise**

traipse ➡ **walk**

trait ➡ **quality, detail, habit**

traitor ➡ **rebel**

➡ = synonym cross-reference • ⇨ = *antonym cross-reference*

trample *vb* tramp, stamp, stomp, tread, flatten, squash, squish, crush

translate *vb* convert, interpret, decipher, decode, paraphrase, render, transcribe, transliterate, paraphrase, transform

translation *n* rendition, paraphrase, adaptation, interpretation, version, transliteration

transparent 1. *adj* clear, see-through, sheer, diaphanous, limpid, lucid, crystalline, translucent
2. *adj* ➡ **obvious**

trap 1. *n* pitfall, snare, catch, hitch
➡ **trick**
2. *vb* ➡ **catch**

trash *n* garbage, rubbish, refuse, waste, debris, litter, rubble, flotsam, wreckage, junk

travel 1. *vb* journey, voyage, tour, cruise, trek, commute, explore, traverse, roam, visit, sail
➡ **go, wander**
2. *n* passage, transportation, traffic, transit
➡ **trip**

traveler *n* tourist, voyager, wayfarer, commuter, fare, pilgrim, wanderer, itinerant, gypsy, vagabond, migrant, nomad ➡ **rider**

tray *n* platter, service, salver, trencher
➡ **plate**

treason *n* treachery, disloyalty, betrayal, mutiny, sedition ➡ **revolution, crime**

treatment 1. *n* care, handling, usage, reception, approach
2. *n* ➡ **cure, dose**

tree *n* sapling, seedling, hardwood, conifer, evergreen ➡ **wood, plant**

If the word you want is not a main entry above, look below to find it.

traitorous ➡ unfaithful

trajectory ➡ curve

tramp ➡ beggar, trample, walk

trance ➡ dream

tranquil ➡ calm

tranquilizer ➡ drug

tranquillity ➡ calm

transact ➡ negotiate

transaction ➡ business, sale

transcend ➡ exceed

transcribe ➡ write, translate

transcription ➡ score

transfer ➡ move, carry, send, movement, delivery

transform ➡ change, translate

transformation ➡ change

transgress ➡ disobey, sin

transgression ➡ crime, disobedience

transient ➡ short, mortal

transit ➡ travel

transition ➡ movement, change

transitory ➡ temporary

transliterate ➡ translate

transliteration ➡ translation

translucent ➡ transparent

transmissible ➡ contagious

transmission ➡ movement, delivery

transmit ➡ broadcast, send

transmittable ➡ contagious

transparency ➡ clarity

transpire ➡ happen

transplant ➡ plant

transport ➡ carry, take, vehicle

transportable ➡ portable

transportation ➡ vehicle, travel, delivery, exile

transpose ➡ change

trapeze artist ➡ acrobat

trash heap ➡ dump

trauma ➡ shock

travail ➡ work

traveling ➡ abroad

traverse ➡ travel

treacherous ➡ dangerous, unfaithful

treachery ➡ treason

tread ➡ gait, step, trample

treasure ➡ appreciate, wealth

treasury ➡ safe, bank

treat ➡ heal, entertain, explain

treatise ➡ report

treaty ➡ agreement

treble ➡ high

trek ➡ travel, walk

tremble ➡ shake, fear, vibration

tremblor ➡ earthquake

tremendous ➡ huge, great

tremor ➡ vibration, earthquake

trench ➡ channel

trench coat ➡ coat

trencher ➡ tray

trend ➡ tendency, fashion

trendy ➡ fashionable, new

trespass ➡ crime, sin, intrude

tress ➡ lock

tresses ➡ hair

trial ➡ try, tryout, experiment, examination, experimental

tribe ➡ family

tribulation ➡ hardship

tribunal ➡ court

tributary ➡ river, branch

tribute ➡ monument, tax

trick 1. *n* stunt, illusion, hoax, artifice, ploy, ruse, device, stratagem, deception, subterfuge, wile, dodge ➡ **joke, trap, pretense**
2. *vb* ➡ **cheat, betray**

trinket *n* bauble, frippery, gewgaw, trifle, bead ➡ **jewel, novelty**

trip 1. *n* journey, voyage, tour, excursion, expedition, cruise, passage, drive, travel, jaunt, outing, spin, pilgrimage, odyssey
2. *vb* stumble, slip, lurch, sprawl ➡ **fall**
3. *vb* ➡ **dance**

trite *adj* insipid, banal, uninteresting, unexciting, vapid, inane, hackneyed, clichéd, stale, musty, overused, tired, stock ➡ **superficial**

trivial *adj* petty, trifling, unimportant, negligible, frivolous, paltry, piddling, insignificant, meager, small, minute, minor, mere ➡ **superficial**

troop *n* troupe, company, squad, unit, corps, garrison ➡ **band, group, crowd, soldier, army**

tropical *adj* tropic, sultry, torrid, humid, muggy, equatorial, lush ➡ **hot**

trouble 1. *n* difficulty, predicament, plight, problem, matter, quandary, fix, pinch, strait, pickle, jam, spot, ordeal, mischief ➡ **hardship, nuisance**
2. *vb* inconvenience, distress, afflict, ail, harry ➡ **bother, disturb, worry**

truce *n* cease-fire, armistice, stand down ➡ **peace**

truth 1. *n* truthfulness, verity, authenticity, veracity, candor, sincerity, openness ➡ **accuracy, honesty** ⇨ *lie*
2. *n* ➡ **certainty**

try 1. *vb* attempt, strive, struggle, essay, endeavor, venture, undertake, tackle, take on
2. *vb* test, sample, check, taste, experiment
3. *vb* prosecute, sue, indict, adjudicate, impeach, arraign ➡ **blame**
4. *n* attempt, bid, endeavor, go, effort, trial, shot, stab, whirl

---

If the word you want is not a main entry above, look below to find it.

trice ➡ **moment**

trickery ➡ **pretense**

trickle ➡ **drop**

tricky ➡ **sly, delicate**

trifle ➡ **trinket, bit**

trifling ➡ **trivial**

trifocals ➡ **glasses**

trigger ➡ **start**

trim ➡ **neat, level, cut, decorate, dress, decoration**

trimester ➡ **term**

triumph ➡ **victory, win**

triumphant ➡ **successful, ecstatic**

trophy ➡ **prize**

tropic ➡ **tropical**

troposphere ➡ **air**

trot ➡ **run**

troubadour ➡ **musician**

troublemaker ➡ **bully**

troublesome ➡ **inconvenient**

trough ➡ **channel**

troupe ➡ **troop**

truancy ➡ **absence**

truant ➡ **runaway**

truck ➡ **vehicle**

trudge ➡ **walk**

true ➡ **correct, faithful, sincere, real, straight**

truffle ➡ **fungus**

truism ➡ **cliché**

truly ➡ **certainly, sincerely**

trunk ➡ **luggage, chest, body, nose**

truss ➡ **support**

trust ➡ **belief, duty, monopoly, inheritance, believe, depend**

trust company ➡ **bank**

trustee ➡ **guardian**

trusting ➡ **naive**

trustworthiness ➡ **virtue**

trustworthy ➡ **reliable, sincere, faithful**

trusty ➡ **faithful**

truth ➡ **certainty**

truthfulness ➡ **truth**

trying ➡ **hard**

---

tryout n audition, trial, reading, screening, hearing

turn 1. vb spin, revolve, rotate, twirl, swirl, whirl, wheel, swivel, pivot, gyrate, wind, coil, hinge, flip ➡ **bend, swing, swerve**
2. n ➡ **curve, corner, round**

tycoon n financier, magnate, capitalist, industrialist, entrepreneur, millionaire, businessman, businesswoman, businessperson

type 1. n kind, sort, class, nature, manner, style, category, species, variety, race, breed, strain, genre ➡ **make**
2. n ➡ **print**

Note that **type**, **kind**, and **sort** are close synonyms and are usually interchangeable. **Sort** is more often used in negative or critical contexts than **type** and **kind**: "He's just the **sort** of person who would cheat." **Class** and **category** are more precise in suggesting the nature of the group referred to: "Platypuses are in a **class** by themselves;" "These books are divided into two **categories**—fiction and nonfiction."

tyranny n oppression, repression, despotism, fascism, totalitarianism, dictatorship, absolutism ➡ **government**

If the word you want is not a main entry above, look below to find it.

tryst ➡ meeting
tsar ➡ emperor
tsarina ➡ empress
tub ➡ barrel, container
tube ➡ pipe, container
tubing ➡ pipe
tuck ➡ fold
tuft ➡ lock, lump
tug ➡ pull
tuition ➡ education
tumble ➡ fall
tumbler ➡ glass, acrobat
tumbling ➡ gymnastics
tummy ➡ stomach
tumor ➡ growth
tumult ➡ noise, excitement
tumultuous ➡ stormy

tun ➡ barrel
tundra ➡ plain
tune ➡ song
tuneful ➡ musical
tunnel ➡ cave, mine, dig
turbine ➡ engine
turbulence ➡ disturbance
turbulent ➡ stormy, wild
tureen ➡ bowl
turf ➡ dirt
turgid ➡ pompous
turmoil ➡ confusion
turn up ➡ appear
turncoat ➡ rebel
turnout ➡ productivity
turnpike ➡ highway
turquoise ➡ blue

turret ➡ tower
tussle ➡ fight
tutor ➡ teacher, teach
twaddle ➡ nonsense
twang ➡ accent
tweak ➡ squeeze
twiddle ➡ tinker
twig ➡ stick, shoot
twilight ➡ evening
twin ➡ duplicate
twine ➡ string, weave
twinge ➡ pain
twinkle ➡ blink, shine, light[1]
twinkling ➡ moment
twins ➡ pair
twirl ➡ turn, swing, bend, hurt, braid, dance

twisted ➡ bent
twisting ➡ indirect
twitch ➡ fidget, jump
two-by-four ➡ board
two-faced ➡ hypocritical
twosome ➡ pair
typescript ➡ print
typhoon ➡ storm
typical ➡ common, normal, model
typically ➡ regularly
typify ➡ embody
tyrant ➡ dictator, bully
tyrannical ➡ dictatorial
tzar ➡ emperor
tzarina ➡ empress

n = noun • vb = verb • adj = adjective • adv = adverb • prep = preposition • conj = conjunction

U

ugly *adj* unsightly, repulsive, hideous, grotesque, loathsome, revolting, repellent, repugnant, horrid, grisly ➡ **plain** ⇨ *pretty*

unanimous *adj* undivided, unified, united, universal, common, undisputed, harmonious, concerted

unaware *adj* ignorant, oblivious, obtuse, unmindful, unconscious, unconcerned, blind, deaf, heedless ➡ **naive**

unbelievable *adj* incredible, unimaginable, implausible, improbable, indescribable, unlikely ➡ **impossible, doubtful**

unbreakable *adj* indestructible, durable, rugged, resistant ➡ **strong, tough** ⇨ *breakable*

uncomfortable *adj* ill-at-ease, discomfited, cramped, painful, distressful, disagreeable, agonizing ➡ **anxious, nervous** ⇨ *comfortable*

unconditional *adj* unrestricted, unqualified, outright, absolute, unequivocal ➡ **complete, certain**

unconscious *adj* insensible, stunned, comatose, out cold, senseless, insensate, inanimate ➡ **asleep, unaware**

If the word you want is not a main entry above, look below to find it.

ubiquitous ➡ universal

ulcer ➡ sore

ultimate ➡ last, best, top

ultimately ➡ finally

ultimatum ➡ rule, order

ultraviolet ray ➡ X ray

umber ➡ brown

umpire ➡ judge

unable ➡ incompetent

unabridged ➡ complete

unaccompanied ➡ alone

unaccountable ➡ impossible

unaccustomed ➡ strange

unadorned ➡ plain, bald

unanimity ➡ unity

unapparent ➡ inconspicuous

unappreciated ➡ thankless

unappreciative ➡ thoughtless

unarmed ➡ vulnerable

unassuming ➡ humble

unattached ➡ single

unattainable ➡ impossible, inaccessible

unattended ➡ alone

unattractive ➡ plain

unavailable ➡ inaccessible

unavailing ➡ useless

unavoidable ➡ certain

unawareness ➡ ignorance

unbalanced ➡ insane

unbearable ➡ intolerable

unbeatable ➡ invincible

unbecoming ➡ improper

unbefitting ➡ improper

unbeliever ➡ skeptic, atheist

unbend ➡ straighten

unbent ➡ straight

unbiased ➡ fair

unblemished ➡ clean, perfect

unbolt ➡ open

unbounded ➡ infinite

unbroken ➡ complete, continual

uncanny ➡ mysterious

uncaring ➡ apathetic, insensitive

unceasing ➡ continual

uncensored ➡ complete

uncertain ➡ doubtful, variable

uncertainty ➡ doubt, suspense

unchanging ➡ continual

uncivilized ➡ primitive

unclad ➡ naked

unclean ➡ dirty

unclear ➡ obscure, doubtful

unclothe ➡ undress

unclothed ➡ naked

uncommon ➡ rare

uncomplicated ➡ plain

uncompromising ➡ resolute, strict

unconcern ➡ apathy

unconcerned ➡ apathetic, unaware

unconfined ➡ free

uncongenial ➡ unfriendly

unconquerable ➡ invincible

unconsciously ➡ accidentally

uncooked ➡ natural

uncoordinated ➡ clumsy

uncouth ➡ rude

uncover ➡ discover, reveal

uncovered ➡ open

uncritical ➡ indiscriminate, superficial

unctuous ➡ self-righteous

uncultivated ➡ wild

uncut ➡ complete

undaunted ➡ brave

undecided ➡ unresolved

undeniable ➡ certain, conclusive

---

under 1. *prep* below, beneath, underneath ⇨ *above*
2. *prep* less than, lower than, inferior to, subject to, subordinate to

underdeveloped *adj* undeveloped, disadvantaged, impoverished, deprived, backward, depressed

underestimate *vb* underrate, undervalue, deprecate, belittle

underground 1. *adj* subterranean, covered, buried, sunken, belowground
2. *adj* ➡ **secret**

undress *vb* disrobe, strip, unclothe, undrape, divest

unemployed *adj* jobless, idle, inactive, unoccupied, out-of-work ⇨ *employed*

unfaithful *adj* false, traitorous, treacherous, disloyal, perfidious, false-hearted, fickle ➡ **dishonest** ⇨ *faithful*

unfortunate *adj* unlucky, unhappy, hapless, disastrous, catastrophic, tragic, adverse, hapless, regrettable, lamentable, deplorable ➡ **sad, poor, pitiful**

unfriendly *adj* quarrelsome, antisocial, unsociable, uncongenial, inhospitable, combative, antagonistic ➡ **belligerent, cool** ⇨ *friendly*

If the word you want is not a main entry above, look below to find it.

undependable ➡ **unreliable**
underage ➡ **young**
underbrush ➡ **brush**
undercover ➡ **secret**
underfed ➡ **hungry**
undergo ➡ **experience**
undergraduate ➡ **student**
undergrowth ➡ **brush**
underhanded ➡ **sly**
underline ➡ **emphasize**
undermine ➡ **weaken**
underneath ➡ **under**
undernourished ➡ **hungry**
underpinning ➡ **basis**
underrate ➡ **underestimate**
underscore ➡ **emphasize**
undersized ➡ **short**
understand ➡ **know**
understandable ➡ **articulate**
understanding ➡ **patient, belief, wisdom, patience, agreement**

undertake ➡ **try, bear**
undertaking ➡ **act, work**
undervalue ➡ **underestimate**
underweight ➡ **light**[2]
undesirable ➡ **bad**
undetectable ➡ **invisible**
undetermined ➡ **unresolved**
undeveloped ➡ **underdeveloped, latent**
undeviating ➡ **straight**
undisciplined ➡ **wild**
undisputed ➡ **unanimous**
undisturbed ➡ **calm**
undivided ➡ **unanimous**
undo ➡ **separate, open**
undoubtedly ➡ **certainly**
undrape ➡ **undress**
undressed ➡ **naked**
undulate ➡ **swing**
undying ➡ **eternal**
unearth ➡ **discover, reveal**
unearthing ➡ **discovery**

unearthly ➡ **supernatural**
uneasy ➡ **anxious**
uneducated ➡ **ignorant**
unending ➡ **long, eternal**
unequal ➡ **different**
unequivocal ➡ **unconditional**
unerring ➡ **infallible**
unessential ➡ **unnecessary**
unethical ➡ **immoral**
uneven ➡ **rough, variable, different**
unexceptional ➡ **average**
unexciting ➡ **trite**
unexpected ➡ **sudden**
unexplainable ➡ **impossible**
unfailing ➡ **faithful**
unfair ➡ **prejudiced**
unfamiliar ➡ **strange**
unfashionable ➡ **unpopular**
unfasten ➡ **open**

unfastened ➡ **open**
unfavorable ➡ **ominous, destructive**
unfeasible ➡ **impractical**
unfeeling ➡ **insensitive**
unfettered ➡ **free**
unfinished ➡ **partial, unresolved**
unfit ➡ **weak, incompetent**
unflagging ➡ **diligent**
unfold ➡ **spread**
unforeseen ➡ **sudden**
unforgettable ➡ **memorable**
unforgiveable ➡ **inexcusable**
unfounded ➡ **superstitious**
ungainly ➡ **clumsy**
ungraceful ➡ **clumsy**
ungracious ➡ **rude**
ungrateful ➡ **thoughtless**
unguarded ➡ **vulnerable**
unhappy ➡ **sad, unfortunate**

n = noun • *vb* = verb • *adj* = adjective • *adv* = adverb • *prep* = preposition • *conj* = conjunction

unhealthy 1. *adj* unwholesome, harmful, injurious, noxious, unsanitary, toxic, bad
➡ **dangerous**
2. *adj* ➡ **sick**

unify *vb* unite, integrate, merge, fuse, consolidate ➡ **join**

union 1. *n* unification, fusion, amalgamation, coupling, confluence, combination, marriage, merger, consolidation ➡ **link, wedding**
2. *n* association, alliance, federation, league, partnership, guild ➡ **organization**

unique *adj* unprecedented, incomparable, singular, peerless, unparalleled, unrivaled, unsurpassed, matchless, idiosyncratic
➡ **different, special, only**

unity 1. *n* identity, homogeneity, sameness, integrity ➡ **similarity**

2. *n* unison, concord, harmony, unanimity
➡ **agreement**

universal 1. *adj* worldwide, international, global, cosmic
2. *adj* ubiquitous, limitless, catholic
➡ **common, general, unanimous**

unnecessary *adj* needless, unessential, irrelevant, extraneous, superfluous, redundant, optional, gratuitous, pointless, extra, surplus, leftover ➡ **useless, excessive**

unnoticed *adj* unheeded, unobserved, disregarded, unseen, overlooked

unpopular 1. *adj* disliked, despised, unwelcome, friendless
2. *adj* unfashionable, outmoded ➡ **old**

unprepared *adj* unready, unsuspecting, inexperienced, napping, unwary

---

If the word you want is not a main entry above, look below to find it.

unhearing ➡ deaf
unheeded ➡ unnoticed
unhinged ➡ insane
unification ➡ union
unified ➡ unanimous, inseparable
uniform ➡ same, suit
unimaginable ➡ unbelievable
unimaginative ➡ dull
unimpeachable ➡ reliable
unimportant ➡ trivial
uninhabited ➡ empty, abandoned
unintelligent ➡ stupid
unintelligible ➡ illegible
unintentional ➡ accidental, automatic
unintentionally ➡ accidentally

uninterested ➡ bored
uninteresting ➡ dull, trite
uniqueness ➡ novelty
unison ➡ unity
unit ➡ troop, team
unite ➡ join, unify
united ➡ unanimous, inseparable
universe ➡ space
university ➡ college
unjust ➡ prejudiced
unjustifiable ➡ inexcusable
unkempt ➡ messy
unkind ➡ mean
unknown ➡ strange, anonymous
unlawful ➡ illegal
unlearned ➡ ignorant
unlettered ➡ ignorant
unlike ➡ different

unlikely ➡ unbelievable
unlimited ➡ infinite
unlit ➡ dark
unload ➡ empty
unlocked ➡ open
unloose ➡ free
unloosen ➡ free
unlovely ➡ plain
unlucky ➡ unfortunate
unmanageable ➡ clumsy, stubborn, invincible
unmarried ➡ celibate, single
unmindful ➡ unaware
unnamed ➡ anonymous
unnatural ➡ strange
unnerve ➡ disturb, scare, discourage
unnerving ➡ scary
unnoticeable ➡ inconspicuous

unobjectionable ➡ harmless
unobserved ➡ unnoticed
unobstructed ➡ open
unobtainable ➡ inaccessible
unobtrusive ➡ inconspicuous
unoccupied ➡ empty, unemployed
unpack ➡ empty
unpaid ➡ amateur, due
unparalleled ➡ best, unique
unpardonable ➡ inexcusable
unplanned ➡ accidental, spontaneous, arbitrary
unpleasant ➡ bad
unpolished ➡ provincial
unprecedented ➡ unique
unpredictable ➡ arbitrary
unprejudiced ➡ fair

unreliable 1. *adj* (*used in reference to persons*) untrustworthy, irresponsible, fickle, undependable ➡ **unfaithful, dishonest** ⇨ *reliable*

2. *adj* (*used in reference to ideas and inanimate objects or things*) deceptive, unsound, misleading, flimsy ➡ **wrong**

unresolved *adj* unsettled, undecided, undetermined, indeterminate, unfinished, pending, incomplete ➡ **doubtful**

unsteady *adj* unstable, wobbly, shaky, insecure, precarious ➡ **variable**

until 1. *prep* till, before, up till, up to, to
2. *conj* till

If the word you want is not a main entry above, look below to find it.

unpretentious ➡ common, humble

unprincipled ➡ immoral, dishonest

unprocessed ➡ natural

unprofitable ➡ useless

unprotected ➡ vulnerable

unqualified ➡ incompetent, unconditional

unquestionable ➡ certain

unquestionably ➡ certainly

unravel ➡ solve

unreachable ➡ inaccessible

unread ➡ ignorant

unreadable ➡ illegible

unready ➡ unprepared

unreal ➡ imaginary

unrealistic ➡ impractical

unrealized ➡ latent

unreasonable ➡ illogical

unrelenting ➡ stubborn

unremarkable ➡ average

unresponsive ➡ apathetic

unrest ➡ disturbance

unrestrained ➡ free

unrestricted ➡ unconditional

unrewarded ➡ thankless

unrewarding ➡ thankless

unrivaled ➡ unique

unruly ➡ mischievous, stubborn, wild

unsafe ➡ dangerous

unsanitary ➡ dirty, unhealthy

unsatisfactory ➡ poor

unsavory ➡ bad

unschooled ➡ ignorant

unscientific ➡ arbitrary

unscramble ➡ solve

unscrupulous ➡ dishonest

unsealed ➡ open

unseat ➡ oust

unseeing ➡ blind

unseemly ➡ improper

unseen ➡ invisible, unnoticed

unselfish ➡ generous

unselfishness ➡ generosity

unsentimental ➡ practical

unsettle ➡ disturb

unsettled ➡ unresolved, variable

unshackled ➡ free

unshaken ➡ faithful

unsharpened ➡ dull

unsociable ➡ unfriendly

unsightly ➡ ugly

unsigned ➡ anonymous

unskilled ➡ amateur

unsoiled ➡ clean

unsolvable ➡ impossible

unsophisticated ➡ naive, primitive, provincial

unsound ➡ unreliable, imprudent

unsparing ➡ generous

unspoiled ➡ new

unstable ➡ unsteady

unsuccessful ➡ useless

unsuitable ➡ improper

unsure ➡ doubtful

unsurpassed ➡ best, unique

unsuspecting ➡ unprepared

unsympathetic ➡ insensitive

untamed ➡ wild, primitive

untangle ➡ comb

unthinkable ➡ impossible

untidy ➡ messy

untie ➡ open

untimely ➡ early, inconvenient

untouched ➡ new

untrained ➡ amateur

untrodden ➡ impassable

untroubled ➡ calm, carefree

untrue ➡ wrong

untrustworthy ➡ dishonest, unreliable, fickle

untruth ➡ lie

untruthful ➡ dishonest

untwist ➡ straighten

unusable ➡ useless, broken

unused ➡ clean, new

unusual ➡ strange, special, striking

unusually ➡ very

unvarnished ➡ plain

unvarying ➡ continual

unveil ➡ reveal

unwary ➡ unprepared

unwavering ➡ resolute

unwed ➡ single

unwelcome ➡ unpopular

unwell ➡ sick

unwholesome ➡ unhealthy

unwieldy ➡ clumsy

unwilling ➡ reluctant

unwind ➡ rest

unwise ➡ imprudent

unwittingly ➡ accidentally

unwrap ➡ empty

unwritten ➡ spoken

unyielding ➡ resolute, tight, strict

up ➡ above, awake

upbraid ➡ scold

upcoming ➡ future

update ➡ renew

upend ➡ upset

upgrade ➡ promote

upheaval ➡ disturbance

uphill ➡ steep

uphold ➡ support

upkeep ➡ support

upland ➡ plateau

uplift ➡ lift

upon ➡ above

upper ➡ best

n = noun • *vb* = verb • *adj* = adjective • *adv* = adverb • *prep* = preposition • *conj* = conjunction

upset 1. *vb* overturn, capsize, topple, upend, invert, tip
2. *vb, n* ➡ **defeat**
3. *vb* ➡ **worry, disturb, anger**
4. *adj* ➡ **angry**
5. *n* ➡ **shock**

upside down *adv* inverted, topsy-turvy, head-over-heels, reversed

urban *adj* city, metropolitan, municipal, civic, cosmopolitan

urchin *n* waif, ragamuffin, brat, imp, gamin ➡ **child**

urge 1. *vb* coax, encourage, goad, prod, spur, egg (on), press, prompt, push, inspire, incite, instigate, provoke ➡ **persuade, suggest**
2. *n* ➡ **desire, beg**

urgent *adj* crucial, pressing, imperative, compelling, desperate, dire, acute ➡ **important**

use 1. *vb* employ, utilize, wield, practice, exercise, exert, apply, expend, exploit, refer to, resort to ➡ **operate**
2. *vb* consume, deplete, exhaust, expend ➡ **finish**
3. *n* application, utilization, utility, usefulness, usage, purpose, operation, employment, consumption, expenditure, exercise ➡ **function, worth**

useful *adj* helpful, practical, handy, beneficial, desirable, advantageous, profitable, pragmatic, utilitarian, versatile ➡ **efficient** ⇨ *useless*

useless 1. *adj* futile, vain, fruitless, unavailing, hopeless, desperate, abortive, unsuccessful, ineffectual, unprofitable ➡ **unnecessary** ⇨ *useful*
2. *adj* worthless, unusable, ineffective, counterproductive ➡ **broken**

usual *adj* regular, customary, accustomed, habitual, ordinary, normal, set ➡ **normal**

usually *adv* ordinarily, customarily, regularly, normally, generally ➡ **often, regularly**

utopia *n* paradise, Eden, Shangri-la, Camelot, promised land ➡ **heaven**

If the word you want is not a main entry above, look below to find it.

upper class ➡ **aristocracy**
upper hand ➡ **advantage**
upright ➡ **vertical, post**
uprising ➡ **revolution**
uproar ➡ **noise, disturbance**
uproarious ➡ **loud**
upscale ➡ **expensive**
upshot ➡ **effect**

uptight ➡ **nervous**
up till ➡ **until**
up to ➡ **until**
up-to-date ➡ **modern, new**
upward, upwards ➡ **above**
urbane ➡ **suave**
usable ➡ **available**
usage ➡ **habit, use, treatment**

used ➡ **old**
usefulness ➡ **use**
use up ➡ **finish**
usher ➡ **guide, lead**
usurp ➡ **take**
utensil ➡ **tool**
utilitarian ➡ **useful**
utility ➡ **use**

utilization ➡ **use**
utilize ➡ **use**
utmost ➡ **most**
utopian ➡ **idealistic**
utter ➡ **pronounce, complete**
utterance ➡ **remark, speech, word**
utterly ➡ **completely**

➡ = synonym cross-reference • ⇨ = antonym cross-reference

vacation *n* holiday, recess, leave, furlough, sabbatical, respite, rest, R & R ➡ **break, leisure**

vaccinate *vb* inoculate, immunize

valid 1. *adj* sound, convincing, logical, cogent, telling ➡ **fair**
2. *adj* ➡ **legal, official**

valley *n* vale, glen, dell, dale, hollow, gap, basin, lowland ➡ **canyon** ➪ *hill, mountain*

valuable *adj* precious, dear, cherished, prized, beloved, inestimable, important, worthwhile, priceless ➡ **expensive, rare**

vandal *n* hooligan, hoodlum, hood, tough, punk, thug, delinquent, savage, barbarian ➡ **criminal, bully, pirate**

variable *adj* changeable, unsettled, mutable, erratic, uncertain, uneven, inconsistent ➡ **arbitrary, fickle, unsteady**

vegetable *n* green, produce ➡ **plant, fruit, herb**

vehicle 1. *n* automobile, car, truck, transportation, transport, wheels (*informal*) ➡ **airplane, boat, taxi**
2. *n* ➡ **tool**

If the word you want is not a main entry above, look below to find it.

vacant ➡ **empty, blank**
vacate ➡ **leave, empty**
vaccine ➡ **medicine**
vacillate ➡ **hesitate**
vacuous ➡ **blank, stupid**
vacuum ➡ **sweep**
vagabond ➡ **traveler, homeless**
vagrant ➡ **homeless, beggar**
vague ➡ **obscure, doubtful**
vain ➡ **proud, empty, useless**
vainglory ➡ **pride**
vale ➡ **valley**
Valhalla ➡ **heaven**
valiant ➡ **brave**
validate ➡ **approve**
validation ➡ **justification**
valise ➡ **luggage**
valor ➡ **courage**
valorous ➡ **brave**
value ➡ **worth, importance, appreciate, respect**

valve ➡ **faucet**
van ➡ **front**
Vandyke ➡ **beard**
vanguard ➡ **front, patrol**
vanish ➡ **disappear**
vanity ➡ **pride**
vanquish ➡ **defeat**
vantage ➡ **advantage**
vapid ➡ **trite**
vapor ➡ **smoke, cloud**
variance ➡ **difference**
variation ➡ **change, difference**
varied ➡ **different**
variegated ➡ **speckled**
variety ➡ **assortment, type**
various ➡ **many, different**
variously ➡ **differently**
varnish ➡ **finish**
vary ➡ **change, differ**
vassalage ➡ **slavery**

vast ➡ **huge**
vat ➡ **barrel, pot**
vault ➡ **jump, safe, grave**
vaulting ➡ **gymnastics**
vaunt ➡ **boast**
veer ➡ **bend, swerve**
vegetate ➡ **rest**
vegetation ➡ **plant**
vehemence ➡ **strength**
vehement ➡ **certain**
veil ➡ **scarf, divider, hide**
vein ➡ **mood, band, blood vessel**
vellum ➡ **paper**
velocity ➡ **speed**
velvety ➡ **fuzzy**
vend ➡ **sell**
vendor ➡ **seller**
veneer ➡ **coat**
venerable ➡ **old**
venerate ➡ **worship**

veneration ➡ **worship**
vengeance ➡ **revenge**
vengeful ➡ **revengeful**
venom ➡ **poison**
venomous ➡ **deadly**
vent ➡ **hole, say**
ventilate ➡ **fan**
ventilation ➡ **air**
venture ➡ **try, bet, adventure, pastime**
veracity ➡ **truth, honesty**
veranda ➡ **porch**
verbal ➡ **spoken**
verbalism ➡ **word**
verbalize ➡ **say**
verbatim ➡ **literal**
verbose ➡ **talkative**
verdant ➡ **green**
verdict ➡ **decision**
verge ➡ **edge**
veridian ➡ **green**

n = noun • *vb* = verb • *adj* = adjective • *adv* = adverb • *prep* = preposition • *conj* = conjunction

verify *vb* determine, prove, confirm, ascertain, ensure, assure, show, demonstrate, establish, authenticate, corroborate, substantiate, vindicate, defend ➡ **decide**

vertical *adj* perpendicular, upright, erect, plumb ➡ **steep**

very *adv* extremely, unusually, greatly, absolutely, immensely, terribly, awfully, rather, really, quite, most, too ➡ **much**

vibration *n* quiver, quaver, quake, oscillation, tremor, tremble, shake, shock

victory *n* triumph, conquest, subjugation, mastery, overthrow, ascendancy, win ⇨ *defeat*

view 1. *n* sight, glimpse, scene, scenery, vision, panorama, outlook, spectacle, perspective, prospect, vista ➡ **look**
2. *n* ➡ **belief**
3. *vb* ➡ **look, study**
4. *vb* ➡ **believe**

violence *n* brutality, destruction, destructiveness, savagery, aggression ➡ **disturbance, confusion, fight, strength**

violent 1. *adj* savage, fierce, furious, fuming, enraged, berserk ➡ **angry, belligerent, mean, wild, destructive**
2. *adj* ➡ **strong, stormy**

virtual *adj* implied, implicit, practical

virtue 1. *n* integrity, morality, honor, trustworthiness, principle, decency, goodness ➡ **truth, honesty, kindness**
2. *n* innocence, purity, modesty, chastity, virginity
3. *n* ➡ **advantage, worth**

visible *adj* observable, discernible, perceptible, perceivable, visual, optical, graphic, illustrative ➡ **obvious**

If the word you want is not a main entry above, look below to find it.

verification ➡ proof
veritable ➡ real
veritably ➡ really
verity ➡ truth
vermilion ➡ red
vermin ➡ bug
vernacular ➡ dialect
versatile ➡ talented, useful
verse ➡ poem, stanza
versed ➡ expert
version ➡ translation, story
versus ➡ opposite
vessel ➡ boat, bowl
vestibule ➡ hall
vestments ➡ clothes
veteran ➡ soldier
veto ➡ rejection, abolish
vex ➡ bother
vexation ➡ nuisance

viable ➡ alive, possible
viaduct ➡ bridge
vibes ➡ xylophone
vibrant ➡ active
vibraphone ➡ xylophone
vibrate ➡ shake, swing
vicar ➡ priest
vice ➡ fault, dishonesty
vicinity ➡ neighborhood, place
vicious ➡ mean
vicissitude ➡ change
victim ➡ casualty, prey, patient, tool
victimize ➡ abuse
victor ➡ winner
victorious ➡ successful
victuals ➡ food
video ➡ movie
vie ➡ compete

viewer ➡ observer
viewers ➡ audience
viewpoint ➡ perspective
vigil ➡ watch
vigilant ➡ alert
vigor ➡ energy, health
vigorous ➡ lively, strong, healthy
vile ➡ bad
vilify ➡ curse
villa ➡ home
village ➡ town
villain ➡ rascal
villainous ➡ bad
vim ➡ energy
vindicate ➡ revenge, forgive, verify
vindication ➡ revenge, justification
vindictive ➡ revengeful

vine ➡ flower
violate ➡ disobey
violation ➡ crime
violet ➡ purple
VIP ➡ celebrity
viper ➡ snake
virgin ➡ new
virginal ➡ celibate
virginity ➡ virtue
virile ➡ masculine, strong
virtually ➡ practically
virtuoso ➡ expert, genius
virtuous ➡ good
virulent ➡ deadly
virus ➡ disease, poison
visa ➡ ticket
visage ➡ face, appearance
viscid ➡ thick, sticky
viscous ➡ thick, sticky

➡ = synonym cross-reference • ⇨ = antonym cross-reference

visit 1. *vb* call on/upon, stay with, drop by/in, sojourn ➡ **frequent, travel**
2. *n* call, stay, appointment, sojourn, visitation, get-together

visitor *n* guest, caller, company, houseguest, tourist

voluntary *adj* intentional, deliberate, willful, willing, freely, spontaneous, optional

vomit *vb* throw up, retch, regurgitate, gag, heave, puke (*informal*), barf (*informal*)

vote 1. *n* ballot, election, referendum, poll, polls, tally ➡ **choice**
2. *vb* ➡ **choose, decide**

vulnerable *adj* defenseless, unarmed, unprotected, unguarded, susceptible, prone, disposed ➡ **weak**

If the word you want is not a main entry above, look below to find it.

vision ➡ sight, view, foresight, imagination
visionary ➡ idealistic, idealist
visionless ➡ blind
visitation ➡ visit
visor ➡ bill
vista ➡ view
visual ➡ visible
visualize ➡ imagine
visually impaired ➡ blind
vital ➡ lively, alive
vitality ➡ energy, health, life
vivacious ➡ lively

vivid ➡ bright, explicit
vocable ➡ word
vocabulary ➡ dictionary
vocal ➡ spoken, straightforward
vocalist ➡ singer
vocalize ➡ pronounce, sing
vocation ➡ profession
vociferous ➡ loud
vogue ➡ fashion
voice ➡ speech, choice
voiced ➡ spoken
voiceless ➡ dumb

void ➡ empty, space
volatile ➡ inflammable, temperamental
volition ➡ will
volley ➡ flood
voltage ➡ energy
voluble ➡ talkative
volume ➡ size, book, measure, productivity
voluminous ➡ abundant
volunteer ➡ soldier
vomiting ➡ nausea
voodoo ➡ magic

voracious ➡ predatory, greedy
vouch ➡ testify
voucher ➡ ticket
vouchsafe ➡ condescend
vow ➡ promise
voyage ➡ trip, travel
voyager ➡ traveler
vulgar ➡ common, dirty, sensational
vulgarity ➡ rudeness
vying ➡ competitive

n = noun • *vb* = verb • *adj* = adjective • *adv* = adverb • *prep* = preposition • *conj* = conjunction

wage *n* salary, pay, allowance, fee, tip, compensation, income, earnings, profit, intake, stipend, revenue, return ➡ **pension**

wagon *n* carriage, buggy, cart, coach, stagecoach ➡ **vehicle**

wait *vb* remain, linger, loiter, stay, tarry, await, abide, dally ➡ **delay, hesitate** ⇨ *leave*

wake *vb* wake up, waken, rouse, arouse, awaken

walk 1. *vb* amble, stroll, march, step, hike, stride, trudge, plod, lumber, file, trek, traipse, tramp ➡ **wander, strut, crawl**
2. *n* ➡ **gait**
3. *n* ➡ **path**

wall *n* partition, fence, parapet, stockade, rampart, palisade, barricade ➡ **divider, dam**

wallet *n* billfold, change purse ➡ **bag**

wander 1. *vb* roam, meander, ramble, saunter, rove, range, drift ➡ **walk, travel**

2. *vb* stray, deviate, meander, ramble, digress, diverge

want 1. *vb* wish, desire, crave, yearn, long, pine, hanker, itch ➡ **envy, hope, prefer**
2. *vb* ➡ **need**
3. *n* lack, dearth, paucity, shortage, scarcity, deficiency ➡ **absence, hardship, poverty**

warehouse *n* storehouse, stockroom, depot, depository, granary, grain elevator, silo, armory, arsenal, magazine

warm 1. *adj* lukewarm, tepid, heated, mild ➡ **hot**
2. *adj* ➡ **friendly**

warn *vb* forewarn, caution, alert, tip off, advise, admonish, exhort, counsel ➡ **scare, tell**

warning *n* alarm, signal, admonition, caution, advice, caveat, premonition, forewarning, omen, threat ➡ **notice, sign**

If the word you want is not a main entry above, look below to find it.

wad ➡ pile

waddle ➡ swing

wader ➡ bird

waft ➡ blow[2]

wag ➡ shake

wager ➡ bet, lottery

wagering ➡ gambling

waggle ➡ shake

waif ➡ urchin

wail ➡ cry

wait on ➡ help

wakeful ➡ awake

waken ➡ wake

walker ➡ pedestrian

walk out ➡ protest

walkway ➡ path

wallop ➡ blow[1]

wallow ➡ fumble

wan ➡ pale

wand ➡ stick

wanderer ➡ traveler

wane ➡ decrease

wanton ➡ thoughtless, wasteful

war ➡ fight

warble ➡ sing

ward ➡ neighborhood

ward off ➡ repel

wardrobe ➡ clothes, closet

wares ➡ product

warfare ➡ fight

warily ➡ carefully

warlike ➡ military

warlock ➡ magician

warmhearted ➡ kind

warmth ➡ hospitality, feeling

warp ➡ bend

warped ➡ bent

warrant ➡ promise, guarantee, deserve

warren ➡ den

warrior ➡ soldier

wary ➡ suspicious, careful

wash ➡ clean, cleaning, laundry

washbasin ➡ sink

washcloth ➡ cloth

washed ➡ clean

washing ➡ cleaning, laundry

washroom ➡ bathroom

washstand ➡ sink

waste 1. *vb* squander, fritter away, dissipate, misuse, mispend ⇨ *save*
2. *vb* ➡ **decrease**
3. *n* ➡ **trash**
4. *n* ➡ **desert**
5. *adj* ➡ **sterile**

wasteful *adj* extravagant, lavish, profligate, prodigal, reckless, wanton, spendthrift

watch 1. *n* ➡ **clock**
2. *n* ➡ **period**
3. *n* guard, lookout, vigil, surveillance ➡ **attention**
4. *n* ➡ **patrol**
5. *vb* ➡ **look**
6. *vb* ➡ **protect**

wave 1. *n* billow, swell, surge, tidal wave, ripple, breaker, roller, whitecap, comber, surf
2. *vb* motion, gesture, signal, beckon, flag, salute
3. *vb* flutter, flap, ripple, sway ➡ **blow, swing**

weak *adj* frail, feeble, infirm, invalid, helpless, powerless, unfit, impotent, puny, delicate, fragile, flimsy, rickety ➡ **breakable, thin, sick, vulnerable** ⇨ *strong*

weaken 1. *vb* flag, wilt, droop, sag, wither ➡ **tire**

2. *vb* cripple, undermine, impair, sabotage, subvert, erode, incapacitate ➡ **destroy**
3. *vb* dilute, thin, water down, adulterate, attenuate ➡ **decrease**

wealth *n* riches, affluence, means, opulence, luxury, prosperity, assets, fortune, treasure, hoard ➡ **money, property, abundance**

weather 1. *n* climate, conditions, clime (*literary*) Use **weather** to refer to what is happening in the atmosphere at a particular time or in general: "I don't like this rainy **weather**." "Is the **weather** being affected by global warming?" Use **climate** to refer to the average state of the atmosphere in a place or region: "Florida has a warm **climate**."
2. *vb* age, season, wear, endure ➡ **harden**
3. *vb* expose, overcome ➡ **bear**

weave 1. *vb* braid, knit, interlace, plait, twine, intertwine ➡ **sew**
2. *n* ➡ **cloth**

weight 1. *n* heaviness, heft, mass, substance, pressure, load ➡ **density, measure**
2. *n* ➡ **importance**

welcome 1. *vb* greet, receive, salute, address, herald, hail ➡ **call, entertain, appreciate**
2. *n* greeting, salutation, reception
3. *n* ➡ **hospitality**

If the word you want is not a main entry above, look below to find it.

wasted ➡ **hungry**
wasteland ➡ **desert**
watchdog ➡ **guardian**
watchful ➡ **alert**
watchman ➡ **doorman**
water ➡ **liquid, wet**
water down ➡ **weaken**
waterfowl ➡ **bird**
waterpipe ➡ **pipe**
waterspout ➡ **gargoyle**
watertight ➡ **tight**
waterway ➡ **channel**

watery ➡ **liquid**
waver ➡ **hesitate**
wax ➡ **shine, finish, grow**
wax paper ➡ **paper**
waxy ➡ **slippery**
way ➡ **course, distance, choice, method**
wayfarer ➡ **traveler**
waylay ➡ **attack**
wayward ➡ **mischievous**
waywardness ➡ **disobedience**

weakness ➡ **fault**
wealthy ➡ **rich**
weapon ➡ **gun**
weaponry ➡ **arms**
weapons ➡ **arms**
wear ➡ **dress, damage, decay, weather**
weariness ➡ **exhaustion**
weary ➡ **tired, tire**
web ➡ **net**
webbing ➡ **net**
wed ➡ **marry, married**

wedded ➡ **married**
wedding ➡ **marriage**
wedge ➡ **block, push, embed**
wedlock ➡ **marriage**
weed ➡ **plant**
weekly ➡ **paper**
weep ➡ **cry**
weigh ➡ **consider, measure**
weightless ➡ **light²**
weighty ➡ **heavy, important**
weir ➡ **dam**
weird ➡ **strange**

n = noun • *vb* = verb • *adj* = adjective • *adv* = adverb • *prep* = preposition • *conj* = conjunction

welfare 1. *n* well-being, prosperity, good ➡ **health**
2. *n* public assistance ➡ **help**

well 1. *adv* properly, thoroughly, competently, satisfactorily, adequately, excellently, splendidly
2. *adv* favorably, kindly, approvingly, highly
3. *adj* ➡ **healthy**
4. *n* spring, reservoir, cistern ➡ **fountain, source**
5. *n* shaft, bore ➡ **hole**

wet 1. *adj* soaked, drenched, saturated, sodden, soggy, dripping ➡ **damp, liquid** ⇨ *dry*
2. *adj* rainy, drizzly, stormy, inclement, misty, showery, snowy, slushy
3. *vb* moisten, soak, dampen, sprinkle, saturate, drench, douse, water, steep, immerse, rinse

wheel 1. *n* tire, roller ➡ **tool**
2. *n* steering wheel, helm, tiller, controls, reins, driver's seat
3. *vb* ➡ **turn**

whip 1. *n* lash, crop, switch, cane, scourge, cat-o'-nine-tails, bullwhip
2. *vb* spank, paddle, lash, thrash, flog ➡ **hit, punish**
3. *vb* ➡ **defeat**
4. *vb* ➡ **mix**

white *adj, n* ivory, milky, snowy, silvery, snow-white, frosty, creamy ➡ **fair, pale** ⇨ *black*

wicked *adj* evil, malevolent, diabolical, fiendish, demonic, devilish, heinous ➡ **bad, immoral, mean**

width *n* breadth, girth, wideness, diameter, span ➡ **measure**

wig *n* hairpiece, fall, toupee, periwig (*historical*), rug (*informal*) ➡ **hair**

wild 1. *adj* untamed, fierce, ferocious, savage, raging, turbulent, fiery ➡ **violent, mean, rough, stormy**
2. *adj* uncultivated, overgrown, rampant, overrun
3. *adj* disorderly, unruly, obstinate, undisciplined ➡ **stubborn**
4. *n* ➡ **country**

If the word you want is not a main entry above, look below to find it.

weld ➡ **join**
well-behaved ➡ **good**
well-being ➡ **welfare**
well-informed ➡ **educated**
well-known ➡ **famous**
well-mannered ➡ **polite, good**
well-meaning ➡ **kind**
wellness ➡ **health**
well-off ➡ **rich**
well-read ➡ **educated**
wellspring ➡ **source**
well-to-do ➡ **rich**
well-versed ➡ **educated, expert**
welt ➡ **sore**

wetness ➡ **humidity**
whack ➡ **blow[1], knock, hit**
wharf ➡ **dock**
wheatfield ➡ **field**
wheedle ➡ **persuade**
wheels ➡ **vehicle**
wheeze ➡ **breathe**
whelp ➡ **dog**
wherefore ➡ **therefore**
whet ➡ **sharpen**
whiff ➡ **smell**
whim ➡ **fancy, impulse**
whimper ➡ **cry**
whimsical ➡ **funny, arbitrary**
whimsicality ➡ **humor**

whimsy ➡ **impulse**
whine ➡ **complain, cry**
whir ➡ **hum**
whirl ➡ **turn, dance, swing, try**
whirlwind ➡ **wind**
whisk ➡ **sweep**
whiskers ➡ **beard**
whisper ➡ **mumble, rustle**
whitecap ➡ **wave**
whiten ➡ **bleach**
whittle ➡ **carve**
whiz ➡ **hurry, genius**
whole ➡ **total, complete, all, healthy**

wholehearted ➡ **sincere**
wholesaler ➡ **seller**
wholesome ➡ **healthy**
wholly ➡ **completely**
whoop ➡ **cry**
wickedness ➡ **immorality**
wide ➡ **broad**
wide-awake ➡ **alert**
widen ➡ **spread**
wideness ➡ **width**
widespread ➡ **common, general**
wield ➡ **swing, use**
wife ➡ **spouse**
wiggle ➡ **fidget, crawl**

will 1. *n* willpower, determination, resolution, volition, conviction, resolve, willfulness
➡ **ambition**
2. *n* testament, bequest ➡ **inheritance**
3. *vb* ➡ **leave**

win 1. *vb* triumph, prevail, succeed, overcome
➡ **defeat** ⇨ *lose*
2. *vb* score, achieve, earn ➡ **get**
3. *n* ➡ **victory**

wind 1. *n* breeze, gale, tempest, gust, zephyr, draft, blast, whirlwind, blow, puff, breath
➡ **air, storm**
2. *vb* ➡ **bend, turn**

windy *adj* breezy, blustery, airy, drafty, wind-swept ➡ **stormy**

winner *n* champion, victor, hero, medalist, prizewinner, conqueror, champ *(informal)*

wisdom *n* judgment, reason, understanding, appreciation, intelligence, intellect, comprehension, sagacity, perception, discernment, sense, common sense
➡ **knowledge, experience, depth**

woman *n* lady, girl, female, gentlewoman, matron, maiden, gal *(informal)*, lass
➡ **human being, humanity, adult**

wood *n* lumber, log, timber, plank, firewood, kindling ➡ **forest**

word 1. *n* term, expression, locution, utterance, vocable, verbalism, articulation, syllable
2. *n* ➡ **talk**
3. *n* ➡ **promise**

If the word you want is not a main entry above, look below to find it.

wilderness ➡ country, desert
wildflower ➡ flower
wildlife preserve ➡ zoo
wile ➡ trick
willful ➡ voluntary, arbitrary
willfully ➡ purposely
willfulness ➡ will
willing ➡ ready, voluntary
willpower ➡ will, discipline
wilt ➡ dry, weaken
wilted ➡ stale
wily ➡ sly
wince ➡ jump
windbreak ➡ hedge
windbreaker ➡ coat
windfall ➡ luck
wind-swept ➡ windy
wind up ➡ finish
wing ➡ limb, branch, fly

wink ➡ blink, moment
winning ➡ attractive
winnings ➡ booty, prize
winnow ➡ sift
wino ➡ drunkard
winsomeness ➡ beauty
wipe ➡ dry, sweep
wire ➡ rope
wiry ➡ thin
wise ➡ smart
wisecrack ➡ joke
wish ➡ want, hope
wistful ➡ thoughtful
wistfulness ➡ desire
wit ➡ humor
witch ➡ magician
witchcraft ➡ magic
with ➡ beside
with child ➡ pregnant

withdraw ➡ leave, retreat, extract
withdrawal ➡ departure, privacy
withdrawn ➡ private
wither ➡ dry, weaken
withhold ➡ subtract, hide, deprive
with-it ➡ fashionable
without ➡ minus
withstand ➡ repel
witness ➡ observer, look
witticism ➡ joke
witty ➡ funny
wizard ➡ genius, magician
wizardry ➡ magic
wobble ➡ shake, swing
wobbly ➡ unsteady
woe ➡ sorrow
woeful ➡ pitiful

wolf ➡ eat
womanhood ➡ maturity
womanly ➡ feminine
women's room ➡ bathroom
wonder ➡ surprise, doubt, miracle, respect
wonderful ➡ great
wont ➡ habit
woo ➡ court
woodcut ➡ print
wooden ➡ prim
woodland ➡ forest
woods ➡ forest
woof ➡ bark
wool ➡ coat
woolly ➡ fuzzy
woozy ➡ dizzy
word-for-word ➡ literal
wordless ➡ dumb

n = noun • *vb* = verb • *adj* = adjective • *adv* = adverb • *prep* = preposition • *conj* = conjunction

work 1. *n* labor, toil, effort, drudgery, exertion, industry, endeavor, pains, elbow grease (*informal*), travail
2. *n* ➡ **job, profession**
3. *n* accomplishment, undertaking, composition, creation, opus ➡ **act, book, picture, poem**
4. *vb* toil, labor, strive, struggle, slave, strain ➡ **act, do**
5. *vb* work out ➡ **solve**

worker *n* laborer, employee, hand, help, colleague, breadwinner, jobholder ➡ **helper, farmer**

worm *n* earthworm, nightcrawler, angleworm, inchworm ➡ **larva**

worry 1. *n* concern, care, anxiety, apprehension, burden ➡ **fear**
2. *vb* upset, concern, trouble, fret, brood, stew ➡ **disturb, bother**

worship 1. *vb* sanctify, venerate, glorify, exalt, praise, laud, adore, revere, reverence
2. *vb* ➡ **love**
3. *n* devotion, prayer, veneration, adulation

worst *adj* meanest, lowest ➡ **bad, least** ⇨ *best*

worth *n* value, benefit, merit, virtue, estimation ➡ **importance, price, use**

wrap 1. *vb* gift wrap, cover, bind, envelop, shroud, clothe, swathe, sheathe, swaddle ➡ **bandage**
2. *n* shawl, muffler, cloak, cape, mantle, stole ➡ **scarf**

wrapper *n* covering, cover, envelope, jacket, dust jacket, folder ➡ **container**

wrinkle 1. *n* crease, rumple, crinkle, crimp, crumple, pucker ➡ **fold**
2. *vb* crease, rumple, crumple, crinkle, crimp ➡ **fold**

write 1. *vb* inscribe, jot, record, scribble, scrawl, transcribe ➡ **sign**
2. *vb* compose, draft, indite, pen, author, publish, edit, compile ➡ **print**

writer *n* author, novelist, poet, playwright, historian, biographer, essayist, humorist, scriptwriter, screenwriter ➡ **reporter, artist**

wrong 1. *adj* incorrect, false, mistaken, inaccurate, untrue, erroneous, invalid, bad, corrupt, amiss, awry ➡ **improper, illogical, immoral** ⇨ *correct, right*
2. *n* ➡ **crime**

If the word you want is not a main entry above, look below to find it.

working ➡ **employed**
work out ➡ **exercise**
workout ➡ **exercise**
workplace ➡ **office**
workshop ➡ **factory**
world ➡ **earth**
worldly ➡ **cosmopolitan**
worldwide ➡ **universal**
worn ➡ **old**
worn out ➡ **tired**
worn-out ➡ **old**

worried ➡ **anxious**
worsen ➡ **relapse**
worthless ➡ **poor, useless**
worthwhile ➡ **valuable**
worthy ➡ **good, noble, praiseworthy**
wound ➡ **hurt, cut**
wraith ➡ **ghost**
wrangle ➡ **argue**
wrath ➡ **anger**
wreak ➡ **inflict**

wreath ➡ **crown**
wreck ➡ **destroy, collision**
wreckage ➡ **damage, trash**
wrench ➡ **pull, hurt**
wrest ➡ **seize**
wrestle ➡ **fight**
wretch ➡ **beggar, rascal**
wretched ➡ **sorry, poor, awful**
wriggle ➡ **fidget, crawl**
wring ➡ **squeeze**

wristwatch ➡ **clock**
writ ➡ **order**
writhe ➡ **fidget**
writing ➡ **print, handwriting, literature**
writing paper ➡ **paper**
wrongdoer ➡ **criminal**
wrongdoing ➡ **crime**
wrongful ➡ **illegal**
wry ➡ **dry**
wunderkind ➡ **genius**

X-Y-Z

X ray 1. *n* radiation, ultraviolet ray, gamma ray
2. *n* radiograph, encephalogram
➡ **photograph**

xylophone *n* marimba, vibraphone, vibes, glockenspiel

yell *vb, n* call, shout, scream, shriek, screech, bellow, thunder, rant, rave, harangue, boo, hiss, jeer, hoot, squall ➡ **cry**

yellow 1. *adj, n* gold, lemon, sandy, saffron, flaxen, blond, blonde
2. *adj* ➡ **cowardly**

yes *interj* aye, okay, OK, affirmative, amen, yeah (*informal*), yup (*informal*), okey-dokey (*informal*) ➡ **certainly** ⇨ **no**

young *adj* youthful, immature, juvenile, adolescent, boyish, girlish, underage
➡ **childish, new** ⇨ **old**

zero *n* nothing, naught, nought, none, nil, love (*in tennis*), zip (*informal*), zilch (*informal*), goose egg (*informal*), cipher

zigzag *adj* crooked, askew, jagged, oblique, meandering, erratic ⇨ **straight**

zone 1. *n* area, region, district, belt, band, quarter ➡ **place**
2. *vb* ➡ **divide**

zoo *n* menagerie, animal farm, game farm, wildlife preserve, game preserve, aviary, terrarium, aquarium ➡ **park**

If the word you want is not a main entry above, look below to find it.

x ➡ tick
yachting ➡ nautical
yachtsman ➡ sailor
yahoo ➡ boor
yank ➡ pull
yap ➡ bark
yard ➡ property
yardarm ➡ gallows
yardstick ➡ measure
yarn ➡ string, story
yawn ➡ spread
yeah ➡ yes
yearn ➡ want

yearning ➡ desire
yelp ➡ bark
yen ➡ desire
yeoman ➡ farmer
yesterday ➡ past
yesteryear ➡ past
yet ➡ but, more, before
yield ➡ surrender, give, growth
yielding ➡ passive
yip ➡ bark
yo ➡ hello

yoke ➡ team, pair
yonder ➡ far
yore ➡ past
youngster ➡ child
youth ➡ teenager, child, childhood
youthful ➡ young
yowl ➡ cry
yup ➡ yes
zany ➡ funny
zeal ➡ enthusiasm
zealot ➡ extremist

zealous ➡ ambitious, patriotic
zenith ➡ top
zephyr ➡ wind
zest ➡ enthusiasm, spice, excitement
zestful ➡ lively
zesty ➡ spicy
zilch ➡ zero
zip ➡ hurry, energy, zero
zipper ➡ clasp
zippy ➡ lively
zoom ➡ hurry

n = noun • *vb* = verb • *adj* = adjective • *adv* = adverb • *prep* = preposition • *interj* = interjection